ONE OF YOUR OWN

D1427010

Carol Ann Lee is an acclaimed biographer and has written extensively on the Holocaust. Following her ground-breaking research on Anne Frank, the Dutch government reopened the investigation into the Frank family's betrayal. She is also the author of two novels and three books for children. Her works have been published in 15 countries.

ONE OF YOUR OWN

The Life and Death
of Myra Hindley

Carol Ann Lee

MAINSTREAM
PUBLISHING

EDINBURGH AND LONDON

This edition, 2011

Copyright © Carol Ann Lee, 2010
All rights reserved
The moral right of the author has been asserted

First published in Great Britain in 2010 by
MAINSTREAM PUBLISHING COMPANY
(EDINBURGH) LTD
7 Albany Street
Edinburgh EH1 3UG

ISBN 9781845967017

No part of this book may be reproduced or transmitted in
any form or by any other means without permission in writing
from the publisher, except by a reviewer who wishes to quote
brief passages in connection with a review written for
insertion in a magazine, newspaper or broadcast

The author has made every effort to trace copyright holders.
Where this has not been possible, the publisher is willing to acknowledge
any rightful copyright owner on substantive proof of ownership

This publication contains references to other websites. While we hope
you will be interested in these websites, you acknowledge that their
content is not subject to our control and we do not endorse or
accept any responsibility for the content of such websites

A catalogue record for this book is available
from the British Library

Printed in Great Britain by
Clays Ltd, St Ives plc

7 9 10 8 6

Dedicated to the memory of
Joe Mounsey, Alex Carr and Dennis Barrow
and for
Ian Fairley, Mike Massheder and Bob Spiers

'Here there is no why'

Concentration camp guard, quoted in Primo Levi,
Survival in Auschwitz

'I had my hair done on Saturday. It looks so nice that I'm sorry I'm
all dressed up and nowhere to go (joke)'

Myra Hindley, letter to her mother, 17 April 1966, two days before
the 'Moors trial' opened at Chester Assizes

CONTENTS

PREFACE

'There's never been a single book on this case that's got the facts right,' former Detective Chief Superintendent Ian Fairley told me. As Hyde police station's newest member of the CID, Fairley was one of three policemen to enter 16 Wardle Brook Avenue on the morning of 7 October 1965, bringing the Moors Murders to an end. His statement underlines one of my primary reasons for writing this book: the facts have never been properly told.

I can't remember when I first heard about the crimes committed by Ian Brady and Myra Hindley. They occurred before I was born but have seeped into the national consciousness over the years, becoming something we absorb as part of our collective history. Although there have been other similarly horrific crimes in the decades that have passed since then, the Moors Murders case remains unparalleled in terms of the strength of emotion it provokes and the sense of utter incomprehension that a woman could abduct children with her lover, then collude in their rape, murder and burial on the moor. Repulsion at Hindley's part in the crimes, above all, gives the case its notoriety.

Myra Hindley died in prison in November 2002 but remains as omnipresent in death as she was in life. There have been acres of newsprint written about her since the 1960s, several books about the case, as well as documentaries and drama series. Those who attempt to say anything in her defence are met with a storm of protest while those who feel that she was evil are accused of being too emotional and unwilling to believe in redemption. The truth, as always, is more complex. It is an unbearable fact that Myra Hindley was capable of love and kindness towards her family and friends, adoring of her niece and the children of those who visited her in prison, yet had been responsible for the sadistic murder of other children. The dichotomy is difficult to process – it calls to mind how the perpetrators of the Holocaust were able to inflict torture and murder on a vast scale, then return home to their families quite clear of conscience. Contrary to what some sections of the media would have us believe, people who commit monstrous acts look no different to the rest of humanity and have likes and dislikes, strengths and weaknesses too. What sets them apart are their choices – acts of appalling cruelty and violence – but otherwise they exist among us as nursery nurses, doctors, office workers, shopkeepers . . . In some cases, they are even children themselves – Mary Bell, Constance Kent, Robert Thompson and Jon Venables, the Doncaster boys who cannot be named . . .

What lay behind Hindley's choices and whether she was genuinely remorseful or not remain points of contention. She and her supporters claim that she acted under duress and had redeemed herself, while her victims' families and a large section of the public believe her crimes were committed out of sheer wickedness and her remorse was simply a facade to win her freedom. This book explores her motivation and what followed it as dispassionately as possible in order to leave the reader to draw his or her own conclusions.

A biography of Myra Hindley understandably draws accusations of sensationalism and unnecessarily raking over painful memories; I hope to have steered clear of the former, while the latter may also be true of almost any study of contemporary history. I've also tried to give a voice to the people who are rarely heard in books of this kind: the victims' families. Myra Hindley's supporters and friends present their views, but it seems to me that a book about someone who has committed murder should reflect – if they wish it – the impact on the people closest to the victims. The book also draws on the memories of the policemen involved with the original investigation, none of whom have ever spoken in-depth publicly about the case. Their recollections result in the overturning of a number of persistent misconceptions. Myra Hindley's recently released prison files give new insights into the woman, her crimes and the institutions that contained her. They include personal papers, prison reports, documents and correspondence, many of which are published here for the first time.

Several books have been written on the Moors Murders case since the trial in 1966, focusing on the crimes and their detection. To date, there has only been one biography 'proper', published in 1988: *Myra Hindley: Inside the Mind of a Murderess*, by Jean Ritchie. Well researched, it was nonetheless written over 20 years ago, before such a vast archive of new documentation was made public, and focused on her life in prison. Duncan Staff's *The Lost Boy* (2007) is the most recent publication on the Moors Murders; he met and corresponded with Hindley and was permitted access to some of her personal papers. Despite its subtitle, 'The definitive story of the Moors Murders and the search for the final victim', there are a few inaccuracies throughout the book – for instance, the date when Keith Bennett went missing is given as 18 June 1964 when it was in fact 16 June, and the photograph purporting to be of Lesley Ann Downey's funeral is actually the funeral of John Kilbride. There are others, some of which are flagged in the text as endnotes.

Myra Hindley remains a gauge of female iniquity; *One of Your Own* is both a study of the woman and her crimes, and an attempt to redress various factual errors that have accumulated over the years.

I am grateful to the many people who have assisted me during the course of writing this book. It is difficult to single out anyone most deserving of thanks, but I must first of all thank Danny Kilbride, who shared at length childhood memories of his brother John and explained quietly and rationally, but no less heartfelt for that, the effect of his loss on his family over the years.

For interviews and source material (and hospitality), I would like to thank Bernard Black and his wife Margaret, Joe Chapman, Allan Grafton, Yvonne Roberts, Duncan Staff (who kindly provided tapes of his documentaries on the case), Father Michael Teader, the Revd Peter Timms and his wife Veronica, and Sara Trevelyan. I am especially grateful to Andrew McCooey for his interview and for extending permission to quote from Myra Hindley's own words. I must also offer a heartfelt thank you to Mrs Bridget Astor, who generously allowed me access to her husband's papers, and to Geoffrey Todd and his secretary, Paula Corbett, for making them available to me. Anne Maguire shared painful memories of the wrongful imprisonment inflicted on her and her husband and two sons, and I am grateful to her for talking to me. I'd also like to thank Angela Handley for putting me in touch with Mo Statham and Anne Murdoch. I owe a special debt of thanks to Peter Stanford, who was particularly helpful and kind in giving me access to his letters from Myra Hindley and a (then) unpublished interview with Lady Anne Tree, as well as for putting me in touch with Bridget Astor, Anne Maguire and the Revd Peter Timms, and for providing a lively interview and ideas for further research. Clive Entwistle, the first reporter to speak to Myra Hindley and the most knowledgeable, gave me a terrifically helpful interview; his documentary, *The Moors Murders* (1999), is exceptional in its detail and accuracy. I must also thank Michael Attwell for his documentary, *Myra: The Making of a Monster* (2003), and Katie Kinnard for sending me a copy of Martina Cole's documentary, *Lady Killers: Myra Hindley* (2008). Thanks, too, to Norman Luck for allowing me to draw on his interview with Dorothy Wing.

I spent a wonderful day with Margaret Mounsey and want to thank her for that and our contact since, and for sharing with me memories of her husband, the redoubtable Joe Mounsey. To Mike Massheder, I offer my thanks for his insights and friendship, and extend the same to Ian Fairley, Tom McVittie and Bob Spiers, all of whom are exceptional men. I'd also like to thank Maureen Spiers for the lunch she provided when I interviewed her husband.

Anthony Ainsworth talked to me about the geography of the moor and provided the introduction to Norie Miles, Winnie Johnson's close friend; sadly, he died a few months after this book was published. Norie Miles has studied the photographs taken by Ian Brady and Myra Hindley and also facilitated an interview with Winnie Johnson. I thank them both, and Elizabeth Bond who looks after Winnie.

Although David Smith did not wish to be interviewed for a book about Myra Hindley, I am very grateful to him for agreeing to an informal chat, and for his and his wife Mary's hospitality. Thank you, too, to their son David and his wife Diane, for providing initial contact.

Together with my son River, I spent two wonderful days at the splendid National Library of Wales, where the papers of Emlyn Williams are kept. The staff there – Manon Foster, Anwen Pierce, Glyn Parry, Caronwen Samuel and others – were unfailingly kind and helpful, and I'd like to thank them not only for their assistance with the Williams' archive, but also for making my son so welcome. I only wish the staff of every archive were as thoughtful and knowledgeable. Thanks, too, to the staff of the National Archive in Kew for their assistance with Myra Hindley's prison files, and National Image Library Manager Paul Johnson especially for his kindness and patience in dealing with the photographs. I'd also like to thank the staff at the Brynmor Jones Library at the University of Hull for providing copies of Myra Hindley's letters held there.

Many literary sources have informed this book, and I am grateful to the authors and publishers for allowing me permission to quote from their works.

Closer to home, I must thank my agent, Jan Michael, and her agent, Jane Judd, for supporting the project from the start. Jan's suggestions on the text were incisive and made a difference to the manuscript generally, and Jane and her husband Brian very kindly let me stay with them while I worked in London. At Mainstream, I offer sincere thanks to Bill Campbell, Peter MacKenzie, Deborah Warner, Ailsa Morrison, Graeme Blaikie, Karyn Millar and all the staff for their hard work and faith in the book.

And literally *closest* to home, I have to thank my friend Tricia Room especially, for ferrying me around various places and discussing ideas. I'm also grateful to my family and other friends for putting up with me while I wrote the book, and to my mother, for listening as I talked about it every day and for looking after River when I needed more time to write. And to River, who knew only the most basic facts of the book, I offer the deepest thanks, for keeping me grounded and bringing joy into my life while I worked on a complex and distressing subject.

I corresponded, briefly, with Ian Brady, and would like to echo Danny Kilbride's words: 'Tell us where Keith is. Stop being a coward. There's a little boy out there on the moor who should be brought home to his family. It can't end like this.'

Finally, there is one other person I would like to acknowledge, whom I did not meet whilst working on this book, but who contacted me after publication. That person is now my partner, Keith's brother Alan Bennett. His support, courage and love mean everything to me and I want to thank him for it all from my heart, with love.

I

Pariah:
20 November 2002

1

A radio station that ran a £500 sweepstake asking listeners to predict the time of Moors Murderer Myra Hindley's death has been branded irresponsible and insensitive by the radio watchdog. The Manchester station Key 103 asked listeners to ring in with the time Hindley would 'meet her maker'... The item followed an afternoon news bulletin announcing Hindley had received the last rites.

The Guardian, 17 January 2003

Her funeral was held at night.

Rain slanted in from the Fens, as it had all day, beating with a thin, hollow sound on the roof of the small 1930s-built chapel. The gardens of remembrance were pitch-black, but the gravel courtyard burned with light and the white draughts of breath issuing from the multitude of journalists who represented every broadsheet, tabloid and TV news company in the country. Closer to the chapel, and guarding the gates, were the legions of police drafted in to search the grounds for intruders, the luminous bands on their uniforms a glare of brilliant yellow among the black trees.

But no one uninvited came. The warning to the public to stay away proved unnecessary, for in a curiously medieval display of suspicion the woman was shunned in death. There were none of the incendiary scenes of rage and hatred predicted by jittery government officials. In life, all that she said and did met with widespread revilement; the ferocity of feeling she evoked gave rise to seething statements by those who could not reach her and physical violence by fellow women prisoners. The few who sought to defend her found themselves attacked. But in death, it was as if her power to terrify and repulse was multiplied – as if mere nearness to her corpse would contaminate the bystander.

Against that backdrop, the burning of her body was not simply a funeral rite. It was an act of ancient justice. The woman herself had sensed that no resting place on earth could contain her bones peacefully; she left instructions in her will that her remains be cremated and her ashes scattered in secrecy.

'I know people would have liked for me to be chucked into a pond three times to discover if I sank or swam,' she wrote, five years before her death.[1] It was a shrewd observation. The nature of her crimes and their unfathomable source tapped into old, unspoken fears.

Whilst she was free and still young, she and her lover visited the Perthshire village of Dunning, where they climbed through a gap in a wall to reach the cross-capped stone cairn that marks the execution place of an obscure witch. A grainy black-and-white photograph captures the woman perched on the monument, grimacing, staring at nothing. The stones behind her are daubed in white paint: 'Maggie Wall, burnt here 1657 as a witch'.

A few weeks later, detectives searching the house the woman shared with her lover dug deep into the garden, uprooting plants and destroying the little rockery where a boulder stolen from Maggie Wall's grave sat, squat as a toad.

No one wanted to drive the hearse carrying Myra Hindley. Discreet enquiries had been made by the Prison Service more than a year before, when her health was already in steep decline. The authorities had anticipated a problem, but the volume of refusals took them by surprise; in Suffolk, within whose boundaries Highpoint Prison lies, every firm of funeral directors declined to handle the body. Their response was echoed by larger companies nationwide. Finally, after months of negotiations, a firm was found in a town 200 miles away who reluctantly agreed, its identity protected by the Prison Service and Home Office officials, who would divulge no more than that the firm was located somewhere in the North. Police then approached West Suffolk crematorium, with a view to holding the funeral service there, but were turned down. An internal prison memo noted: 'Ipswich crematorium also refused to cremate Myra . . . I will make further enquiries regarding costs and funding and try to find out how the funeral of Fred West was managed, as this is the closest parallel I can think of.'[2] Eventually, Cambridge City crematorium consented to the service, providing strict conditions were met.

In her will, Myra had requested the presence of 12 close family and friends, though the chapel secured for her funeral could accommodate 60 mourners. Her mother, brother-in-law and 27-year-old niece informed the authorities that they wouldn't be attending. A couple of invited friends were also expected to avoid the ceremony, which, like all the funeral arrangements, was funded by Myra's estate (reports that she had willed other monies to charities, including the National Society for the Prevention of Cruelty to Children, were refuted; the NSPCC said it had no record of her as a benefactor and that donations from her estate, if offered, would be returned immediately). Another memo, strictly confidential, posited a question: 'Will Ian Brady be allowed to attend the funeral? For guidance: he is not related to Myra Hindley and has had no continuing contact with her.'[3]

Myra's death from natural causes – bronchial pneumonia brought on by hypertension and coronary heart disease – occurred on Friday, 15 November 2002 in a remote corner of West Suffolk Hospital, Bury St Edmunds. Afterwards, Room J on Ward G2 was torn apart by staff with instructions to incinerate every article, from the bed linen to Myra's clothing. A spokesman told the press that the hospital administration was sensitive to future patients and therefore 'the room has been cleared of everything that was used during her care and has been redecorated'.[4] The smell of fresh paint drifted down the corridor, but not as far as the mortuary, where Myra lay isolated from the other dead and under constant police guard.

The anonymous firm of undertakers came for her on the evening of 20 November. Her 5 ft 8 in. 'heavily built' body was laid out in a light beech coffin with gold handles.[5] Once the lid had been secured, they covered it with white lilies and orange gerberas, then carried the coffin through to the waiting hearse, driven up to one of the rear exits. Cellophane-wrapped chrysanthemums and bouquets of carnations filled the glass compartment where the coffin would rest. After a few minor security checks, the hearse departed under police escort.

A reporter noted that a doctor standing at the exit doors muttered 'good riddance' before returning to his rounds.[6]

One of the attendant policemen told the reporter that the floral tributes would be destroyed, although the cards were to be kept for

Myra's ailing mother, living in sheltered accommodation in Manchester under an assumed name. In the courtyard where the two men stood hunched against the rain, the glorious flowers were momentarily visible as the hearse turned onto the road for the crematorium. In a low voice, the policeman said, 'There should have been thorns.'[7]

The mourners arrived in two cars shortly before half past seven, directed to the back of the crematorium to escape the media's probing questions and cameras. Myra's mother was too frail to make the journey, but Andrew McCooey, Myra's steadfast solicitor, was there, as was her barrister, Edward Fitzgerald QC, the leading human rights lawyer who married a granddaughter of Lord Longford, Myra's most vocal campaigner.

Among the other mourners was Bridget Astor, widow of *Observer* editor David Astor, whom Myra regarded as her adoptive father. Bridget recalls, 'It was a very quiet affair. There were only about eight or ten people in all. Tricia, a former partner of Myra's and still a close friend, didn't go either, despite what the press said. She rang me up afterwards and said, "Tell me every detail." I went with my daughter Lucy, who had once visited Myra with me. We travelled to Suffolk by train with the two lawyers, Andrew McCooey and Edward Fitzgerald. There were two other people at the chapel who looked as if they didn't want to talk to us, but they were definitely among the mourners. An elderly lady and another woman. I just felt they were hostile in some way. I remember thinking, "What have the police done with the crowds of troublemakers?" There weren't any. That was interesting. I saw the barriers, those cattle-fence things. The funeral was very dignified.'[8]

Three members of the crematorium staff were brought in for the service. The mourners sat talking quietly, listening to the persistent drumming of the rain on the chapel roof. Outside, where camera crews stood rank and file behind the steel barriers, exhaust fumes from vehicles passing on the main road coiled and vanished in the beam of generators. In lay-bys, long-distance truck drivers settled down in their cabs for the night, while others woke from their naps and continued on their journeys. Most had no knowledge of the funeral about to occur; those who did sounded their horns or shouted as they passed the crematorium gates. But that was all.

A set of headlights swung onto the driveway of the chapel, followed by a second, and the press threw down their cigarettes, stamped the numbness from their feet and began jostling for an uninterrupted view of the black Volvo carrying Myra's coffin. The tyres of the police escort vehicle ground over the gravel, then waited to let the hearse pass. Flashguns lit up the clock tower of the crematorium and the stark rows of winter trees lining the path. The hearse drew up to the chapel porch and the pallbearers stepped out, clutching their coats against the wind and rain.

Father Michael Teader, Myra's priest and close friend, appeared from inside the chapel, his white cassock billowing in the wind. A solitary lamp hung creaking in the porch, and the priest stooped below its flickering light to sprinkle holy water on Myra's coffin before the pallbearers raised it onto their shoulders. They entered the chapel beneath a stone arch engraved with the Latin text: *Mors Janua Vitae – Death is the Gateway to Life.* The doors of the chapel silently closed; the press had had their last encounter with Myra Hindley.

Afterwards, Andrew McCooey described his former client's funeral as 'very quiet, in the sense that there weren't too many people . . . The priest did give a very proper service for the people who were there. His theme was basically the parable of the prodigal son returning home and that really was it.'[9]

Father Michael addressed the mourners from the lectern beside the coffin on the blue-clothed catafalque. 'I used the story of the prodigal son at her funeral because I felt she was the prodigal daughter,' he explains seven years later. 'She'd gone away from the decency of humanity and from God, but somewhere she made the decision to return to us and to the Church. God forgave her and she became a different person.'[10] He conducted a short Mass, and the music Myra had requested on her deathbed, Albinoni's *Adagio*, briefly masked the pattering rain. When the service ended, the curtains were drawn while the crematorium staff bore the coffin to the incinerator, where it was heated to 1,000°C and razed to a pile of ash. The crumbling residue was covertly removed through a side entrance, carried to a prison van and driven away from the black, wet Fenlands.

There had been endless press speculation about Myra's ashes. Cambridge City Council, on whose property she was cremated, issued a statement: 'The cremated remains will be taken as soon as they are available after the funeral back with the Prison Service. They will take possession of them and will make the arrangements in consultation with the family as to what happens with them.'[11] The Prison Service put out a statement of their own: 'Myra Hindley did not say exactly where she wanted her ashes placed because she was worried that the news might leak out. She left it to Father Michael to scatter them in a peaceful and secret place.'[12] In truth, Myra had specified where her ashes should be scattered, and by whom. Her powdery remains were handed first to the Prison Service and then to her family, who gave them to her ex-partner, Tricia Cairns. On a clear day in February 2003, she scattered Myra's ashes at Stalybridge Country Park, an area of woodland and water at the foot of Saddleworth Moor. One tabloid claimed to have photographed the ashes and printed a picture of a leafless shrub shrouded in white dust. The possibility that someone would attempt to photograph Myra in death seemed strangely inevitable; an internal memo from Suffolk Constabulary noted: 'Photographs of Hindley alive are greatly valued. Those of her dead are believed to be worth more.'[13]

For it was, after all, by a photograph that the world knew Myra Hindley best: an image that captured 'the most evil woman who ever lived', 'the devil's daughter', 'a Medusa', a 'peroxide-haired Gorgon' and 'a disgrace to womankind'.[14] A photograph sealed her transformation from convicted murderess to something that modern language could not adequately convey: she was both the stuff of age-old nightmares – hence the references to mythical female horrors – and the depraved product of modern society. 'She was the end of innocence.'[15]

Throughout her years in prison, Myra fought against the impact of the photograph, launching persistent campaigns to rehabilitate herself in the public eye. She grew bitter when they failed. In an open letter to *The Guardian*, she wrote: 'The truth of this continuing Gothic soap opera is that most people don't want to accept that people like myself can change. They prefer to keep me frozen in time together with that awful mugshot so that their attitudes, beliefs and perceptions can remain intact.'[16] Each fresh story of her efforts to educate herself, to express remorse, or of her conversion to 'good Catholic girl' was accompanied by the same infamous photograph. Towards the end of her life she admitted defeat: the crude black-and-white mugshot from October 1965 was impossible to efface. It defined her, no matter how fervently she and her supporters insisted she had changed, and would serve as her epitaph.

She was 23 when the photograph was taken in the basement cells of Hyde police station. Six months later, the 'Moors' trial closed at Chester Assizes and Myra began life in prison. She and her lover, Ian Brady, were known then to have killed two children and one teenager; they were also strongly suspected of killing a twelve-year-old boy and a sixteen-year-old girl, but the police investigation was contentiously shelved, although the case itself remained open. Two of their victims were discovered buried on the vast, bleak moor between the villages of Greenfield in Lancashire and Holmfirth in Yorkshire. The crimes had gone undetected until David Smith, Myra's then brother-in-law, told the police that he had witnessed a murder in the newly built council house Myra and Ian shared, and that Ian had boasted of other victims, on the moor. David Smith insisted that Myra was no mere accessory to her lover's crimes but an active participant. She denied his claims for almost a quarter of a century; although she never admitted an equal role in the murders, she did eventually confess that the children had been willing to go anywhere she and Ian suggested, simply because they trusted *her*. Like all children of that era, they had been diligently warned about strange men, but it never crossed their young minds to fear a woman.

The murders were cold and calculated, committed, in the parlance of the day, 'for kicks'. When the known details were made public, there was both seismic shock and outrage, and calls for the two accused to be hanged. But there could be no question of that; the Murder (Abolition of the Death Penalty) Act had been passed one month after their last victim was killed. The convicted pair were sent to prison for life instead.[17] Ian Brady accepted that he would never be free and apparently succumbed to mental illness; Myra worked obsessively at winning parole, sustained by a number of high-profile figures who crusaded publicly on her behalf, and she kept her sanity.

Widespread indignation greeted Myra's reaction to her punishment. Her desire for freedom seemed unaccountably arrogant in view of the relentless suffering endured by the families of her victims. Her resistance to insanity once she had – or professed she had – come to terms with her crimes defied common logic. The idea that she could have committed such appalling acts of cruelty over a sustained length of time, then emerged with a sound mind and the good heart her campaigners accredited to her was deemed unthinkable.

And yet, in reverse, it *had* proved possible: a few years before the murders began, in the close-knit streets of Gorton where she was raised, young Myra was regarded by local mothers as a dependable, cheery babysitter. As a teenager, she defended her sister and school friends against neighbourhood bullies. Despite claims by both Myra and those who have written about her, there was nothing substantive in her background to hint at the crimes she committed in her early twenties. Her roots were as normal and absent of wickedness as that most homely of local dishes, the Lancashire hotpot.

But if that is the case, then might it not also follow that her crusaders may have been right and that a succession of Home Secretaries acted unethically in keeping a repentant and rehabilitated woman imprisoned? After her death, should Myra Hindley be viewed with more compassion than she was in life? Or is the summing up of her character by the detective in charge of the original Moors Murders investigation closer to the unpalatable truth: 'She was an evil girl – if you ask me who was responsible for what [she and Ian Brady] did, I'd say it was six of one and half a dozen of the other.'[18]

In her unpublished autobiography, Myra declared: 'I am a child of Gorton, in Manchester. Infamous, I have become disowned, but I am one of your own.'[19] Towards the end of her life, she gave her birthplace and site of her crimes another name. One of the few journalists to whom she spoke relatively unguardedly recalls: 'The one phrase that really sticks in my mind is that she referred to Manchester as "Victim Country". She was talking to me about a friend who lived in the area and she said, "She lives in Victim Country."'[20]

The red warren of Gorton's terraced houses where every working day began and ended with the din of the foundry buzzer; the soot, brick and iron of the streets and the high-railed playgrounds of old Victorian primary schools where countless knees had grazed and beaded with blood on the asphalt . . . And then the moor: the stark swell of the land, with its pallet of myrtle green, charcoal and indigo; the black stone ruins and barrelling winds, and birds that spark up from the heather like tinder. Two very different geographies overlaid with a chilling name:

'Victim Country'. Her journey through it, from wartime slum-kid to funeral pariah, was down a long and crooked path.

II

Gorton Girl:
23 July 1942 – 21 December 1960

2

The Mancunians in particular are rooted in the myth right up to their heads; they're narrow-minded, conventional people who believe everything they read or see or hear – and they're vengeful.

Myra Hindley, letter, February 1985

'Once upon a time,' she wrote, 'I was simply Myra Hindley, a very normal child.'[1] In her memory, Gorton was 'a tough but respectable working-class district. There was a lot of poverty but virtually no crime and a strong ethos of Victorian prudery.'[2] Today, the Gorton of Myra's childhood no longer exists. It was swept away in the 1960s and 1970s, when town planners ordered its demolition as part of the city's slum-clearance programme. Most of the inhabitants were resettled on overspill estates in council houses and tower blocks that were supposed to provide them with a better standard of living; what was lost was a watertight sense of community, replaced by crime levels and rigid disenchantment as high as the electricity pylons dominating the skyline.

Ghosts of the old Gorton remain – the odd, mouldering pub and recognisable street name – but the rest has gone. It was once a neighbourhood interchangeable with countless others throughout the north of England, an urban village where the inhabitants all knew each other and life revolved around the neighbourhood. There were few, if any, feelings of inferiority; everyone was in the same boat. Apart from the weekly wage, the only other source of income was an occasional win on the horses or (for the truly blessed) a windfall on the football pools. Communities were close-knit because different branches of one family lived in the same street or nearby; children ran between virtually identical homes of grandparents, aunts and uncles. This invisible gridwork extended to leisure, where outings were taken en masse, with whole streets hiring a charabanc to ferry them to the nippy coast for the day. The era of cheap foreign holidays was but a speck on the horizon; Gorton's clans looked forward to public holidays and traditions to lighten their working lot – Easter, Shrove Tuesday, Whitsun, Guy Fawkes, Christmas, New Year's Eve. Otherwise the days were indistinguishable: when the buzzer of the foundry sounded every morning and afternoon, a labour-filthy line of men poured down Gorton Lane, leaving or returning to condemned houses where their wives strove to manage an equally heavy workload of domesticity.

It was into these unambiguous surroundings that Myra was born, as she wrote in her autobiography, 'an ordinary baby', in the middle of the Second World War.[3] Her mother, Nellie Hindley, went into labour on the sweltering midweek afternoon of 22 July 1942, and travelled six miles by bus from Gorton to Crumpsall Hospital, a former workhouse. Nellie was 22, delicate in appearance though headstrong in character, and had been married for little more than a year when she fell pregnant with her first child. Her husband, Bob, was serving in the war overseas and so it was on her mother Ellen Maybury's arm that Nellie leaned as she made her way to F Block, the hospital's maternity wing stretching over four floors.

In the early hours of the morning, Nellie gave birth to a healthy daughter whom she called Myra, a name that had been popular since the mid nineteenth century. A hundred years after it came into common usage, 'Myra' fell into sharp obscurity, a phenomenon entirely due to the deeds of the girl born that stifling night in the red-brick Victorian building in north Manchester.

Nellie entrusted the baby into Ellen's care while she returned to her job as a factory machinist earning a meagre wage. Ellen now became 'Gran' to all the family and was to be the most constant figure in Myra's life, providing her with a proper home and the stability of unconditional love. In common with most children of her age, Myra grew up in a house where the mantelpiece bore a sepia photograph of a soldier killed in the Great War: Gran's first husband, Peter. When the war ended, Gran married a coal carter, Bert Maybury, and with her son and daughter from her first marriage, James and Louie, settled into a cramped house at 24 Beasley Street in Gorton. Three more children followed: Anne, Bert junior and, in 1920, Myra's mother

Nellie. Louie died of peritonitis shortly after her marriage to an Irishman called Jim, and Myra was fascinated to hear how Gran's hair had turned white overnight from grief.

Myra's parents met in 1938. Eighteen-year-old, wilful Nellie began a fiery courtship with twenty-five-year-old Robert (Bob) Hindley, who was tall, dark-haired and sinewy. The Mayburys were Protestant, and though the teenage Nellie was indifferent to religion, she was scathing of the Catholic Church, a ubiquitous presence in Gorton. Bob was born and raised a Catholic: he had been educated by monks at the school in the shadow of St Francis' Monastery on Gorton Lane. Religion was rarely a cause for argument during the early days of their courtship – that came when Myra was born – but Nellie and Bob had furious rows and equally passionate reconciliations. They married in 1940 and moved into the two-up, two-down house on Beasley Street that was packed to the creaking rafters with occupants: Gran's husband had died, but her other children – James (Jim), Annie and Bert junior – had not yet left home.

Bob Hindley wasn't part of the household for long. A flair for sport at school led to enrolment in the Parachute Regiment; he took part in regimental boxing matches and won the championship. During the war, he worked as an aircraft fitter and left the damp streets of Gorton for the broiling heat of North Africa, Cyprus and Italy. 'I must have been conceived during his period of leave from the army after a night on the booze,' Myra reflected years later. 'It would have been better if I wasn't born at all.'[4] On his next leave, Bob and Nellie had a fierce quarrel over the baby. He wanted Myra to be baptised, but Nellie was against it. They reached an uneasy compromise: Nellie agreed that Bob could have his wish provided Myra would not have to attend a Catholic school. Bob relented, and on 16 August 1942, Myra was duly baptised at St Francis' Monastery. Her Uncle Bert's girlfriend, a sensible young Catholic woman named Kath, was godmother. Myra's father had already returned to his regiment.

The Luftwaffe flew regular sorties over the streets of Gorton, targeting the foundry and damaging the schools adjacent to the monastery. The backyard of Gran's house held an Anderson bomb shelter, but it was seldom used by Gran and her tenants, who felt safer in the communal shelter at the end of Beasley Street. Although Bob was at war, and Myra's Aunt Annie and Uncle Jim had each left home after marrying, there were still five people living in Gran's tiny house: Bert and his girlfriend Kath, Nellie, baby Myra and Gran herself. The family ran so often to the communal shelter that as soon as the air-raid sirens began to sound their ear-splitting wail, each person embarked on their individual task: Gran and Kath would dash straight out to join the neighbours flooding towards the shelter, while Nellie scooped Myra up from her cot, swaddled her in a blanket and handed her to Bert, who was a fast sprinter. In her autobiography, Myra records the story of how on one occasion Nellie leapt upstairs to retrieve her daughter and, in her panic to escape, flung the baby down to Uncle Bert, who was waiting to catch her at the foot of the stairs. He missed – and Myra flew through the air, landing safely in a thick pile of washing in a tub on the stairs. From then on, Nellie always clutched Myra in her arms as she hastily negotiated the stairs.

Life at Beasley Street was cosily populated by women, apart from Bert, who had inherited his parents' gentleness and easy-going nature. 'Like most families at this time, we made the best of what we had,' Myra recalled. 'I was strongly influenced by my uncle Bert, who was a father figure. He was kindly and caring.'[5] She couldn't recall him ever losing his temper and one of her earliest memories was of being thrown deftly into the air by Bert under the washing hung up in the parlour while she screamed with delight. 'I always went to [him] for help and advice. I respected him,' she mused, 'but somehow I seem to have inherited my dad's strength of character.'[6]

After VE Day, when Bob Hindley came home permanently, three-year-old Myra's reaction to her father was cautious, even slightly fearful. He did his best to win her love and trust, but it rapidly degenerated into a formidable battle of wills: his, and those of his spirited daughter.

In her autobiography, Myra recalls that her father found it difficult to adjust to civilian life; his wartime experiences were bottled up inside him, something he either couldn't or wouldn't articulate. Like his own father, he began working as a labourer at Gorton Foundry, which had withstood the Luftwaffe bombs to retain its dominance as 'a thudding reverberant wilderness of brick and iron' in Gorton Lane.[7] Bob's return had several repercussions, one of which was a new home for his family. Myra sobbed when her mother told her they were going to live in their own house but was slightly placated when she saw how close it was to Gran's – literally round the corner, at 20 Eaton Street – and virtually identical, although with the twin benefits of electricity and a tiled fireplace. The similarities were odious: an army of cockroaches that scuttled under furniture and into cracks in the walls whenever a light flicked on, and rooms that were just as poky and mottled with damp. The back bedroom, which should have accommodated Myra, had a leaky ceiling and rotting floorboards. She slept in a single bed in her parents' room, resenting the change and the person responsible for it: 'I hated him for forcing us to move away from Gran's . . . having to listen to him snoring and blowing off was a nightmare.'[8]

Bob persevered in building a relationship with Myra. Both he and Nellie were proud of her looks; the resemblance to her father grew more marked as Myra entered her teens, but as a toddler the determined Hindley chin was offset by large grey eyes and a heavy mop of blonde curls. Nellie always ensured that Myra left the house in clothes that were clean, neat and as pretty as their meagre income allowed. If Nellie tried to put a hat on Myra, Bob objected, enjoying the compliments his daughter's curls drew. He was careful to spend time alone with her, visiting nearby Belle Vue, the huge entertainment complex where crowds flocked to the pleasure gardens, roller coasters, Speedway stadium, greyhound racing, pubs, dancing and zoo. Curiously, Myra remembered those visits with less emotion than a trip father and daughter took into the city centre, where in Lewis's department store she suddenly needed the toilet but was too frightened to go into the Ladies alone. Sympathetic to his daughter, Bob asked to see the manager and insisted that Myra be permitted to go into the Gents with him. He refused to listen to objections and eventually the manager gave in.

Bob also took Myra to his relatives, who lived less than a mile away in Longsight. The little girl didn't warm to her paternal grandmother, whom she addressed as Nana Hindley; Bob's mother had dyed curls, wore garish make-up, liked to air her opinions and was a complete contrast to softly spoken, naturally pretty Gran. Her maternal aunts and uncles lived almost on the doorstep: Annie and her husband lived in Gorton's Railway View, while Bert and Kath had married and lived a mile away in Clayton. Jim, to whom Myra was never close, lived in Dukinfield, four miles from Gorton.

Despite the sleeping arrangements at Eaton Street, on 21 August 1946, Nellie gave birth to a second daughter. Myra's sister Maureen had a shock of dark hair and petite, birdlike features. There was no jealousy on Myra's part at the new addition to the family; she worshipped her sister and called her by Bob's nickname for the baby: Moby. Sometimes she called her Mo Baby or just Mo, pet names that lasted into adulthood. Like Myra, Maureen was baptised into the Catholic faith at Bob's insistence. Unlike her, she was not a baby who slept well and most nights were splintered with her sudden wails and lengthy bouts of crying. Nellie found it increasingly hard to cope. Weekday mornings were the worst; Myra helped occupy the baby while Bob dressed and Nellie prepared breakfast.

Another mouth to feed stretched the warring parents' resources to the limit and Bob started bare-knuckle fighting in the evenings to bring in extra money, even though he was disadvantaged by a war wound. Promoters sponsored the matches, which were held in local halls in 'blood tubs' – a moniker which suited the brutish nature of the fights, with their ill-matched contestants and dearth of fair rules. But after an accident at the foundry left him unable to walk without a pronounced limp, Bob retired from fighting and spent his days with other unemployed and elderly men in Gorton's pubs. There were three pubs on adjacent corners of Gorton Lane, in the shadow of his old workplace: the Bessemer, the Shakespeare and, Bob's preferred bolthole, the Steelworks Tavern (the Steelie). His transformation from brawny, newly demobbed breadwinner to jobless semi-invalid got to him most when he drank – his behaviour after last orders was a running thread in Myra's post-trial writings and conversation.

She summarised Bob's violence in an article she submitted to *The Guardian* in 1995: '[He] went off to the pub every night and being a taciturn, bad-tempered man, almost always got into a fight . . . and staggered home bruised and bleeding. I was often sent to the pub to retrieve his jacket which he'd taken off before fighting; it was the only "good" one he had. When my mother berated him for the state he was in, he began knocking her about and when I tried to prevent him, I was hit too.'[9]

Her parents began to row again fiercely at home, and Gran was Myra's ally when the fights became physical: 'Gran was protective of me and we would both protect Mam by attacking him, even before

I started school . . . I remember Gran bashing him with a rolled-up newspaper while I tried to pull his legs from under him.'[10] She laughed as she recounted the story to her prison therapist, explaining how she 'concentrated on the leg with the war wound, which was the weakest one'.[11] Nellie was no cowering victim; as her daughters grew older, she would drink copiously in the Steelie's lounge while Bob stayed in the vault with the men, and she was always as quick as her husband to launch into rows with a punch, but his build, strength and boxing skills made him a fearsome opponent.

Myra created a hostile picture of her father in her re-written autobiography and later conversations, incorporating everything from 'his oily, greasy hands . . . clutching a piece of bread' to an incident when he struck her after finding her smearing shaving foam on her face and scraping it off with a kitchen knife.[12] She maintained that she was singled out by her father for hidings, while her sister was never hit. In her autobiography, there is no mention of violence at her mother's hands, but Myra told her ex-partner Tricia Cairns a different story; according to her, Myra was beaten so badly by her mother that her ears bled, but she spared her mother in print because Nellie stood by her at the trial and afterwards.

While there is no reason to doubt Myra's accounts of being hit by her parents, the slant she put on the stories appears to depend on what purpose was served by their telling. She quickly learned through her encounters with prison doctors that dwelling on a troubled childhood worked in her favour and might be viewed as a mitigating factor in her own psychological make-up. In her *Guardian* article, written as she was approaching another bid for parole, she mused, 'With hindsight I can see that my sense of family values and relationships were seriously undermined by [my father's] influence on me as a child . . . he was far from being a good role model.'[13] She was silent both on the subject of her father's sufferings – although that clearly doesn't excuse his behaviour – and the feminine role models that cushioned her life: indulgent Gran, perhaps her mother Nellie, and certainly aunts Annie and Kath.

The notion that this was the point at which Myra 'accepted' violence, with fatal consequences, is endorsed by Professor Malcolm MacCulloch (former medical director of Ashworth Hospital, previously Park Lane Hospital) in Duncan Staff's book about the Moors Murders, *The Lost*

Boy. In the absence of a fluent explanation behind the crimes from the protagonists themselves and 'in keeping with our culture's Freudian cast of mind', Staff's book is one of many which tries to stitch the fabric of the past into a satisfactory psychological pattern from which the murders then emerge. The credibility of such theories is somewhat undermined by the unfortunate commonness of Myra's childhood experiences.

Although there can be no justification for the mistreatment Myra witnessed and endured as she grew up, or the beatings that Nellie took from her husband, what occurred in the Hindley household was relatively routine in that era and environment; Myra was honest enough to admit as much in her *Guardian* article: 'Friday and Saturday nights were known as "wife-beating" nights: the men worked hard all week and many spent the weekends drinking. Pub closing times were dreaded, because we all knew what would happen. Women ran out into the street, trying to escape from being beaten. All of the kids used to jump out of bed and rush outside to try to stop our fathers hurting our mothers, and we were often turned on too.'[14]

Children were regularly clouted by their parents – and other adults – for the mildest of misdemeanours. Unlike Maureen, who didn't challenge her parents until she was old enough to leave home, as Myra grew up she answered back when her parents rebuked her and was deliberately cheeky, despite knowing that a whack would follow. If Bob and Nellie sought to intimidate Myra by blows, they did not succeed: by the time she was a teenager, Myra was on the whole doing and saying exactly as she pleased. In her late teens, she began dealing with Bob's attacks on her mother by meting out even harsher beatings on him. Her father was weakened then by his war wound and work injury; he would fight with his wife but never retaliated against Myra, except to hold up his arms to defend himself when she punched him and hit him about the body with his own stick. There are hints that her attacks came from something other than a need to protect her mother; by the time she was approaching her twenties, she was known in Gorton as a fighter, and Jim Burns, the uncle to whom Myra was never close, described her 'temper and meanness as a child' as having become 'major faults'.[15] Father and daughter were in many senses cut from the same cloth, as Myra confided in a trusted friend 40 years later: 'If my father were alive, people would notice how much

I resemble him in looks – at least I did when I was young, and I know I took after him in temperament in many respects too.'[16]

She privately admitted that if Ian Brady suffered as a result of his fractured upbringing, she could not validly claim the same: 'I didn't have any traumas in my childhood as he may have done. I didn't have a grudge against the world or society. I had no excuse for my actions.'[17]

3

Progress and conduct: satisfactory.
Personality: not very sociable.
Attendance: consistently unsatisfactory.

Myra Hindley's school report,
Ryder Brow Secondary Modern, 1954

'Any good in me comes from my gran,' Myra wrote to her idealised father figure, David Astor, three years before her death. 'She was a wise, gentle, polite and kindly lady who had not had an easy life and worked her fingers to the bone to make ends meet. She loved me dearly and I loved her more than anyone in the world.'[1] After years of accommodating her children and their spouses, Gran felt as if she rattled like a pea in a bucket alone in the house on Beasley Street. She suggested to Nellie that four-year-old Myra move in to keep her company, perhaps hoping it would help diffuse the tension between Nellie and Bob. He was opposed to the idea, Myra recalled: 'I wanted to go back to Gran's but Dad wouldn't let me . . . eventually he said I could but had to come home for meals.'[2] She doesn't explain why her father was against the move; it may well have been that he feared his daughter would become spoiled by living with her overindulgent grandmother. Myra had three disparate examples of adult behaviour guiding her through her childhood: her strict father, her extremely lenient grandmother and her inconsistent mother, who would let Myra do as she liked one minute, then wallop her for relatively little the next.

Myra's permanent departure from home to Gran's house is often perceived as an unnecessary upheaval of Dickensian cruelty, instilling her with 'a lurking sense of rejection' and the fact that 'there had never been any question of Moby being the one to go' made her banishment seem complete.[3] In reality, there was no discussion about which child should be sent to live with Gran for the simple reason that the request for Myra came from Gran herself; Maureen was then a very young baby who needed her mother. The two houses were so close that Myra could skip between them in a matter of minutes, and she certainly wasn't the only child in Gorton to live with a grandparent: it was a practical arrangement in the overcrowded terraces where working mothers had to rely on family members to mind the kids. And Myra was pleased with the move. Living with Gran meant respite from her bickering, irritable parents. She continued to eat at home because her father insisted upon it but was soon telling her mother that Gran was a better cook, and received a slap for her cheekiness. She was 'forced to eat meals, especially fish, which I hated. I would eat it and be sick rather than get a good hiding.'[4] When she was older and refused to eat what was on her plate, Nellie resorted to serving a side dish of chips at every meal, determined that Myra would leave home with some food in her tummy.

A year later, Myra and Gran moved to 22 Beasley Street. Their new home was scarcely an improvement on the last. As before, the front door opened straight into the front room or 'parlour', where there was a stove and an open staircase, and the second of the two ground-floor rooms was a gloomy space with a lean-to scullery where cold water wheezed from a single tap into a Belfast sink. Upstairs, the wintry back bedroom overlooked the toilet shed in the yard and faced the back window of the Hindley house on Eaton Street. The room was too cold to be functional; Gran slept downstairs next to the stove, while Myra had the front bedroom, sleeping on a tick mattress on a lumpy bed. The furnishings were few: a wardrobe, a chair, a rickety marble-topped chest of drawers and a handmade rag-rug to brighten the floorboards. Gran followed the usual custom of piling old coats on the bed at night for warmth, together with bricks she'd heat in the stove and wrap in newspapers before pushing them under the blankets.

Myra began school in 1947. Gran accompanied her on the three-minute walk there and back to Peacock Street Primary, a sooty, two-storey building opposite the foundry. By the age of seven, Myra was allowed to trot to and from school on her own; she was an independent little girl and sensible enough to be relied upon not to wander off. She soon made friends, though most of the boys and girls were children she already knew, having played with them on the street. A few of them thought her bossy and spoilt, and one lad decided to see how tough she really was by scratching his nails down her face. Myra ran away, crying – and it wasn't Gran to whom she rushed for comfort but her father, who gave her a few tips on how to get the better of her tormentor, then sent her back out to put the theory into practice. In her autobiography, Myra describes the confrontation that followed: 'I set off up the street to meet my persecutor and I quickly concentrated on the things Dad had told me and shown me. As Kenny's hands came up, I shot out my left hand, fist bunched, towards his head. As I had predicted both hands went up to protect his face and I lifted my right hand and slammed it into his tummy, hitting his tummy. With a gasp, Kenny Holden's knees crumpled and, before he could recover, I slammed my left fist into the side of his head. Kenny was so shocked he sat down heavily on the floor and burst into tears. I stood looking down at him, triumphantly.'[5] Her detailed account is imbued with gratification at having beaten her opponent, even though the event itself was long past.

After she had trounced Kenny, her father ruffled her hair and said he was proud of her. He decided to teach Myra how to stick up for herself by passing on a few more boxing techniques. She never forgot his advice: 'Don't put both your hands up. If you can't deflect the first punch with one arm, keep the other one ready to protect your stomach.'[6] Professor MacCulloch cites this as an example of Myra being brutalised by her relationship with her father, but Bob Hindley knew that bullies wouldn't pick on his daughter if she were an equal or bigger threat to them. Myra recalled, 'He would make me fight back if anybody tried to hurt me. I think he would have liked me to be a boy.'[7] Bob's advice stood her in good stead, not only during childhood but also in prison, where she was frequently the target of attack. Tricia Cairns, who grew up in Gorton but didn't meet Myra until she was in prison, admits that you either fought back on the streets or risked being bullied. Myra was able to protect herself and other, more timid children, but only used the skills her father taught her in self-defence.

Myra's relationship with Bob was still unsteady; his awkward efforts at affection were never a success. She told her prison therapist that when she was eight: 'I was sitting in front of the fire in my nightie, and Dad picked me up and sat me on his lap. He suddenly kissed my forehead. I was so shocked it made me jump and I knocked his fag out of his hand. It burnt my shoulder and I ran out of the house screaming that he had burnt me with a fag end ... Poor man, he was only trying to be nice to me, which wasn't often, and I accused him of child abuse. Mam had a go at him for hurting me, so he gave her and me a beating for causing such a fuss.'[8]

She maintained that from then on, rather than letting her parents see when she was upset, she developed 'a strength of character that protected me a lot from emotional harm ... from a very early age I learned to keep [emotions] under control, to refuse to cry when being chastised, except in the privacy of my bedroom at Gran's house, to never let my feelings show, to build up layers of protective buffers, to tremble, rage, cry and grieve inwardly.'[9]

Living with Gran proved a godsend to Myra; there were no raised voices or hands itching to slap in the house on Beasley Street – just softly spoken, doting Gran. Photographs from the time show Myra with a disarming, ready grin and, regardless of her parents' bitter squabbling, she has the look of a confident, happy child, full of mischief and humour. Gorton was her world, familiar as her own reflection.

Beasley Street was in a cluster of terraces set within Gorton Lane to the north, the privately owned houses of Furnival Road to the south, crofts to the west and Casson Street recreation ground to the east. The area was dominated by the two buildings on Gorton Lane that served as the twin custodians of local life – religion and work: the monastery and Gorton Foundry, with trains shunting by on the railway line behind that led into London Road station (renovated and reopened as Piccadilly Station in 1960). Stippled about the neighbourhood were a broad variety of working men's clubs, pubs and cinemas. Home was the domain of women, while the streets belonged to the children. Life was a constant routine: the fish-and-chip tang of Friday and Saturday nights, *Housewives' Choice* blaring from tinny radios, stray dogs barking, the whiff of Woodbines from the corner shop – even the starlings settling on the rooftops seemed rooted to Gorton.

Despite the drunken rows Bob and Nellie conducted on the street, the Hindleys regarded themselves as respectable. Nellie was vigilant about her daughters' clothes and cleanliness, and though she didn't 'hold' with religion, each Sunday Myra was allowed to walk hand-in-hand with her auntie Kath to worship at St Francis' Monastery, joining a congregation that poured in from every corner of the city. Because Kath fasted before morning Mass, Myra did the same, and entered the great church feeling light-headed with hunger and piety. The monastery captivated her, from the hallowed, luminous beauty of the stained glass to the cool grace of the stone arcades. Each Sunday, Myra sought a place at the end of a pew, hoping to catch a drop of the rich, spicy incense as the priest swung it back and forth along the aisle, and she listened with eyes tightly shut and head bent as the hypnotic cadences of the Latin Mass – which she didn't understand – rose and fell. When she was a bit older, she visited the monastery alone through the week, lighting candles and peeping at the folded pieces of paper bearing scribbled prayers. She loved watching the Whit parades too, when whole communities dressed in their best proudly bore embroidered banners through the crowded streets.

Myra was less spellbound by school. She joined other skiving children to play in derelict houses or to run down to the reservoir where 'we would skim stones across the water or try to build rafts out of old doors'.[10] Gran knew about the truanting but ignored it, even when the authorities stepped in; it seems that none of Myra's family took a great interest in her education. Myra recalled: 'I remember the school board man coming to Gran's house. She would tell him I was ill. I don't know what ailment I didn't have as a kid . . .'[11] But Gran was an asset in other respects: 'She helped with my schoolwork,' Myra remembered. 'I liked reading and writing the best. Gran was the main reason I became good in English.'[12]

Myra discovered a passion for books. She enjoyed *Swallows and Amazons*, and all Enid Blyton's books, particularly the Famous Five series, identifying with the tomboy character of George, whose best friend was her dog. Gran acquired a collie named Duke, whom Myra loved. Duke disappeared once and was missing for several days. The local newspaper wrote an article about it, and Duke was found, chipper and unharmed, and reunited with his owner and her ecstatic granddaughter.

Myra's favourite book was one she had to study at school: *The Secret Garden* by Manchester-born author Frances Hodgson Burnett. She read the book again and again in her bedroom at night by candlelight, rapt by the story, whose setting is an isolated mansion reached by a 'rough-looking road' through a 'great expanse of dark apparently spread out before and around them . . . a wind was rising and making a singular, wild, low rushing sound like the sea'.[13] Curled up on the tick mattress in Gran's house, Myra imagined she was Mary, the girl in the book, whose guardian reassures her that it isn't the sea she can hear but 'the wind blowing through the bushes . . . It's a wild, dreary enough place to my mind, though there's plenty that likes it – particularly when the heather's in bloom.'[14] It's the moor through which they drive, and the girl in the story is instinctively afraid of it: 'On and on they drove through the darkness . . . Mary felt as if the drive would never come to an end and that the wide, bleak moor was a wide expanse of black ocean through which she was passing on a strip of dry land. "I don't like it," she said to herself. "I don't like it," and she pinched her thin lips more tightly together . . .'[15]

Myra's best friend was Joyce Hardy, a lively little girl with blonde hair in an urchin cut. Joyce lived on Beyer Street, just behind Peacock Street Primary, and after school she and Myra would play marbles together and buy sweets, if they could afford them, from the herbalist. They used to perform a trick made popular by the comedian Harry Worth: standing in the glass doorway of the dry cleaner's, extending one arm and one leg to make it look as if they were levitating in their reflection. They invented games based on ones they already knew; Britain in the early 1950s was an ascetic place in which very few people could afford bought entertainments and most had never seen a television. Children were baffled when adults 'reminisced about eating oranges, pineapples and chocolate; they bathed in a few inches of water, and wore cheap, threadbare clothes with "Utility" labels . . . Austerity had left its mark, and many people who had scrimped and saved through the post-war years found it hard to accept the attitudes of their juniors during the long boom that followed.'[16]

The 'long boom' didn't begin until well after Myra left primary school. In her final year at Peacock Street, she was nicknamed 'Beanstalk' because she was so tall and lanky. Her hair had grown long and poker-straight, and she caught nits from someone at school. Gran parked her by the sink, rubbed vile-smelling liquid into her hair and dragged a steel comb through the dark-blonde lengths. She got rid of the nits, but when Myra went outside to play she was spotted by Eddie Hogan, who jeered, 'Nitty Nora!' Myra was furious. She raced up and pummelled him to the ground while a crowd of yelling children gathered. Gran, hearing the commotion, came out and hauled her off Eddie, who limped away, ashamed at having been beaten by a girl. Myra records this fight, too, in her autobiography, adding with characteristic remembered glee, 'Eddie never called me Nitty Nora again.'[17]

Despite her poor attendance record, Myra's school marks were good. Records show her IQ rating as 109, above average, and she sat the 11-plus exam at Levenshulme High. Upon arrival, she was overwhelmed by the prospect of grammar school and stared at the pupils in their immaculate uniforms, trying to fathom how her parents would afford such extravagance. She failed the entrance exam, hinting in her autobiography that she did so deliberately.

Nellie wanted her daughter to attend Ryder Brow Secondary Modern, close to home, but some of Myra's friends were going on to the Catholic school attached to the monastery and Myra was eager to join them. Bob supported his daughter, but Nellie was vehement: no Catholic school for Myra – that was the deal. Bob tried to sway his wife by inviting an old school friend of his, Father Roderick, to drop by to discuss the matter. The visit was a disaster, as Myra recalled in a letter written while she was on remand; Father Roderick declared that because Bob and Nellie had married in a registry office rather than a church, Myra and Maureen were nothing but bastards. Bob barely managed to restrain his fists as he propelled the priest towards the door. Myra shot off to tell Gran that she was a bastard like her and her mother before her. No amount of pleading, sobbing and shouting on Myra's part after that could persuade Nellie to send Myra anywhere but Ryder Brow.

Myra began attending the school – a three-quarter-mile walk from Gran's house – in September 1953. Although she was unhappy at being separated from some of her closest friends, the more affluent backgrounds of a few classmates inspired her with ambition. She recalled, 'I felt like a fish out of water at first. All of the other kids seemed to have big smart houses and smart clothes, but I still lived in the same house, with a loo down the backyard. This had quite an effect on me at the time and I remember thinking: one day, I'll have all of that.'[18]

Myra settled in sooner than she had expected and found a new best friend, Pat Jepson, whom she already knew. Pat lived on Taylor Street, just round the corner from Gran's house. The two girls spent their evenings and weekends together, playing games on the crofts around Belle Vue. Pat recalls: 'I don't remember Myra crying or being a bad sport . . . Myra was a strong character. If we were going anywhere, she picked the place to go . . . She wasn't a violent person, but if she said something it was taken that it was done.'[19]

Still taller than average, and skinny, as puberty crept in, Myra developed large hips, and local lads would rile her by shouting 'Square Arse' – though few risked saying it within walking distance. 'Myra wouldn't let herself be pushed around by any of the boys,' Pat remembers, 'She was so tough she frightened some of them off. She was so much a tomboy that I sometimes thought that she wanted to be a boy. On the other hand, she was very intelligent and could hold her own on any subject.'[20]

Myra was in the A stream throughout her time at Ryder Brow, although she wasn't an enthusiastic pupil. English remained her favourite subject, and she loved poetry, but otherwise sat listlessly in the classroom. The headmaster, Trevor Lloyd-Jones, tried to engage her by suggesting that she keep an official class diary. She did as he asked, but without any interest. He set her a second task: writing an essay for a classmate to illustrate. Myra had a gift for creative prose – her essays were often read aloud – and she threw herself into the project. The resulting story, 'Adventure at Four Oaks Farm', was exceptional. She let her imagination follow where Blyton and Ransom had led, filling an entire exercise book with the tale of a group of intrepid children. Her friend Jean Hicks drew the accompanying pictures. When Myra handed it in, Lloyd-Jones was delighted and said he was going to have it bound and put in the school library. Her sister Maureen – then at primary school – recalled Myra writing two other essays that were highly praised by the teachers, one about a leopard in a jungle, the other about a shipwreck.

She was clever and could have excelled at school but was too idle and had no one to properly motivate her. Practical work was never her strong point: she couldn't draw and her attempts at needlework were wretched. Myra's friend Pauline Clapton explains that Myra's talents lay elsewhere: 'Myra could run very fast and she would have a go at any game. She was always the best in the gym class. She was in the school rounders team and I remember she made up a song that started, "How would you like to be/in the Ryder rounders team with me?"[21]

Anne Murdoch was also in the school rounders team: 'I didn't like Myra one bit. She hung around with a gang of girls and was dead cocky. We got off to a bad start: during an early rounders match, I hit the ball and pelted down the field and could hear her screaming at me, "Run faster, go on, faster than that, bloody RUN!" I was fuming and faced up to her, "If I'd run any faster I'd have ended up on my head." She didn't like being challenged. "Don't you *dare* speak to me like that," she said. "I'll hit you with my bat if you're not careful." I walked off. After a while we got on all right, but we were never friends. She was still a terror during rounders, though – if Myra stumped you out, you didn't dare argue. She'd fix you with that glare of hers.'[22] Naturally gifted at field events such as javelin and discus, Myra was a strong defence in netball because she was so quick and lithe. Her nimble climbing won her another nickname: Monkey. Boys admired her sporting abilities, but she wasn't pretty enough to grab their attention otherwise. She was more popular with girls, entertaining them by playing the mouth organ and making up little ditties. Linda Maguire, then head girl at Ryder Brow, remembers Myra as 'funny and always singing, with long, lanky hair'.[23]

Her attendance record didn't improve, however. Myra begged her mother and Gran to write notes justifying her absences, and when they refused she wrote them herself. On one occasion, she and Pat Jepson skived school and sneaked round to Gran's house, expecting it to be empty. When they heard footsteps at the door, they fled. In a fit of remorse, Myra decided to confess to Nana Hindley that she and Pat had played truant. Bob's mother reacted with unusual calmness and proposed that Myra and Pat should spend the rest of the day cleaning Gran's house on Beasley Street and Nellie's on Eaton Street. Gran agreed to the idea when she heard, although she knew exactly what Bob's mother was insinuating – that she and Nellie didn't keep their homes in order. But she let it pass and set Myra and Pat to work.

The teachers at Ryder Brow admitted defeat over Myra's truancy; one morning Trevor Lloyd-Jones asked the class to give Myra a round of applause: she had successfully attended school for five days in a row. Myra shrugged it off with a grin.

Although she disliked school, Myra wasn't unsociable. Her unwillingness to become involved in classroom discussions was due to boredom, not hostility. As a teenager, she got on well with most of her peers and the younger children. She was always happy to spend time with her sister Maureen, who was small, dark-haired and dainty. Maureen copied everything Myra said and did, and the two of them were as close as siblings could be. Maureen was also a nippy little fighter when she needed to be, but was occasionally bullied. In a 1977 letter, Myra reminisced to a friend that she often 'leathered' kids who picked on her sister and recalled an instance where one girl had been tormenting Maureen for weeks without anyone else realising; when Myra found out, she chased the girl across a field: 'She glimpsed me pelting across and started running like the clappers, but I grabbed her before she had time to lock herself in her backyard and pasted hell out of her. Her big brother, who was in my class, came out and, scared though I was of him, for he was the bigger bully, I went for him before he came for me. To my amazement – to say nothing of relief – he threw his sister and himself into the backyard and bolted the door ... Returning home, filthy and scruffy, I got yelled at by Gran and clouted by Mam, who, when Maureen explained, was full of contrition, but, bristling with indignation, I stole without compunction two of my mother's Park Drives and decided to run away from home – until about 10, when I returned because I was starving hungry.'[24]

As a teenager, Myra was a keen babysitter, and she and Pat Jepson spent many hours looking after neighbours' children. Mrs Joan Phillips was a regular customer. 'They were a grand pair of lasses,' she recalled. 'They were often round the house, drinking tea and talking about clothes and boys. They never used to take a penny for babysitting – they wouldn't hear of it – but I used to take the two of them to the pictures now and again as a treat ... My husband used to say he liked Myra to babysit because we could go out in peace, knowing everything would be all right if she was there. My boys loved her because she would spoil them. She used to bring them chocolate and let them stay up late, and when it was light in the evenings, she used to play football with them on the bit of wasteland near our house. In her last year at school, she and Pat Jepson used to play wag and come round to our house to hide. Myra was wonderful with our Denis. He was only a year old. She used to turn a kitchen chair on its side and put him in-between the legs to teach him to stand up and then to walk. She used to take Gordon, who was about six or seven, to see the cowboys at the children's matinee on a Saturday at the Cosmo or the Essoldo. Often I would come in and find she'd have Gordon all scrubbed clean and in his pyjamas ready for bed – I think it was the only time he liked being washed, because she made such a game of it. She was like that, Myra, always full of fun, and if she wasn't chattering on about boys or records, she would be singing the latest tune. You never saw her depressed.'[25]

Myra was only miserable when she was forced to spend time at home with her rowing parents. Once she repeated something she had picked up at school, telling her father he only had one bad habit. When he asked what it was, she replied flatly, 'Breathing.' The comment wounded Bob; he got up from his chair and left the house in silence. Nellie, for once, said nothing either.

Allan Grafton, who lived on Casson Street and was two years younger than Myra but got to know her during football sessions at Ryder Brow, remembers Bob Hindley in a different light: 'I played football on a Sunday for the Steelworks Tavern and Bob Hindley was our sponsor. He was really a super guy, and what happened to his daughter later killed him. When we came back from playing football, he'd be sitting in the vault, first seat behind the door, and he used to buy all the lads a drink. Every Sunday the monks from St Francis' Monastery would come round selling their wine – St Francis wine. The monks would get up early, tread the grapes for the wine, do the service and then three of them got on pushbikes and rode up to the Steelworks Tavern in their cassocks to sell their wine and have a few beers. Bob Hindley never let them buy their own drinks – he paid for all the monks' booze. We'd be just getting in from football as the monks were ready for going and the landlord used to shout for us to nip out of the pub on Gorton Lane to watch these three drunken monks, cassocks flying, wobbling on their bikes back to church. Bob was smashing with them, and with us. Obviously, I only knew him as a person outside the house, but I never once saw him in a fight. He was a kind, generous man. Myra's mother on the other hand – she was a bawler and a shouter. You'd hear her yelling every day, "Mau-reeeeen! Come in for yer tea!" She was tall and slim, and always used to walk about with her arms folded. Myra did the same, and Maureen.'[26] Allan remembers Myra as 'one of the lads. We used to practise football on Ryder Brow field and she'd hang out with us. Afterwards we'd pile into a pub just off Ryder Brow called The Haxby for pints of shandy. We were underage, but the landlord never bothered because we didn't cause any trouble. Myra always came in with us. Because she was such a tomboy the lads never took much interest in her. She could look after herself anyway; she was good company, but she said what she thought and didn't hold anything back.'[27]

When she wasn't with her friends or sister, Myra was content to be at home with Gran. All the neighbours knew Ellen Maybury well, and liked her. One of the most frequent visitors was Hettie Rafferty. She was a similar age to Gran and had a ready laugh, though their conversation was often morbid; they liked to speculate on which of them might die first and discussed their acquaintances' various ailments. When a penniless friend died, Gran cashed in part of her own funeral insurance to buy the man a coffin. She then 'laid out' his body and kept the coffin in her front room prior to burial.

Myra arrived home to find the house reeking of embalming fluid and Gran and Hettie Rafferty sitting with the coffin. Sensing her alarm, Gran suggested that Myra see for herself how peaceful the old man looked. Myra edged forward and peered in the coffin, where the old man appeared to be asleep. She reached out to touch his hand, then withdrew quickly from the feel of his cold skin. The following day the coffin had gone.

There were other reminders of mortality that winter, 1954. One afternoon Gran had a visitor whom she hadn't seen for many years: her daughter Louie's widower, Jim. Gran welcomed him in with a smile and invited him to stay for tea, but after he'd gone she broke down, vividly remembering the daughter who had died at such a young age. Her depression lingered, but she tried to deflect Myra's concern by telling her she was worried about her eyesight. Myra insisted that she visit a doctor, and when Gran took her advice, she discovered that she had cataracts and needed an operation.

Myra was distraught when Gran was admitted to hospital. She was supposed to stay with her parents, but after dark she slipped out and ran back home to Gran's, where she spent a fitful and forlorn night in the front room, wearing Gran's old coat for comfort. Nellie told Myra that children weren't allowed on the ward, but Myra begged her mother to sneak her in somehow. To placate her, Nellie styled Myra's hair and put a bit of make-up on her; she passed the scrutiny of the nurses and hurried to the ward but burst into tears when she saw Gran sitting up in bed with her head swathed in bandages. Gran told her that the operation had been a success. When visiting hours were over, Myra decided to do something constructive and pressed her mother and Aunt Annie into decorating the front room. She and Gran had recently moved again, and their new home had electricity, a copper boiler in an outhouse for heating water and a bedroom that Gran could finally call her own. It was their third house in the same street, but the address was different because the street had been renamed; Myra and Gran now lived at 7 Bannock Street.[28] Myra's relief when her grandmother arrived home was palpable. Gran's vision was better than it had been in years and her face lit up when she saw the vibrant red wallpaper in the sitting-room and the special meal Myra and Nellie had prepared.

Myra's fear of losing her grandmother had been dispelled, but the following year she suffered a disturbing bereavement when her close friend Michael Higgins drowned. His death came out of nowhere, on a perfect summer's day, and had a profound and lasting effect on her.

Michael Higgins was not the sort of boy Myra usually befriended. Now nearly 15, Myra was feisty and outspoken. She let it be known that she fancied the head boy at school, Ronnie Woodcock, and she had been smoking for a while, openly lighting cigarettes on the bus that chartered pupils from Ryder Brow to the public baths. Michael, in contrast, was a small and diffident 13 year old, who lived on Taylor Street and attended Catholic school. Despite their obvious differences, Michael and Myra became inseparable; she told him that because they had the same initials, they were fated to be friends and their lives destined to be entwined. 'I felt very protective towards Michael,' Myra told her prison therapist. 'He was always bullied and I would stick up for him. We spent a lot of time together.'[29]

Michael emerged from his shell when he was with her. Myra's sturdy presence gave him the nerve to do things he wouldn't normally dare. They couldn't afford to go to the Speedway at Belle Vue very often, so would sneak in without paying. Speedway was then Britain's second most popular spectator sport and every large town had a track.

Myra and Michael discovered that by scrambling over various walls and fences, and crossing the railway line, they could squeeze in at a secret spot without being noticed. Myra was bold enough for the two of them and would brag her way into the riders' enclosure by telling security guards that she had been sent by her nana, 'Kitty' Hindley (Bob's mother worked at Belle Vue, where she met the married lover whom Nellie called her 'fancy man'). Michael was thrilled when they gained access; he and Myra begged the drivers for autographs, adding considerable value to the Speedway programmes Michael collected.

Myra's bravado led to another prank that could have landed them in serious trouble. Together with Eddie Hogan – whose 'Nitty Nora' slur had long been forgiven – she and Michael would go into local stores and, while Myra chatted away to the shopkeeper, Michael and Eddie filled their pockets with sweets. Years later Myra referred to her 'criminal apprenticeship' as involving a few minor acts of juvenile theft, including stealing some potatoes from a local greengrocer 'to roast on a bonfire we had made, and on another occasion I ran off with some Christmas cards. I was waiting to pay for them, but I kept getting ignored, so I ran off. I also remember stealing some alleys (marbles) from Woolworths.'[30]

Creeping into Gorton Tank was a more dangerous activity. She and Michael liked to clamber about the trains in the huge railway yard, but on one occasion they were seen and chased out. As they fled, laughing, Myra felt a searing pain shoot up her leg; her ankle was caught in a steel trap and blood poured from the serrated wound. Michael raced for help and found her uncle Bert, who carried Myra home. In her autobiography, Myra recalls that while she was lying on the sofa waiting for the doctor to arrive, she asked Michael plaintively if he thought she might die. He laughed at her: 'Course not! You're too young.'[31]

Of all their escapades, swimming in the disused reservoir in Mellands Fields on the outskirts of Gorton was the most perilous. The water was fenced off, hidden behind thick trees and fertile allotments, and only the most foolhardy ventured in. Two years earlier a girl had been saved from drowning there and several people had committed suicide in its murky, weed-filled depths. Another Gorton resident recalls, 'We were strictly forbidden from going to the res. My mam always told us, "Don't go in, mind, cos the Jenny Green-teeth (weeds) will drag you under.'"[32] But Myra and Michael went in, swimming until their limbs ached, then lying drowsily on the grassy bank in the sunlight, letting the water pearl off them.

Friday, 14 June 1957 was the day of the Whit parade. The city was in the middle of a heatwave and Myra could feel the perspiration trickling down her neck as she and Pat Jepson and Pat's sister Barbara stood watching the procession. Michael had been given the honour of carrying one of the embroidered banners. Myra cheered as he passed them, and waved at Eddie Hogan, who marched alongside Michael. When the procession had gone by, Myra accompanied Pat and Barbara to tea at their aunt's house in Reddish, having turned down Michael's idea of swimming in the res. Myra and her friends were dressed in their best – new white outfits bought for Whitsun.

On the way home, they stood on the open rear platform of the bus to get some air, but the draught from the road was hot and gritty. Myra saw a boy pedalling furiously to catch up with the bus and realised it was a lad who lived near Pat and Barbara on Taylor Street. He was shouting at them. The girls jumped down as the bus slowed and the boy told them breathlessly that there had been an accident at the reservoir in Mellands Fields. Myra didn't wait for him to finish; she turned and started running. Pat and Barbara raced to keep up with her, as she flew down the streets and headed across the playing fields to the reservoir. A huddle of people were walking slowly towards them, where the sun glittered on the water behind the trees. Someone detached themselves from the crowd and responded to Myra's high-pitched, panic-stricken questions.

That afternoon, Michael had been swimming with Eddie Hogan and a younger boy called Walter King. After a rest on the sun-drenched bank, Michael and Walter dived back in. Walter noticed after a while that Michael appeared to be thrashing about and 'in difficulties' but shouted at him to stop fooling around.[33] Then Michael shot out an arm and pulled Walter under the water. Walter struggled free and resurfaced, gasping for breath. He looked frantically for Michael, but there was no sign of him in the still water.

From the grassy bank, Eddie Hogan watched in disbelief; he, too, thought Michael had been 'larking about'.[34] An older boy who had seen the two lads go under realised it wasn't a wind-up and dived into the reservoir to look for Michael. Someone else alerted the police.

Within minutes, uniformed figures from the fire brigade, as well as several policemen, were wading into the dark water. The wide reservoir varied in depth from ten feet to twenty-five and could be numbingly cold, even on a hot summer's day. Grappling lines were brought in and Michael's parents were told that their son was missing.

At ten to seven in the evening, a Lancashire County Police frogman finally broke the surface of the reservoir with Michael's body in his arms.

'It was just lying on the bottom,' he told the inquest later, 'face downwards. The water was dark and clouded with mud. The deeper he went down, the colder it got.'[35]

On the bank, Laurence Jordan, who lived near Myra, watched in horror: 'I saw them bringing out this chalk-white body. You could see the whiteness of the body against the blue uniform of the police. His arms were outstretched . . . They hurriedly put him in the mortuary van.'[36] Michael's mother stumbled into the ambulance to be with the body of her 13-year-old son.

Myra was hysterical. Pat recalled: 'It was the only time I ever saw Myra cry.'[37] Pat and Barbara took her home with them, but Myra couldn't stop sobbing and kept repeating that she should have been with him, that if she'd gone with him that afternoon he would still be alive. Mrs Jepson told Myra not to blame herself – there was nothing anyone could have done. 'If I'd been there, I might have saved him' became Myra's refrain, one she still repeated forty years later.[38]

Her other friends who had witnessed the accident congregated in a cafe nearby. 'It went round like wildfire,' Allan Grafton remembers. 'We all went to the sarsaparilla bar on Gorton Lane. We used to go there a lot. They had pumps, seats and a bar as you went in, but it was all soft drinks and you could get pints of sarsaparilla, dandelion and burdock, that sort of thing. We sat there talking about it until the place shut, unable to take it in. His death that summer was absolutely shattering for the neighbourhood.'[39]

Myra dreamed of Michael that night, of trying to swim under the dark, reedy water to save him. She pestered her mother to make a black armband and wore it as she traipsed from door to door collecting money for a funeral wreath. Touched by her distress, Mrs Higgins gave Myra a few of Michael's belongings – his Speedway programmes and a comb – but to everyone else there was something eerie about the intensity of Myra's grief. Her face took on a white, pinched look.

Mrs Higgins worried about the effect of her son's death on the girl and asked her to visit the house when the coffin was brought in before the funeral, thinking that might bring her some peace. Years later, Myra remembered seeing Michael in his coffin: the sliver of light under his eyelids, and his mother gently sliding the rosary from his fingers to give to her. Allan Grafton also went along: 'His mother and father invited the kids in, all of us who'd known Michael, to see him in the coffin in the front room. I went in and came straight out again – I couldn't do it. I thought I'd be all right, but I looked at the faces of my friends who had already been in and I thought, no, this isn't for me. I went to his funeral, though. Quite a few of us went.'[40]

A requiem Mass was said for Michael at St Francis' Monastery. Every pew was filled to capacity, but Myra's name was not on the list of mourners published in the *Gorton & Openshaw Reporter* on 21 June 1957. She explained later, 'I couldn't go to his funeral because I was frightened. His death was hard to come to terms with. It made me realise how final death is. He was the first person who had gone from my life for good.'[41] She waited at a distance during the internment at Gorton cemetery, back turned to the mourners, while Pat described what was happening.

The local newspaper reported that the inquest into Michael's death found that he had drowned after getting cramp from the cold water. The verdict of accidental death was no comfort to Myra: 'My faith was being seriously tested by this. I wanted some kind of sign to tell me it wasn't just the end of everything.'[42] She told her prison therapist that her grief was profound but had no pernicious influence on her otherwise, and she was revolted by 'fools [who] said that Michael's death made me start to hate the world we live in, to hate society. Those cretins just need to find one reason for my crimes.'[43] She conceded only that it 'brought about a drastic change in my personal beliefs and really it has never left me'.[44]

Day after day, she sat alone at his grave, bringing flowers she had picked from hedgerows and gardens. She prayed with Michael's mother at church but 'cried openly and was inconsolable for weeks after his death, until I was told there was something wrong with me; I was abnormal, I'd be ill, I had to pull myself together, I'd become "soft in the head". Well-meaning words, no doubt, but they only served my need and ability to bury my emotions as deep as I could.'[45]

In her autobiography, she recalls being at the Jepsons' house on Taylor Street and watching the rain trickle in silver lines down the windows. The rain appeared to shimmer and when she looked beyond it, to the opposite side of the street and the 'Bug Hut' Plaza cinema, she saw Michael standing hunched in the shadow of the fire escape. He wore his black overcoat and stared straight at her. Myra leapt up and wrenched open the front door; cars splashed past and people walked quickly by with umbrellas, but the gap beneath the fire escape was empty. Michael had gone.

She returned to the house, disturbed and drenched to the skin. The memory of Michael haunted Myra for the rest of her life: 'Sometimes I can still see him in that murky water, reaching out for me.'[46]

4

Myra used to go to church. She liked dancing and swimming.
She liked the normal way of life. She had many girlfriends.
And she liked children.

Maureen Hindley, evidence at 'Moors trial', 1966

Myra Hindley's first appearance in the press was in honour of her achievements. On 19 July 1957, the *Gorton & Openshaw Reporter* featured a column about Ryder Brow school sports day. Myra had covered herself with glory; on an afternoon of 'keen competition' she excelled: 'Individual Championships . . . Senior Girls, Myra Hindley, 10 awards'.[1] The overall winner in her year among the girls, Myra's triumphs included coming first in high jump, second in javelin and third in the 220-yard run.

Her last term at school occurred in a period of sweeping social change. The Suez Crisis of the previous year proved that although Britain's days of Empire were at an end, the gloom of austerity was beginning to disperse, with rationing no longer in force and sales of consumer goods such as washing machines and televisions escalating. Wages and living standards were on the rise, and one of the first signs of significant change in people's lives was how they shopped: in the major cities, housewives abandoned their daily queuing at individual stores and embraced the supermarket – which, in their infancy, were still nothing like the vast emporiums they are today. Convenience foods in cans and foil containers proliferated, while new products like fish fingers, tinned steak-and-kidney pies and pre-sliced white bread appeared on the shelves. The tea bag was launched in 1952, and a decade later Nescafé's instant coffee became a contender for the nation's favourite drink. Youngsters guzzled fizzy pop: Coca-Cola, Vimto and Tizer. Old essentials such as sugar lumps, candles and turnips were replaced by camera films, telephone rentals, dog food and nylon stockings, while high-street stores – WH Smith, Burton and Woolworths – flourished. 'Deep in the national psyche,' wrote journalist Christopher Booker, 'was the knowledge that a very real watershed had been passed ... the dam had burst.'[2]

Nowhere was the upheaval more evident than in Myra's age group; she was a teenager when the phrase first came into common use in Britain, when girls began to be freed from the drudgery of housework as appliances took over and National Service was abolished for boys in 1960. The popularity of coffee bars springing up in every town centred around jewel-bright jukeboxes where the latest single flipped into riotous life for sixpence a throw. Britain's first Top Twelve Chart, cribbed from the American Billboard Chart, appeared on the pages of *The New Musical Express* in 1952, although for a while ballads sung by old-fashioned crooners held the top spots until Bill Haley and the Comets exploded into the chart in 1954 with 'Rock Around the Clock' and 'Shake, Rattle and Roll'. Almost overnight, rock 'n' roll – black slang since the early 1920s for sex – became the soundtrack to British teenagers' lives.

In 1955, four million singles were sold in Britain; by 1963, that figure had risen to sixty-one million. In September 1956, when Myra was 14, the film *Rock Around the Clock* was released in British cinemas and, in Manchester, the press reported: 'A thousand screaming, jiving, rhythm-crazy teenagers surged through the city . . . sweeping aside police cordons and stopping traffic.'[3] Two months into the new year, the first episode of a youth-orientated music show aired on the BBC, with Pete Murray addressing the nation's teen boys and girls: 'Welcome aboard the *Six-Five Special*. We've got almost a hundred cats jumping here, some real cool characters to give us the gas, so just get with it and have a ball.'[4] Over ten million viewers tuned in to the show, which set a trend; ITV launched their equivalent, *Oh Boy!*, a few months later, and in 1959 the most popular programme of its kind, *Juke Box Jury*, burst onto screens, with its celebrity panel declaring new singles a 'Hit' or a 'Miss'.

Although Myra's voice joined those yelling along to *Rock Around the Clock*, her idol was Elvis Presley, who had his first number one single in Britain with 'All Shook Up' in the month she left school: July 1957. She saw his first film, *Loving You*, twice a night for a whole week when it was shown at Manchester's Apollo, queued for every record he released, collected souvenirs and put together a scrapbook of newspaper and magazine clippings about the swivel-hipped singer.

Furthering her education was the last thing on her mind; she wanted to find employment and have money to spend: 'I couldn't wait to leave school and start work, which I did days after my 15th birthday. [They] were the happiest days of my life, except for those of my childhood when I didn't have to go to school. I had a wide circle of friends with whom I went dancing, swimming and roller-skating and also spent a lot of time in local libraries, where I could browse and read in peace and quiet.'[5] She was pleased when Lloyd-Jones gave her an excellent reference, and took a test to assess her suitability for a College of Further Education: 'I was delighted when I passed because I wanted to learn secretarial skills. I didn't want to end up in a dead-end job like most women seemed to.'[6] She rejected a place at teacher training college in Didsbury and applied for a position as a junior clerk at an electrical engineering company, Lawrence Scott and Electrometers, on Louisa Street.

She was offered the post but was a couple of weeks short of her 15th birthday – the firm's required age limit for staff – so Auntie Kath found her a temporary position with a catalogue company in the city centre until then. The pay was good: £3 per week and tax-free. For a fortnight, Myra packed shoes and ran errands for the sales representatives, then on 26 July began work at Lawrence Scott, where the salary was less but the prospects considerably better. Her duties were limited to some light typing, running more errands and making tea. She enjoyed being part of a team and bantering with colleagues. When she mislaid her first week's wage packet and told the other girls about it, they organised a whip-round to replace the money with a few bob extra thrown in to cheer her up. Their generosity was soon withdrawn when she came into work one day with a tearful story about losing her pay packet again. The girls weren't fooled, and some of them turned against her, calling her 'a hard cow'.[7]

Other colleagues continued to be friendly. One of the girls, Margie, had a flat and invited her over for an evening. Hearing that Myra was thinking about changing her hair colour (she was fed up with being dishwater-brown), Margie immediately offered to bleach it. That same night Myra changed her image forever: when the peroxide was rinsed off and her hair blow-dried into a puff ball, the result was shockingly different. Myra stared at her reflection in the mirror, aghast. The awkward, lank-haired school-leaver had gone; in her place was Myra Hindley, slinky candyfloss blonde.

Myra knew her appearance would cause a stir at home and at work. It did: her mother was incandescent with rage and struck her across the face, telling her she looked cheap. But to Myra's relief she said nothing about dyeing it back again, and Bob contented himself with a few choice words about bottle blondes. The men at her workplace were more appreciative, and for the first time she had a glimpse of the power a sexually attractive woman could wield. She started going into the association room, where her colleagues – mainly the men – played table tennis and listened to the latest singles. When one lad offered to teach her how to play the game, Myra readily agreed and joined the company team, as they bussed about the city for table-tennis tournaments that usually ended in the pub. One of the older women advised Myra to be careful with her alcohol intake if she didn't want to get herself a reputation.

The workforce at Lawrence Scott made a point of socialising together after clocking off and funded their nights out with a weekly kitty. Myra's first evening out with her colleagues was at Levenshulme Palais, where she wore a blue knitted dress, blue shoes and matching handbag. She managed to stay sober but spent the entire night jiving and smooching on the dance floor with a welder called Ray. His blond hair was gelled into a quiff and he drove a fast motorbike when they went out on dates. They split up when Myra refused to sleep with him; she feared falling pregnant like her friend Dodo, whose boyfriend was a Teddy boy.

She'd learned the rudimentary facts of life from gossip with other girls, knowing that there was no point raising the subject with her mother, who hadn't even known when Myra began menstruating: 'The smell of toasted bread reminds me of my first period. I was sitting in front of the fire eating toast when it happened, and I panicked and ran to Gran . . . We never talked about sex in our house and Mam didn't warn me about periods. In fact, I never had any sex education at all. I don't think anybody did in those days.'[8] The impulsive element in her personality was limited to experimenting with her looks and skiving from work. She relished her wage packet and socialising with colleagues (whose netball team she had joined), but the actual business of working left her cold. On the rare occasions when she could be bothered to put in an appearance, she idled away the hours in the loos, puffing on Park Drives and keeping a casual lookout while some of the girls busied themselves with their sideline – buying and selling from catalogues.

One member of the household was lost that year when Duke was fatally run over. Myra was distraught. Gran immediately bought another collie and gave it the unimaginative name Lassie. Myra lavished the dog with attention but pined for Duke, who had been a loyal childhood companion.

Myra began to grow increasingly dissatisfied with her life. Holidays were still uniformly domestic, but the whiff of foreign possibilities was there in newly popular French recipes and Italian fashions and the ubiquitous coffee bar with its air of European sophistication. Myra had overhauled the way she looked, but her lifestyle was unchanged. There was a brief escape with Margie to Butlins in Ayr (funded by second jobs in a jam factory for both girls), but then it was back to Gorton and the tacky glamour of local dance halls. 'Myra liked jiving, it was the only kind of dancing she would do,' Pat Jepson recalled.[9] Myra and Pat attended Stan's Dancing School off Knutsford Road, where classes on Wednesday, Thursday and Saturday cost 1s 6d. They tried out the jive sessions at Chick Hibbert's on Ashton Old Road, although the place was more dive than jive, and frequented the seedily glamorous Ashton Palais, where rockers often roared up on their motorbikes to start fights in the car park. On one occasion Myra and Pat travelled to a dance in Ashton-under-Lyne (five miles from Gorton), then missed the last bus home and had to stay at a friend's house. Pat remembers: 'I got a clout, but Myra's mother batted her in the street and she wasn't allowed out for a week.'[10]

Sivori's, the espresso cafe opposite the town hall on Hyde Road, was *the* place to be seen in. Allan Grafton recalls, 'Everyone used to meet there. Myra was hanging around with a different football team then, the Mission Lads. We used to tease her about her hair. She was loud and brash, but still OK, though if you said too much, you'd more than likely see the back of her hand.'[11] Myra and Pat dawdled by the jukebox, sipping hot Vimto and nibbling on Holland's pies. They had their own uniform, favouring pencil skirts, cardigans that buttoned up at the back and ballet pumps. Myra disliked the full-skirted fashions; she preferred tight skirts and sweaters worn over cone-shaped bras and roll-on girdles – the Hitchcock Blonde look.

She visited Ashton market with a group of friends, buying herself a complete outfit from one of the stalls. She was learning the age-old art of accentuating her good points – a strong face and slim legs – and camouflaging the bad – a beaked nose and broad bottom. She favoured scarlet lipstick and heavy, spit-slicked mascara worn with eyeliner as sooty as the bricks of Gorton Foundry.

After the initial row over hair colour, Nellie agreed to bleach Myra's roots and she returned the favour by curling her mother's hair using fire-warmed tongs. Eventually, Myra decided to have her hair professionally coloured and styled. There was a salon on Taylor Street called Maison Laurette where she and Pat experimented with beauty treatments; Myra paid 10s 6d to have her hair bleached a dazzling white-blonde. The salon owner, Mrs Laurette Howells, showed her how to create the beehive look by putting rollers in her hair every night and protecting them with a headscarf until the following morning.

'I thought I was fairly attractive to men,' Myra reflected, 'although some might argue, and I had a series of short-term relationships, but none that really satisfied me.'[12] Her friend Pat Jepson recalls, 'Myra never bothered much with boys. Of course she used to go out with them but not a lot. Myra looked very grown-up ... I think she thought the boys around our way were too young for her.'[13] Yet one neighbour complained to Nellie Hindley that Myra was always kissing lads outside her back door on Almond Street.

The summer of 1958 brought a week's holiday for Myra with Pat's family in Blackpool, but she was still at odds with herself. Michael's mother asked her if she'd considered what the Church might do for her and Myra began taking instruction in the Roman Catholic faith from tall, bespectacled Father Theodore at St Francis' Monastery. Nellie swallowed her disapproval and joined the family to watch the Bishop of Salford anoint Myra. Auntie Kath was delighted, having always guided Myra's interest in the Church, and presented her with an expensive prayer book. On the flyleaf was the dedication, 'To Myra, from Auntie Kath and Uncle Bert. November 16th 1958. Souvenir of your first Holy Communion.'[14]

Seven years later, the small ivory prayer book would yield a clue that cemented the Moors Murders case, establishing it as the most notorious exhibit ever presented in a murder trial. Its discovery condemned Myra as the benchmark of female evil in modern times.

'When I used to pray in front of the pietà, I used to touch the hand of Our Lord, which hung from Our Lady's sorrow-racked embrace, and although slightly scared because the church was only dimly lighted by candle-glow, and empty, which awed me a little, I used to quickly kiss His hand before leaving the church,' Myra recalled in a prison letter.[15] Her immersion in Roman Catholicism gave her a temporary sense of calm and she was touched when the Higgins family asked her to be godmother to Michael's nephew, Anthony John. But her devotion to the Church soon waned. Within a few weeks, she had stopped attending Mass, and when she encountered Father Theodore in the street hung her head in embarrassment and mumbled excuses.

Pat Jepson was engaged and saving for her wedding. Myra described herself then as 'emotionally immature, relatively unsophisticated and sexually inexperienced – I was still a virgin and intended to be so until I got married'.[16] The boys she dated tried to rectify that, but Myra was prudish to the point of not allowing even her family to see her undressed and shrieked when her sister walked in on her at bath-time. 'Don't be daft,' Maureen responded, typically down to earth. 'It's only your sister.'[17] But Myra didn't want anyone seeing her in the tin bath that was brought into the kitchen on Saturday nights. She found a steady boyfriend, however, in Ronnie Sinclair, one year her senior, from nearby Dalkeith Street. They met when she was 12 and he tugged the ribbons from her hair at the 'Bug Hut' cinema. He was working as a tea-blender at the Co-op when Myra agreed to go out with him in late 1958. In preparation for marriage – whether to Ronnie or someone else – she took over all the housework from Gran, as practice for running her own home, and paid a neighbour two shillings a week for 'bottom drawer' items from a catalogue. She also paid two shillings every week into a Christmas club.

In spring 1959, Myra was made redundant due to financial difficulties at Lawrence Scott. She was unemployed for just one week; in March 1959, she began work as a junior typist at Clydesdale's Furniture Shop in Gorton. The wages were poor, but Nana Hindley came to the rescue by securing weekend jobs for Myra, Margie and a few other ex-Lawrence Scott girls in the catering department at Belle Vue. Allan Grafton and his friends visited the huge entertainment complex every weekend: 'On Saturday nights, everyone would go to the Speedway and then into Belle Vue amusement park. At 10.30 p.m., the crowds converged on the Lake Hotel boating lake, where there was a fantastic weekly firework display. Apart from paying a small fee to go to the Speedway, everything was free.'[18] Myra served customers from food trolleys, but she hated the stink of fish and chips on her clothing and was glad when she and her friend Irene were offered work in the German-styled 'bierkeller' instead. The head barmaid advised them to dress up, keep smiling and serve short measures without getting caught. Myra and Irene were happy to go along with it, especially when they were given free packets of cigarettes as a bribe.

Ronnie presented her with an engagement ring on her 18th birthday, which Myra duly displayed to her family and friends, careful to point out the three tiny diamond chips set in it, while hoping they wouldn't find out it was second-hand. Bob offered to pay for the wedding with his compensation money from the foundry. Nellie was less enthusiastic; she wanted Myra to enjoy life while she was still young and didn't like the idea of her settling down with the first boy who proposed. Her mother's misgivings roused Myra's own. She looked at Nellie, trapped in a 'boring domestic role' of the 'downtrodden wife. I wanted my mother to stand up for herself, but she was weak and allowed Dad to bully her. I hated that.'[19] Myra began silently criticising Ronnie as a result, put off by the grease under his fingernails – 'like Dad's' – and secretly condemning him as 'boring and mundane. He cared a lot about me, which mattered, but he didn't like dancing and we spent most of our time at stock car races, which was his hobby.'[20]

Pat Jepson was the first of her friends to marry. Others followed, and Myra abhorred how their lives seemed to shrink: 'When I began to witness many of my friends and neighbours, some of whom "had to get married", having baby after baby, almost tied to the kitchen sink and struggling to make ends meet while their husbands went out every night, drinking and betting away their wages just as my father had done, I began to feel uncomfortable and restless.'[21] She disliked their husbands, drinkers who flirted endlessly with other women, and came to the conclusion that 'very few men could be trusted'.[22] She felt her friends had been 'trapped into family life, with no money and no freedom'.[23]

Just after her birthday, Myra caused the gossips' tongues to wag when she had a pink rinse at Maison Laurette. She told Mrs Howells that she was thinking of working abroad as a nanny or else as a Butlin's Redcoat. Myra had social aspirations: she strove to subdue her Lancashire accent, intended to learn how to drive and craved foreign holidays. 'I wanted a career, to better myself, to travel and struggle to break free of the confines of what was expected of me,' she recalled. 'Although so much was unattainable, I still dreamed and made plans and kept everything to myself. I didn't want to leave home, because I loved my family, but I wanted more scope and space, and they would think I was "getting above myself" if I confided in them.'[24] She enrolled in judo classes to burn off the excess energy triggered by her ambitions, but at the Gresham Street club she attended once a week, Myra quickly became the girl whom nobody liked to partner because she took so long to release her fierce grip.

She was drifting, and she knew it. Yet her relationship with her mother improved: the two of them often went shopping together and mealtimes at home were not the argumentative chore they had been in the past, though Myra scarcely tolerated her father. She counted her sister as her best friend, though Maureen was proving more streetwise than Myra. Despite her tiny frame, she would take on anyone in a fight and was a member of the Gorton street gang. She had the same beehive as Myra, although hers was ink-black, accentuating her pale skin. She wore similar clothes to Myra and copied her sister's heavy black eye make-up. Maureen was instantly recognisable, even at a distance, tottering down the street in stilettos, pencil skirt and sweater, black beehive stiff as a board, arms crossed or thin fingers clasping one of the Park Drive cigarettes she'd cadged off Myra, who had started smoking Embassy Tipped because she considered them to be a classier brand. Maureen talked nineteen-to-the-dozen and would dance at the drop of a hat, in the streets with her friends, at Sivori's in front of the jukebox or at home with Myra to the distorted crackle of the blaring record player.

Myra envied Maureen's carefree, even lackadaisical attitude to life. By her own admission, she was filled with 'conflict and confusion'.[25]

She left Clydesdale's and on 15 February 1960 started working as a typist for Bratby & Hinchcliffe, Engineers and Automatic Bottling Manufacturers, in Gorton Lane. She liked her colleagues Anita and Mary but loathed her boss, who banned his staff from talking to each other during working hours. She started arriving late again, or not at all. When Anita left to work for Burlington's, a catalogue warehouse in town, Myra and Mary jumped at the chance of joining her there when two other jobs came up, but Anita rang to say that Burlington's was even worse than Bratby & Hinchcliffe, with guards patrolling the warehouse to pounce on any shirkers. 'I decided to look elsewhere,' Myra remembered. 'I wanted job security, but also personal satisfaction was important to me. I wasn't going to follow my friends into domestic drudgery. I wanted different from the norm.'[26] Mary decided to stick with the job she already had, but Myra went back to studying the 'Situations Vacant' pages of the *Manchester Evening News*. Mary pointed out an advert for Millwards Merchandising. 'She had worked there herself in the recent past,' Myra recalled. 'She told me something about the firm and mentioned some of the people I'd be working with, if I got the job. She told me about ... a tall and good-looking, very quiet and shy, smartly dressed "intriguing man" who had appealed to her.'[27]

She was interviewed at Millwards on 21 December 1960. The company had been supplying chemicals, mostly to the cotton industry, since 1810 and occupied a large, detached house off Levenshulme Road. The entrance was at the back, down a potholed lane and past a cluster of brick outhouses. Despite its unkempt appearance, the house had once been an elegant family home called Rose Cottage. The boss's office was in the old drawing room. It retained an ornate fireplace and French windows that led into the garden, now filled with chemical containers.

The head of the firm, Tom Craig, greeted Myra warmly and showed her through to a small room where he set her a simple typing test and chatted to her for a while. He was an affable, middle-aged man who was keen to get along with his staff. There were about 15 employees – bookkeepers, typists and manual workers. Tom offered Myra the job on the spot. The wages were reasonable – £8 10s – and the hours regular: 9 a.m. to 5 p.m. through the week and alternate Saturday mornings. Since it was the end of the afternoon, Tom invited her to meet the rest of the staff, leading her through to his office, which he shared with two men. One was a retirement-age clerk sitting at a desk. He stood up with a smile as Myra entered and introduced himself as Bert Matthews. Tom explained that Myra would probably be taking most of her dictation from him.

The other man was standing by the filing cabinets. He was much younger than Bert and Tom, in his early twenties, tall and thin with a sallow complexion and dense, dark-brown hair combed into a short quiff. He wore a smart, three-piece suit and the look he gave Myra was unreadable. Tom introduced him as the stock clerk, Ian Brady.

III

This Cemetery of Your Making:
21 December 1960 – 6 October 1965

5

There are hundreds of women who can relate to how I felt
about him ...

Myra Hindley, conversation with prison therapist

Myra's description of her meeting with Ian Brady was inevitably
coloured by hindsight: 'Before his name was mentioned, I already knew
it was him. I can only describe my reaction to him as an immediate
and fatal attraction, although I had no inkling then of just how fatal it
would turn out to be.'[1] She was struck by his 'dark hair, deep-blue eyes
and fresh complexion' and the 'well-manicured fingernails' that were
'in stark contrast to my boyfriend's, which were always greasy'.[2] Dirty
fingernails signified manual work; she intuitively responded to a man
whose job required the use of his brain more than his hands, although
she had never been attracted to her previous male co-workers.

Ronnie was on night shift the evening after her interview at
Millwards, leaving Myra free to go out with her friends. She told
them about the encounter, comparing Ian to Elvis and James Dean,
regarding his indifference as a challenge: 'He gave no indication that
he noticed me, appearing to be the strong silent type. I was determined
I would make him notice me.'[3]

She began working at Millwards on Monday, 16 January 1961,
putting extra care into her appearance for Ian's benefit. She caught
the bus opposite the Steelworks Tavern and arrived on time for once.

Her desk was in a chilly little office of its own, meaning she had
minimal contact with the other staff, apart from taking dictation,
but there was a strong social bond between the employees, who met
regularly for nights out and had a weekly football pools syndicate.
During lunch breaks, the men would play cards, chess and dominoes,
and consult the racing pages of the press. Nearby was a bookies and
most afternoons one of the men would pop out to put their bets

on. Tom allowed them to listen to the major races on the radio or someone would phone through to the betting shop for the results. Ian was a keen gambler but careful, though Myra heard him shouting on the telephone at the bookie if he lost money. His betting name was Gorgonzola; eventually, he shortened it to Gorgon. She listened to him talking to colleagues about the books he read and realised they regarded him as highbrow and tedious. Other than that, she learned scarcely anything about him. He hardly spoke to her and barely seemed to notice she existed, despite her efforts.

Her infatuation deepened and she broke off her engagement to Ronnie, telling Pat that he was 'too childish and we're not saving enough money for marriage'.[4] But secretly she was frightened of ending up in a dull marriage, one whose tedious dynamics were reflected in the kitchen-sink dramas playing in every British cinema, usually set in the North. A real-life *Saturday Night and Sunday Morning* wasn't for her. 'Things could have been right with [Ronnie], but I got bored,' she recalled. 'Looking back on it, this loving relationship was the type that I desired but in the end it wasn't very attractive.'[5] Her ex-fiancé was distraught; he rang Millwards repeatedly in an attempt to persuade Myra to think again – until Tom warned him to expect a visit from the police if he didn't stop. Myra was relieved when the phone calls ceased but secretly pleased that Ian had witnessed Ronnie's desperation.[6]

Myra was free to indulge her fixation with Ian. She recalled, 'For almost a year, during which I broke off my engagement, he took virtually no notice of me. When he did, it was either a covert "come on", which sent my hopes soaring … or an ostentatious apathy towards me, making cruel and sarcastic remarks or totally ignoring me except when he had to ask me to take dictation and type letters for him. It was a year of emotional torture which I'd never experienced before. I went from loving him to hating him and loving and hating him at the same time. When he smiled at or was nice to me, I felt blessed and floated on air.'[7] The attraction was straightforward enough, apart from his appearance: 'Ian was older and seemed wiser than me, so cultured, so exciting and different from others.'[8]

Despite her antipathy towards her father, she noted similarities between the two (apart from the fingernails): 'They both had strong, dominant personalities. Each was his own man, living independently from the rest of the family and doing his own thing. My father ignored me, so perhaps subconsciously I wasn't going to let that happen with Ian.'[9]

She began keeping a diary, hiding it in her desk drawer, which she was careful to keep locked. By the time she put pen to paper, she was 'head over heels in love'.[10] It was six months since she had begun working at Millwards.

> July 24: Wonder if Ian is courting. Still feel the same.
> July 25: Haven't spoken to him yet.
> July 27: Spoken to him. He smiles as though embarrassed. I
>   am going to change, you'll notice that in the way I write.
> July 30: Ian and Graham [a colleague] aren't interested in
>   girls.
> August 1: Ian's taking sly looks at me. Still not sure if he likes
>   me. They say he gambles on horses and cards.[11]

She found out his address by eavesdropping on a telephone conversation Ian had with the bookie: 18 Westmoreland Street, Longsight. She slipped out that evening with a plan: 'I often took my baby cousin [Aunt Annie's son, Michael] out in his pram, and when I discovered where Ian lived, I began taking Michael down the long street he lived in, hoping I'd see him and he'd stop to talk to me, but I never did. I asked one of my friends to come with me to the pub on the corner of his street in the hope that he might be there, but he never was. I'd become utterly obsessed with him, though tried desperately not to show it.'[12] The friend was May Hill; she and Myra had known each other for years. The two of them whiled away several evenings in the Westmoreland pub until it became obvious Ian wasn't a regular customer. Myra returned to wandering past the bay window of his house alone, singing 'On the Street Where You Live' under her breath. Then she admitted defeat and contented herself with reporting nonsensical snippets about Ian in her diary:

> August 3: Ian likes Boddington's [*sic*] Bitter Beer.
> August 6: Irene Eccles has clicked with a lad she met in
>   April.
> August 8: Gone off Ian a bit.
> August 10: Tommy is scared of Ian.

August 12: Been to Friendship pub (not with Ian).

August 13: Wonder what 'Misery' will be like tomorrow?

August 14: I love Ian all over again. He has a cold and I would love to mother him. Going to a club.

August 19: Visited Belle View [*sic*]. Tony Prendergast and Eddie were there.

August 24: I am in a bad mood because he hasn't spoken to me today. He still has not made any approach.

August 29: I hope he loves me, and will marry me some day.[13]

Myra told her prison therapist that she would 'daydream about what life would be like with a man like Ian. He was so different to the men I had known before . . . I wanted him badly.'[14] His persistent and probably deliberate refusal to pay her any attention lent him an unreachable air, elevating him above the realms of normality. 'Some of my friends would feel this way about pop idols or film stars, but my idol was sitting in my office behind his desk,' Myra recalled. 'I'm not sure that Ian knew how much I wanted to be with him, but I can accept that perhaps he knew what effect he was having on me and baited me until the time was right.'[15] She still knew next to nothing about him, other than the little she observed at work, but, even with the benefit of hindsight, she admitted, 'I didn't know of any of his activities but even if I did I would have ignored them. All that mattered was that I was with him.'[16]

Her diary continues:

August 30: Ian and Bert have had a row. Tommy sided with Bert and said Ian loses his temper too soon.

September 2: Sivori Milk Bar in Clowes St.

September 4, 5, 6: Ian's moodiness.

September 6: Don't know anything about Ian (parents, background, etc.).

September 9: Ian mentioned Hadfield to George, I suppose near Glossop. Ian wearing a black shirt today.

September 10: In Siv's Tony and Eddie were arguing about a girl.

September 14: Marge went in to see Eddie about his tape-recorder.

September 16: Irene's 21st Birthday Party. Hodge, Tony P and Eddie. I could fall for Eddie.

September 20: Still hoping for date with Ian.

September 23: Saw Eddie drunk (Sportsman's pub, where we go every Sat).

October 2: Ian has been to Glasgow.

October 8: Ian never talks about his family.

October 9: Eddie lives in the next street to Ian.

October 13: Ian hasn't spoken to me for several days.

October 18: Ian still ignores me. Fed up. I still love him.

October 19: Ian lives with his mam and dad and hardly ever goes out.

October 21: Malcolm phoned Ian at work and Ian arranged to go to him for drinks.

October 23: I fancy Eddie. I could fall for Ed.

October 25: Ian and Tommy had a row. Ian nearly hit Tommy. Ian swearing. He is uncouth. I thought he was going to hit Nellie [Mrs Egerton, the cleaner, of whom Ian was surprisingly fond; he presented her with a bottle of port every Christmas].

October 28: Royal Oak Pub in Wythenshawe.

November 1: Months now since Ian and I spoke.

November 2: Met Bob, pub crawl, went up to Ashton-under-Lyne, Dukinfield, Denton. Quite a good night.

November 3: Ian swearing at work, using crude words.

November 4: Rodney had drinks at Plough. Rodney said, 'All Ian is interested in is making money.'

November 6: Ian still not speaking. Called him a big-headed pig.

November 7: Have finished with Eddie. He is courting another girl.

November 28: I've given up with Ian. He goes out of his way to annoy me, he insults me and deliberately walks in front of me. I have seen the other side of him and that convinces me he is no good.

December 2: I hate Ian, he has killed all the love I had for him.

December 11: Visited Empress Club, Stockport, with Joan, Irene, Dave.

December 13: Pauline's party.
December 15: I'm in love with Ian all over again.[17]

The breakthrough Myra longed for occurred when she decided to show an interest in one of Ian's passions: literature. Her own love of reading remained, but she preferred to dip into light novels and magazines like *Valentine* and *Honey*. Hoping to impress Ian, she borrowed *The Collected Works of William Wordsworth* from Gorton Library. Having studied it at school, she was confident she could discuss it if necessary without having to read it from cover to cover. When she took it out at lunchtime in Millwards the next day, Ian glanced up from his game of chess and noticed the thick book in her hands. After a while, he asked her if it was any good. She replied that it was marvellous, *The Prelude* especially. He took it from her and flicked through the pages, murmuring that he might borrow it himself. Myra was silently euphoric. A few days later she appeared at the office carrying *Songs of Innocence and of Experience* and discovered that Ian was a keen admirer of William Blake. During one of their gradually more frequent conversations, Ian asked her about musical tastes. She was sharp enough to reply that she liked a bit of everything. He confided that he wasn't a pop fan, but recorded music from television programmes or albums borrowed from the library. He'd bought a Philips tape recorder on hire purchase and Myra immediately did the same, then asked him to lend her some of his music.

The office Christmas party took place shortly before the holidays. Finishing work at noon one weekday, everyone trooped over to the Haxby, where Myra sat with the women but kept her eye on Ian, who drank heavily. When the pub closed in the afternoon, the Millwards crowd returned to the office, where the desks – one laden with snacks and alcohol – had been pushed back to leave a space for dancing; someone had brought in their record player. Myra sipped rum and Coke, and watched her colleagues pairing off to bop enthusiastically. She was swaying slightly when Ian suddenly appeared at her side and asked her to dance. He kept stepping on her feet as they moved awkwardly about the floor, and then Tom interrupted to ask Ian if he still wanted a lift home. To Myra's joy, he replied that he was going to walk her home instead. It was pitch black outside when they left the office, weaving a path through Sunny Brow Park, the pond a pale oval in the darkness. As they came out onto Haworth Road, Ian invited her to meet him later that night. Myra was still reeling from having danced with him and recalled, 'I shook from head to toe, I could hardly breathe.'[18] She saw him onto his bus, then rang her friend Margie: 'I was on cloud nine. I rushed to a phone and cancelled a night out with the girls I always went out with. They were really pleased when I told them I was going out with Ian, for I'd talked about him incessantly.'[19]

Keyed up with excitement, she arrived home to find Maureen and their cousin Glenys nattering to Gran. Myra begged her sister to nip out to the chemist to buy her some perfume and mascara while she freshened up and had a quick tea. After reapplying her make-up and lacquering her hair, she left Bannock Street and headed to the bus stop where Ian had suggested they meet. When the bus turned down from Gorton Lane, she saw him standing on the open rear platform; he reached out his hand and she stepped up next to him. They spent the evening bussing from pub to pub: the Three Arrows in Gorton, the Thatched House in town and another one whose name escaped her when she tried to remember it afterwards ('we were both drunk').[20] Her only clear memory of their conversation was that Ian had declared himself an obsessive fan of *The Goon Show* and kept launching into impressions of the characters played by Spike Milligan, Peter Sellers, Harry Secombe and Michael Bentine. Myra was vaguely familiar with the radio show, which ran from 1951 until 1960 and was filled with juvenile jokes, nonsense songs and catchphrases. If she'd known more about Ian, she would have understood its appeal; satirist Jonathan Miller described it as 'a send-up of British imperialism' that did 'an enormous amount to subvert the social order'.[21] But his love of *The Goon Show* was all Ian revealed about himself that evening.

They missed the last bus back to Gorton and ended up walking home through dimly lit Ardwick. When they arrived at Bannock Street, Ian asked if he could come in, but Myra refused: 'I told him my gran might still be up.'[22] He made a clumsy attempt to kiss her before saying goodnight. She climbed the stairs to her bedroom in an exultant daze.

At Millwards, Ian behaved as if nothing had happened between them, but in a quiet moment he asked her to the pictures the following Saturday. Myra marked the date triumphantly in her diary: 22 December 1961. History records that the film they saw was *Judgement at Nuremberg*, but Myra recollected it as Nicholas Ray's biblical epic *King of Kings*, narrated by Ian's favourite actor, Orson Welles.[23] They sat through the film in complete silence, apart from Myra's sniffing, as she tried not to cry, then they walked on to the Thatched House. This time, Ian was more forthcoming, as, needled by the film, he talked about his hatred of religion. He dismissed the Bible, Catholic Mass, incense and confession as drivel for the intellectually weak; his views 'demolished' Myra's attempts to counter-argue: 'He convinced me that my faith, that all religions, were superstitions instilled in us as conventional norms. Religions, he said, were a crutch people used to hobble through life on, the opium of the people. And I believed him because I thought I loved him, and his arguments were so convincing he demolished my tiny precepts with a single word . . .'[24] She must have told him something about her own past since he asked why God had allowed Michael Higgins to die. She couldn't answer. Michael's death had undermined the foundations of her faith, which she had tried to rebuild without success, and Ian's words crumbled them to nothing.

According to Myra's autobiography, she and Ian became lovers that night, on the bumpy settee in Gran's house on Bannock Street.[25] She described the loss of her virginity as an act of semi-violence, which she instigated by kissing Ian ferociously. It crossed her mind to wonder whether he was as inexperienced as she was, but she didn't question him. There is no mention in her diary of the occasion at all.

Although she asserted later in life that for months after their first date she became 'a Saturday-night stand', she spent Christmas Eve with Ian. The two of them were on Gorton Lane when they heard church bells tolling for midnight Mass.[26] Despite Ian's hatred of religion and her own diminished beliefs, she wanted to attend the service – if only for the atmosphere. He flatly refused to enter a Roman Catholic church but allowed her to lead him to St James's Anglican church. After the service, they walked through the churchyard and, according to Myra's autobiography, Ian 'walked across the grass to the edge of the graves, where he casually urinated'.[27] He took a draught of whisky from the bottle he had concealed under his coat and announced, 'That's what I think of Christianity.'[28]

In her unpublished and re-written autobiography, she added a final line, almost as an afterthought: 'Little did I realise then that his graves would be marked by photographs and not headstones.'[29]

Ian's conduct on Christmas Eve failed to repulse Myra; she wanted to see the new year in with him and records in her diary (where the incident in the graveyard doesn't feature):

> December 31: Went to see *El Cid* with Ian. Ian brought a
> bottle of German wine and a bottle of whisky, to let New
> Year in. Dad spoke to Ian as if he'd known him for years.
> [Ian] is so gentle he makes me want to cry.[30]

But Myra's mother didn't like Ian; he reminded her too much of her husband, and shortly before her death she recalled, 'I wouldn't have him in the house.'[31] Myra confronted her at some point, reproaching Nellie for being prejudiced against Ian's Scottish roots, but her mother's dislike arose from parallels she saw with Bob, Ian's affectations – his love of long words and air of superiority – and, quite simply, because 'I just never liked him.'[32]

A week into the new year, Myra's diary ended as tersely as it had begun:

> January 1: Should have gone to Pauline. Too tired.
> January 2: I hope Ian and I love each other all our lives and get
> married and are happy ever after. I have been at Millwards
> for 12 months and only just gone out with him.
> January 6: Went with Mam to the Shakespeare, Haunch of
> Venison [Dale Street] and the Royal George [Lever
> Street].[33]

Bert Matthews retired early in the new year and Ian was promoted to his job. Whether by coincidence or design, most of his work was done with Myra. Her desk was shuffled in next to his, although he insisted on standing up for dictation. If their relationship seemed slow to her at first ('If he didn't want to see me, I had no choice. I had taken so long to get him to take me out; I wasn't going to ruin things'[34]), it deepened after he used his increase in wages to put down a deposit on a Triumph Tiger Cub motorbike. He'd seen an advert in the local newspaper for one with a front windshield and told Myra he intended to use it for travelling to work each day and 'in hot weather, including fast trips to Glasgow'.[35] She recalled, 'When he bought a motorbike, he came one weeknight unexpectedly and we went for a ride. After that, because he never made a date, I began staying in every night, terrified that I might be out when – if – he came round. I became estranged from most of my friends, who had become disgusted with me for "letting him tread all over me".'[36] Myra's friends encouraged her to invite Ian out with them, but Myra didn't ask him, either sensing that he would refuse or preferring to be alone with him. 'I'd become totally besotted with him,' she wrote in her 1995 *Guardian* article, 'always trying to fathom out the mystery he'd become to me, the aura that emanated from him.'

There were countless occasions when Ian would arrange to meet her, then fail to appear: 'I asked where he was going or where he had been [and] he would answer: never mind. Some women might ask why I stayed with such a self-centred man, but at least when he was with me he made me feel good, when he wasn't I was content to stay in and wash my hair or babysit.'[37] Eventually, he told her that he liked to 'people-watch' at the Rembrandt pub on Canal Street or the Union Hotel on the corner of Canal Street and Princess Street. Myra was aware that the two venues attracted an almost exclusively homosexual clientele, but she either discounted the possibility that Ian might be an active observer or chose to ignore it; either way, she accepted his often compulsive desire to go there.

As the months passed, Ian's 'aura of mystery and secrecy', which had proved such an irresistible lure for her in the first place, began to dissipate as the two of them called in at the Waggon and Horses pub at the end of Hyde Road daily after work.[38] In the snug, old-fashioned surroundings of the pub, with its thick wooden beams and polished horse-brasses, Ian divulged remnants of his fractured past.

6

I have never experienced the need to corrupt anyone. I simply
offered the opportunity to indulge extant natural urges.

Ian Brady, *The Gates of Janus*

The destruction of the church at the end of Gorbals' Camden Street
by a German bomb was among Ian's most vivid childhood memories.
As the stained glass shattered into a million brilliant filaments, then
vanished into dust, the impact blew out 'all the tenement windows'.[1]
But Ian wasn't troubled: 'To all of my age, it was an exciting time,
not one of fear or danger. The blackout was also hilarious, families
bumping into one another and tripping over cats as they negotiated
the streets and alleys to reach cinemas.'[2]

What remained of Glasgow's Gorbals after the war was destroyed
by the town planners of the 1960s in much the same way as Gorton
disappeared.

A once elegant neighbourhood, by the turn of the twentieth century
the Gorbals landlords had grown avaricious, and then negligent, as
migrants crowded into the city. By the 1930s, it was the notorious
slum made infamous in Alexander McArthur's pre-war novel *No
Mean City*, where the chief character, Johnnie Stark, is the Razor
King, stalking through streets riddled with 'gangs, winos, poverty,
overcrowding, sickness, defective drains, bed-bugs and three-shilling
prostitutes'.[3] Twenty years later, another resident confirmed that 'the
hard drinking and open-razor fights still went on, and the area, with
its magnificent buildings and crumbling tenements, was much the
same as it had been in the 1930s'[4].

Ian Brady was born Ian Duncan Stewart at Rottenrow maternity
hospital in Glasgow on 2 January 1938. His mother, 28-year-old
Maggie Stewart, was an unmarried tearoom waitress, although the

hospital recorded her as 'Mrs' Stewart. She appears to have had no close family and lived with a friend at 8 Huntingdon Place. Ian's father, according to Maggie, was a journalist who died three months before the birth of his son. She told an early biographer, 'Why Ian's so clever with reading and writing is his dad was a reporter – but not on the *Glasgow Herald*.'[5] For reasons of her own, she kept his identity a secret from her son. Interviewed later about his father, Ian could only add that he had heard 'of a move to Australia' and didn't know his name.[6]

After her son was christened, Maggie found a rented room in a tenement on Caledonia Road. She struggled to find someone to care for the baby while she returned to waitressing but wouldn't consider giving him up for adoption. After four months, she decided the best means of ensuring Ian's safety while remaining part of his life was to find a suitable foster family. Ian referred to it as a 'commercial' arrangement, and it was the only viable solution if Maggie was to continue earning a living.[7] Mary Sloan, a 34-year-old cotton-mill worker, responded to Maggie's predicament with the offer of a home for Ian. Mary's husband of 15 years was 39-year-old John Sloan, a grain-store employee. They had four children of their own – Robert (thirteen), Jean (eleven), Mary (six) and John junior (two) – and lived in the heart of the Gorbals, at 56 Camden Street, a two-room flat in a tall tenement with shared washing facilities and an outside toilet. It was poor and cramped, but the family were regarded as warm, respectable people by those who knew them.

Ian's earliest memories revolve around the flat on Camden Street. He recalls lying mottled with measles in his cot, in the warm light of the kitchen range, while his new family gathered around the radio. Each Christmas they hung a stocking at the foot of his bed, although they could ill-afford to fill it. Ian loved them all, and called Mary and John his ma and pa, although his natural mother was a constant presence, visiting him at least every Sunday. He soon grasped that the slim, pretty woman who now called herself Peggy was his real mother. She spoiled him with gifts and clothes bought from her wages at the hotel, bringing him a kilt and ruffled shirt for Sunday best and a pair of black velvet trousers to wear during the week. He was known as 'the smartest wee lad on the street'.[8]

From the age of five, Ian attended Camden Street Primary, a quarter of a mile's walk from home. Despite stories of temper tantrums that erupted in repetitive head banging, Ian insists that his childhood was largely trouble-free and 'the best [period] in my life . . . I had many friends and won school prizes, including one for English.'[9] His sole act of rebellion occurred at Sunday School when the teacher asked the children if they believed in God; Ian's voice quavered, 'No.'[10]

Later, he would fume at psychologists who pointed to his illegitimacy and being fostered as the origin of his crimes: 'I had a happy childhood and loved the family. The dichotomy in parentage was not pivotal – I was aware of it from an early age . . . I enjoy remembering aspects of the past . . . Searching for the fashionable stereotypical excuses and scapegoats in childhood would be fruitless in my case.'[11]

War broke out in 1939 and, two years later, in March 1941, German bombers besieged shipyards and munitions factories in the Clydebank area until it became the most consistently shelled spot in Britain. Ian found the 'crump' of missiles thrilling, suffering no personal losses during the bombardment. His home life was stable, due to the Sloans' care and attention, and regular visits from his mother, who worked as a lathe operator in a factory. When the war ended in 1945, Ian was seven years old. Half a century later, he retained 'vivid recollections' of VE Night, particularly the terrific 'street bonfires'.[12]

There followed a brief spurt of cruelty towards animals, but that ended when he encountered a fallen horse in the street. It was a cold, misty morning and the Clydesdale had been pulling the drayman's cart when it slipped on the cobbles and broke a bone in its leg. Ian was transfixed by the pain and helplessness in the horse's eyes. He ran away from the distressing spectacle, sobbing.

The Sloans acquired a pet dog around the same time and Ian adored it, subsequently developing a powerful affinity with animals. Police chief Peter Topping, who interviewed him in the 1980s, recalls, 'He was always upset if he read about cruelty to animals and he did not like the articles and books which claimed he had been cruel to a cat when he was a child. "I prefer animals to people," he would say.'[13]

At school, Ian's poor performance in team games earned him the nickname 'Big Lassie'. He relished his other nickname, 'Dracula', which arose from his taste for horror films. Academically, he shone and won praise for his neat, meticulous writing. His recollection of the last years at Camden Street Primary are disjointed: he told one correspondent that 'the child's games in the playground seemed futile to me and I had stood alone at the edge of crowds, never fitting in', but in his own book he claims the opposite: 'In childhood years I was not the stereotypical "loner" so beloved by popular media. Friends formed round me eagerly in the school playground . . . Apparently I had a descriptive talent and contagious enthusiasm.'[14]

His best friend, John Cameron, lived in the flat below the Sloans and told a much-repeated story: '[Ian] always carried a flick-knife and was a great one for a carry-on. He once tied me to a steel washing-post, heaped newspapers round my legs and set fire to them. I can still remember feeling dizzy with the smoke before I blacked out.'[15] He added, 'Mind you, we were all rough lads in those days. But Ian was the toughest of the lot.'[16]

A seminal event did occur in 1947, when the Sloans took a picnic to Loch Lomond, some 20 miles north of Glasgow. It was Ian's first experience of a vast, open and empty landscape; the wide expanse of water and wild blue splendour of the hills and mist-trailed, wooded glens mesmerised him. He explained years later what he could not then put into words, how endless, bleak panoramas 'expanded' his spirit: 'Confronting a sea, a moor, or standing on a mountain, you can almost hear the unknown, invisible presences: you know they are there, almost within touch, speaking an arcane language, and you feel the power rise up within as you become a receiver.'[17] It was spiritual rather than religious, a godless, self-affirming and inherent 'surge of ultimate energy and power [that] makes you laugh with pure delight or cry with gratitude'.[18] His foster family, ready to return home, found him standing on one of the hills, feet firmly planted in the grass, staring ahead as though hypnotised by the shadowy rise and fall of the land. He was unusually garrulous throughout the journey back to Glasgow.

That same year, as part of the slum clearance programme that saw ugly tower blocks replace old tenements, the Sloans were resettled on an overspill estate in Pollock. Families were vetted before being allocated houses there, hence its status as a 'select' estate; 21 Templeland Road was a three-bedroom house on a street of semi-detached properties with indoor bathrooms and rear gardens. Ian shared a bedroom with Robert, who was in his twenties by then, and John, who was two years his senior. He was delighted with the move; apart from the vastly improved living conditions, nearby there were woods and the

River Cart. The couple next door, Thomas and Elizabeth Chalmers, remembered the Sloans as 'terribly nice people who kept themselves to themselves', dedicated gardeners whose plot was 'a mass of roses'.[19] Ian willingly helped out in the garden and looked after the vegetable patch. He loved home comforts and has strong, happy memories of childhood Hogmanays.

He changed schools after the move, transferring to Carnwadric Primary on Capelrig Street, a two-mile bus journey from home. He attained good marks and made new friends; however, his mother began missing their Sunday meetings in 1948, when she began a relationship with Patrick Brady, an Irish ex-army man. Weeks drifted by in which she had no contact with her ten-year-old son, and when Patrick moved to Manchester for work, Peggy went with him, leaving Ian in the care of his foster family. Communication between them was by letter alone.

Ian attended the wedding of his foster brother Robert Sloan the following year. Afterwards, there was a family holiday in Perthshire, where the Sloans rented a cottage in Dunning and Ian stumbled across the memorial to Maggie Wall, the witch who had burned there three centuries earlier. Ian loved the cottage, with its low ceilings and oil lamps, and the stone bridge nearby across the river. He happily accompanied the family to the witch's monument, on walks through the fields and on a day trip to the salt-eddied coast of St Andrew's, and another to the harbour village of St Monans, where he scrambled over the bulbous stones of the ancient castle ruins.

Returning to Glasgow, Ian passed his exams and was admitted to Shawlands Academy in 1950. The pupils, who wore a navy-blue uniform with gold piping, were mostly from wealthy families; before the new estate in Pollock was built the school was deemed 'posh', but the local authorities insisted on adding a new wing to accommodate children from the estate. Ian invited new classmates to meet his old friends from Camden Street, taking pleasure in observing 'how quickly they sloughed off middle-class values and enjoyed real life in the Gorbals'.[20] His teachers regarded him as 'withdrawn, quite a clever boy', while a classmate saw 'a boy who didn't like company but nae dunderhead. He read all kinds of books about the Nazis and never stopped talking about them. Even when we were playing war games, he made a great point of being a "German" . . . When Ian used to shout, "*Sieg Heil!*" and give the Nazi salute, people would laugh.'[21] He began collecting Nazi memorabilia, pestering other boys whose brothers were in the army to fetch him anything from Germany. He renounced God forever at the age of 12, when his beloved dog fell ill. His prayers that it wouldn't die went unanswered and he declared himself a committed atheist.

On 16 May 1950, Ian's mother married Patrick Brady at Manchester's All Saints Registry Office. They lived in Ancoats, and Patrick worked as a meat porter in Smithfield Market. Peggy retained minimal contact with her son. He didn't travel south to attend the wedding, holidaying instead with the Sloans at Troon, a large town on the south Ayrshire coast.

Returning to Glasgow, Ian committed his first break-in at the house of a naval man, although he claims he 'did not take anything, but simply looked around'.[22] It was in this period, Ian recalls, that 'matters changed imperceptibly. Gangs formed round me . . . I took it as a natural process . . . That our activities became criminal was also accepted as natural. The more money we stole, the more fun we had. Only when we were caught did a minority drift away, mainly at the behest of their restrictive parents . . . replacements joined us and we continued to enjoy the fruits of our activities.'[23] His 'activities' landed him in Juvenile Court in May 1951, accused of housebreaking and attempted theft, to the bemused shame of his foster parents. The courts were lenient and placed him on two years' probation.

Ian's appearance altered radically as he hit his teens: he grew tall and gangly, with a thick mop of dark brown hair, which he wore in a high quiff. He dressed sharply – one photograph shows him with a group of grinning lads on a seafront wearing a dark suit, black shirt and light tie. He found a girlfriend: Evelyn Grant, whom he met on the Shawlands bus. They shared a seat and he treated her to trips to the pictures, where he would immerse himself in the film.

On 16 July 1952, while still on probation, he appeared in Govan Juvenile Court on a housebreaking charge. His sentence was minimal – more probation – but according to journalist Fred Harrison, who interviewed Ian at length in Gartree Prison, he was growing increasingly disturbed; he claimed that while out cycling one day he felt inexplicably dizzy and saw a warm green radiation, like a thick mist, ahead of him, which he named the Face of Death.[24] He professes to have made a pact with it, agreeing to commit 'sacrifices' in return for its unspecified favours.[25] On a visit to Glencoe, where the horrifying clan massacre took place in 1692, he apparently experienced the same light-headedness and hallucination, and assumed that the Face of Death lived on nearby Rannoch Moor, a wilderness of black peat, lochs and abundant heather.[26]

Ian left school in 1953 at the age of 15. He worked as a butcher's assistant for a while, then as an engine cleaner with British Rail, and as an apprentice plater before moving on to the Harland and Wolff shipyard as a tea boy. Shunting from job to job, none of which engaged his intellect, he became dissatisfied and frustrated, craving the accumulation of what he called 'working capital'.[27] His courtship of Evelyn came to an unruly end when he threatened her with a flick-knife after she went dancing with another youth.

Then on 29 November 1954, at the age of 16, Ian appeared before Glasgow Sheriff Court, charged once again with theft and housebreaking. The Sloans were overwhelmed and convinced that he would be sent to prison, but the Glasgow courts accepted the more unusual solution suggested by Ian's probation officer, and his future was no longer their concern. The Scottish justice system had washed their hands of him and were – as Ian himself phrased it – 'deporting' him.[28] In December 1954, he caught the train south to Manchester, where his mother was waiting anxiously at Victoria Station. He hadn't seen her since he was ten, but she seemed determined to do her best for him now. He hadn't yet met his stepfather either, but he had already taken his surname, shrugging off 'Ian Sloan' like an old coat – his third name change since birth. An awkward, long-limbed 16 year old, he left the railway station with his mother and stepped out onto Manchester's bitterly cold streets as Ian Brady.

Peggy and Pat had recently moved from Ancoats to Moss Side; their home at 13A Denmark Street was sparsely furnished with bulky, old-fashioned pieces that made the rooms appear pokier than they already were, but everywhere was neat and clean. To Peggy's relief, Ian got on well with his stepfather, who found him a job as an errand boy with Howarth's Fruiterers at the market. The two shared a love of racing and sat listening to the radio commentaries together to find out if their modest bets had paid off. Otherwise Ian was insular, aware that his heavy Glaswegian accent sounded foreign in the city of flat vowels.

The Bradys moved often within the neighbourhood during the mid 1950s: from Denmark Street to Grammar Street (later Cannel Street) and then to 36 Cuttle Street, a particularly drab terrace near the Grey Mare Lane market. Mrs Alma Singleton, who lived at number 19, already knew Peggy and described Ian as 'a boy too good to be true'.[29] She remembered him as 'a quiet lad. When I went in, he would look up and nod, and then he would blush. He always seemed to be embarrassed when he met anyone. Maybe he was a bit awkward with his mother's friends because no one knew she had a grown-up son until he appeared.'[30] Every lunchtime Peggy popped home from her job in an engineering works to prepare dinner, and in the afternoon Mrs Singleton stopped by to light the fire. Whenever she saw Ian, he was usually sprawled in a chair, wearing the checked shirts that he kept for work, and reading a book. 'Anyone could tell Ian was Mrs Brady's son,' Mrs Singleton recalled. 'When he was about the house, her eyes followed him everywhere. She thought the world of him.'[31] He was kind and respectful towards Peggy and quiet about the place, but he appeared to have more money than he should, and never struck up conversations with the neighbours or the market workers, except to make disparaging comments about the black residents of Moss Side.

He missed Scotland deeply, and recalls that within months of arriving in Manchester he made the first of frequent trips to visit the Sloans. His younger foster sister Mary married a soldier in the Highland Light Infantry at Christmas 1955. Ian liked him and later accompanied the couple and their two small children on holiday to Ayrshire.

But he had fallen foul of the law again, and on 9 November 1955 was convicted of stealing 44 lbs of lead seals from banana boxes. A driver at the market had asked him to stack the lead onto his lorry and had sold it to a scrap dealer, who contacted the police. The driver, when questioned, implicated Ian, who was called to Manchester Crown Court for sentencing. He pleaded guilty, anticipating a fine, and flipped a coin to decide how he would respond to the outcome: whether to go straight or become a career criminal. He was stunned to be sentenced to two years in borstal – and because all the borstals were full, he faced incarceration in Strangeways until a place became available.

The decision enraged him. A later psychiatric report reflected: 'He felt that this was a time of deep crisis in his life and that in some way a decision had been made. He felt increasingly cut off from other people in the emotional sense – he could no longer feel concern for them or feel warmly towards them. He retained affection for his foster family.'[32] Ian admits that he found it increasingly hard 'to accept the values of others. It seemed futile and pointless, their living, like trying to obtain something in a dream. I felt as if I was awake, and they were asleep . . . by the time I was seventeen or eighteen, everything started to become increasingly unreal. People seemed like puppets and marionettes. Their lives cotton wool, marshmallow, unreal . . . that was the beginning of the end for me.'[33]

In Strangeways, Ian made an effort to socialise with those inmates who he thought might prove useful to him later and struck up friendships with a small group of men from Leeds and Bradford. On 10 January 1956, he was transferred to Hatfield Borstal, a camp of wooden huts sunk into flat Yorkshire marshes. Borstals were run by the Prison Service, aiming to reform delinquent youths under the age of 23. Education was central, together with stringent routine and authoritarian discipline; one writer described them as 'breeding grounds for bullies and psychopaths'.[34] Hatfield Borstal, nine miles from Doncaster, opened in 1950 and was a former army training camp for boys of 'better than average intelligence with a relatively light criminal record'.[35]

Ian's mother and stepfather visited him there, unaware of his crystallising ambitions to become wealthy through crime. He was barred from National Service following a psychiatric examination and punished for running a betting syndicate and selling self-made alcohol to his fellow detainees. Eventually, he was 'expelled' for attacking a warder when drunk and transferred to a much harsher borstal housed within Hull Gaol, a squat Victorian former military prison two miles east of the city centre. During his two years there, the authorities discovered that Ian had a knack for figures and gave him some basic training in bookkeeping. He refined his plans to masterminding bank robberies and payroll snatches, and noted the names of two fellow inmates, Gil Deares and Dougie Woods, as prospective fellow thieves.[36]

'Gradually I began to adopt a more studious, professional attitude towards crime,' he recalls, adding with characteristic grandiosity, 'My instinctive form of relativism developed into a pragmatic philosophy. I began to choose my followers.'[37]

Released from Hull Borstal on 14 November 1957, he returned to his mother, who tried to convince the neighbours that he had merely fallen into bad company. 'He still blushed every time you spoke to him,' Mrs Singleton recalled. 'Anything seemed to embarrass him. He didn't want to be noticed, but you couldn't help feeling sorry for him. There were at least half a dozen lads of his age in the street, but he never spoke to any of them. He didn't seem to have any friends and he never brought anyone to the house.'[38] Her daughter, Carol, found him attractive, as did other girls in the neighbourhood; he was tall and dark, always smartly dressed, and wore his aloofness as plainly as the dark overcoat he favoured. No one ever saw him in the local pubs, but Carol Singleton spotted him staggering up Cuttle Street occasionally and her father met him clinging drunkenly onto a lamp post one night, unable to support himself.

Ian's borstal report featured one positive aspect: 'Application, Good at Figures'. But for several months he was unemployed.[39] He found menial work eventually but was made redundant after a short time. In April 1958, through the intervention of his welfare officer, he was taken on as a labourer in Boddingtons Brewery, rolling out barrels and cleaning vats. Despite his clandestine ambitions, his only brush with the law after leaving borstal until he met Myra was when he was fined £1 for being drunk and disorderly. On 3 October, he lost his job as part of the brewery's cutbacks but was given a reference as a 'conscientious worker and good timekeeper'.[40] He returned to fetching and carrying at the fruit market, contemptuous of the world around him and aching for change.

The Bradys moved on again, leaving Cuttle Street for 97 Grey Mare Lane, just around the corner, before finally settling in Longsight: 18 Westmoreland Street was a dingy terrace, ill-lit at night, with broken flagstones underfoot.[41] Peggy tried to make the house more attractive, and Ian helped her decorate throughout, bit by bit, when they could afford it. Mrs Singleton visited them, bringing her baby daughter Lesley. When Peggy called Ian to see the baby, he mumbled that it was bonny and excused himself.

He had discovered Dostoevsky's *Crime and Punishment* on one of his frequent trips to Longsight Library. 'That's me, that's what I'm all about,' he declared 30 years later, telling police that everything he had ever done was in *Crime and Punishment*.[42] The novel concerns Raskolnikov, a poor, failed student who commits a murder that is at once mercenary and a challenge of will but finds redemption in the love of a virtuous prostitute. Raskolnikov rationalises murder, suggesting that man has the 'inner right to decide in his own conscience to overstep . . . certain obstacles', such as the conventions of accepted morality.[43] Ian discarded Raskolnikov's salvation and the novel's ethical core, using it instead to justify his own dark thoughts.

Having found one celebrated writer whose works he could interpret to make his own desires more palatable, he sought out others and soon encountered the novels of the Marquis de Sade, whose books brim with sexual cruelty and urge the reader to view murder not as a criminal offence but as a pleasure to be indulged. From de Sade he moved on to the philosophies of Nietzsche, telling himself that a killer was 'attracted and stimulated by the excitement of challenging the norm, of stepping into forbidden territory like a solitary explorer, consciously thirsting to experience that which the majority have not and dare not'.[44] A post-trial psychiatric report on Ian concludes: 'He found an affinity for literature of a sadistic nature and had sympathy with fascist ideology and Nazi practices. He says he was exhilarated by their loss of feeling, as it appeared a liberation or freedom, but at the same time he was distressed.'[45]

In February 1959, one month after his 21st birthday, Ian replied to an advertisement for a stock clerk. Wearing the new suit his mother and stepfather had bought him, he caught the bus on Hyde Road to Millwards. He was offered the position following an interview with Tom Craig, who had his reservations over the young Scotsman with the borstal record but decided to give him a chance. Ian began work at Millwards on 16 February 1959, earning £9 a week. Staff found him neat, punctual and usually polite, apart from a dire lack of gamesmanship; lunchtime bridge sessions were dropped because he was so foul-tempered with his partner when they lost, and would sit glowering for the rest of the day if he had a bad hand at pontoon. Otherwise he was quiet, eating his egg-and-cheese sandwiches alone, reading *Teach Yourself German* or *Mein Kampf*.

Tom Craig regretted having employed him: 'He was so bad-tempered about anything that upset him. If you ticked him off about something, he would fly into a rage. He had a shocking temper and his language was dreadful, but I used to pass it over just to keep the peace. He was reasonable at his job, but he would have been sacked long before if it hadn't been that difficult to get staff . . . I can't say I ever got to know him at all. In an office, the lads usually chat a bit about football or something like that, but Brady wasn't interested in anything like that. Sometimes in the morning he might join in a conversation about what was on TV the night before, but I noticed he only talked about the crime films or the *Hitchcock Hour*, things with a bit of horror or brutality in them. He often had a book with him – I don't remember any of them, but they were always those paperbacks with a bit of filth in them. I think it was his first clerical job and he was just adequate and no more. He wasn't the sort of fellow I liked to have around.'[46]

Although he was a keen reader, privately Ian returned again and again to *Crime and Punishment*, sharpening his beliefs and ambitions through the character of Raskolnikov. He failed to recognise the sorrow behind the would-be assassin's lament: 'What filthy things my heart is capable of . . .'[47] Instead, he interpreted it as a switch to flick on the 'black light' of his darkest secret: a sexual attraction to children.[48] But he couldn't satisfy it alone.

7

She walked along with her nose in the air. She was ladylike but very stuck up with it, too. She had known me all her life, but she always passed without speaking. He looked as if he wouldn't say boo to a goose. He always wore dark glasses and never walked by her side. He always walked behind her going along the street.

Mrs Lily Yates, former neighbour
of Myra Hindley, interview, 1966

Ostensibly at least, Myra and Ian appeared to be a normal if unsociable couple. The staff at Millwards weren't deceived by protestations that they were merely friends; Myra confided in one girl that they were having a relationship, and everyone else knew without being told. The two of them spent their lunch hour at their desks, talking quietly and eating sandwiches, or went out together for fish and chips. Although Ian was undemonstrative towards Myra in public – he never held her hand or put his arm around her – the impression they gave was of an unassailably intimate couple. Even years afterwards, when Myra was diligently constructing an image of herself as a gullible handmaiden to a master, she admitted that he was often loving and affectionate in private. Capable of genuine kindness towards her and habitually generous with money, he treated her to meals at Oriental restaurants and brought home impulsive gifts. He cooked more often than she did at Bannock Street, when they were alone after Gran had retired to bed, and if they had a disagreement he would apologise with another gift, which they referred to as 'anniversary presents'.[1] He called her Kiddo or the Germanic-sounding Hess, while she named him Neddie in homage to the *Goon Show* character played by Harry Secombe, which she learned to love as ardently as Ian.[2]

They were keen cinema-goers. Ian always tried to reserve seats that had an uninterrupted view of the screen but recalls when, if there was a full house and they had to wait, 'the doorman would come walking along the queue declaring that two of the best seats (also the most expensive) were available [and] I hated having to walk past the queue in order to accept them; I felt that I was deliberately snubbing or insulting them by my action. "I can afford the most expensive; you can't."'[3] He vividly remembers sitting with Myra in the front circle at the spectacular Gaumont cinema on Oxford Road to watch *West Side Story*. They were spellbound by the riotous colour and energy of the film; it flashed by 'in what seemed like half an hour', Ian recalls.[4] They shared the national interest in the spy dramas that reflected the political climate of the times and, having read Ian Fleming's novels, were both eager to see the first Bond film, *Dr. No*, when it premiered in October 1962. *New Statesman* cursorily dismissed the spy as 'an invincibly stupid-looking secret service agent', but the British public embraced the film, relieved to have an alternative to the gritty new-wave realism of the working-class North.[5] Ian and Myra loved it, and saw the follow-up, *From Russia with Love*, when it was released the following year.

After the cinema, they would head back to Bannock Street and share a bottle of Liebfraumilch, which Ian placed next to the fire until the heat forced the cork from the bottle. On other evenings, when Gran was in bed, they indulged in the new British obsession: television. Replacing the radio as a daily staple in people's lives, by 1962 the television had gone from being a luxury to a social necessity. *Coronation Street* was an immediate ratings winner upon its launch in 1960, as was the long-running, gentle police drama *Dixon of Dock Green*, superseded in 1962 by the more hard-hitting *Z Cars*. *The Wednesday Play* outraged the moral majority with its pragmatic depictions of sex, poverty and crime. But the programme Ian and Myra never liked to miss was *That Was The Week That Was* (*TW3*), a satirical news show that began in November 1962 and reached the peak of its popularity in April 1963. David Frost was the chief presenter, but it also starred Bernard Levin, an opinionated journalist with whom Ian later corresponded, and Malcolm Bradbury, Jack Rosenthal, John Braine and Dennis Potter contributed sketches.

Each evening, Ian would pretend to return home, sharing a curious streak of public prudery with Myra, not wanting the neighbours to know that they spent the night together. Mrs Margaret Withnall, who lived nearby, wasn't fooled: 'When Ian started visiting Myra, he used to leave the house and say goodnight at the front door, but several times we heard him sneaking in later.'[6]

The couple's public prudery was at odds with their private lives and values. Literature featured heavily in their love-making; they borrowed books on philosophy and torture from local libraries. Barbara Hughes, a trainee librarian in the district, grew used to seeing them: '[Myra] wore quite short skirts, even before the miniskirt was in fashion, so the first impression was that she was tarty, a bit common. That's why I thought they were not suited. When he returned his books at the Longsight branch, he never said please or thank you. He always walked straight to the True Crime shelves, crash hat under his arm. They frequently came into Levenshulme Library, chatting together, but they never spoke to the staff.'[7] They went elsewhere in search of more explicit books. Myra told her solicitor, Jim Nichol: 'When we went to the Central Library in Manchester and upstairs into the reference library, [Ian would] give me a list of books to pick out, such as *The Cradle of Erotica*, which was pornographic, Havelock Ellis, Kinsey, etc. and show my library card to get them and casually leave all but one on the desk he'd chosen to sit at, some distance away from mine. There was one book, *Sexual Murders*, which could only be taken out on a special ticket. I had to go to the main desk and ask for it, and get it stamped out on my card and give my name and address.'[8]

Together they read Henry Miller, Harold Robbins and de Sade, incorporating scenarios into their own sex lives. '[Ian] took the lead most times,' Myra divulged to her prison therapist. 'He enjoyed rough sex and light spankings became whippings ... He excited me in a way that no other man had done before.'[9] Although she used alcohol to lower her inhibitions, she never drank to excess, not wanting to dull her senses: 'I needed to drink to perform for him or to do the things Ian wanted to do. He liked me to dress up like a tart, for us both to wear hoods. He enjoyed anal sex the most ... He also enjoyed having a candle inserted up his backside. It gave us both pleasure, especially me, because then I was in the dominant role.'[10] The pornography they used wasn't always of interest to her, but she 'went along with it for Ian's sake. I didn't reach orgasm, but I was very excited by seeing him satisfied.'[11] De Sade – whose writings by then had largely fallen into obscurity – remained a mutual favourite. They read aloud to each other from his books, which feature rape, bestiality, incest and necrophilia, and deliberated on the lines: 'If you enjoy wickedness, it shows that nature intended you to be wicked and it would be wicked not to be' and 'If crime is seasoned by enjoyment, crime can become a pleasure . . .'[12] Myra admitted to journalist Duncan Staff that Ian's sadistic desires, inspired by de Sade's writings, aroused her. They took a substantial risk by never using a reliable form of birth control, although a family planning leaflet was found among their belongings after their arrest, and Myra recalled, 'On one occasion . . . I thought I might be pregnant. I was very happy at the thought, but in the end I wasn't. Perhaps it might have been disastrous if I had been.'[13]

Ian had never seen the appeal of conventional relationships and scorned those around him whose aims in life were 'to marry, breed, further burden themselves by mortgage . . . own a family car, and live in excruciating moderation and boredom till death do they depart'.[14] Myra briefly entertained the idea that their affair might lead to marriage but was glad to have found someone who echoed her own loathing of 'dreary domestic bliss and the norm'.[15] She and Ian had 'a very good understanding with one another' which she felt was far superior to her married friends' lives.[16] Finally, she had met a man 'on a similar intellectual level' to herself.[17] In her eyes, Ian was 'cultured, he listened to classical music, he read classical literature. They were things that interested me too, but I'd had no one to share them with.'[18]

Ian encouraged her to use her mind, to realise that politics weren't something that happened in London but had a personal and daily effect on her life. His belief that the working classes were deliberately kept in a state of subjugation by the government and that 'the very wealthy and powerful are the lawmakers [but] no one accumulates such a high degree of wealth and power by honest and legal means' made sense to her.[19] Myra recalled: 'One thing which we shared was a dissatisfaction with belonging to the working class and being trapped in it.'[20] He was fanatical about Nazism and despised Churchill for his part in the Third Reich's downfall. He bought German records from mail-order companies, ending his letters with the flourish, 'Thank you, Meine Herren.' Both he and Myra were gripped by *Hitler's Inferno*, a compilation of war songs, speeches from the Nuremberg rallies and beer hall music. Fuelled by Nazi-inspired hatred, he and Myra detested the waves of immigrants who arrived in Britain between 1955 and 1962 from the West Indies, East Africa and South Asia in search of work and better lives for their families. Ian and Myra regarded the newcomers as 'filth' and 'spongers', while the rest of humanity were 'morons' and 'maggots'.[21] Animals were preferable to people; the two of them lavished attention on Ian's dog, Bruce, and Gran's dog, Lassie, whom they dubbed 'Ches'. They read the *Manchester Evening News* for names of those convicted of animal cruelty, then secretly damaged their property or subjected them to physical attack.

The revolution in Myra's intellect manifested itself in her appearance. Ian was obsessive about the cut and fabric of his suits, which he either bought from Burtons or had made to measure by a Jewish tailor (temporarily setting aside his virulent anti-Semitism). His clothes were classic in style; Myra had always followed the fashion pack with her pencil skirts and neat blouses, which tended to look ageing on her, but she began dressing provocatively, ditching the flat ballet pumps for stilettos or knee-length boots, and wearing her skirts shorter and her trousers tighter, and topped it all off with a leather jacket. She drew her inspiration from Ian's crush on Irma Grese, the notorious female concentration camp guard who was executed in 1945, and kept a photograph of Grese in her handbag.

At Millwards, foreman George Clitheroe noticed Myra 'starting to become overbearing, and wearing kinky clothes. They used to laugh and joke together over dirty books.'[22] Tom Craig was disappointed in her: 'She was a good shorthand typist, I'll say that for her, and she was always smartly dressed. She wore these short skirts and boots and fancy stockings. But she would have been fired if it hadn't been difficult to get a replacement. With most of the girls in an office you have a bit of a lark around, you pull their legs and everyone tries to get a bit of fun out of their work. But Myra was heavy going. You got no response from her at all. She was surly at the best of times and aggressive if you spoke to her the wrong way. She didn't come in contact much with the other girls, but she still managed to have a bad effect on everybody. The pair of them were just plain surly and unsociable.'[23]

Outside the office, Myra was the curt public face of the closed unit she and Ian presented to the world. He provided the funds, but if they travelled by bus, she bought the tickets; if they frequented a pub, she paid for the drinks; and if they visited an off-licence for cigarettes, she requested the brand in newly clipped vowels. She even placed bets at bookies while Ian sat outside in his sunglasses to wait for the ticket stub. Otherwise, she rarely spoke to anyone; in Gorton, the neighbours called her Miss Hoity-Toity because she wouldn't acknowledge them. One school friend recalls: 'She went from this happy-go-lucky girl to not wanting to speak to anybody, not wanting to be with anybody. You'd shout to her and she'd completely ignore you.'[24] Even Pat Jepson felt sidelined as Myra withdrew from their friendship and 'start[ed] to speak posh'.[25] Pleasantries from her were so rare that when she rewarded Mr Spencer from the chip shop with a smile and a thank you after he repaired the primus stove she and Ian used on their travels, he passed the news on to his customers.

Only the affection Myra and Ian felt for their families survived the cohesive rejection of everyone else. Ian mourned the death of his foster father, John Sloan, from lung cancer in 1962 and returned to Scotland for the funeral, but postponed the introduction of Myra to his mother and stepfather for months. Peggy still washed and cooked for Ian, and was delighted when he mumbled that he had found a girlfriend, but he never brought Myra indoors, asking her to wait for him instead on the corner of Westmoreland Street while he changed his clothes or finished a meal. The neighbours became accustomed to seeing 'Blondie' sitting on the low wall in front of the house, stonily smoking a cigarette and ignoring all polite nods until Ian appeared and the two of them disappeared on his Tiger Cub motorbike.

Dance halls and coffee bars held no attraction for the couple; they craved the countryside beyond the city, travelling into Derbyshire and Staffordshire on Ian's motorbike, stopping at the old-fashioned pubs he loved. Myra recalled, 'We had some pleasant, relaxing times in country places that he'd found on his travels on his bike; we'd pack a picnic lunch, flasks of coffee and bottles of wine and spend whole days in peace and tranquillity . . .'[26] They recorded their explorations on camera: Myra wearing a motorcycle helmet and sitting on the old stone stile that led into Shallcross Wood; Ian standing with his dog hoisted onto his shoulder below the great jutting fin of a vast rock formation; Myra teasing the dogs with a twig held high at Ladybower reservoir, where a pair of drowned villages lay beneath the still surface of the water. One day they took a different route, passing east through the city suburbs to the old mill villages out towards the dark shoulder of Saddleworth Moor, an undulating, vast and empty landscape that reminded Ian of his boyhood visit to Loch Lomond. He was enraptured as the moor rose and fell on either side of the twisting road, where long expanses of water lay glinting in the hollows of heather-marled valleys. They came to regard the moor as their kingdom, riding through it slowly enough to catch the thick smell of the black soil on the air or walking for miles across wind-soughed hills to mysterious rock formations callused by time. They ate and drank on the moor, had sex in its cotton-grass vales and named its soaring outcrops for themselves.

And it was on the moor in 1963, lying together on a plaid picnic blanket in the sun, that they began to discuss what Ian called 'switching on the dark' inside oneself: the execution of a classic bank robbery – and the perfect murder of a child.[27]

'For years people have assumed that Ian totally corrupted me, but he didn't,' Myra admitted a few years before her death. 'I have to own the part that I played in things, to accept that I wanted some of the things to happen.'[28]

Her initial infatuation with Ian Brady isn't difficult to understand; it was based on simple sexual attraction to a man she perceived as good-looking, intelligent and arcane. But, within a short while, everything else that he was had become clear to her and rather than being repulsed by the discovery, she found it stimulating. Why she was 'attracted to his "theology" of fascism and nihilism' and went on to participate in the murders are questions that have never been adequately answered, and it is – as writer Helen Birch phrases it – 'around this absent centre [that] knowledge and understanding fail'.[29] Psychoanalysts inevitably point to Myra's upbringing as fully culpable, but the 'absent centre' was within Myra herself. She told her prison therapist a few years before her death that the 'predatory instinct' already existed within her before she met Ian, around whom her naturally obsessive nature revolved.[30] This, coupled with a strong, dominant element in her character and a desire to rise above her background, drew her to the atrophy of established morality offered by her relationship with Ian.[31] She described him as having 'a powerful personality, a magnet-like charisma', but she is the only woman to have ever felt that way about him.[32] What he did have was the insidious ability to awaken in her an extant urge to 'kick against social and moral convention', as she herself phrased it.[33] She admitted finding it 'exciting to swim against the tide, to do things that others would never dream of . . . I just don't know how much, but I have always wanted something different, more exciting. I have never been satisfied with any situation for long.'[34]

The discussions she and Ian had on the moor quickened her blood. 'Not killing people initially, but criminal activities,' she told her prison therapist, 'the perfect robbery, its planning and execution.'[35] She described her participation in the crimes as 'exciting' and owned up to experiencing an adrenalin rush beforehand.[36] She maintained that her incentive was a form of social sedition: 'I did not gain any sexual gratification from the murders. The prime motivation for the murders, for Ian Brady, was the feeling of power and control. In my case, it was rather compensation in the sense of being different from other people and being set apart from the world.'[37]

She had a sense of having been asleep until she met Ian; his stated desire to 'shed the boring, accepted realities that suffocate the majority and embrace or confront what lies beyond' – of being able to see 'far and deep' – was the base element in the alchemy of their relationship.[38] Before he met her, Ian had used literature as a means of validating his darkest impulses to himself; as a couple, they continued to do the same, discussing the philosophy of Nietzsche and Wittgenstein. Ian introduced her to moral relativism, the concept that there is no universal ethical code by which a person should have to live his or her life, only societal and cultural conventions that can and should be cast off. Decades after their arrest, when they were each preoccupied with constructing dissimilar accounts of their involvement in the crimes, they agreed on one issue: having practised a form of self-hypnosis to liberate them of guilt and to deflect outside suspicion. 'One important aspect of our relationship was that we shared equally the ability to shut down our feelings and our emotions,' Myra explained. 'Ian talked of controlling the subconscious urges or presenting a cold exterior. This ability plus the use of alcohol influenced our sexual experience and would eventually influence everything in our lives . . . We had to be able to blend into our surroundings like chameleons. To exist on two different planes, convincing others that we were normal, not capable of committing crimes . . . He taught me how to conquer my emotions, to do things on autopilot and disregard the consequences. I was a willing apprentice.'[39]

Until then, Ian's impulses had been internalised, but the relationship with Myra justified them: 'Before I met Myra it was all inside me, and the feeling of unreality kept me down . . . I feared it. The energy was kept in. When I met her, she made me feel confident. She believed in me and looked up to me so much that I lost all fear, and the energy projected outwards and I lost control . . .'[40] Their initial plans revolved around robbery, although it may have been a ruse on Ian's part to discover whether or not Myra was truly capable of carrying out the criminal activities they discussed. Ian retained the names of several men whom he had known in Strangeways and borstal, and Myra recalled his mooting Gil Deares as a possible accomplice in a bank raid.[41] They debated seizing money from couriers, and Ian suggested that Myra should stake out the electricity showroom on Hyde Road in preparation. Among the thousands of papers in the relevant files at the National Archives is a note from Ian to Myra on the subject, dated 16 April 1963. Written during his absence from work, after he had injured his ankle crashing the Tiger Cub into railings at Belle Vue, it reads: 'Well Myra, Ich habe meinen Fuss verboten [sic] . . . However, let us capitalise on the situation, I shall grasp the opportunity to view the investment establishment situated on Stockport Road, next Friday, to go over details.'[42] He digresses with a slur about Jews before ending: 'please excuse this atrocious scribble as I am writing this in a yoga stance (filthy swine) upside down. Well Myra, just wanted to put you in the picture. I'll sign off now, as I am writing to Tommy [Craig], poor soul. See you soon, love from I.'

Lying on their picnic blanket on the moor in the spring sunshine, they came up with a line that became their secret catchphrase: 'Money and food is all I want, all I want is money and food.'[43] Myra scrawled the words on the walls of their office in Millwards, beneath the scenic pictures she'd torn from calendars to remind her of the moor.

As the weather grew warmer, the conversation switched from robbery to murder. According to Myra, Ian had given her Meyer Levin's *Compulsion* to read, a fictionalised account of the 1924 Leopold and Loeb murder case. Aiming to commit the perfect crime, wealthy students Nathan Leopold and Richard Loeb, both of Chicago, USA, abducted and killed a 14-year-old boy. Keen adherents of Nietzsche's

Übermensch theory, the two young men burned their own and their victim's clothes after the murder and thoroughly washed down the abduction vehicle but were caught when Leopold's distinctive glasses were found at the crime scene. During their sensationalised trial, defence attorney Clarence Darrow gave one of the most celebrated speeches in court history, pleading for their lives to be spared by arguing that their crimes were innate and that they should not be hanged simply because they had fashioned their lives upon philosophy. The two were sentenced to life for the murder and 99 years each for kidnapping.[44] One commentator noted that what amazed most in the case was that two killers 'met and fitted each other's needs like pieces of a jigsaw puzzle'.[45]

Myra claimed that Ian had handed her the book – in which one character is called Myra – to read as a blueprint for the murder he and she would commit; he told her that Leopold and Loeb had failed to plan properly and that had proved their downfall. Ian denies having read the book at all – he claims the inspiration came from the 1959 film *Compulsion*, in which his favourite actor Orson Welles played the defence attorney. 'To the perfect crime!' runs the opening line.

The rape and murder of children were something Ian and Myra talked about during sex. Myra admitted, 'Sex with children was an interest he had that influenced his offending behaviour, but it was a sadistic trait, gaining excitement from their suffering.'[46] She resolutely denied sharing his paedophilia, but the discussion of it was part of their sex lives and they observed children at play with a view to the crimes they would eventually commit. In the months before she passed her driving test, Myra borrowed a black Ford Prefect van from greengrocer Benjamin Boyce – who knew her as a reliable babysitter – and drove around Manchester with Ian in the passenger seat to watch children. They parked outside her old school, Ryder Brow, and Ian slid down in his seat to take surreptitious photographs of schoolboys through the railings, with Myra sitting next to him. She later confessed to driving about Gorton's streets, stalking children, and imagining what she might say to lure them into the van. 'I was considered to be good with children, an excellent babysitter and able to put children at ease,' she reflected. 'Could I therefore be considered capable of child abduction or violence towards children?'[47]

The moor would be the burial ground for their victim. They chose Hollin Brown Knoll, a shelf of land behind a knot of black boulders protruding from the roadside. It was where they lay on the picnic rug, discussing plans. From the heather-strewn plateau, it was possible to see for miles over the moor and across to where the land sloped down to Greenfield reservoir in the hollow. Their cemetery unfolded before them like a map. '[Ian's] attention to detail was such that major landmarks on the horizon, viewed from a particular vantage point on the roads across the moors, provided a perfect grid reference for his trained mind,' Myra recalled. 'Ian had spent months planning the murders and plotting each location.'[48] They rehearsed the burial meticulously, ascertaining what was possible: 'We used to climb up to and over the big rocks,' she remembered, 'where he would tell me he was going to practise carrying a body, tell me to make myself as limp as possible, then he'd hoist me up and over his shoulder, with my arms and head hanging over one side and my lower body and legs over the other side. The blood used to rush to my head until I thought I was going to faint. Sometimes he would stumble over a small rock or large tuft of grass and we'd both fall . . .'[49]

In a letter from Gartree Prison, Ian described himself and Myra as 'demon folk'.[50] They felt themselves to be above the 'normal mundane consciousness of most of society', residing not in the ordinary world but with 'demons and angels'.[51] Myra told one journalist that she and Ian had been separated by a 'chasm' from the rest of humanity.[52] In his writings, Ian expands on the idea that certain murderers believe in 'a form of personal philosophy (predominantly nihilistic in character) so devoutly that it has the psychological power of a religion . . . Metaphorically gods in their own kingdom . . . eventually taking the lives of those who have entered their own private domain, witnessed their darkest desires and therefore, must never be allowed to leave or testify.'[53] Myra had doubted the existence of God since Michael Higgins' death; her brief dalliance with the Church at the age of 16 hadn't healed the rift within her: 'Perhaps I was almost convinced about God's non-existence without Ian's influence. He simply made it even more plausible. We became our own gods.'[54]

Almost half a century after the murders began, Ian quotes W.H. Auden in his book *The Gates of Janus*: 'The sky is darkening like a stain/Something is going to fall like rain/And it won't be flowers.'[55]

The poem, titled 'The Two', features a couple whose presence is both sinister and seemingly deadly in a town where they guard a gate in a rock. Nearby is a green field whose ground, if removed like a lid, would reveal something deeply unpleasant. At the end of the poem, a funeral car departs and the twin shadowy figures warn the people of the town to be careful, never to forget that they are being watched and that time is ticking, inexorably, on.

The murderer uses the poem to illustrate the propensity of individuals to slip into criminal activity, and perhaps as an allusion to the events that began happening in the summer of 1963, when something did, undeniably, fall like rain.

8

Out of my mind I was, really. It was a dark world. I always had a living hope that she were about somewhere . . . [Myra's] sister was a near neighbour. Lived next door but one, Maureen. She went visiting there. Myra Hindley was talking to me normally and saying she was sorry about Pauline, knowing she'd done that . . .

Mrs Joan Reade, interviewed in *The Moors Murders*
documentary, Chameleon TV, 1999

In May 1963, Ian and Myra took a series of pornographic photos of themselves. Ian bought the equipment – a more technical camera, a tripod and lighting paraphernalia – and developed the photographs in an improvised darkroom. The pictures show them having sex, Ian urinating on a curtain, Myra in crotch-less black pants, both of them wearing white hoods with eyeholes cut out and Myra bearing whip marks on her skin. Thirty-five years later, the photographs became a bone of contention between the two of them regarding their original purpose – whether the photos were intended for private use or for sale – and also the degree of manipulation involved. Ian insisted that Myra had posed willingly in the knowledge that he would attempt to sell the photographs and said that the whip marks were 'drawn on with lipstick . . . not raised welts'.[1] Myra emphasised the opposite and was relieved to learn that the photographs had not been destroyed, hoping they would give credence to her claim of having been 'under duress and abuse before the offences, after and during them, and all the time I was with [Ian]'.[2]

The photographs, she asserted, were taken after Ian had drugged her with the intention of distributing them to her family and work colleagues unless she fell in with his murderous plans – but she didn't explain how he would manage to do so without incriminating himself, particularly given his strong streak of public prudery. According to Myra, the day after he had drugged her, she woke up at lunchtime with a pounding hangover only to be harangued by Gran for getting into such a state. Going outside to clear her head, she borrowed her neighbour John Booth's motorbike and drove for miles until she lost control and crashed into a bus. The next time she saw Ian, he apparently told her that he had mixed her grandmother's Nembutal tablets with red wine to sedate her. She claimed later that she had been too terrified of him to go to the police, or even to end the relationship.

The issue of the photographs formed part of a carefully orchestrated campaign by Myra's supporters in an effort to change the public perception of her role in the crimes. In letters to her solicitor and journalists deemed sympathetic to her, she wrote at length about how Ian 'used to threaten me and rape me and whip me and cane me. I would always be covered in bruises and bite marks.'[3] An inventory of the alleged incidents can be found in Myra's 3 June 1998 letter to her solicitor Jim Nichol; it was evidently written in response to a request from one of her legal team. In the letter, she declares that prior to the first murder, Ian had also drugged her grandmother: 'When I went upstairs to give my gran the cup of tea I'd made for her, as I did each morning before I left for work, I couldn't wake her up. I ran round the corner to my mother's house and she came back with me; she couldn't wake Gran either, although she could see that she was breathing. I ran to the family doctor's, who was nearer to us than the nearest phone box, and begged him to come back with me and see what was wrong with my gran. When we got home, where my mother was still trying to wake her, the doctor examined her and told us both that she was alright, that she had probably forgotten, the night before, that she'd taken her sleeping tablets and had taken them again. She would sleep them off and be okay and that he'd call in and see her the following day.'[4] When Myra questioned Ian that night, having phoned in sick from work: 'He said that unless he convinced me he was serious about murder, it would be my fourteen-year-old sister Maureen next, and then my mother, and said he might also stand in my bedroom until Gran came out of hers – she passed my bedroom to go down the stairs – and push her down the steep stairs, which would undoubtedly kill her . . .'[5]

In the same letter, she claimed to have applied to the NAAFI in order to escape Ian. The episode is repeated elsewhere, though several books date her intention to go abroad as having occurred before she and Ian met, while others contend that she didn't even trouble to fill in the application form. In Myra's version of events, she travelled to London for an interview after a botched abduction attempt; she hadn't been able to find a child whom she felt it was safe to approach, and when Ian lost his temper with her, she responded to an advert to join the NAAFI. During her interview in London: 'I had to have a medical. Maybe six weeks beforehand [Ian] had bitten my breasts so badly that, although the teeth marks had faded, the bruises were still there. The doctor asked me immediately how I got these. My body was covered in bruises from where he had bitten me so I told a half-truth; I said I had been involved in a motorbike crash, which I had – I was the pillion passenger – and I said I had sustained quite a lot of bruising. She must have believed me because I got the job. I wish I had gone.'[6]

Returning home with a two-year contract to work in Germany, she claims she was met by Ian, Nellie, Gran, Maureen, Aunt Annie and cousin Glenys: 'He had got them all together. He was standing behind me and everyone started crying and saying, "Please don't take the job." We were a really close family. And I was thinking, "For Christ's sake, it's because I want to protect you that I am trying to leave." Then he put his hand on my shoulder – and he never touched me in public – and he said to everybody in general, "Don't worry, she has two weeks in which to make her mind up." He squeezed my shoulder and I knew then that he wouldn't let me go. When everyone had gone home and Gran had gone to bed, he stripped me, gagged me and beat me with a cane, raped me anally, which he often did because he knew I cried with the pain and hated him doing that to me. Then he turned me over and urinated inside me. Before leaving, he warned me that if I ever tried to get away again, I'd be the sorriest person alive.'[7] She told her solicitor that having originally wanted to leave for her family's sake, she now decided to stay for them because 'I couldn't go to the police about him for there was no proof of anything, and whilst I feared and often hated him, I was so emotionally obsessed with him I just couldn't change my feelings for him.'[8]

At the time of Myra's letter to her solicitor, none of the incidents could be verified; however, one person came forward to speak on

Myra's behalf after her arrest in 1965: her friend May Hill. May was one of the few people with whom Myra had retained contact, and the two of them occasionally met at the Bessemer or Steelworks Tavern for drinks. When May's boyfriend finished with her, she and Myra spent the evening drinking heavily at the pub and on the way home May blurted out that no one liked Ian. When they reached May's house, Myra asked for pen and paper, then sat down at the kitchen table to write a letter that she refused to let May read. She sealed it in an envelope and pushed it under the carpet in the sitting-room before leaving. The following Saturday, Myra claims, Ian revealed the pornographic photos he had taken of her and told her she had no choice but to do as he wished. Immediately afterwards, Myra asked May to return the letter to her, which she did. Two years later, when the news about the murders broke, May informed the police about the letter, in which Myra had written that she was 'frightened of Brady' and was 'contemplating going abroad and joining the Women's Auxiliary Air Force in order to get away from that man'. William Mars-Jones QC related in 1967: 'He had administered a drug to her and she had no idea what he had done while she was unconscious. When she came to she found him leering over her and she was frightened. She said in the letter that in the event of her disappearing or in the event of the disappearance of three men, whose names and addresses she gave, [May] was to go to the police with the letter . . .'[9] Myra wouldn't discuss the letter with the police until the mid 1980s, when she disputed having mentioned three men but confirmed her fear that Ian might kill her and bury her by the rocks on Hollin Brown Knoll.

Myra's letter to her solicitor continued: 'Some weeks later, he stopped talking to me at work, except to tell me to take dictation, and didn't come near the house . . . for a whole week he ignored me, then on the Friday afternoon not long before we all finished work, he came through to my small office and dropped a note on my desk before going upstairs to the bathroom . . .'[10] That night, she alleged, he called for her and they travelled to a favourite country pub in Whitefield, but instead of stopping, he drove the motorbike down a lane and produced a Stanley knife. After arguing with her about a lift she had accepted from another man, he 'laughed, put the knife away, told me never to accept a lift from Brian again and we drove back to the pub . . . [That night] he raped me anally, urinated inside me and, whilst doing so, began strangling me until I nearly passed out. Then he bit me on the cheekbone, just below my right eye, until my face began to bleed. I tried to fight him off strangling me and biting me, but the more I did, the more the pressure increased. Before he left, when he'd seen the state of my face, he told me to stay off work the next day . . . My gran almost fainted when she saw me, and went to get my mother, who asked me if "he" had done that to me . . . I told them what he had told me to say [that she had been hit by a stray beer bottle in a pub fight] but I knew they didn't believe me.'[11]

Among the many other instances she listed was an account of how, after reading de Sade, Ian attacked her when she refused to have sex with him: 'He said he would soon wake me up. He went into the kitchen and came back with a sweeping brush and, using the handle and head in turns, beat me until I was a bleeding bruised mess. I'd learnt not to cry out when he was hitting me, for my gran had been wakened several times and shouted down the stairs.'[12] She went on: 'He did many other things to me, such as forcing my mouth open and urinating in it, or urinating all over my body, in my ears, up my nose, everywhere he could think of. I was so humiliated . . .'[13] When she asked Ian 'why he kept strangling me so much, so many times – this was before the offences took place – he told me he was "practising" on me. I said one of these days he was going to go too far and would kill me, but he just laughed and said he wouldn't – he needed me. That wasn't an affectionate remark; I knew what he needed me for.'[14]

Towards the end of this litany of violence, she suddenly comments, 'I must be totally honest and say he wasn't always cruel and sadistic towards me . . .', then recounts the walks, picnics and days out that she and Ian had enjoyed together.[15] The abrupt change in tone jars, and undermines everything that has gone before. Unsurprisingly, Ian denies Myra's claims; he admits only to having struck her twice, and recalls just one instance when his jealousy almost erupted in violence, but not towards her: 'We had come out of a cinema and gone for a late-night drink in a town centre bar in Manchester. As we were drinking, a group of five or six men came in together and sat at right-angles to us. The one nearest kept staring at M[yra] with a stupid grin on his face. I gave him a few warning glances, but he continued . . . Casually, I slipped my hand into my overcoat pocket and, with thumb and forefinger, opened the lock-back knife I always carried, made entirely of stainless steel, devoid of ornament and with the functional purity of scalpel. I glanced at the bottles on the table in front of me, selecting which ones to choose as additional weapons. I felt marvellous, delighted and ready to hack the halfwits. I turned towards them. "Who the fuck are you staring at? You looking for trouble?" Words to that effect. I waited for the first move and intended to deal with the starer first . . . Suddenly, apologies were coming from the men, including the starer. I felt a mixture of disappointment and relief."[16] Myra also remembered the incident, admitting, 'Ian started shouting and offering to take them all on. I was secretly pleased.'[17]

Aware that her failure to go to the police about the murder plot was one of many insurmountable hurdles she faced in changing public opinion, Myra attempted one explanation in an open letter to *The Guardian*: 'I knew by the time he began talking about the perfect murder that I was going to help him, that I had very little choice. Again, even if I went to the police there was no proof, only my word against his. And then he would know what I'd done if the police had told him I'd made these allegations against him, and although I knew he wasn't stupid enough to do anything to draw attention to himself, I also knew that he would bide his time while he thought of what to do and how to do it without raising suspicion. I would have had to leave my job, which wasn't a problem; I could go away and lose myself somewhere, but how could I possibly tell my family all that had happened and been said by him without terrifying them? They couldn't move; a family just can't uproot itself and move somewhere and find places to live, jobs, etc. and still live in fear, looking over their shoulders all the time. I knew I was trapped and would have to do what he wanted of me.'[18]

She gave an alternative, more prosaic answer in an interview with detectives in the 1980s: 'It was out of fear in the beginning and after that just to remain safe, and hoping that between murders he would display affection and never fancied anybody else.'[19] More frankly, she told a close friend, 'I simply could not envisage life without him any more . . . It was, at best, a tenuous, unsettled relationship, but I cannot deny that I didn't prefer it to an existence from which he was absent.'[20]

Ian offered his own explanation in a letter to Jack Straw, then Home Secretary: 'Myra Hindley and I once loved each other. We were a unified force, not two conflicting entities. The relationship was not based on the delusional concept of *folie à deux*, but on a conscious/subconscious emotional and psychological affinity. She regarded periodic homicides as rituals . . . marriage ceremonies theoretically binding us ever closer. As the records show, before we met my criminal activities had been primarily mercenary. Afterwards, a duality of motivation developed. Existential philosophy melded with the spirituality of death and became predominant.'[21] He confided more forthrightly in journalist Fred Harrison, stating that what happened between himself and Myra was 'a meshing into one . . . We didn't need to speak. Just a gesture – something had got to be done, something would happen. I'd just look, or just make a gesture with my hand and the thing would happen. It was so close, we knew exactly what was in each other's minds. We were one mind.'[22] And despite her efforts to distance herself from Ian, unwittingly, Myra echoed his words in prison therapy sessions: 'We were of one mind, not troubled by our consciences.'[23]

1963 was the summer of the Beatles. Their first single, 'Love Me Do' – which prompted one music executive to enquire upon initial hearing, 'Is it Spike Milligan in disguise?' – reached number seventeen in the hit parade of October 1962.[24] Five months later, they topped the charts with 'Please Please Me' and that summer Britain was caught between twin obsessions: Secretary of State for War John Profumo's affair with Christine Keeler, and Beatlemania.

Seventeen-year-old Maureen Hindley was fanatical about the Beatles; she would let out an ear-piercing shriek at any mention of the band. After leaving school, she worked in a bewildering succession of low-paid jobs until Myra secured her a position at Millwards as a filing clerk, swearing her to secrecy over the obvious relationship with Ian. Despite working with her sister's boyfriend and seeing him almost every night at Bannock Street, talkative Maureen barely managed to elicit more than a curt nod from Ian. But she had noticed a change in Myra: 'She stopped going to church. She said she didn't believe in it. She didn't believe in marriage. She said she hated babies and children and hated people. She never used to keep things under lock and key, but she started after she met Brady. She kept books, her tape recorder, all her tape recordings and all her clothing locked up in the wardrobe.'[25] Gran seemed resigned to the changes in her household; increasingly frail, there was little she could do about anything that concerned her granddaughter. The neighbours complained angrily about Ravel's *Boléro* thumping through the walls – Ian and Myra played it incessantly – but Gran could only offer an apology on her tenants' behalf and left it to Maureen to question their taste in music.

Among Maureen's wide circle of friends was 16-year-old Pauline Reade. In Gorton's tightly packed network of streets, invisible threads bound Pauline loosely to her murderers. She attended primary and secondary school with Maureen and had briefly dated Maureen's boyfriend, David Smith, who lived with his father at 13 Wiles Street, next door but one to the Reade home at 9 Wiles Street, a 'dog-leg' from the Hindleys on Eaton Street. Pauline worshipped at St Francis' Monastery and knew Myra, who used to walk to work with Pauline's mother, Joan. Amos Reade, Pauline's father, was a regular customer in the Steelie, where he sometimes drank with Bob Hindley.

Pauline was a trainee baker at Sharples on Gorton's shopping thoroughfare, Cross Lane. She worked alongside her father, rising with him at the crack of dawn, and was delighted when her photograph appeared in a Christmas 1962 issue of the *Gorton Reporter*; using her baking skills, she was one of three winners in a Christmas cake competition. Exceptionally pretty and slim, with dark hair and an effervescent light in her blue eyes, Pauline was beginning to come out of her shell a little. She enjoyed a holiday at Butlins Filey in 1961, loved dancing – proudly accompanying her dad to a works dinner dance in Tottenham in early July – and composed poems and songs. Beneath the budgie's cage in the Reades' front room was a piano; Amos could play and Pauline had lessons from a neighbour. She got along well with her shy brother Paul (her senior by one year) and her friends were the girls she had known all her life, including Barbara Jepson, sister of Myra's friend Pat. She was closest to Pat Cummings of Benster Street, and the two girls often conferred on their outfits before attending dances, keen to ensure they dressed alike. Pat remembers Pauline as 'very quiet. When she came to our house, she would ask me to walk her home if it was dusk. She was very frightened. She was not the sort to get into a car with a stranger.'[26]

On Friday, 12 July 1963, Ian and Myra decided to commit their perfect murder.

The sun had shone all day and the early evening air was warm. When Pauline finished work at the bakery, she was alone; her father had already gone home for a quick nap before heading to the Steelie for a pint. She called on her friend Linda Bradshaw in Bannock Street to ask if she'd like to go with her to the dance that night at the British Railways Social Club in Cornwall Street. Although the club was only half a mile from home, Linda's mother refused to allow her to go because alcohol was available there. Pauline tried Pat Garvey next; the two of them had gone to a dance the previous week wearing identical white skirts from C&A. But Pat wasn't allowed either, for the same reason. Pauline trailed home and asked her mother if she could persuade one of her other friends' mothers to agree, otherwise she would have to go alone.

In Bannock Street, Ian and Myra arrived home from Millwards on the Tiger Cub and ran through their meticulously thought-out plans for the evening.[27] Myra still hadn't qualified as a driver, although Harold Rainger, a local driving instructor, gave her lessons and she drove about regularly in Ben Boyce's black Ford Prefect van since he'd bought himself a new vehicle; she had arranged to help Ben pick up his broken Dormobile later that night. Myra would drive Ben's old van around the streets of Gorton until she found a potential victim, with Ian following behind on the Tiger Cub. If Ian agreed with her choice, he would indicate by flashing the headlamps on his motorbike and they would then drive up to the moor on the pretext of needing to find a lost glove, offering the victim a set of records as a reward.[28] Everything was premeditated, nothing left to chance. 'He'd told me what to wear and had counted the buttons on my coat,' Myra wrote later. 'He'd counted the buttons on his coat and jacket and shirt and made a list of everything . . . He was so methodical and precise, he thought of everything, every possibility, absolutely everything.'[29]

While Myra and Ian ate dinner, in her bedroom on nearby Wiles Street Pauline dressed carefully for the dance. With her wages from her apprenticeship at the bakery, she had recently bought a 'Twist' frock – a pink shift dress with a square neck and a hemline that finished just above the knee. She added new white court shoes whose gold lettering gleamed on the insoles as she slipped them on, white gloves bought from Gorton market and only worn once before, and then a light-fitting powder-blue 'duster' coat. After adding 10s to her pocket, she went downstairs. Her mother lent her a locket, fastening the clasp at the base of Pauline's neck, beneath her dark hair. At half-past seven, Pauline left home. Amos had just arrived from the pub, and Joan served him fish and chips before dashing out to catch up with her daughter; their son, Paul, had gone to the cinema with friends for the evening.

Pauline and her mother called first on Barbara Jepson on Taylor Street, but Mrs Jepson still wouldn't let Barbara go to the dance. They tried Linda Bradshaw next, on Bannock Street, where, just a few doors away, Ian and Myra were preparing themselves for the night ahead. Pauline made a fuss of the Bradshaw twins in their pram while her mother tried valiantly to convince Linda's mother to relent, but Mrs Bradshaw couldn't be swayed. As they left Bannock Street, Pauline insisted that she was bound to know people at the dance once she got there, and although Joan Reade hated the idea of allowing her daughter to go alone, she trusted her to be sensible and come home on time. A quick peck on her mother's cheek and Pauline was gone, a quick, fragile figure in her pastel-coloured clothes, disappearing in the slanting copper light of evening.

A few minutes later, Myra climbed into the van parked on Bannock Street and switched on the ignition, as Ian started up the Tiger Cub. They drove slowly down Taylor Street and turned right into Gorton Lane. The Plaza cinema, where Myra had glimpsed the ghost of Michael Higgins, shrank in her wing mirrors as the van trundled past Casson Street rec. Myra's old primary school loomed on the right, and she saw a small girl walking alone towards them on the pavement. She slowed the van and squinted at the child. She recognised her: eight-year-old Marie Ruck lived with her parents and brother Kevin next door but one to Myra's mum on Eaton Street. Myra put her foot down on the accelerator; the risk was too great. She told Ian the same thing when he indicated sharply for her to stop and explain why she hadn't picked up the little girl. He accepted it and told her to drive down Froxmer Street towards the railway line and Ashton Old Road.[30]

Pauline passed the Hindley home on Eaton Street, crossed the road and took a shortcut through the backyard of the Shakespeare, where the warm smell of beer and Woodbines wafted from the air vents, and turned down Gorton Lane.

Pat Cummings couldn't believe that her best friend Pauline, always so reserved until she knew someone well, would dare go to the Railways Social Club dance alone. She called for another friend,

Dorothy Slater, and the two girls set off to spy on Pauline, intending to catch up with her near the club. They hid on the croft behind Benster Street to watch for her and were amazed when she walked by, her pale-blue duster coat swinging around her. It was a little after eight o'clock. They trailed her along Gorton Lane, the black dust motes of the foundry opposite swirling in the sunlit draught of a vanished car. Pauline turned down Froxmer Street, heading for the long stretch of Cornwall Street. The girls waited until she was almost at the end of Froxmer Street, then dashed across the croft to where it opened onto Railway Street, expecting to meet up with Pauline there.

Myra turned the van into Froxmer Street. Pauline was a short distance ahead, a little over halfway to the club, where the dance had already begun. Myra spotted her immediately, recording in her autobiography: 'I saw a young girl walking down the street on her own with nobody else in sight. [Ian] flashed his light and I slowly drew up just behind the girl, opened the passenger door and called to her to ask if she could spare a minute. She turned round and to my horror it was Pauline Reade.'[31]

To detective Peter Topping, Myra insisted that there was no truth in an earlier claim that Pauline was deliberately chosen as a victim. Ten years later, however, she told her prison therapist that there was one fact concerning the abduction she wanted to reveal 'to put the records straight', which, if she had admitted to it earlier, 'could have sealed my fate forever'.[32] Having previously said that *Ian* had decided Pauline was 'suitable', she then admitted, 'That wasn't the case at all. *I* chose to pick Pauline up because it was an easy option, less chance of failure and someone who was known to me. If I could do this without conscience, I could do anything . . .'[33] Pauline was known to Myra, but her disappearance was less likely to cause a fuss than that of an eight-year-old girl who was a near neighbour of Myra's parents. In an open letter to *The Guardian*, Myra wrote: 'I knew I had a choice: I could either just wave at Pauline and drive past her, in which case she would have lived and I would have had to endure the consequences of Brady's rage. This all happened in split seconds; I looked at Pauline and saw my sister there and my gran and my mum. I made the choice of having to sacrifice Pauline so that my own family would be safe. I felt sick with fear and self-loathing as I asked her if she wanted a lift. She readily accepted and I opened the passenger door to the car for her to get in.'[34]

On Railway Street, Pat Cummings and Dorothy Slater waited impatiently for Pauline to appear. Eventually, they gave up and walked home, puzzled by their friend's disappearance and assuming she had turned back. In Wiles Street, too, Joan Reade was fretting, wishing she had never allowed Pauline to go to the dance alone.

Myra drove past Ian, parked on his motorbike outside the Vulcan pub, which was known locally as 'the Monkey' and was where the young apprentices from Gorton Tank drank. She asked Pauline if she fancied taking a detour to the outskirts of the city to look for a glove that had strong sentimental value. Although they were yards from the Railways Social Club and could have been there in a couple of minutes, Pauline agreed, accepting Myra's offer of several records as a reward for helping.

It was still light as they drove along the A635 through Stalybridge and Mossley towards the moor. Myra recalled afterwards how Pauline's fragrance suffused the air inside the van; the scent of summer flowers, fern and moss reminded Myra of her own perfume, Saville's June. Pauline asked after Ian; Myra was aware of him tailing them in the mirror, but she said he had gone out and hoped to join her later to look for the glove. The road twisted and dipped through the blackened stone of Greenfield's mill cottages, and Pauline asked Myra if she was all right – as they turned up onto the moor road, she was gripping the steering wheel so tightly that her knuckles were white, and she had hardly spoken. Myra murmured that she was nervous about the van. The light was failing and gradients of shadow rippled across the steeply sloping land. The rocks of Hollin Brown Knoll protruded like black molars against the sky as Myra pulled into the lay-by on the opposite side of the road. She turned off the engine and climbed out of the vehicle.

Myra and Ian each gave different accounts of what happened that night on the moor. According to Myra, Ian's Tiger Cub had passed them somewhere and was already concealed behind a cluster of rocks.[35] Myra feigned surprise to see him, and agreed when he suggested that she should park the van in a safer spot, just beyond the sharp bend, while he and Pauline began hunting for the glove.

In her writings, Myra claimed that she returned to the van. As she pulled away, she saw Ian leading Pauline over the rocks to where the black peat and plum-hued heather gave way to silken cotton grass, the soft white heads of the flowers vivid as stars on the dark ground. Pauline stumbled in her court shoes, and Myra averted her eyes, concentrating on parking the van. She turned off the engine again and stared out across the undulating landscape, down to the valley where lights flickered on in the small cottages. Beyond Greenfield lay the city and Gorton, where Joan Reade had opened her front door to let in the still, warm air, worrying about her daughter and expecting Paul home from the pictures soon. As Joan glanced up the street, she spotted something lying on the cobbles. She went across to investigate and realised it was one of Pauline's white gloves. The unease fluttered in her chest; she hadn't noticed the glove earlier, when she came back from saying goodbye to Pauline. She picked it up and returned to the house, placing the glove in the drawer of the kitchen sideboard, then went up to bed, a knot of anxiety settling on her chest.[36]

In Ian's account, both he and Myra climbed onto Hollin Brown Knoll with Pauline on the pretext of searching for a lost glove belonging to Myra. He claims that Myra not only witnessed Pauline's rape and murder, but, as he told writer Colin Wilson, also 'took a very active part in the sexual assault of Pauline Reade'.[37] He makes the same assertion in a 1990 letter, alleging that Myra carried out 'some form of lesbian assault' and caused injuries to Pauline's nose and forehead.[38] He also claims to have struck Myra during the course of the murder, when he sensed that although he had dropped to the depths of depravity, Myra had 'dropped even further' by taking the locket Pauline wore around her neck and taunting her with the words, 'You won't need that where you're going.'[39] In *The Gates of Janus*, Brady declares: 'It is human nature that, if caught, the pupil will blame the master for his criminal conduct. But should the criminal enterprises succeed, I can assure you, from wide personal experience, the pupil's zeal and devotion to criminal activities can *outdo* that of the master like that of a convert.'[40]

Myra was equally adamant that she remained in the van throughout and that Ian collected her after he had killed Pauline, banging on the window to indicate that she should accompany him to see the body. She followed him over the rocks, where the ground was heavily disturbed; that summer, trenches had been dug across the moor for a new trans-Pennine methane gas pipeline. The ditches remained unguarded at night, and Ian led Myra around the deep gullies in the waning light to where Pauline lay on her back on the cotton grass.[41] Myra stared down: Pauline's clothes were dishevelled and her throat had been cut so fiercely that she was almost decapitated. Blood seeped thickly from the wound. Pauline wasn't dead, but dying; a gurgling noise came from her as the last vestiges of life slipped away. 'Did you rape her?' Myra asked. 'Of course I did,' Ian replied.[42] He told Myra to wait with the body while he fetched the spade he had hidden earlier in one of the pipeline trenches. Myra recalled being surprised by the throat wound because Ian had said that he intended to strangle the victim.

During Ian's absence, Myra kept her eyes averted from Pauline. She realised she could hear nothing but the soughing of the wind across the moor; the gurgling had stopped. 'I moved as far away from her as possible,' she wrote in her autobiography. 'I stood and looked at the dark outline of the rocks against the horizon of the dark sky and three people died that night: Pauline, my soul and God.'[43]

Ian returned, complaining that he hadn't been able to find the spade at first, which they'd bought from a hardware shop in Gorton for the sole purpose of burying the body. He told her to go back to the van and watch the road; his clothes were saturated with blood. Myra stumbled over the uneven ground to where she'd parked the van and saw that Ian had removed the keys to the vehicle, which she'd left unlocked. She slid into the driver's seat and waited for him. Eventually, he appeared from behind the rocks carrying the dirty spade and the knife he'd used to cut Pauline's throat. He placed the spade in a plastic bag in the back of the van and wrapped the knife, wiped almost clean on the cotton grass, in a piece of newspaper which he lay on the dashboard. He mentioned that for a while when he was killing Pauline she'd struggled so much that he'd thought he might need Myra's help.

He told her to drive to the other lay-by, where the Tiger Cub was parked, and swore as she botched the three-point turn. They reached the lay-by and dragged two long planks of wood from the back of the van, using them as a makeshift ramp to get the motorbike inside the vehicle as they'd practised. After securing the back doors, they returned to their seats. Myra turned the ignition and asked Ian the time. He told her it was ten-thirty.[44]

She could feel the dull weight of the Tiger Cub as she steered the van down the A635 from the moor. Later she claimed that as they came to the outskirts of the city, Ian was the first to speak; he told her that if she'd shown any indication of wanting to back out, she would have ended up in the grave he'd dug for Pauline. She replied quietly that she knew that. As they weaved through the city suburbs, she contemplated her involvement in Pauline's murder: 'I felt doubly doomed; first by the crime itself and also because I believed it was impossible to envisage or hope for any other kind of existence.'[45]

The van trundled quietly through Gorton's dark streets. Heading slowly down Gorton Lane, Myra saw two figures walking towards them from the direction of Cornwall Street: Joan and Paul Reade, searching for Pauline. 'That's her mother and brother,' Myra told Ian as she turned the van onto the croft near Bannock Street and let the engine die.[46] They dragged the Tiger Cub out and walked round to Bannock Street, where the glowing fire hissed and spat quietly in the otherwise silent house. Ian brought the knife and spade in through the back door and locked them in a cupboard. Myra had forgotten her promise to Ben Boyce about recovering his broken Dormobile; she swore when Ian reminded her with a small push towards the front door. He fastened the buttons on his overcoat to hide the blood seeping deeper into the fabric of his shirt. At Ben's house, Myra apologised for being so late, telling him that she'd had problems with the Ford Prefect. The three of them drove out to nearby Abbey Hey. Ian kept up a steady stream of conversation and helped Ben attach the tow rope to the Dormobile. Myra climbed into the van to steer it, while Ben drove the vehicle in front. She claimed later that on the journey home she was so preoccupied with the events of the evening that she kept running over the tow rope and bumping into the other van.

After saying goodnight to Ben, Myra and Ian returned to Bannock Street. Ian was determined they wouldn't make the same mistakes as Leopold and Loeb; every trace of what he called 'forensic' had to be eradicated. He'd compiled a list of everything they needed to account for, beginning with the van. Myra handed him a bucket of boiling, foamy water and shone a torch while he sponged the vehicle clean, inside and out, including the tyres. When he was satisfied that it was clean, they shut themselves in the house and laid out a plastic sheet on the sitting-room floor. Ian crouched on the sheet to cut up his clothes into small pieces that would burn more easily on the fire; he burnt his footwear as well. Myra's clothes weren't as soiled as his had been and she could wipe off any traces of moorland soil from her shoes. He attempted to break the handle from the knife, but it wouldn't snap, so he threw it on the fire whole. Myra scrubbed the cupboard with hot, soapy water to remove any smatterings of blood and soil from where the murder weapon and spade had lain.[47]

Later she claimed that after cleaning up, Ian produced a bottle of Drambuie, which he'd bought to toast the crime: 'He sat down next to me on the settee, sipping his drink and saying that after all the years of dreaming of it he'd actually done it: he'd committed the perfect murder. He asked me how I felt about it. I told him I'd never in my wildest dreams imagined that something like this could have happened and began to cry ... He put his arm round my shoulder and kissed me clumsily on the cheek, telling me it was all over now; I'd learn to live with it and he'd try to control his temper and not hit or hurt me. I was so relieved I clung to him, still crying, and promised I'd do everything I could to cope with what had happened and do my best not to antagonise him, although I rarely did and he still hit and hurt me. He stroked my hair – I thought the merest touch would repel me, but in spite of what had happened this new tenderness touched the core of my heart and flooded it with all the love and emotions I'd felt for him for so long.'[48]

In his own book, Ian writes that the serial killer feels, in the aftermath of the first murder: 'I am no longer of your world – if, as you might suggest, I ever was.'[49] Years earlier, Myra had used precisely the same words in a conversation with her prison therapist: 'After Pauline's death, Ian and I were no longer of this world. I was frightened but equally felt safe in the knowledge that I was a worthy apprentice.'[50]

9

Curiosity about murder and how it feels, this exists in everybody at some level. I could never kill anybody but witnessing a killing, although difficult at first, becomes bearable. I couldn't believe how exciting it would feel to do something really bad, how free you can feel when all is lost ...

Myra Hindley, conversation with prison therapist

Myra claimed that her self-professed childhood ability to control her emotions was fundamental in the psychological exercise she and Ian employed before the murder and afterwards: 'I had learned and continued to learn to hide my real feelings when necessary and only show them when it was safe to do so ... [This] enabled me to lead an apparently normal existence whilst being involved in the offences.'[1] They feared being caught but 'had to combat these feelings in order to repeat the experience'.[2]

In his writings, Ian argues that the serial killer's motive stems from 'power and the will to power', which is synonymous with sex in his mind.[3] Having gone 'unchallenged' by either God or more secular authorities, the serial killer begins to regard 'the rest of humanity as subnormal and weak ... He has created a microcosmic state of his own in which he alone governs.'[4]

Myra confirmed that Ian's murderous delusions of power were 'an aphrodisiac' to him, and in therapy sessions she admitted that their best performances sexually were in the periods immediately after the murders: 'We celebrated our bonding with drink and sex. I would lay myself open to Ian in a physical demonstration of our unity ... Ian and I became further bonded by the blood of our victims.'[5] She again denied experiencing any 'sexual gratification' from the murders, instead gaining 'a sense of security due to the fact that one could not be safe without the other . . . There were times when we would be paranoid about each other, but loyalty was a duty we both respected. There was no room for weakness or treachery.'[6] The secret they shared 'bound us together more closely than any ties of affection possibly could'.[7]

Privately, Ian had moments when he was aware that something had disintegrated horrifically inside him, but he guarded those moments alone: 'I would sometimes wake in the morning and my higher self would not be there, the compelling self had vanished and it would just be me, and I would be like everyone else, and I would think that I was a madman, and I would get up and look at myself in the mirror and my eyes would look like someone else's, and it would return, like being possessed by evil spirits, but it is not; it is too much of yourself inside you . . .'[8]

While Ian and Myra drifted into a drunken slumber before the dwindling fire, Pauline Reade's parents and brother scoured the streets frantically, then called the police. When the first strands of daylight filtered across the city, instead of waking to Saturday's routine of an early breakfast and walk to the bakery with his daughter for the morning shift, Amos found himself going over the events of the previous evening in minute detail with the police.

Throughout much of the day, Joan walked about the streets in a state of utter shock, searching for her daughter, Paul at her side. She encountered Pauline's friend Linda at a bus stop and her pent-up nerves erupted: if Linda had gone to the dance as Pauline had asked, her daughter wouldn't be missing. Linda ran home, crying bitterly until her own mother explained that Mrs Reade was lashing out in her terror about Pauline. When Pat Cummings heard that her best friend hadn't gone to the dance or returned home that night, she went straight to the Reades' home and helped Joan cook a dinner that no one had the appetite to eat. Pat couldn't hold back her tears; she had nightmares for months afterward about the split second when Pauline turned down Froxmer Street in her new blue coat and vanished into thin air.

In Bannock Street, Myra woke at quarter to seven that morning. The fire had gone out long ago. She nudged Ian and he awoke with a curse about the bloodstains on the collar of his black coat draped across a chair. He took the coat to the sink and ran the tap, dabbing at the stains with a damp cloth. The water whirled in the plughole, faintly pink. Myra brewed tea while he retrieved the blackened knife from the fire; he wrapped the contents of the grate in a newspaper and deposited them in the dustbin, but kept the knife in a sheet of the *Manchester Evening News* to dispose of later.

After breakfast they drove into town on the Tiger Cub; Ian waited while Myra took his coat into a dry-cleaner's, booking it in under the surname of the American president, Kennedy. When she returned, they drove south-east from the city centre along Stockport Road until Ian stopped for cigarettes. He came back with the fags and a Crunchie bar, confiding that he'd bought them with four half-crowns he'd taken from Pauline's coat pocket. Myra was appalled; fearing any remaining coins might be traced to them, she told him to replace them near the grave. Ian bristled at the idea but grudgingly relented that she might be right. They drove on towards Macclesfield and turned up a lane. A group of children were playing nearby; Ian gunned the bike to a quieter spot where he unrolled the knife from the newspaper and threw it into a babbling river, followed by a few heavy stones to keep it submerged. He used his lighter to burn the newspaper before they headed home.

The following morning they drove up to the moor on the Tiger Cub to scatter the coins on Pauline's grave, then visited the Odeon cinema in Oldham. A double bill was playing: *The Day of the Triffids*, based on the bestseller by John Wyndham, and *The Legion's Last Patrol*, starring Stewart Granger. That month, Ken Thorne and His Orchestra had a number four hit with the trumpet-led 'Theme from *The Legion's Last Patrol*'. Ian bought the record for Myra, to 'commemorate' their perfect crime, and claims that if either of them hummed the tune afterwards, it was a private reference to Pauline's murder.[9]

When they returned to Bannock Street, Nellie, Maureen and Glenys were there, discussing Pauline's disappearance with Gran. Fear and confusion ran through Gorton in response to one of their own going missing. Allan Grafton recalls, 'We all knew each other and that's partly why Pauline's disappearance made people so nervous. Everyone tried to keep an open mind about it because people didn't just vanish in those days – if they did, it was with good reason. But with Pauline no one knew what to think. It threw everything off kilter. Her family were absolutely positive she hadn't run away, and we believed them. But if she hadn't run away, what had happened to her? There was no explanation, no clue.'[10] The police investigation had drawn a blank and, in the absence of fact, rumours were rife that Pauline had eloped with a fairground worker or run away to Australia. On 19 July, the *Gorton & Openshaw Reporter* ran a column about Pauline under the headline 'Gorton Girl Went to Dance: Missing', describing her as 'an attractive, dark-haired Gorton girl'.[11] Joan Reade was quoted: 'This is a complete mystery. Pauline has no boyfriends and there has not been a row at home. We would rather know that she was safe and have her back home, no matter what she may have done.'[12] Mention was made of the money Pauline had on her person at the time of her disappearance and Myra felt vindicated that she had insisted on replacing the coins Ian had stolen.

On 23 July 1963, less than two weeks after Pauline's murder, Myra celebrated her 21st birthday. Ian bought her a gold-plated Ingersoll watch that she kept until the end of her life. Ben Boyce told her she could have the van as a gift from him, although it needed an MOT, tax and insurance. Myra placed a tax disc borrowed from Ben on the windscreen and drove the van around until she was reported to the police and received a summons. Since it was still registered in Ben's name, he pleaded guilty to permitting the offence. One weekend, Myra and Ian painted the van's interior white to remove any last traces of 'forensic'. They drove to the moor regularly; in her autobiography, Myra writes that being near Pauline's grave calmed Ian and gave him a renewed sense of his perceived dominion.

They were both fully aware of the local press interest in Pauline's disappearance. In a letter, Myra related an anecdote about how she had been sitting in Gran's chair, alone, when she found a notice in the personal column of the newspaper: 'It said: "Pauline, please come home. We're heartbroken for you." I began to cry, rocking myself back and forth with the paper clutched to my chest. I didn't hear his bike, nor knew that he'd come into the house. [Ian] asked me what was wrong, but I couldn't answer; I couldn't stop shaking and crying, for I was devastated about what had happened to Pauline, and for her mum and dad. I really liked Mrs Reade and used to feel sorry for her because she had problems with her nerves and always looked as though she was on the edge of a breakdown. He grabbed the paper off me and soon saw what I'd seen. He put the bolt on the front door in case Gran came back, did the same to the back door, and began to strangle me. Before I lost consciousness, I heard him remind me of what he'd said after Pauline's murder, and that threat still stood.'[13]

The *Gorton & Openshaw Reporter* tried to keep up public interest in Pauline's disappearance. On 2 August 1963, the front page featured a photograph of Pauline looking strikingly pretty, leaning against a car and laughing with her best friend Pat while her brother Paul strummed a guitar. The article quoted her mother Joan: 'She used to go dancing often. I was not worried at first, but I became alarmed when she failed to return . . . There will be no trouble for Pauline when she does come home', and included a disheartening comment from the police in charge of the investigation: 'The search has drawn a complete blank and we are very anxious about the situation.'[14] Seven days later, the newspaper tried again, asking, 'Have You Seen Pauline?' and offered an update on the search: police had drained a large section of the canal in the vicinity of Cornwall Street and Ogden Lane, used tracker dogs, dragged ponds and visited fairgrounds, coffee bars and cinemas, and questioned people, but there was still no trace of the missing girl.

Pauline's family conducted their own desperate, haphazard search of the city. Allan Grafton recalls: 'I was a postman at the time, living at my mam and dad's house in Casson Street, and I used to catch the five o'clock bus to start work at half past five every morning. It's pretty lonely, standing at a bus stop at that time. My bus left from Gorton Lane and most mornings I'd see Pauline's dad, Amos, pass by. I'd ask, "Any luck, Amos?" and he'd say, "No, Allan, no luck." He was out looking for her. I'd see Joan walking about, searching for Pauline, as well. The family were at the end of their tether.'[15]

Every Tuesday Pauline's mother offered a novena for her daughter at St Francis' Monastery. Otherwise, her time was consumed with the search. 'I was always looking,' she recalled. 'I even did Avon's job, going from house to house, thinking I'd find her in one of the houses. I was always ready with my coat on, to run out as soon as daylight came. I went miles on my own, travelling on the buses and thinking I'd seen her and running, getting on one bus and running after another bus. I never thought Myra Hindley or Ian Brady were to do with it at all.'[16]

That summer the couple travelled on the Tiger Cub to Scotland for a holiday. Before their departure, Myra called in at the local police station to ask if they would mind watching out for her van, which was parked on the croft behind Bannock Street. She was a familiar face at the front desk there, asking for coins for the gas meter and checking whether the police had seen Gran's dog Lassie, who wandered about the neighbourhood.

On a previous trip to Scotland, Ian had shown Myra where he'd been brought up: they visited the derelict tenements of the Gorbals and drove out to Templeland Road, but he didn't introduce her to his foster mother and siblings, despite spotting Jean Sloan at a distance. They'd climbed the stairs of a tower block to observe Ian's old home more clearly and a girl emerged from one of the flats and swore at them, wanting to know what they were doing. Ian had answered her with equal aggression but told Myra afterwards that he would never hurt a fellow Scot. In summer 1963, they visited Glasgow again, then drove north to Loch Lomond and sailed on the *Maid of the Loch*, Britain's last large paddle steamer. From the promenade deck, Ian snapped away with his camera, while Myra admired the scenery that had enraptured him as a young boy.

Returning to Gorton, Myra answered the door one day at Bannock Street to find a policeman standing there. She didn't mention in her writings whether or not his uniformed appearance frightened her, instead recalling, 'Outside was one of the tallest, most good-looking men I'd ever seen. He said he'd come to talk to me about the van and could he come in for a few minutes?'[17] He introduced himself as Norman Sutton and asked whether, in view of the legal trouble over the van, she would sell it to him. When Myra agreed, suggesting £20 for it, he told her he would be happy to pay £25 but couldn't exchange money while he was on duty and asked if she would consider an evening out with him so that he might hand over the money later. Myra accepted, and recounted the incident to Ian during a picnic. He laughed hysterically and Myra admitted later that she found it amusing too, in view of the murder they had committed.

She arranged to meet Norman after the night-school classes she had enrolled in at her old school, Ryder Brow. She took maths on Friday and English on Wednesday, taught by her old English teacher, Miss Webb, who remembered her. During their conversation, Myra brought up her date with Norman, adding that he was a policeman. Miss Webb said that if Myra ever felt inclined to join the force, she could put in a good word for her because a friend of hers worked at Mill Street station. After the class, Myra found Norman waiting for her on his motorbike, and they drove to a pub in West Gorton, where he said he remembered her from Belle Vue; his mother, May, was the manageress there. After last orders, he drove Myra home. She asked him in for a cup of tea and, in Gran's front room, she explained that she was seeing Ian. He asked if she was serious about Ian. She nodded, but when Norman kissed her she didn't rebuff him. They had sex, and Myra claimed later that he asked her to marry him – though he was already married – at which point she felt an overpowering urge to tell him about Pauline's murder. She quelled the urge and they ended up discussing whether she should apply to join the police force, then made plans to meet after her next evening class.

Myra recalled: 'I went to Mill Street for an interview, and was considered suitable for training, and given forms to fill in, a formal application to join the police and a list of questions to answer. When I told Ian what I had done, he thought it was hilarious. Then he said, "Join the force, you'll pick up a lot of useful information." That made me change my mind.'[18] There is no record of Myra's attempt to become a policewoman because she didn't complete a formal application, but an officer who worked at Gorton station at the time confirms: 'She was given a number of brochures which outlined the opportunities open to a woman officer. That much is certain, but it's impossible to confirm whether or not she actually went for an interview.'[19] After his hilarity about her application to the police subsided, Ian asked Myra if she was sleeping with Norman. Her silence provided him with an answer. She alleged that Ian threatened to kill Norman, who later stated that Ian *had* arrived at Bannock Street one night while he was there and warned him off, but without resorting to violence. Myra and Norman continued their affair for months unharmed, visiting pubs and attending dances, despite the combined threat of Ian's rage and Norman's wife finding out about the relationship.

In October 1963, Ian met Maureen's boyfriend Dave Smith. Although they knew of each other, they had never spoken; Myra disliked Dave, who was regarded as a local tearaway, almost as fervently as Maureen disliked Ian. But during an office party at Millwards, one of the men had flirted with Maureen, who then told her boyfriend about the incident. Dave arrived at Millwards one lunchtime to confront the man, but he had already left after a tip-off from Maureen. Tom Craig responded to Dave's demand, 'I want Maureen', with a firm, 'Well, you can have her at five.'[20] Returning shortly before five, Dave saw the man in question sprint across the car park and chased after him, but was given the slip. He appeared in the car park again out of breath and still fuming. Ian had seen the skirmish and was amused. He asked Myra to shout Dave over with the offer of a lift home. Dave climbed into the van, where Myra introduced the two; whenever Dave visited a friend who lived opposite Myra in Bannock Street, it always made him laugh to see the tin cans Ian had fixed to the back of his motorbike to ward off joyriders. Ian knew of Dave in much the same way as Allan Grafton, who recalls: 'We used to see Maureen quite regular with Dave Smith. The two of them were always knocking about the streets. Dave was a loner, really. He moved away from the gang of lads and had the old Teddy boy hairdo, the jet-black DA at the back, winkle pickers, skin-tight jeans and leather jacket.'[21] Ian and Dave chatted on the journey home, but for the time being their contact remained limited to a nodding acquaintance.

On 7 November 1963, Myra finally passed her driving test after failing it three times. When she bought a car a few months later, she and Ian began eating their lunch in the vehicle during workdays, and they used it for travel more often than the Tiger Cub when they went out together. On shopping trips, Ian would hunker down in the passenger seat while Myra pushed a trolley around one of the new supermarkets, and he stayed in the car when she went into the betting shop to complain that Ian had been short-changed by tuppence on his winnings. The bookie remembered, 'He sent Myra all the way round here – about 300 yards – in the car to collect it. I gave her the coppers, but in the meantime he'd been working out the odds and decided it was three pence he was underpaid. It's hard to believe, but the next I know he's come all the way round for a penny. He came in and thumped the counter, shouting about it – all over a penny.'[22]

A post-trial psychologist's report stressed the importance of the vehicle in their relationship. Apart from its use during the abductions and, on a later occasion, as a hearse to carry the body of one of their victims to the moor, it was like 'a shelter to them. It carried them about safely. [Ian] instanced one occasion when they sat in the car and watched the crowds go by – he knowing what they had done and exhilarated by the secret – they were cut off in the car and the outside crowd were in ignorance of the occupants. This was a powerful and liberating feeling.'[23] The incident mirrors Ian's recollection of parking outside Strangeways, where he had been incarcerated five years earlier; he and Myra 'just sat there, a nice sunny evening, in the car, smoking cigarettes, drinking wine. That wine tasted beautiful because we were watching people in prison.'[24]

Myra joined a gun club in November. She told Peter Topping that the idea that they 'needed' guns came from Ian, but his borstal record vetoed his application for a firearms certificate. He had drawn up loose plans again for a major robbery. Myra made enquiries about joining Cheadle Rifle Club to George Clitheroe, the warehouse foreman at Millwards, who was president of the club and captain of the team. He suggested she accompany him to the indoor shooting range at Cheadle. She went along eight times in all, and four times to an open-air range at Crowden on the road from Manchester to Woodhead. George wasn't impressed by Myra's shooting skills. He was annoyed by her constant querying, 'Will it kick?' whenever she was about to fire and her habit of closing her eyes as she squeezed the trigger, which accounted for her poor aim. When she mentioned wanting to join a pistol club, he tried to dissuade her, telling her she didn't have the right temperament for it because she was too quick to flare up whenever anyone criticised her. Unbeknown to George Clitheroe, a few months later Myra bought a Webley .45 for £8 from John Boland and a nickel-plated, two-inch-barrel Smith & Wesson .38 for £5 from Alan Cottam, two members of the club.[25] She asked if they could get hold of a Luger for her and bought a target rifle from a Manchester gunsmith's. Ian treasured the guns, sitting for hours painstakingly cleaning them, and he and Myra roamed for miles on foot until they found suitably isolated valleys at Woodhead, Saddleworth and Wessenden Head where they could practise shooting at old railway sleepers, oil drums and tin cans.

Myra told a journalist that once, when Ian was cleaning the rifle, she looked up to find him 'pointing [it] at me with his finger slowly pulling the catch back. I didn't know if it was loaded or not, but it petrified me, until one day I said, "Shoot me and put me out of my misery." He just laughed. Another time, he was sitting reading and I was cleaning one of the handguns, a Webley .45. When he looked up,

I was pointing it at him. I told him it was loaded – which it wasn't – and a real look of fear crossed his face. He made a slight movement and I loudly released the safety catch. The tension was palpable and, just as my hands began to shake, I threw the gun across to him and asked how it felt to have a gun pointed at him as he'd done to me so many times. Then I began to cry and he smacked me across the head twice with the handle of the gun, told me I was getting too out of line [and] not to go too far or he would put me in my place once and for all.'[26]

In mid November, Ian and Myra began plotting another murder. Myra claimed that the impetus to kill again came from Ian alone and that she tried to resist. In her account, she and Ian were sitting in Gran's front room, watching the variety show *Sunday Night at the London Palladium*, when he suddenly said he wanted to 'do another one'.[27] Myra insisted later that she had told him she didn't want to be involved, but he said she would 'only' have to coerce the victim into a hired car. This time, he wanted a child, both because of his sexual attraction to children and because Pauline had fought him and he wanted someone smaller. Myra claimed that he began strangling her until she agreed to do as he asked, and that she felt as if the pattern of her life had been mapped out, but she couldn't stop loving him nonetheless.

She slept with policeman Norman Sutton once more, then told him their affair was over. He paid her for the van and that was the end of their relationship. 'If we'd met before Ian and I did,' she wrote years later, 'I knew that the love that had grown between us would have blossomed. I would have had no hesitation in marrying and having children with him.'[28]

Myra attempted to hire a car from Warren's Autos on London Road in Ardwick to use for the abduction, which was planned for 16 November, but since she only had a slip of paper confirming she had passed her driving test, rather than an actual licence, her request was refused. When her licence arrived, she booked a car from the same firm on 16 November for the following weekend. The vehicle she chose was a white Ford Anglia and it cost £14 10s to hire.

On Friday, 22 November 1963, Myra drove Ian to Central Station, where he deposited a suitcase filled with incriminating material in the left luggage department.[29] Railway stations were among Ian's favourite places; he had often walked to Piccadilly Station from his house in Westmoreland Street in the early hours of the morning and enjoyed the 'old-world romanticism of travelling by steam locomotive, and the mysterious, sooty atmosphere of railway stations vibrant with bustle and purpose'.[30] That evening, as he strolled through the concourse, he became aware of a conversation between two commuters: 'I heard one say to the other, "Did you hear about Kennedy?" and then the word, "dead". The girl [Myra] was in the car park and as soon as I got in, I switched on the radio and found out he was dead.'[31] The US president, John F. Kennedy, had been assassinated that afternoon in Dallas, Texas.

A few years later, Shelia Kilbride, the mother of the young boy murdered and buried on the moor the following day, reflected with immeasurable sorrow: 'I think the country was so swept up with Kennedy, they thought: now's definitely the night . . .'[32]

10

I remember the night before, watching the news about the Kennedy assassination on the telly. Everybody was shocked, everybody was talking about it. You never heard of things like that then. All the bad stuff seemed to escalate after that . . .

Danny Kilbride, brother of
John Kilbride, interview with author, 2009

The three-bedroom, red-brick house at 262 Smallshaw Lane in the market town of Ashton-under-Lyne was home to the Kilbride family. There were nine of them: parents Patrick and Shelia, and their children: John, Danny, Pat, Terry, Shelia, Maria and Chris. 'Our upbringing was the same as everybody else's,' Danny recalls. 'It was strict, you had to be in by a certain time and if you did anything wrong, you got your arse walloped, but that was how things were back then for everyone. As kids we ran errands for neighbours and did as we were told. My dad was a builder and flagger who always worked, right up to him being about 60. My mum was a real homemaker, though we didn't have much. But we were a happy family. We went to church every Sunday and had lots of relatives living nearby. It was close-knit.'[1]

John, the eldest child, was a sunny-natured boy of 12 in 1963. He was of average height for his age, with brown hair and the large, almost luminous eyes of all the Kilbride children. He was well-known in the neighbourhood for his gap-toothed smile and habit of walking with his hands in his pockets, singing or whistling. Since September 1962, he had attended St Damian's Catholic Secondary and loved it there. 'John was 11 months older than me,' Danny explains. 'We were the same age every year for four weeks, so we were close. He went up to St Damian's before me and used to say, when I was ready for going up, "Oh, you'll like it, Danny." He made some new friends at that school because the kids came in from different towns, though there were lads and lasses from his old junior school class. He was a kid who was well liked, always cheerful. He loved his football – we all supported Ashton United and used to go to the matches on a Saturday. And he liked going to the pictures, that was his thing – our John loved the films.'[2]

All the Kilbride children had small duties about the spotless house, where Danny and John shared a room. As the eldest, John was the most trusted. Every day he walked round to visit his gran, Mrs Margaret Doran, in nearby Rowley Street, to see what she needed doing about the house and garden. She suffered from gallstones and couldn't stoop easily; she welcomed John's help and his company, watching out for him 'walking along the path at the side of the football ground across the road, in his usual cheerful way'.[3]

On the morning of Saturday, 23 November 1963, Danny remembers: 'I got up early to do my paper round, same as always. I came home just after nine, and John had been up to my gran's, doing some shopping for her. He came back after he'd helped her out. My interest then was the garden – I liked being out there, and I had a couple of sheds with budgies and finches in. I spent time with them like I always did, cleaning them out, feeding them and so on.'[4]

In Gorton, Myra pulled on black trousers, a polo-neck jumper and leather jacket, then caught the bus to London Road. At Warren's Autos, the white Ford Anglia was in the forecourt, gleaming from its wash and service. Myra drove to Westmoreland Street, where Ian was waiting with his dog, Bruce. He muttered about the 'too clean' car, as she'd known he would, but handed her a present: Gene Pitney's 'Twenty-four Hours from Tulsa', then slowly climbing the Hit Parade with its end line about never being able to return home again. They drove south, 35 miles away from the city, to Leek in Staffordshire, and spent the morning at the Roaches, a serrated rank of grit-stone crags.

In Ashton-under-Lyne, after lunch, three of John's friends called for him. 'They were going to the pictures,' Danny remembers. 'All three of them were called John. I still see one of the lads, John Ryan. He was the last person to see John before Brady and Hindley picked him up . . .'[5] John threw on his jacket with the football buttons his mum had sewn on for him and headed out with his friends to the

Pavilion cinema. The film they wanted to see – *The Mongols*, starring Jack Palance as the son of Genghis Khan – was an A-rated film that children could only watch with adult supervision. John and his friends found a kind-hearted man to take them in. They sat together in their one-shilling seats in the vast auditorium, whispering to each other as the lights dimmed.

Leaving Staffordshire, Ian and Myra travelled north through the Peak District as far as Huddersfield, where they stopped for coffee and a Danish pastry. Myra had already bought a black wig from Lewis's department store in Manchester; she tugged it over her skull and into place, concealing her blonde hair, and added a headscarf to keep the wig secure.[6] Suitably disguised, she visited a hardware shop while Ian waited in the car, and bought a small kitchen knife, a length of cord and a spade. With their purchases in the boot of the Ford Anglia, they headed across the moor and onto the outskirts of Manchester. Driving from cinema to cinema, they found one showing a film they had already seen, *From Russia with Love*, which would give them an alibi if necessary. Myra removed her headscarf and slipped off the black wig before they reached Longsight, dropping Ian and his dog at home.

By four o'clock, he was at Bannock Street on his motorbike. He helped Myra line the boot of the hired car with sheets of polythene from Millwards, then placed the rifle, spade and a torch in the boot. The skies were ink-black as they left Gorton; Myra stopped the car under a streetlamp and pulled on the wig and headscarf, hiding her blonde hair again. They discussed where she should park on the moor after the abduction and arranged that she should leave Ian with the victim while she drove down to Greenfield, where she would wait for half an hour – taking the rifle from the boot and placing it on the passenger seat – then return to the moor and flash her headlights three times as a signal. Ian would respond with three flashes of his torch.

Satisfied that they knew what they were doing, Myra turned the Ford Anglia onto the A635 and drove through the darkness towards Ashton-under-Lyne.

The Mongols finished at five o'clock. As the crowds spilled out of the cinema onto the pavement, John and his friends decided to see if they could earn a few bob running errands on the market. 'I knew John and his mates used to help out there,' Danny recalled. 'They did it for spending money because most parents couldn't afford much – you were lucky if you got a packet of toffee. And there were quite a few of us, so it was hard for our parents. I used to give the biggest part of my paper money to my mum.'[7] Their parents were unaware of the errand-running; John's father *was* there that afternoon, buying himself a pair of shoes, but left at quarter to five. John and his friends rolled up to the stalls about 20 minutes later.

The market spread across the square and into a long hall whose clock tower was a familiar landmark. Over 100 stalls were lit up that evening; the market sold everything from custard tarts, fresh fish and oven-bottom muffins to cheap perfume, diamond-mesh tights and school uniforms. The striped awnings were decked out with bits of tinsel, 'snow' made from cotton wool and plastic Santas to remind people to start thinking about their Christmas list. John and his friends split up to ask the stallholders if they needed a hand with anything. John Ryan later told a hushed courtroom: 'We went and fetched a trolley from the station for a man on the market. I got sixpence for this. John got about threepence or sixpence, I'm not sure exactly. Then we went to a man who sells carpets in the open market . . . There were two lads, one from the same class as me. After I had some talk with them, I decided to go home. When I set off to catch the bus, John Kilbride was not with me. I last saw him near the carpet dealer's stall. There was no one with him.'[8] The hands on the clock tower pointed at half past five.

Inside the ladies toilets in the market hall, Myra adjusted her black wig in the mirror. She recalled later that the other women washing their hands and reapplying their lipstick didn't pay her any attention as she tied the knot of the headscarf tighter beneath her chin. Then she left and weaved her way through the aisles between the stalls to where Ian waited in the chill night air. He told her he'd already spotted a young boy who seemed to be alone. Linking arms to give the impression of a contented couple, they joined the bustling crowds and headed towards a wall where John sat nibbling broken biscuits from a plastic bag, the treat he'd bought with his earnings. Myra made the initial approach: 'You're out late for such a young lad, aren't you?'[9] Ian added that they had children of their own and could imagine that John's parents might be worrying about him. In answer to their smiling questions, John told them his name and said that he lived on Smallshaw Lane. Myra offered him a lift, and John readily agreed, pushing the bag of broken biscuits into his pocket as he jumped off the wall. Ian and Myra promised John a bottle of sherry, claiming they had won it in a raffle, and the three of them climbed into the car. John sat in the front passenger seat next to Myra. She locked the doors.

As the engine purred into life, Ian mentioned that they'd have to collect the fictitious sherry from their home in Greenfield. John was unruffled by the proposed detour; he sat gazing out of the window as the familiar streets rushed by, giving way to dark lanes and autumn trees. On the approach to Greenfield, Ian added that they ought to try and find the glove Myra had dropped on the moor – it had sentimental value. He addressed his comments to John, who didn't reply, engrossed in the unknown road as it snaked down into the village and then coiled upwards onto the bleak, black moor.

In the town the three had recently left behind, the Kilbrides were beginning to experience the first tremors of nauseous, bewildered panic. 'John was usually home for five o'clock at the latest,' Danny remembers. 'Six o'clock came, half past, then seven. He didn't come back. I was sat there waiting, we all were, the kids watching telly. My mam and dad thought at first that he'd gone to one of his friends and he was going to get his arse smacked when he came home for giving us all such a fright. That was the attitude at first. We thought he might have gone out with his mates to the local woods, something like that. I went down to a couple of my cousins' houses to see if he was there. But he'd vanished.'[10]

On the moor, Myra steered the car into their regular parking place to the right of Hollin Brown Knoll. On the other side of the lozenge-shaped rocks lay Pauline's body in the peaty soil. In her account of that night, Myra recalled that Ian asked John if he would help him look for the glove and fetched the torch from the boot. In the pocket of his overcoat were the knife and string Myra had bought that afternoon. John stood awkwardly in the car doorway until Ian beckoned him to follow down a slight incline to the left of the car as it faced Greenfield. Myra watched them walking away, the small boy and the tall man, in the muted light of a half-moon that gleamed on the reservoir in the valley below. She turned the car onto the road.

'Everything imaginable went through our heads – more so for my parents,' Danny recalls. 'Then it got to about nine o'clock and my mum knew he wouldn't stop out that late, not even for a prank, we all did. So my mum went to my auntie's, because we didn't have a phone, and she called the police from there.'[11]

Myra drove down as far as the small roundabout at the foot of the moor road, where bright lights and the chink of glasses came from the Clarence, a four-square pub in the fork of the road. She parked in an unlit spot opposite the pub and got out to retrieve the rifle and ammunition, placing them on the passenger seat, then climbed back behind the steering wheel and sat glancing from the pub to her watch until half an hour had passed. She spun the car around the roundabout and drove up the winding road to Hollin Brown Knoll, flashing the headlights as she pulled in. Through the darkness she saw three blinks from Ian's torch and turned the car until it faced Greenfield again. Ian appeared, slightly out of breath. He unlocked the boot and thrust the spade in.[12] Myra got out of the driver's seat and saw that he was holding a shoe. Ian told her it must have come off John while he was raping the child; he'd noticed it after filling in the grave. Then he said he hadn't been able to kill John with the knife because the serrated blade was too blunt and he'd had to strangle him with the cord instead. He put the weapons next to the spade in the car boot before walking round to the passenger seat. Myra slid in beside him and they drove away from the moonlit moor.

In Ashton-under-Lyne, Danny Kilbride turned the TV sound button to mute when the police entered the front room. The newsreels of Kennedy being shot played silently in the background as Danny witnessed his mum breaking down under the weight of her fear: 'All I saw my mother do for the next two years was cry.'[13]

Ian told Peter Topping that after he killed John, he looked up at the sky, shook his fist and shouted, 'Take that, you bastard!'[14] Afterwards, he was angry with himself for acknowledging God, following years of denial. In *The Gates of Janus*, Ian writes that for a serial killer 'nothing less than challenging God or the indifferent universe will satisfy. A form of reversed hope, as it were: "Show me your power, your existence, by stopping me" . . . To be ignored is to be deprived of human dignity and meaning.'[15]

Shortly before her death, Myra wrote of John Kilbride's murder: 'I knew I'd never be able to come to any kind of terms with this; that it would haunt me for the rest of my life, as would the murder of Pauline Reade. That is why I've said several times that I am more culpable than Brady is, even though he committed the crimes. Not only did I help procure the victims for him, I knew it was wrong, to put it mildly, that what we were doing was evil and depraved, whereas he subscribed to de Sade's philosophy, that murder was for pleasure. To him it had become a hobby, something one did to get absorbed into, interested and often fascinated with, and it had become literally a deadly obsession.'[16]

In Bannock Street, she helped Ian remove all traces of John's murder. Adhering to every stage of Ian's written plan, they cleaned the soil-encrusted spade in the sink and locked it in a cupboard with the rifle. John's shoe was consigned to the fire, together with Ian's own clothes. This time, the handle snapped easily off the knife and Ian burned it, disposing of the blade by some other method. The plastic sheeting in the boot of the car was thrown away and the car was given a thorough wipe down, inside and out again. When every item on the murder plan had been ticked, the two of them settled down by the fire, where John's shoe was turning to ash, and drank: three bottles of wine followed by whisky chasers. Myra wrote later: 'With the killing of John Kilbride, a child, I felt I'd crossed the Rubicon. [Ian] said good, admitting to having crossed the Rubicon was tantamount to admitting what he'd tried to drum into my head: that what was done was done, and couldn't be undone, there was no going back and even after the first murder we were irrevocably bound together and more so after the second one. Just then he looked up at the TV – there was either a football match on or late sports news. He said: "Look at that massive crowd. Who would miss one person, two, three, etc., from all the millions of people in this country?" I didn't say their parents and family – he never gave them a thought and I knew I'd really have to steel myself to do the same.'[17]

While Myra and Ian drank themselves to sleep, in Ashton-under-Lyne police station, scene-of-crime officer Mike Massheder was in the darkroom. He recalls that evening vividly: 'Everyone knows where they were when Kennedy was killed, and John Kilbride went missing a day later. I was working late in the darkroom and I had a radio fixed up on one of the shelves and the announcement about the little lad came on there, crackling over the airwaves.'[18] It was his exceptional photography skills that, two years later, led to the discovery of John Kilbride's grave.

The following day marked the start of the search proper. Detective Chief Inspector John Down took charge of John's disappearance. At first light, the police swooped on the market, peering into lorries and questioning stall-holders, opening boxes and probing the area around the square. 'The police took it seriously right away,' Danny recalls. 'They searched everywhere: people's attics; sheds; the market, of course. In the days to come, I went all over the place with my mum, looking for him. My dad was working, but we used to get on the bus and go to different towns to see if there was any sign of him. But there was no reason for him to run away, so we knew it was hopeless, but we had to do *something*.'[19]

In Gorton that morning, Ian left Bannock Street and returned to his mother's house in Longsight. Myra tried to quell the worst of her hangover as she returned the Ford Anglia back to Warren's Autos, where foreman Peter Cantwell noticed it was spattered with mud. In his evidence to the court during the Moors trial, he remarked, 'It looked as if it had been through a ploughed field.'[20] When Myra arrived home, Gran rebuked her for drinking too much then fetched her a cup of tea and an aspirin. Myra climbed the stairs to sleep off her hangover.

On Monday, 25 November, the *Manchester Evening News* ran a headline story about John's disappearance: 'Dogs Join in Massive Comb-Out for Boy'. Myra and Ian read the newspaper while sitting on a bench together in Sunnybrow Park, not far from Millwards, where the office buzzed with the news of another missing youngster. Reading about his crimes gave Ian a sense of satisfaction; he states in *The Gates of Janus*: 'The audience is the value and quality of the act. During the process of artistic creation, in the killer's psychic dimension beyond good and evil, the audience is merely a possible offstage threat. If his "play" is a success, he will read the critical reviews with interest, not least as a technician in search of dangerous, structural flaws.'[21] Over 700 statements were taken from stall-holders and people frequenting the market in the search for John, which was highlighted on the local television news. Five hundred posters were distributed bearing his smiling image and the words: 'Have You Seen This Boy?' Danny recalls, 'I remember seeing the posters wherever I went. When I got on the school bus, I'd see his picture at the bus stop. It was horrible – something you can't imagine. And there was still no sign of him.'[22]

On Tuesday, 26 November, the police appealed to the man who had accompanied John and his friends to the cinema to come forward; he did, immediately, and was eliminated from their enquiries. The following day, Myra and Ian returned to the moor for what Ian termed 'a reconnaissance', checking that the recently dug grave hadn't been disturbed. On the same date, the *Manchester Evening News* drew attention to the search again, reporting that the police would welcome anyone over the age of 18 to join them in the hunt for John.

Patrick and Shelia Kilbride struggled valiantly to keep their anguish from their other children and to retain a semblance of normality while their world changed irrevocably. 'John went missing on Saturday and I went back to school on the Wednesday,' Danny recalls. 'It was terrible. Until then, I'd enjoyed school, but every Monday morning there was an assembly when we'd all stand in the hall and the headmaster said – this was the following Monday – "Let's say a prayer for John Kilbride." And every single kid in school turned round and stared at me. It was just … terrible. But I also understood and appreciated what he was doing. The first time I went into the school canteen afterwards, the dinner lady who was dishing out puddings tried to give me double helpings – that was her way of doing something kind. But I said, "No, don't do that." I knew she was only doing it because of who I was and that was something I didn't want – to be singled out from my mates. Most people were kind. The others were very few and far between. The kids at school … well, my true friends were fine with me, but I got one or two lads – one especially – pushing me about and saying, "You haven't got your big brother to protect you now, have you?" I felt like ripping his head off.'[23]

The search widened. On 29 November, the *Ashton Reporter* devoted its front page to John: 'Boy Vanishes Sixth Day'. The *Manchester Evening News* included a photograph of frogmen wading into the foaming River Tame, noting that the search was also being 'concentrated east of Lees Road, an area of bleak moor lands, part of which has already been combed'.[24] Lees Road was close to the A635 between Mossley and Greenfield. Years later, Myra told Peter

Topping that she had been aghast to read how close the police were to finding the graves. On Sunday, 1 December, in a biting cold wind, 2,000 volunteers poured across crofts, derelict buildings and parks in the search for John.

When Shelia Kilbride was told that a boy resembling John had asked a news vendor in Bury about Ashton United's progress, she caught the bus to Bury and went from door to door, holding out a photograph of her son. At home, she was unable to break the habit of including John at the table: 'For a long time, I put an extra plate out, counting the seven children . . .'[25] A businessman offered £100 as a reward to anyone who could offer information leading to John's whereabouts.

In her memoirs, Myra recounted how one evening she and Ian were watching television at Bannock Street when *Sunday Night at the London Palladium* came on: 'I can't remember if the host was Bruce Forsyth or Norman someone, but whoever it was his catchphrase was: "I'm in charge." Brady casually said to me: "What do you think I get out of doing what we've done?" And I immediately said because he was in charge. It was having the power over someone's life and death. He smiled and said good, you know where I'm coming from now.'[26]

The 'Mass Hunt for a Boy', as *The Reporter* phrased it on 6 December, continued apace. The 'biggest search ever mounted for a missing person' meant that 'owing to pressure of work the Police Dance at the Mecca ballroom is cancelled'.[27]

By mid December, the situation was desperate enough for the press to start interviewing clairvoyants. Dutchman Emile Croiset, a parapsychologist who had worked with the police in the Netherlands on missing persons cases, was called in. His information was too vague to be even remotely useful, but a psychic based in Ashton-under-Lyne gave an accurate description of John's grave. Annie Lansley saw John 'out in the open, some way down a slope, with the skyline completely barren, not a tree in sight, a road on the right and near a stream'.[28] But her 'vision' remained no more than a talking point for the next two years.

On 21 December 1963, Myra again hired a car from Warren's Autos for a reconnaissance trip to the moor. She disputed the accusation, made by journalist Fred Harrison, that she and Ian called at the Kilbride home in the weeks after John's murder, posing as detectives and taking away some of his clothing while Ian promised John's mother, 'I'll see you next week. Johnny will be with you.'[29] She did, however, admit that Ian had a compulsion to visit Smallshaw Lane, and that the two of them would sit for a long time on the Tiger Cub, watching the Kilbride house. On other occasions they drove up to the moor, sitting in the lay-by at Hollin Brown Knoll and gazing across the rolling hills to John's grave. There, Myra claimed, Ian found a measure of peace, while in Smallshaw Lane, John's family were striving to get through each day.

'My mum and dad let me stay whenever the police called,' Danny recalls. 'I was allowed to read the papers as well, whereas the other kids weren't. I was the eldest, plus I'd got a good brain on me. My mum would talk to me about John's disappearance, but my dad didn't. I don't think he handled it very well. If anybody said anything to him about it, he'd thump them. If he heard someone whispering behind his back, he just snapped. The police had him in twice, to question him about John, and he fought them: "They won't bloody well accuse *me* . . ." But he *did* snap and I can't blame him for that, because the police would come and drag him out of the house. They had to get a firm hold of him because he wasn't going otherwise. He got locked up for battering some bloke in a pub for insinuating something.'[30]

For other families, apart from the usual seasonal festivities, Christmas 1963 was dominated by the Beatles, whose music and merchandise were everywhere. Christmas audiences gathered around the TV set to watch Ian's favourite shows – *TW3*, the *Hitchcock Hour* – and two new programmes, which proved immediate hits: *The Avengers* and *Doctor Who*, the latter's fame rising steeply ever since the first episode aired on the night John Kilbride went missing. On 27 December 1963, a photograph appeared in the local press, demonstrating the stark contrast in the Kilbrides' Christmas: it showed Shelia and Patrick sitting around the decorated table with all their children but one, and a gap in the chairs where John should have sat.

'My mum laid a place for John and bought him presents that Christmas and the next,' Danny confirms. 'She bought him birthday presents and cards as well. But she just used to cry all the time until they found him. She couldn't help herself. No matter who was there, she'd collapse. My dad felt the same, but he hid himself away. I caught him a couple of times sobbing on the back step. I talked about everything to my brother Pat, because he was nine and a half when John went missing, but the others were too young. I kept trying to work out what had happened. I knew John wouldn't run away because he had so many friends and was a happy kid. He was going out with a young girl at the time; she was upset. They were only just getting into their teens; it was light, innocent stuff. But after two or three months, I knew our John wasn't ever coming home again.'[31]

On New Year's Eve 1963, Ian and Myra climbed on the Tiger Cub and drove to the moor. In the lay-by at Hollin Brown Knoll, Ian held his whisky bottle aloft until it glittered in the soft light from the full moon and shouted, 'To John!'[32]

11

When I saw a photo of Keith Bennett, I was shocked at how young he looked. Once he was in the van, I never saw his face again. Only the back of him, walking along with Ian.

Myra Hindley, letter,
quoted in *Modern Times: Myra Hindley*

Britain was almost halfway through the 1960s, but despite the much-vaunted social and cultural changes taking place 'there was no such thing as a single national experience ... the soundtracks to *The Sound of Music* and *South Pacific* comfortably outsold any Beatles albums of the decade ... more people attended church than went to football matches [and], far from turning against a supposedly repressive Establishment, most people were content to vote for socially conservative, Oxford-educated politicians'.[1] John Lennon spoke of the absence of an actual revolution: 'The people who are in control and in power and the class system and the whole bullshit bourgeois scene is exactly the same ... nothing happened except that we all dressed up.'[2]

The North was fast falling into industrial decline, and the cinema reflected the geographical shift in focus from Liverpool and Leeds to London in the last authentic new-wave film, *Billy Liar*. Critic Alexander Walker commented, 'With Julie Christie, the British cinema caught the train south.'[3] In the same way that they used literature to make their sexual preferences more palatable, Myra and Ian took their discontent with the stagnation of life in Manchester's suburbs to an incomprehensible end. They spent hours on the moor, ruminating on how the murders had enabled them to rise high above the limitations of their working-class backgrounds, telling themselves that social dissatisfaction justified their crimes, which Ian described as 'merely an existential exercise'.[4]

In February 1964, Myra bought a second-hand Austin A40. At Millwards, her new acquisition caused a stir; Tom Craig recalled, 'Everyone thought she'd gone ambitious.'[5] Only 37 per cent of households owned a car by 1965; it was the apex of all affluent symbols and indicated not merely a certain level of prosperity but status as well. One of the first trips Myra and Ian took in the Austin was a reconnaissance visit to the moor. It had snowed, but the steep road up to Hollin Brown Knoll was still open to traffic. In the car with them was a small black-and-white puppy, one of a litter that Lassie had given birth to in January. Myra loved the little dog with a passion and called him Puppet or Pekadese. Ian had bought him a tartan collar and held the inquisitive animal on his knee as they parked in their usual place, the ice on the road making the turn hazardous. In warm clothing, they walked across the moor with Puppet tucked inside Myra's coat, heading to the high ground where Pauline was buried. Ian took a photograph of Myra standing nearby, cuddling Puppet. Then they returned to the road and made their way carefully down the slope to John's grave. There, in the watery sunlight, with the snow melting on the moor, Myra crouched on the sludgy ground above John's body. In the photograph Ian developed a few days later, Puppet peeks out from inside Myra's coat while she stares intently at the flat stones at her feet, an eerie half-smile playing about her lips.

In prison therapy sessions, Myra discussed how they collected 'souvenirs' of their crimes but attempted to distance herself from the practice: '[Ian] would have liked the victims to have suffered for the rest of their lives after he had abused them. He could only savour past experiences through the items that he kept under lock and key. Returning at a later date to rekindle the excitement . . . Some of the photographs that we took on the Moors were constructed with the location of the graves taken into consideration, [but] Ian did not need a camera's image, he could reproduce the image in his own head.'[6] They slotted the photographs he had taken of their victims' graves among holiday snaps and family pictures in a tartan album.

That Easter, Myra and Ian drove to Scotland; they slept in the back of the Austin and toured the sites of Ian's 1949 holiday to Dunning with the Sloans. They visited St Andrews and St Monans, and walked from the small village of Comrie through beech woods to the Devil's Cauldron, a sheer drop of rushing white water that surged from a cavern into a wide pool. On the journey home, they paused in Glasgow, and Myra discovered Dali's *Christ of St John of the Cross*; in her letters, she mentions visiting Kelvingrove Art Gallery and Museum with Ian and falling in love with the painting.

On 6 May, Myra part-exchanged the Austin for a white Morris Mini-Traveller. A two-door estate car, the rear bench seat folded flat to convert the back into a load-carrying area. On the moor, she and Ian took photographs of each other standing like sentinels on the high boulders at Hollin Brown Knoll, with the car parked in the lay-by below. In one picture, Ian wears dark glasses and turns his head towards Pauline's grave, smiling faintly. In another, Myra stands on the same boulder, grinning broadly at the camera, her body angled towards the opposite side of the road, where John Kilbride lay buried. A transistor radio sits at her unsuitably clad feet; she remembered later that Mary Wells' Motown hit 'My Guy' was playing at the time. They also photographed the Mini-Traveller on its own, with the tumbling boulders behind.

John Kilbride would have celebrated his 13th birthday on 15 May 1964. His mother bought him presents and wrote on his card: 'For John, if he is found by today, May 15th 1964, All my love.' She kept all John's belongings safe, including his guitar and toy submarine, and the Flintstones annual he'd received with such pleasure the Christmas before his disappearance. She prayed regularly at St Christopher's Catholic Church and continued to scour the streets for him. Likewise in Gorton, Pauline Reade's parents carried on their search for their missing daughter.

At the beginning of June, Ian told Myra he was 'ready to do another one'.[7]

Keith Bennett celebrated his 12th birthday on 12 June 1964. His home at 29 Eston Street was cheerfully crowded with family: mum Winnie, stepfather Jimmy Johnson and Keith's younger siblings, Alan, Margaret, Ian, Sylvia and stepsister Susan, who was the same age as Keith and very close to him. 'She and Keith went everywhere together,' Winnie recalls. 'I can just see their little faces now, asking me if I'd give them the money for the pictures. And if they liked the film they'd stay in the cinema and see it twice . . . And Margaret, she was only about three at the time, but she was devoted to Keith. Used to follow him around like a little dog.'[8] Winnie's own childhood was deeply scarred by the death of her seven-year-old sister, who burned to death when her dress caught light on the front-room fire; Winnie was ten at the time. Her life since hadn't been easy – she had separated from Keith's father when Keith was very young – but she regarded Jimmy as the love of her life, and their wedding in 1961 brought their two families together. Keith got on well with his stepfather and called him 'Dad'.

Like most boys, Keith was keen on football; he and his brother Alan, with whom he shared a bedroom, spent hours kicking a ball in front of the house and had painted two goal lines on the brick wall at the end of the street. Winnie describes Keith as a kid anyone could love: 'There was no harm to him. He enjoyed life and was very interested in nature. He used to pick up leaves and caterpillars and bring them home, and he collected coins.'[9] He was small, with sandy-brown hair, and wore spectacles for acute short-sightedness. He participated in the school swimming gala when he turned 12 and swam a length of the old Victorian baths for the first time, receiving a certificate for his achievement. That day he had dropped his glasses and broken a lens. His mother had set them aside to be mended.

The Bennett children often stayed the night with their gran, 65-year-old Gertrude Bennett, who was a cleaner at Toc H rugby club in Victoria Park. She lived on Morton Street, which was known locally as 'the concrete' because the ground was laid with tarmac, while the surrounding streets were cobbled. Kids loved it because they could get up a bit of speed on their bikes and scooters without juddering about or catching their wheels between the cobbles. 'The concrete' was in Longsight, between the Daisy Mill Works factory on Stockport Road and the railway line, and three streets from Westmoreland Street, where Ian Brady lived.

Winnie had arranged for Keith, Alan, Ian and Margaret to stay with her mother on the night of 16 June while she went to the eight o'clock bingo at St Aloysius School in Ardwick. That morning, Ian and Myra made their own plans for the evening ahead. They had already deposited a suitcase at the left luggage department of a railway station, and Ian had presented Myra with Roy Orbison's 'It's Over', which hit the number one spot in the music charts the following week with its deeply mournful refrain about the loss of a loved one.

The day passed in a haze of sunshine, and it was still warm when

Myra drove to collect Ian from Westmoreland Street, pausing on the journey to pull on the black wig. When she arrived at Ian's home, he climbed into the back of the car and said he would rap on the glass divider to indicate a potential victim. Myra accelerated out of the street, glancing at the groups of children playing outside their houses in the evening sunlight. It was just after half past seven.

Winnie and Keith left Eston Street shortly after Alan, Ian and Margaret. Winnie was a few weeks away from giving birth to her fifth child, and a little slower at walking than usual. Keith was slightly ahead of her as they turned past the school on Plymouth Grove West, but she followed him, wanting to be certain that he crossed busy Stockport Road safely without his glasses. He met a couple of girls whom he knew from school and larked about behind them, pretending to be fierce. 'I shouted to him to be careful in case he hurt them girls,' Winnie remembers. 'He just give me one of them big grins of his, as much to say don't worry, mam. And them's the last words I spoke to him.'[10] She watched him walk across the zebra crossing on Stockport Road. When he reached the other side, he turned and waved, then she lost sight of him as he turned into a side street next to the Daisy Works. His path took him down Upper Plymouth Grove, bypassing the back entry into Westmoreland Street.

The white Mini-Traveller glided towards him. Myra wound down her window to ask if he would mind helping her carry a few boxes from an off-licence. When his eyes flickered towards Ian, she said he was helping too.[11] Keith agreed, and climbed into the front passenger seat.

None of the children fought the initial approach, Myra claimed, years later: 'It was probably because of me being a woman – they never had any fear.'[12] They hadn't driven very far through the sunlit streets before Ian asked Myra to stop and invited Keith to join him on the back seat. As Keith edged in beside him, Ian mentioned that Myra had lost a glove recently near Greenfield and that they'd appreciate Keith's help in finding it. Ian kept talking as they drove away from the city, through Stalybridge and Mossley and the last huddle of cottages at Greenfield. The road wound through the falling landscape with its uncanny, elaborate rock formations and indigo summer veil of heather. It was still light, the copper glow of a warm evening, as Myra parked the car and watched Ian, who had a camera slung about his neck, lead

Keith onto the sloping moor.[13] She picked up a pair of binoculars and locked the car, then trailed Ian and Keith who went, she recalled, 'like a little lamb to the slaughter'.[14]

They walked along a stream, keeping mainly to the right-hand bank, but occasionally crossing the water. After a while, Ian turned and pointed towards a rise in the land; Myra followed where he indicated, onto the plateau, and put the binoculars to her eyes. The moor was empty. She sat down, no longer able to see Ian and Keith, who had gone into a dip. 'I don't know how long I was there,' she recalled. 'It seemed like ages. It could have been 30 or 40 minutes.'[15] She stared at a cluster of rocks, her back turned away from the direction in which she'd walked. Later, she claimed to have heard nothing as she sat there, other than the soughing of the wind across the moor.

When Ian returned, he was carrying the soiled spade. Myra asked how he had killed Keith and he replied that he had raped him, then strangled him with a length of cord – exactly as he had John Kilbride. He added that he had taken a photograph of Keith's body before burying him. He began walking, and Myra followed him along the stream, watching him bury the spade in a bank of shale.[16]

Back in Gorton, they worked their way quickly through Ian's list of necessary precautions following the murder. He sponged down the car and burned his shoes and hers, because she had been standing next to him when he had buried the spade. He cut up his clothes and handed them to Myra, who threw them on the fire, together with the cord used to end Keith's short life. When everything on the list was done, she drove Ian back to Westmoreland Street for the night. They would meet at Millwards the next day.

Keith's family didn't realise he was missing until Wednesday morning. They didn't own a telephone and when Keith failed to arrive at Morton Street, his grandmother assumed he had stayed at home instead. But at half past eight the following day, when Gertrude Bennett brought Alan, Ian and Margaret back to Eston Street, Winnie looked at her in puzzlement: 'I said, "Where's our Keith?" because normally she brought him with her on her way to her job ... She said he hadn't come to her last night. She said she'd been expecting him, but then she thought I must have made some other arrangements. We both started to panic ... I went up to the school and the clinic, where I thought he might have gone about his broken glasses. But there was no sign, so I went to the police.'[17] Like Danny Kilbride, Alan Bennett immediately sensed that something terrible had happened to his older brother. He left the house and went into the street with his football, kicking it repeatedly against the wall where the white lines stood out on the red-brick, and remained there for a long time, not knowing what else to do.

After work, Ian gave the Mini-Traveller a more thorough clean. He set up his makeshift darkroom and developed the photograph he had taken of Keith. Myra admitted to looking at it with Ian and recalled that it showed Keith lying on the ground with his trousers down and blood on him. Ian told her he was going to destroy the picture because it was out of focus.

Ian retrieved the suitcase of incriminating material from the left luggage department alone. Myra told Peter Topping that she didn't know what was in the suitcase but believed the contents included an address book with the names of the men he had met in borstal and Strangeways, and a notebook in which he'd doodled the name of John Kilbride, though she claimed not to know about the notebook until after the trial. She related an implausible story about how she had been intrigued by the suitcase, which was kept under the bed, but never attempted to open it because she found that Ian had placed a hair over the lock, a trick she said she'd learned to look out for after reading James Bond novels.

The press soon picked up on Keith's disappearance. On 19 June, the *Manchester Evening News* featured an article on page 17. Under the headline 'Tracker Dogs Join Hunt for Lost Boy', readers learned that Keith's home 'is in an area where several murders have occurred and missing persons have gone untraced'.[18] The search focused on Longsight, but there were no leads, as the press reported on 20 June: 'Particular watch is kept on railways because he is keen on trains and frequented the railway sidings at Longsight.'[19] The inevitable rumours began; two children gave separate but clearly inaccurate accounts of having seen Keith outside Longsight Library on the morning after his disappearance. There was speculation that he had run away, even though, like John Kilbride and Pauline Reade, he had no reason to want to leave home. The *Manchester Evening News* sent a photographer round to Smallshaw Lane, where Winnie had gone to meet Shelia Kilbride, instinctively feeling that Keith's disappearance was linked to John's, although the police had nothing to support that idea. The subsequent article was headed, 'Missing Boys and the Two Mothers Who Wait'.[20] Winnie visited the Kilbrides occasionally after that, and she met Joan Reade.

Gertrude Bennett, Keith's grandmother, blamed herself for not having raised the alarm when he didn't arrive at Morton Street. Winnie went into premature labour and gave birth to a healthy son, but her anguish about Keith was compounded by the police suspicion that centred on her husband, Jimmy. Detectives searched their home, tearing up the floorboards and inspecting the concrete in the backyard for signs of disturbance. They took Jimmy Johnson in for questioning four times over the next two years, once calling at the house early on Sunday morning while the family were still asleep. 'They accused me of killing him because I was his stepfather,' Jimmy recalled. 'I don't blame them. I'm glad they explored every possibility, they had a job to do. But it was terrible at the time. I was very fond of the lad and to be accused of doing away with him was too much.'[21] The strain began to affect their marriage, Winnie recalls, and eventually she became so distraught that she confronted the police: 'I said to the head of CID, "Do you think I'd have stayed with my husband if I thought he had anything to do with Keith? You're splitting my family up. And if that happens, you'll have my death and the death of four kiddies on your conscience because I'll kill myself and take them with me."'[22]

The police scaled down their interest in Jimmy Johnson, but Winnie's fragile spirits were almost shattered by a stranger's malice: 'I was walking along Stockport Road one day with my mother and two of the kiddies when a woman stopped me. She said, "You're Keith's mum, aren't you? Do you want to know what's happened to him? He's been chopped up and fed to pigs." I was upset for days after that.'[23] The rest of the family suffered in different ways: the girls persistently asked where Keith had gone and cried themselves to sleep, while Alan found his brother's absence as insistent as his presence had been.

On 3 July 1964, the *Gorton & Openshaw Reporter* ran the front-page article: 'Longsight Boy Still Missing'. Mention was made of the house-to-house enquiries and the dragging of a brook near Mellands Camp on Mount Road in Gorton. Winnie gave a hauntingly prophetic statement: 'I'm very worried now, for the longer it is, I fear there's less chance of him being found.'[24] A week later, the same newspaper featured Pauline Reade on its front page: 'One Year Ago: Girl Went Dancing and Disappeared'. Ten days later, the local press ran a renewed appeal for information about Pauline to tie in with a television broadcast by the police. But no one came forward.

Winnie's desperate hope that her son might be found alive lasted only until the leaves began to fall from the trees that dotted the route Keith had taken that evening: 'My senses told me he was dead, but I just couldn't believe it. And then one night when my new baby was about three months old, I was feeding him and half falling asleep while I was doing it. And in my drowsy state I heard Keith call to me, as clearly as anything. "Mam!" he shouted. And then I knew for certain he was dead.'[25]

On Saturday, 15 August 1964, Maureen Hindley married David Smith at Manchester's All Saints Registry Office. Maureen had given up her job at Millwards; she was seven months' pregnant. Her mother refused to attend the wedding out of shame at her daughter's 'predicament', while Myra told Maureen she didn't approve of marriage *or* David Smith and remained at home. However, that evening, a knock came at the door of 13 Wiles Street, where Maureen was living with Dave and his father, two doors down from the Reade family. Myra stood there; she knew the newly-weds would probably be in, since they couldn't afford a honeymoon or even a reception, and she invited them to Bannock Street. 'Ian would like a drink with you,' she said.[26]

The couple freshened themselves up before going round. Maureen and Dave were always careful about their appearance; she didn't usually go out without her thick eye make-up on, even though she sometimes left her hair in rollers, while Dave dressed like James Dean, had Tony Curtis hair and a distinctive, self-confident walk. He had a slight stammer, and Maureen sometimes finished his sentences for him. Ian was waiting for them in the front room with a bottle of red wine next to the fire. Dave hadn't paid much attention to Myra or Ian until then: 'Brady was always aloof and was just the Scotsman who would turn up on a Friday night and sleep with [Myra], and they'd go off to work together on Monday morning. Myra was very hard, she rarely smiled, she was just Maureen's older sister.'[27] But that evening, with Gran safely tucked away upstairs in bed, Myra was chatty and Ian seemed more genial than usual. Dave was pleasantly surprised:

'Everybody was dressed up, but no one was going anywhere. It was civilised and that impressed me.'[28]

Ian betrayed his real interest in Dave by opening a conversation with, 'I believe you've got a record.'[29] Born in Manchester on 9 January 1948, on the surface Dave was the epitome of the era's folk-devil: a juvenile delinquent. He was 13 years old when he and Maureen began their relationship (she was then 15) and had just left remand home.

His unmarried mother, Joyce Hull, had disappeared when he was two years old, leaving Dave to be brought up by his paternal grandparents, Annie and John Smith, who lived in a neat terraced house in Ardwick. Dave believed Annie was his mother and had no idea that his uncle Jack was actually his father. Discovering the truth when he was seven marked a change in Dave's behaviour; he became unruly, smoking and drinking despite his tender age. Then one evening Jack arrived and announced that he was taking his son to live with him. Their new home in Gorton's Wiles Street was so filthy that Dave had to visit Gorton Baths to wash himself properly. He hated his landlady; a male relative of hers shared Dave's bed on occasion and began abusing him. Dave lay silently terrified, too traumatised to tell anyone what was happening.

He started truanting from school, and after a vicious physical fight with his father – who would take out his drunken frustration on his son, beating him on that occasion with a dog chain – found himself in Rose Hill Remand Home at the age of 11. Dave returned to Gorton having learnt nothing but several new techniques for self-defence, and appeared in court on an assault and wounding charge, followed by another summons four years later. He was sent to Stanley Grove Secondary School in Longsight but was expelled after thumping the headmaster. All Saint's School in Gorton Lane took him in, but the fighting continued and it wasn't long before he was expelled again and sent to another school. By then, he was interested in girls, and for several weeks he and his next-door-but-one neighbour Pauline Reade were an item, much to the dismay of her parents. They were relieved when Dave turned his attentions to Maureen Hindley. He remembers Maureen as 'a giddy person. I could talk to her. She was a fighter – rough. No one in the area had beaten Maureen in a fight. She was not an easy lay.'[30]

On 8 July 1963, Dave was hauled before the courts again, when he and his friend Sammy Jepson – brother of Myra's friend Pat Jepson – were caught stealing electrical goods. Dave was placed on probation for three years for housebreaking and larceny, and store-breaking and larceny. When Pauline Reade disappeared, their brief relationship and his criminal convictions led detectives to interview him twice, but Dave had nothing to tell them; he was completely wrapped up in Maureen, although their relationship was fiery and made more difficult by his inability to hold down a job. By mid 1964, he was working as a labourer for Jim Miller, who ran a property repair business from his home in Railway Street, but he was fired shortly before the wedding. Jim reinstated him briefly, but it wasn't long before he fired Dave permanently, unwilling to put up with his hopeless timekeeping.

Despite their new relationship as sister and brother-in-law, Myra didn't warm towards Dave. In time, she grew to hate him and the refrain the police came to associate with her during their investigation into the murders – 'I didn't do it, Ian didn't do it, ask David Smith' – formed the foundation of her relentless determination to ruin his life.

12

Joe liked to get his teeth into things. When he went to Ashton, he became very interested in the Kilbride case. He didn't like the idea of having a missing child on his patch. And he didn't like loose ends, didn't Joe. He liked to get things tidied up. He'd inherited the case and felt that if there was any more to be done, he would do it.

Margaret Mounsey, widow of Joe Mounsey,
interview with author, 2009

Myra called on the newly-weds again the following day, inviting them on a jaunt to the Lake District. They set off in the Mini-Traveller at half past two, Maureen sitting in the front seat next to Myra, chatting nineteen-to-the-dozen, while Dave sat in the back with Ian, listening to him expound on the enforced subordination of the working class. The car was packed with wine, beer and cigarettes. Ian and Dave drank freely, and the alcohol made Ian garrulous.

At Lake Windermere, the car parks were overrun with other day-trippers, so Myra suggested they head on to Bowness, further along the shore. They managed to park the car there and Ian paid for a steamship trip on the lake, then lunch in a restaurant and drinks at various pubs. It was after eight o'clock when they climbed back into the car; Ian and Dave were three sheets to the wind but, at Preston, Ian tapped on the glass partition to stop at another pub. Pints of bitter were downed and Ian bought a small bottle of whisky for the rest of the journey. In the back of the Mini-Traveller, Ian raged about capitalism and the futility of working for a living. Dave let him talk, impressed by the generosity Ian had displayed that day and his exhaustive, articulate philosophy. It was one o'clock when they arrived at Bannock Street, where, as Dave later phrased it for the benefit of the courtroom: 'We had a meal and most of it was drink.'[1] The sun was stealing across Gorton's grey rooftops when he and Maureen departed for home.

From then on, the Smiths socialised regularly at the weekends with Ian and Myra, either at Bannock Street or Wiles Street, and Saturday was 'fish and chip night'. Dave recalls: '[Myra] would be talking to Maureen. Girly talk. The girls would get bored and go to bed. Leave us drinking and listening to big band music, Hitler tapes . . . a pretty bad atmosphere altogether, to be honest.'[2] Ian enlightened Dave about his own past, describing his months in borstal as a kind of criminal apprenticeship, and the 16-year-old youth was happy to listen, sprawled by the fire with a pack of cards on the table and a drink in his hand: 'Myra didn't like it too much, relegated to girls' talk with baby sister, but I didn't care . . . I think I just felt contented enough to be impressed out of my mind.'[3]

Dave was curious about his new pal's relationship with his sister-in-law: 'Both he and Myra were fond of dogs, but I cannot remember ever seeing Brady show any sentiment at all over any human being, nor can I remember him ever showing any affection towards Myra. Never once have I seen him put his arm around her or speak to her affectionately. She was just there and he just seemed to accept her. On the other hand it was quite obvious that Myra was very fond of him.'[4] But there was no sense of her being dominated by Ian or showing meekness; on several occasions Dave witnessed Myra losing her temper violently, both towards her father – whom she would beat with his own walking stick and punch about the head when she discovered him in a drunken stupor after he had attacked her mother – and, to a lesser extent, Ian: 'He liked eating tinned macaroni cheese and she hated it. I've seen her fling a tin on the floor and scream at him that it was worse than dog food and what was he, a baby?'[5] One withering glance from Myra was enough to warn Ian he was straying into dangerous territory during his inebriated rants. Myra was easier company when Ian wasn't there; on the evenings when she dropped him off in Manchester to go 'people-watching', she would often call on Dave and Maureen and revert to a more girlish version of herself. She was openly affectionate to Maureen and the two of them would discuss fashion and gossip, then dance in the front room, the dial turned up to ear-splitting volume on the record player.

Nonetheless, Myra was jealous of Dave's friendship with Ian and was convinced he wasn't good enough for her sister. In her autobiography, she describes enacting a form of revenge when Dave appeared at Bannock Street looking for Maureen, who had run off after a row. It was bucketing rain and Dave was drenched. Myra pretended that she was going to visit her sister at an address in Blackpool and offered to drive Dave there. They sped out of Gorton and headed north-east. Dave fell asleep on the journey; he awoke when Myra shook him to say there was a problem with the car. They were parked on the hard shoulder and the rain was still pelting down. He got out obligingly when Myra asked him to listen to the noise coming from the car outside, then spun round in shock as she slammed the door behind him, locked it and sped away, the wheels spitting gravel, leaving him standing there in the downpour with no immediate means of getting home.

Dave disputes the incident on the motorway ever took place. Recalling his evenings with Myra and Ian, he reflects: 'On looking back, it's easy to see the obvious, but to do that is a big mistake ... Nothing stuck out as plainly evil. Time wasn't easily measured in separate days, it just flowed into one mass event.'[6] During one of their get-togethers in Wiles Street, he and Ian went outside in the dark to urinate by the garages behind the house. As they strolled back, Ian put an arm around Dave's shoulder and nodded towards the Reades' home, where a light burned in an upstairs window, and asked softly, 'What do you think happened to that girl?'[7]

In 1955, almost 70,000 homes in Manchester were declared unfit for human habitation. The slum clearance programme, largely interrupted by the war, had been resumed fully in 1954, aiming to transform the city into an ultra-modern metropolis: 8,000 homes were demolished in Manchester before 1960, and another 3,000 in Salford. Expansion of the programme in 1960 led to four areas being earmarked for clearance, including Gorton, where once-proud industries such as the Beyer Peacock Works were already closing down. Europe's biggest council estate, Wythenshawe, was starting to rise on land bought from the Cheshire authorities, and satellite towns were planned, with scope for 55,000 homes, based on the Garden City principle. The new neighbourhoods were intended as self-contained communities, with shops, schools, surgeries, parks and so on, but what emerged were crime-ridden districts comprising unsightly red-brick council houses and high-rise flats that the architects themselves wouldn't have dreamt of living in. Families who had lived en masse in the same streets were split up, with older members often isolated in other neighbourhoods.

Hattersley, 12 miles east of the city, was the largest town of them all, with homes for 14,000 people. Myra was pleased when Gran was allocated a house there because she saw it as a step up in the world. Her mother was less impressed.

Bob had suffered a stroke, and he and Myra enjoyed a short respite from their habitual antagonism. 'For the first in my life, I saw him almost helpless,' she recalled. 'Unable to walk, sitting almost constantly in his, the only, armchair in the house or lying in his bed in the living room ... I felt sorry for him, compassionate and even tender towards him. I could never love him but seeing this strong, brutal man reduced to the helplessness of a baby made me feel strong and almost maternal towards him. I waited on him, fetched and carried for him, because I wanted to and not because I had in the past.'[8] Nellie had been having an affair with a man named Bill Moulton and had no intention of moving as far as Hattersley with her invalid husband. She held out for another offer from the council.

Among those residents packing their belongings reluctantly were the Reades. Joan hated leaving Gorton, distraught at the idea that Pauline, if she returned, would not know their new address.

Gran and Myra were given a half-timbered house at 16 Wardle Brook Avenue, the end of a short terrace. The road through the estate ran in front, sloping ten feet as it passed number 16, which stood behind a brick wall. Avoiding the path along the terrace, Myra would park her car directly below the house, then climb up the slope and vault the fence. Beyond the front garden and the road, planted with saplings, was a grassy patch of land next to the New Inn pub on the main road, Mottram Road. The rear garden faced onto the houses of Wardle Brook Walk. The view to the front, past the back walls of the New Inn, was of fields and farms. On the horizon, clearly visible from the upstairs rooms of Wardle Brook Avenue, was the moor.

Seven skyscrapers reared above the red-brick council houses. At night their stairwells were lit, creating 'tall pencils of light'.[9] The static sizzle of the electricity pylons crackled over the neighbourhood, whose streets bore old-fashioned names: Sundial Close, Pudding Lane, Fields Farm Walk. Among the new houses stood Sundial Cottage, a low stone building with tiny windows and a lintel engraved '1697', inhabited by two elderly sisters who kept chickens and goats, and sold eggs and milk to their new neighbours. The roads through the estate were unfinished when the first residents arrived, so workmen had to lay down planks of wood so that mothers could wheel prams safely across the churned-up ground. Since there were no facilities, at different times during the week grocery vans and mobile chippies trundled about the estate, stopping with a 'pip-pip' to let residents know they were there, and housewives would appear, clutching their purses. The milkman delivered medicines together with the milk for those who couldn't reach the surgery in Hyde, and offered lifts to people on the back of his float. Buses were crowded with people whose jobs were in the city centre; Hattersley Road West was known by the drivers as 'Debtors' Retreat'.

Many residents were happy with the move from Gorton: fresh air, gardens and inside bathrooms were a welcome novelty, and the houses felt palatial in comparison to the poky terraces they had left behind. Inside 16 Wardle Brook Avenue was a small entrance hall with stairs to the left, and a kitchen and sitting room. There were windows at either end of the sitting room and a modern fireplace, and a serving hatch through to the kitchen with its smooth Formica worktops. Upstairs were a double bedroom and a single bedroom, and a bathroom with plumbed-in bath, basin and toilet.

Myra was eager to furnish the house with new belongings. Together with her friend May Hill, whose family were living directly behind them at 2 Wardle Brook Walk, she visited Ashton-under-Lyne for a pair of fireside chairs, curtains and rugs. Ian fitted lino under the rugs in the sitting room and slept most nights on the red bed-settee there. Myra placed a vase of plastic chrysanthemums on the sideboard under the back window, a magazine rack under the telly, a mirror above the fireplace and horse-and-foal figurines on the mantelpiece. She hung a couple of lithographs of dogs on the distempered cream walls, added a pair of coffee tables to complete the furnishings, and stood Gran's budgie Joey's cage next to the front window. In the hallway, she and Ian installed a cigarette-vending machine. Every Sunday a man would pop round to empty the half-crowns from the machine and refill it to its 20-packet capacity. Myra smoked 40 Embassy Tipped a day, while Ian favoured Disque Bleu or, when he was feeling flush, good-quality cigars. Throughout the rest of the house, boldly patterned curtains hung at the windows and the floors were fitted with lino. Myra's bedroom was spartan because she shared the sofa bed with Ian almost every night. He eventually fitted a lock on the door to her room, where she kept more than just her clothes in the wardrobe. The 'souvenirs' of their crimes were hidden there, along with the guns.

Each weekday morning at twenty past eight, Myra would set off in the car for work. She left it outside a house near Millwards, but the elderly resident asked if she would mind parking elsewhere; the woman explained that she was virtually housebound due to arthritis and liked to sit in the window to look at the view. Myra released a tirade of abuse, telling her that she was nothing but 'an interfering old busybody', and refused to move the car.[10] Shortly afterwards, a policeman appeared at Millwards, asking for Miss Myra Hindley. When he explained that he had come to see her on behalf of the elderly lady and would be obliged if she could find somewhere else to park her car, Myra relented immediately, doubtlessly thankful that the car was the only matter he wished to discuss.

Together, she and Ian earned approximately £24 a week and from that, they paid rent, fuel bills, ran the car and motorbike, and paid for various items on the never-never. Myra ran into arrears on her purchases from a catalogue and was stretched to her financial limit, but she and Ian somehow managed to find money for trips away and funded a drinking habit that was more expensive than most: wine, gin and whisky. Myra often ran out of cigarettes, despite the vending machine at home, and would cross to the New Inn for supplies, where one of the bar staff recalls: 'She was very ladylike and never drank. She would just say "Twenty Embassy Tipped, please" in a posh voice. She didn't sound like she came from Manchester.'[11]

Most of the neighbours in Hattersley were former Gorton residents like Myra, but she was selective about the people to whom she spoke, and both she and Ian were known as a quiet couple. Kitty Roden, whose husband Tom was distantly related to Myra through marriage, lived on Wardle Brook Walk behind Gran's house but rarely got a word out of Myra. The Rodens' neighbours, May Hill and her family, were friendly with both Myra and Gran. Mrs Hill, who had always liked the singalongs and a bitter lemon at the Bessemer pub in Gorton, was blind; Gran often had a cup of tea with the family and she placed a bet for Mrs Hill every day at the New Inn. Neither Gran nor Myra liked Mr and Mrs Fryer, their neighbours at the end of the terrace. Gran would refer to Mrs Fryer as 'the queer one' and Myra never spoke to the couple.[12] Their immediate neighbours at number 14 were well-to-do, gracious, friendly and – to Ian and Myra's dismay – black. Phoenix Braithwaite had been a painter in Jamaica; in Manchester, he found work at an engineering firm. He was married to Tessa and they had three affable children under the age of five: Donna, Carol and Barry. Phoenix recalled that Myra and Ian 'didn't try to get on or make friends'.[13] He and his family would occasionally elicit a nod from the surly pair, but Myra dismissed the whole family as 'filth'.[14]

The Mastertons at 12 Wardle Brook Avenue fared better with the couple. Chatty forty-three-year-old Elsie from Gorton was on her third marriage and had six children, ranging in age from eighteen-year-old James to three-year-old Peter. It was Elsie's 11-year-old daughter Patty (who had her father's surname, Hodges) who made the initial approach a few weeks after moving in, when she called at number 16 to ask if her mother happened to be there.[15] Patty responded delightedly to Puppet and Lassie frolicking about her ankles, and Myra invited her in, though Elsie was elsewhere. She asked Patty if she'd like a ride in the car because she was due to collect Ian from his mother's house in Longsight. Patty readily agreed: 'I went with her in a little minivan. We both stayed in the car after it had stopped, and eventually Ian joined us. Myra said she didn't go into his house because his mother kept her talking.'[16] Unaware of Myra's white lie, Ian was as pleasant to Patty as Myra had been and the three of them struck up a friendship. The Mastertons didn't have a television set, and Patty was thrilled to be allowed to watch whatever she liked with Gran, Myra and Ian, who were the only people to call her 'Pat'.

The two households often visited each other. Patty's brother James owned a motorbike and quizzed Ian about his Tiger Cub. Elsie told her husband that Ian and Myra were married, knowing that he would have 'put his foot down' about socialising with them otherwise; she speculated to herself that Ian might be already married and waiting for his divorce. She was flummoxed when Myra refused to try on a dress her daughter Edwina had made for her in front of Ian, and invited her to number 12 instead, where the dress – tightly fitted to

Myra's statistics of bust 38, waist 26, hips 42 – proved a hit with its wearer, who had a husky, low-pitched laugh: 'She never laughed in a happy sort of way,' Elsie recalled.[17] In return for Myra encouraging Patty to show an interest in reading at the Central Library (where Patty took out books for Myra on her ticket), Elsie kept an eye on Gran while she was at work and regularly picked up her prescription for Nembutal. Gran was an outpatient at Ashton Hospital, where she had check-ups for insomnia and heart murmurs, and was given regular iron injections.

'I thought [Myra] was a smashing girl,' Elsie later told a BBC interviewer. 'A bit hard, but any promises she made she always kept. She was a very accurate sort of person ... I knew her pretty well from last September because I used to see quite a lot of her at night, owing to my daughter being very friendly with her, and she was very good to the other children ... She was the type I could have imagined forging anything or something but never to do any harm to children because I thought a person who loved animals as much as she did would be incapable of that. And she made such a fuss of children.'[18] Patty wasn't the only child Myra and Ian befriended upon their move to Hattersley: they took two of Elsie's younger children out for rides in the car and went shopping with them, and were friendly with ten-year-old Carol Waterhouse and her brother David, who lived nearby. Carol called on Myra at her mother's request to ask to borrow an onion and, like Patty, she got talking to her. Together with her brother David, she would clean Myra's car in return for a little money, and when Ian suggested a trip to Saddleworth, Carol and David leapt at the opportunity. Ian kept his sunglasses on as they walked across the moor to a stream, crossing it on stepping stones down to a small waterfall, where he took photographs of the two children.

Although they took Carol and David to the moor a couple of times, their most frequent companion by far was Patty, who initially accompanied them on Myra's invitation. In her statement at the trial, Patty recalled: 'When we got there on the first occasion, we just sat in the van; it was light and we just sat there talking. We went up on the moors about once or twice a week. They took wine with them nearly every time. We went to the same spot except for a couple of times when we went further down the road. There were occasions when they brought soil back from the moors. They put the soil on the back garden. This happened ten times, sometimes in the day and sometimes at night. I had some of the wine. It was given to me sometimes by Myra and sometimes by Brady . . . I would have about four glasses of wine on a visit to the house. On two occasions I went for walks on the moors with Ian and Myra. Both times we started off from the same place . . .'[19] The place was Hollin Brown Knoll, where they would sometimes picnic, and during one of their walks across the heather on a sunny day, Ian encouraged Patty: 'If you're thirsty, have a drink from that brook – nice pure water.'[20] The girl did as he suggested, not knowing that the brook flowed next to John Kilbride's grave.

After their arrest, Ian and Myra never spoke of the incomprehensible dichotomy between the murders and their behaviour towards their neighbours' children and Ian's foster nephews – of whom he was very fond, often hiding money in their bedrooms as a treat for them. In his book, Ian writes in a preposterously self-inclusive passage that 'most normal adults find the company of the young a refreshing change from the far too serious adult world. It invigorates and reminds one of happier golden days. We draw raw energy, spiritual stimulation and delight from the relative innocence and spontaneity of the young.'[21] But the neighbourhood children were probably taken to the moor for the particular purpose of having them unknowingly tread on the graves.

Following the move to Hattersley, Myra retained her close relationship with Maureen, and often went shopping or to the pub with her mother Nellie. Once a fortnight, she took Gran to spend the day with Jim, Gran's son, at his home on Combermere Street in Dukinfield. Gran, however, was increasingly unhappy in the house on Wardle Brook Avenue; at the end of September, she told Elsie that Myra hadn't said a civil word to her in months and that she would rather be in an old people's home than living with her granddaughter. She confided that Myra had told her not to expect rent when she was on holiday for a week that month. Elsie told her to stand up to Myra, reminding her that she was the tenant and her granddaughter and boyfriend were the lodgers, to which Gran replied, 'Don't tell Myra!'[22]

In October, Maureen gave birth to a girl, whom she and Dave named Angela Dawn. They were both ecstatic at becoming parents, and Dave was a devoted father, happy to feed and change his daughter, play with her and take her out in her pram through Gorton's semi-demolished streets. Jim was pleasantly surprised by the display of his niece's husband's softer side and told everyone in the family that Dave was 'wonderful' with the baby.[23] That same month, at Manchester Juvenile Court, Dave was bound over to be of good behaviour for twelve months after being convicted of two cases of common assault, for which he was fined £3 each. Myra and Ian seemed less interested in the baby than in the litter of puppies Dave's dog Peggy had in October. Myra gave one, a six-week old pup named Duke II in honour of her childhood pet, to Patty.

John Kilbride had been missing for one year on 23 November 1964. Newspapers and television appeals requested that anyone with information of his whereabouts should come forward. Leading the renewed investigation was Ashton-under-Lyne's new CID chief, Detective Chief Inspector Joseph Mounsey.

Mounsey was one of two policemen who altered the course of the Moors case by refusing to budge when other senior detectives wanted to scale down the inquiry. He had followed his father into the police force after he was demobbed in 1947, spending a few years as a uniformed bobby on the beat in Morecambe, where he idled away his time 'admiring myself in Burton's window'.[24] A year after his marriage in Cyprus to former policewoman Margaret Barrett, the couple left the island – where he had been involved in the hunt for terrorists – and returned to Lancashire. He was promoted to Detective Chief Inspector in 1964, settling at Ashton-under-Lyne, where he described himself as 'a typical copper with size ten boots'.[25]

Margaret Mounsey recalls: 'One of Joe's strengths was knowing the value of having a good team around him. He enjoyed getting stuck into things with people he could trust. They don't work a murder inquiry like they used to; Joe was a dedicated, old-fashioned detective.'[26] Among his loyal, skilled and enthusiastic squad was Mike Massheder: 'Johnny Down, who led the investigation into John Kilbride's disappearance originally, retired. Frank Taylor filled in for a while and then Joe Mounsey took over. One of the first things he did was to take all the detectives out to the pub. He always used to come up to the darkroom and say, "Mike, can you do so-and-so?" and I'd say, "Well, I'm a little bit pushed ..." and he'd say, "It's all right, I'll go. If you can, you can, if you can't, you can't, no problem." Then he'd come back a few minutes later: "Mike, do you think you could just ..." and I'd find myself saying, "Aye, go on then, what is it?" It'd be two o'clock in the morning, I'd be in the darkroom, and thinking, "Bloody hell, he's got me *again*." His team would do anything for him. One of his sayings was, "Never complain, never explain." He was a grand boss, the very best.'[27]

Mounsey quickly picked up on the stagnant Kilbride case. Margaret recalls: 'When Joe moved into the area as the new head of CID, he looked through the back cases for anything outstanding, and that's when he read the case notes on John Kilbride. He called on Mrs Kilbride, just generally taking an interest and seeing exactly what was involved. He had the posters reprinted and got the whole campaign into the little boy's disappearance up and running again.'[28] Mounsey shared Mrs Kilbride's unspoken conviction that something terrible had happened to John and shared her certainty that her husband had no part in John's disappearance. His tenacity in the Kilbride case led to John becoming known at Ashton police station as 'Mounsey's Lad'.

Danny Kilbride recalls, 'None of us had any hope then that John would come back, but what Mounsey did was to get things moving towards finding out who was responsible. He decided to reconstruct John's last known movements at Ashton market to try and jog people's memories. He needed someone to take John's part and I said straight away, "I'll do it." I was 12 at the time and I looked a lot like him. We did the reconstruction around the time of the first anniversary of John going missing.'[29] Despite Mounsey's efforts, no one came forward with fresh information about John's whereabouts.

As Christmas approached, the shops were flooded with Dalek merchandise; having made their first appearance on *Doctor Who* the previous Christmas, Dalek-themed toys were all the rage, and only Beatles and James Bond products came close to beating them in popularity. In Hattersley, Myra told Elsie that she loved the glowing, light-laden Christmas tree that stood in the front window of number 12; however, just a few days before Christmas, there was a fracas at the Masterton house when a neighbour 'went berserk' and attacked Elsie's eldest son, Jim.[30] Anita, Jim's girlfriend, rushed to Myra's house for help and Myra reported the incident to Hyde police while Ian cleaned the blood from Jim's face. When the situation had calmed down, Elsie told Myra that Patty and the other kids had been invited to a Christmas party at the Braithwaites' house. She recalled: 'Myra hated the Jamaican next door. She said to me, "Dirt is better than him . . . You're not letting them go are you? I wouldn't let my children go nowhere near a black's party. Tell them I'm taking them to see Santa Claus." But my little girls went and Mr Braithwaite was very kind. He kept playing records and jiving about like a teenager.'[31]

Shortly before Christmas, Myra and Ian visited a Tesco store near Ancoats one lunchtime to take advantage of the special offers on wine and spirits. On their way there, they saw posters advertising Silcock's Wonder Fair, to be held on the recreation ground off Hulme Hall Lane.

During Christmas Eve afternoon, Patty took Puppet for a patter about the estate – Gran insisted he wore his little coat to keep him warm – while Edwina and Myra were across the road at the New Inn; Ian was at his mum's house until the evening. Patty spent the rest of the day at number 16, and that night Ian and Myra told her to fetch Elsie in for a drink. They exchanged presents: Patty gave Ian a box of chocolates and she had made Myra a jelly in the shape of a rabbit. Myra's gifts for Patty and her siblings were 'done up lovely', as Elsie phrased it.[32] They discussed Elsa, then nine, who was going to have her ears pierced by Ian. Myra was against it, and offered Elsie the money to have her daughter's ears professionally pierced instead. She refilled their glasses with gin; Patty was given some too, together with a small amount of whisky and the sweet apricot wine she and Myra loved. Elsie noticed that Myra seemed unable to tear her eyes from Ian and kept his whisky glass topped up. She recalled: 'Ian talked and talked and I couldn't understand half of what he said.'[33] He smoked cigars and let Myra finish the tabby ends. Elsie asked Ian what made a man go berserk. Ian thought for a while, then answered, 'It's nothing to do with his brain, it's just how much provocation he can stand.'[34]

Later, when Ian and Patty were watching telly and the dogs were sleeping in front of the fire, Elsie followed Myra into the kitchen, where she was putting a pork joint in the oven for Christmas lunch. During their conversation, Elsie confided that she was pregnant again and Myra closed the serving hatch 'so that Ian won't hear'.[35] She asked Elsie if she was going to do 'something to shift it', to which Elsie replied with a shocked, 'No fear.' Myra told her, 'Ian and I have a very good understanding . . . I'd rather have puppies than babies.'[36] She also told

Elsie that everything was taken care of for the house to be put into her name if Gran died. The elderly lady was already in bed, but Myra took her up a cup of tea when she called down for one.

It was after eleven o'clock when Elsie decided to go home. As she got to her feet, Myra asked whether she'd mind if Patty went with them to the moor, to see in Christmas Day. Elsie agreed on the understanding that they wouldn't stay too long; it was bitterly cold. Patty already had her coat on, and went out with Ian and Myra to the car. They drove to their usual spot, by Hollin Brown Knoll. It was a crisp, clear night, starlit above the reservoir. 'We sat in the van when we got there,' Patty recalled. 'Myra took some sandwiches. I might have had a little bit of wine. We stayed there until about 12.30 a.m. Myra said, "Shall we go home and get some blankets and come back for the night?" and Ian said, "All right." Myra then drove me back home. It was about 1.30 a.m. when I got in. Shortly after I got in the house, I heard the van drive off.'[37]

While Patty drifted to sleep in her warm bed in Hattersley, and Elsie dressed in a Santa costume to sneak into the kids' rooms to fill their Christmas stockings, Myra and Ian sat cocooned on the moor, discussing the murder they intended to commit on Boxing Day. Ian referred to the posters they'd seen for the fair in Ancoats. But this time they wouldn't take the victim straight to the moor to be raped and murdered; they would take the child to the house instead, where, Myra recalled, they planned to take 'blue photographs'.[38] When the sun came up over the moor on Christmas morning, the couple headed back down the winding road to Hattersley, where Ian unwrapped the most expensive of the presents Myra had bought him: a tape recorder.

13

Shut up or I'll forget myself and hit you one. Keep it in.

Myra Hindley, tape recording of
Lesley Ann Downey, Boxing Day, 1964

Lesley Ann Downey was ten years old in 1964. She was the only girl in a family of three boys: Terry, fourteen, Thomas, eight, and Brett, four. The children lived with their mother Ann, and her partner, Alan West, in a new council flat at 25 Charnley Walk, Ancoats. Ann had largely been brought up by her grandfather following her mother's death; her father was a sergeant-major. Her disjointed childhood made her determined to give her own children a stable home, but her marriage to Terence Downey had broken up in early 1964. Although Terence had remarried, he remained in touch with his children. Ann was working in the city as a waitress when she met Alan West, a lorry driver from London who provided the stability she wanted for her family. Their new home on Charnley Walk was in the shadow of Bradford Road gasworks in the redeveloped quarter of Ancoats, a once thriving industrial region of cotton mills and foundries.

Lesley, a porcelain-faced little girl with bobbed, wavy dark hair, was an extremely shy child who – like Pauline Reade – only came out of her shell when singing and dancing. Her favourite song was 'Bobby's Girl' and she had a poster of Chris Montez, the 'Let's Dance' vocalist, on her bedroom wall. She had gone with her brother Terry, an apprentice butcher, to her first dance a few months before at the church hall, where a skiffle group were playing. Lesley bashfully admitted to finding one of the boys in the group lovely, and Terry asked for a lock of the lad's hair, which Lesley kept in a box on her dressing table. Although quiet by nature, she had several close friends at school and at the Trinity Methodist Church's Girls' Guildry, where she was a member. When she went away with her Sunday School group to north Wales, she was terribly homesick and spent her money on a small bottle of freesia perfume for her mother. The only lingering sadness in Lesley's life concerned the family dog, Rebel; he was given to her uncle for safekeeping following the move to Charnley Walk. Lesley missed Rebel every day and visited him whenever she could.

A fortnight before Christmas, Alan treated Lesley, Tommy and Brett to an outing to Henry's Store on Manchester's Market Street, where they met Santa Claus. Lesley, undergoing one of the swift growth spurts that occur between childhood and adolescence, had her photograph taken there, among the tinsel and twinkling lights, looking very much the proud 'big sister' next to her younger brothers. Within a month, that same photograph – cropped to show only Lesley – had been distributed to thousands of city shops and cafes in the search for her.

On Christmas morning, Lesley unwrapped her presents with delight: a small electric sewing machine, a nurse's outfit, a doll, an annual and various board games. After breakfast, she carried her little sewing machine to Trinity Methodist Church, where the local children were encouraged to bring their favourite presents to have them blessed. As the skies darkened that afternoon, a few flakes of snow floated down with the faint music from Silcock's Wonder Fair, pitched on the recreation ground half a mile away on Hulme Hall Lane. Lesley was due to visit the fair with friends on Boxing Day, while her older brother Terry had already been with his friends, winning a string of white beads and a matching bracelet on the shooting gallery. He'd left the plastic jewellery on Lesley's dressing table while she was sleeping; they were the first things she saw when she opened her eyes the following morning. She clipped the necklace on immediately and rolled the bracelet onto her wrist.

In Hattersley on Boxing Day morning, Ian handed Myra a record in a paper sleeve: 'Girl Don't Come' by Sandie Shaw, who had scored a huge hit earlier in the year with 'Always Something There to Remind Me'. Upstairs, the wardrobe in Myra's room had been emptied of incriminating materials; Ian had already deposited a suitcase at the left luggage department of a railway station as part of the preparations. There was no need to invent an excuse to get rid of Gran because it was Jim's birthday, and Myra was taking her to his home in Dukinfield after breakfast. While they were gone, Ian set up his camera and photographic lights in Myra's room and checked that all the equipment was in working order. He slid his reel-to-reel tape recorder under the divan bed.

In the maisonette on Charnley Walk, Lesley played with her new toys and looked forward to her visit to the fair that afternoon. Whenever her mother, Ann, opened the kitchen window, the tinny music and stallholders' booming, magnified shouts wafted up from the recreation ground. Lesley elicited a promise from her mother that she would show her how to make clothes for her two favourite dolls, Patsy and Lynn, on the new sewing machine later that day. Shortly before four o'clock, she pulled on her coat and left the flat with Tommy to knock on the Clarks' door downstairs. Mrs Clark and her children – Lesley's friend Linda, and her younger brother and sister, Roy and Ann – had planned to spend an hour at the fair, but Mrs Clark declared herself too tired to venture out. Undeterred, the children left Charnley Walk without her, agreeing to return at five o'clock. At ten years old, Lesley was the eldest of the small group walking along the frosty, twilit streets.

Myra returned from Dukinfield after lunch, having arranged to pick up Gran at nine-thirty that night as usual. By late afternoon, she and Ian were driving out to the Tesco store they had visited a few days before Christmas; the posters for Silcock's Wonder Fair, emblazoned with a big wheel, were everywhere. They did their shopping, packing it with deliberate carelessness in a few cardboard boxes. With the groceries in the back of the car, Myra pulled on the black wig and headscarf, careful that no one should see her. She started the ignition and they drove on to Hulme Hall Lane, parking the car in a quiet side street, away from the whooping crowds milling about the recreation ground. She and Ian overloaded a couple of boxes, locked the car and began walking towards the dazzling, flashing lights of the fair.

By five o'clock, Lesley's small group had run out of money and knew they should be heading home. Lesley was still breathless from a ride on the cyclone as they threaded their way past the soft toy prizes dangling from the stalls. Away from the main booths and whirling waltzers, they trod on dank grass and entered the dimly lit streets where a pale, thin flurry of sleet fell. As they trooped towards home in the shadow of the gasworks, Lesley suddenly said, 'I'm going back', and turned and ran up

Iron Street before anyone could stop her, past the red-brick wall and in through the dark opening, met by a surge of deafening music and glaring lights.

At six o'clock, Lesley was still at the fair. Bernard King, an 11-year-old boy who attended the same school, spotted her from where he stood beside the spinning waltzers. She was by the dodgems, alone, gazing at the bright, speeding cars as they thudded about the rink, the jolt of buffers colliding. Bernard passed Lesley to get to the cyclone and that was the last he saw of her.

The sliding guitars of the Rolling Stones' recent number one single, 'Little Red Rooster', blared from the fairground speakers as Myra and Ian watched Lesley from the darkness behind the dodgems' rink.[1] They waited several minutes, observing her spellbound expression as purplish sparks of electricity flickered on the wire mesh overhead from the car rods, and when they were sure she was alone, they made their approach.

Groceries spilled from the overfilled boxes Myra and Ian carried awkwardly in their arms; as Lesley turned to look, Myra smiled and asked if she would mind giving them a hand taking the boxes back to their car nearby. She promised Lesley a reward for her help and the little girl readily agreed, following where the couple led through the glittering fairground to the dim side street where their car was discreetly parked. Myra asked Lesley if she might help them unload the boxes at home, and again the little girl nodded, climbing into the front passenger seat. They piled the boxes around Lesley to hide her from view, then drove away from the hectic noise and light of the fair to the quiet, dark streets of Hattersley.

After saying goodbye to the other children, eight-year-old Tommy rushed up the stairs at Charnley Walk and burst through the door of the flat, expecting to find Lesley already there. His mother stared at him, aghast, as he stuttered out his sister's decision to return to the fairground alone. Ann sent Tommy back down to Mrs Clarke's flat to see if Lesley was there; when he returned white-faced with shock, she and Alan threw on their coats and dashed out with instructions for Tommy and Terry to stay with four-year-old Brett. They ran down Iron Street, Christmas lights twinkling in every window they passed, and headed onto the recreation ground, where the Ferris wheel revolved endlessly on the skyline. One of Lesley's favourite songs,

'Let's Dance', belted out across the heads of the shrieking, excited crowds. But Lesley – like Pauline, John and Keith before her – had vanished.

Inside the house at Wardle Brook Avenue, Myra told Lesley to take the boxes upstairs. Ian was already in the bedroom; Myra intended to follow, but the dogs dashed into the hall. She later maintained that she had wanted to shut the dogs in the kitchen, and, as she ushered them out, closing the kitchen door on their whines, she heard Lesley screaming.

In the account Myra gave over 20 years later to Peter Topping of Lesley's final hours, she stated that the little girl was screaming because Ian was trying to undress her. She climbed the stairs and in the bleakly furnished room, where a window apparently hung open to let in the bitter winter air, she saw Lesley crying as Ian attempted to remove her coat. 'I know I should have tried to protect the child and comfort her, but I didn't,' Myra told Topping. 'I was cruel, I was brusque and I told her to shut up because I was frightened people would hear. I just panicked.'[2] She claimed not to know that Ian had set up the tape recorder she had bought him that Christmas below the divan; a sheet hung down from the bed, hiding the machine. She also told Topping that the tape was recording before Ian started photographing Lesley in the nude, which would appear to be true, borne out by Lesley's own muffled words on the tape.

The sequence of events is partially verified by the tape recording: it begins with the sound of Ian moving about the room, pushing the dogs out and checking that the microphone works, then Myra's voice is heard as she brings Lesley into the room – these are the two sets of footsteps heard on the recording, before a handkerchief was forced into Lesley's mouth, to gag her.

Beneath the divan, the spools of brown tape revolved inexorably.[3]

> Ian: 'This is track four. Get out of the fucking road. Get in the fucking basket.'
> *Sound of door banging, crackling, heavy footsteps, recording noises, blowing sounds in microphone, more footsteps. Myra's voice, quiet, indecipherable. Light footsteps walking across the room, whispered conversation and, at the same time,*

footsteps. Distant speech containing the word 'upstairs', then two sets of footsteps.

Lesley: [screaming] 'Don't. Mum. Ah.'

Myra: 'Shut up.'

Lesley: 'Please God, help me, please, oh.'

Myra: 'Come on.'

Whispering and footsteps.

Myra: 'Shut up.'

Lesley: 'Oh please, please. Oh. [faintly] Help, oh. I can't go on, you've got hold of my neck. Oh. [screaming] Help.'

A gurgling noise. Heavy breathing, sounds of distress, laboured breathing.

Myra: 'Ssh. Ssh. Shut up, shut up.'

Screams and gurgles. Lesley crying.

Myra: [whispering] 'Keep [unintelligible]. You will be right. Sit down and be quiet. [whispers]'

Ian: 'Go on.'

Whispers. Footsteps on the stairs, then entering the room.

Lesley crying, muffled.

Ian: [whispered] 'Here.'

Myra: 'Hush, hush, go on.' [indecipherable]

Lesley crying.

Myra: 'You are all right. Hush, hush. Put it in your mouth – hush and shift that hand.'

Lesley crying.

Myra: 'Put it in your mouth and keep it in and you'll be all right. Put it in. Stop it. If you don't – ssh.'

Lesley crying.

Myra: 'In your mouth. Hush, hush. Shut up or I'll forget myself and hit you one. Keep it in.'

Lesley whimpering.

Ian: 'Put it in.'

Myra: 'Put it in.' [spoken quickly]

Ian speaks, but words indecipherable except for 'hand'. Then footsteps.

Ian: 'Put it in. Keep it in. Stop it now, stop it now.'

Myra: 'I'm only doing this and you'll be all right. Put it in your mouth. Put it in – in.'

Further words spoken by Myra but indecipherable except for 'put it in'.

Myra: 'Will you stop it. Stop it.'

Myra's voice indecipherable, Lesley whimpering.

Myra: 'Shut—'

Ian: 'Quick. Put it in now.'

Lesley whimpering and then retching.

Ian: 'Just put it in now, love. Put it in now.'

Lesley retching.

Lesley: [muffled] 'What's this in for?'

Ian: 'Put it in.'

Lesley: 'Can I just tell you summat? I must tell you summat. Please take your hands off me a minute, please. Please – Mummy – please. I can't tell you [grunting]. I can't tell you. I can't breathe. Oh. I can't – Dad – will you take your hands off me?'

Ian whispering.

Ian: 'No. Tell me.'

Lesley: 'Please God.'

Ian: 'Tell me.'

Lesley: 'I can't while you've got your hands on me.'

Lesley mumbling.

Ian: 'Why don't you keep it in?'

Lesley: 'Why? What are you going to do with me?'

Ian: 'I want to take some photographs, that's all. Put it in.'

Lesley: 'Don't undress me, will you?'

Myra: 'That's right, don't—'

Lesley: 'It hurts me. I want to see Mummy, honest to God.'

Ian: 'Put it in.'

Lesley: 'I'll swear on the Bible.'

Ian: 'Put it in and hurry up now. The quicker you do this, the quicker you'll get home.'

Lesley: 'I've got to go because I'm going out with my mama. Leave me, please. Help me, will you?'

Ian: 'Put it in your mouth and you'll be all right.'

Lesley: 'Will you let me go when this is out?'

Ian: 'Yes. The longer it takes to do this, the longer it takes you to get home.'

Lesley: 'What are you going to do with me first?'

Ian: 'I'm going to take some photographs. Put it in your mouth.'

Lesley: 'What for?'

Ian: 'Put it in your mouth. [pause] Right in.'

Lesley: 'I'm not going to do owt.'

Ian: 'Put it in. If you don't keep that hand down, I'll slit your neck. [pause] Put it in.'

Lesley: 'Won't you let me go? Please?'

Ian: 'No, no, put it in. Stop talking [then] What's your name?'

Lesley: 'Lesley.'

Ian: 'Lesley what?'

Lesley: 'Ann.'

Ian: 'What's your second name?'

Lesley: 'Westford. Westford.'

Ian: 'Westford?'

Lesley: 'I have to go home for eight o'clock. I got to get [pause] Or I'll get killed if I don't. Honest to God.'

Ian: 'Yes.'

Quick footsteps of Myra leaving the room and going downstairs. Then a click, and a door closing, then Myra's footsteps coming upstairs, followed by eight longer steps.

Ian: 'What is it?'

Myra: 'I have left the light on.'

Ian: 'You have?'

Myra: 'So that . . .'

Indecipherable, then Lesley crying.

Lesley: 'It hurts me neck.'

Ian: 'Hush, put it in your mouth and you'll be all right.'

Myra: 'Now listen, shut up crying.'

Lesley: [crying] 'It hurts me on me—'

Myra: [interrupting] 'Hush. Shut up. Now put it in. Pull that hand away and don't dally and just keep your mouth shut, please. Wait a bit. I'll put this on again. Do you get me?'

Lesley: [whining] 'No, I . . .' [indecipherable]

Myra: 'Ssh. Hush. Put that in your mouth. And again, packed more solid.'

Whispered, indecipherable sentences.

Lesley: 'I want to go home. Honest to God I'll [her speech is muffled] before eight o'clock.'

Myra: 'No, it's all right.'

Ian: 'Eh?'

The music begins: a country-style tune, followed by 'Jolly St Nicholas' *and* 'The Little Drummer Boy', *during which a voice speaks. Three loud cracks are heard and the music of* 'The Little Drummer Boy' *grows fainter. There is a sound of footsteps, fading.*

The tape ends.[4]

The music, Myra insisted to Topping, came from a radio that was playing in the room. The prosecution lawyers at the trial were equally vehement that the music did *not* come from a radio but had been added deliberately to intensify the horror of the recording.[5] The three loud cracks at the end of the tape occurred when Ian opened the tripod and set up the camera; he then stopped the tape recorder and removed the plug from the sole socket in the bedroom to switch on the bright photography light. Lesley was forced to undress and either Ian or Myra bound a scarf around the lower half of the little girl's face, making it almost impossible for her to breathe. Ian then took a series of photographs of the child.[6]

Myra described her actions that night as 'assisting Ian in the preparation of Lesley Ann'.[7] Her prison therapist noted that she did so in the same way 'a parent may describe preparing a child to take a bath or dress for school. Her voice remained monotone as she referred to the binding and gagging of the victim and her positioning for photos and "acts of indecency".'[8] Initially, Myra told her prison therapist that she left the room when the photographs were being taken and sat on the stairs, drinking a bottle of wine, but in subsequent therapy sessions and during her confession to Peter Topping, she admitted to running a bath for Lesley at Ian's request *after* the photographs were taken to get rid of any dog hairs or fibres on the child. She claimed she then waited in the bathroom while Ian raped and murdered Lesley.

After 20 minutes, she apparently let out the water because it had gone cold and ran some more, at which point Ian entered the bathroom and Myra walked through to the bedroom. Lesley was lying on the bed, with the scarf still tied about her mouth. The little girl was dead;

there was a lesion on her neck, where she had been strangled with cord, and her legs were streaked with blood. The sheet beneath her was also bloodstained. Ian returned and carried Lesley into the bathroom, where he washed the blood from her, then lay her on the bed again to remove the scarf. He told Myra to clean the bath.

Ian's version of Lesley's death is very different. Author Colin Wilson, who has corresponded with Ian for many years and penned the introduction to *The Gates of Janus*, recounts Ian's claim that '[Myra] strangled Lesley Ann Downey and later deliberately played in public with the cord used to kill the child.'[9] In a letter to Jack Straw, Ian made the same accusation: 'She insisted upon killing Lesley Ann Downey with her own hands, using a two-foot length of silk cord, which she later used to enjoy toying with in public, in the secret knowledge of what it had been used for.'[10] The truth about Lesley's death will probably never be known; what is certain is that she fought valiantly for her life before it was extinguished and that afterwards Myra self-admittedly 'witnessed Lesley being placed in the bath, there was blood everywhere and I helped Ian to clean up'.[11]

Ian wrapped Lesley's small body in the bedsheet, together with her clothes. Outside, the flurry of snow was thickening and beginning to settle. At eight o'clock, Ian carried the bundle concealing Lesley's body out to the car. They intended to bury her that night, but as they approached the moor the snowfall was heavy enough to cause problems on the road. They watched other cars sliding about on the ice and returned to Hattersley, where Myra rang the AA from a public call box to ask about road conditions in Saddleworth. She related their advice to Ian: no travel unless absolutely necessary. But she still had to pick up Gran, having promised to do so that morning. Ian fumed, reminding her that Lesley's body lay in the back of the car. They drove on to Dukinfield, two hours later than promised; it was almost half past eleven when Myra, alone, knocked on Jim's door. He recalled: 'She came into the house and said, "I'm sorry, Gran, I can't take you back. The roads are too bad." I started to have an argument with Myra. As a result of going outside frequently to see whether Myra had come, I knew what the roads were like. It had been snowing, but there was only a light sprinkling of snow in the street where I lived.'[12] Jim was angry; his son had died six months before his 21st birthday after a blow to the skull and neither Jim nor his wife Nellie wanted anyone else to sleep in his room, which they had turned into a shrine. Jim remembered: 'The argument went on for about a quarter of an hour and ended when Myra said, "I can't take Gran and that's that." Then she walked out. As a result, Gran stayed at my house on a bed made of cushions on the floor in the living room.'[13]

At Wardle Brook Avenue, Myra parked the car and Ian scrambled up the slope with Lesley's body, which he placed in Myra's bedroom. She claimed afterwards that she never slept in that room again and hated going in there, even if just to dust it. Ian spent a while setting up his darkroom to develop the photographs he had taken of Lesley. They looked through them together and listened to the tape recording. Myra later insisted that she never saw the photographs or listened to the tape again, but begged him to destroy them.

Despite the volume of words Myra wrote about her life, she failed to account conclusively for Lesley's murder. Her prison therapist noted that the killing of Lesley was 'difficult and painful for Myra to relate . . . because of three factors. It occurred at Christmas, which is normally a period of peace and joy. It happened not on the desolate moors but in the home that she shared with Ian, and thirdly she had witnessed events first hand "up to the point of death".'[14] Myra told her prison therapist that Christmas was always 'the anniversary of many bad memories, not least of all the killing of little Lesley Ann, which gives me the deepest shame . . .'[15] By her own admission, she would later concede that the lengthy description she gave of Lesley's last hours in a statement to the Home Office was a pack of lies. She knew that the abuse and death of Lesley Ann Downey could not be explained without incriminating herself unreservedly: the tape recording condemned her forever as having been party to the little girl's unmitigated, prolonged torment.

On Boxing Day evening, while Myra and Ian curled up together on the sofa bed in front of the fire, with Lesley's lifeless body in the bedroom above, Ann Downey grew almost demented with anxiety about her daughter's whereabouts. She and her partner Alan had spent the evening running between the flat on Charnley Walk and the fairground. They called on Mrs Clarke, and Ann screamed at her for not having accompanied the children that afternoon, then left the flat to report Lesley's disappearance at Mill Street police station. Finally, they returned again to the fair after it closed, picking their way around the mute, empty rides and shuttered stalls, shouting for Lesley.

Gritting lorries rumbled along Mottram Road early the following morning as Ian carried Lesley's body to the car again. Myra drove to Hollin Brown Knoll. She recalled: 'There was thick snow covering the moor and the road was icy and there was very little traffic. When he'd checked up and down the road and made sure there was no traffic, he picked up the child's body, which was wrapped in a sheet, hoisted the bundle onto his shoulder and made his way up and over the rocks until he was out of sight. I waited for him in the [car].'[16] Ian returned to the car for a spade, burying Lesley just behind the jutting rocks, on a part of the moor known as Higher Wildcat Lowe. When he reappeared at the roadside, pushing the spade into the back of the car, he told Myra that he'd buried Lesley's clothes with her in the grave, at the child's feet.[17] They drove home, and Ian washed the spade before making a start on dinner. At half past ten, they arrived in Dukinfield to collect Gran. Elsie popped in later and Ian left to visit his mother in Longsight. He didn't return to Hattersley that evening but was probably aware of the extensive search taking place in Ancoats for Lesley since it was reported on the local news and in the press. The fairground had been torn apart by detectives, who aimed to interview every visitor. Crofts, empty houses and abandoned factories were scrutinised and the canal dredged.

On Monday, 28 December, the *Manchester Evening News* picked up the story: 'Tracker Dogs Join Giant Search for Girl.'[18] The following day, Millwards opened for the first time since the holidays and Tom Craig recalled that Ian and Myra turned up for work as usual, and that Ian kept asking after his daughter – whose name happened to be Lesley Ann. On 30 December, Lesley's friend Linda Clarke appeared on the Granada television children's programme *The Headliners* as part of the appeal. The *Manchester Evening News* kept the story on its front page, noting that police also feared the worst for a 15-year-old girl called Diane Minham, who went missing on Christmas Eve on her way home from a dance in another area. On New Year's Eve, the *Manchester Evening News* reported: 'Lesley: 100 Police with Dogs in Big Hunt'.[19] Six thousand posters bearing Lesley's image had been printed, along with five thousand flyers to be handed out in cafes, pubs, shops, etc. Lesley's Uncle Patrick had 200 posters printed at his own expense and distributed them personally. Over 6,000 people were interviewed and the search spread out. Sightings of Lesley came in from Blackpool to Belgium.

Myra and Ian saw in the New Year at Wiles Street, partying with Maureen and Dave, Bob and Nellie. Ian had brought along whisky, wine and rum, and was in jocular mood, kissing Maureen on the cheek to wish her luck in 1965, even stroking baby Angela Dawn's soft hair. On New Year's Day, the *Gorton & Openshaw Reporter* devoted most of its front page to the inquiry: 'Have You Seen 10 Year Old Lesley? Big Search for Lost Girl'.[20] The article mentioned the disappearances of Pauline Reade, John Kilbride and Keith Bennett. Myra bought the newspaper herself, and when Patty Hodges visited them that morning, Ian's tape recorder picked up the ensuing conversation.[21] Between idle chatter about Paul McCartney, telly, Sandie Shaw's hairdo, *Ready Steady Go!* and confusion on Patty's part over how to pronounce 'omelette', Myra drew her attention to the search for Lesley:

> Myra: 'Want to read the paper? Do you ever get that – to read all about the news?'
>
> Patty: 'Is it about Gorton?'
>
> Myra: 'Gorton, Openshaw, Ardwick, Bradford, Clayton and all over.'
>
> Patty: 'You see that girl [Lesley] at Ancoats?'
>
> Myra: 'Yes – just now.'
>
> Patty: 'She lives near my friend.'
>
> Myra: 'She lives near her house?'
>
> Patty: 'Yes.'
>
> Myra: 'Did she know her?'
>
> Patty: 'I don't know.'[22]

Ian and Myra retained the recording among their 'souvenirs'.

The search for Lesley continued, with policewomen visiting schools to warn children about Stranger Danger. Alan West was eliminated from police inquiries after a series of harrowing interviews and a thorough search of the family home at Charnley Walk. Ann kept her daughter's bedroom exactly as she had left it, with Lesley's dolls Patsy and Lynn slumped next to each other on the bed. Mary Waugh, who ran the grocery nearby, started a collection to offer a reward to anyone who could provide police with the breakthrough they needed. She raised £100, an enormous sum in those days. Ann called in at Mill Street police station at least twice a week on the off-chance that they had news about Lesley's whereabouts. She told the press: 'It's a nightmare. I can't sleep or eat. If I close my eyes, I can see her all the time.'[23] She clung to the forlorn hope that if Lesley had been abducted, then it was 'by some childless couple who would take care of her, love her'.[24] Three weeks into the new year, Ann issued an appeal through the *Gorton & Openshaw Reporter*: 'To whoever is holding my Lesley, if only they knew the agony that myself and my family are going through. Her little brothers keep asking when she is coming home . . . I plead with all mothers never to let their children out of their sight because they do not know the heartbreak of losing them until it happens.'[25] The voice of Lesley's elder brother Terry joined his mother's: 'Whoever is holding our Lesley, please look after her because she will be very sad and ill being away from Mum.'[26]

A little over a year later, Maureen Smith told a hushed courtroom about an incident that occurred in February 1965, when she and Myra were climbing into bed during one of their frequent get-togethers: 'Mrs Downey [had] offer[ed] a reward of £100 to anybody who could give any information as to where her daughter, Lesley, was. I said to Myra: "Her mother must think a lot of the child."'[27] Prompted by William Mars-Jones QC as to Myra's response, Maureen said flatly, 'She laughed.'[28]

14

In light of the evidence, I hope that you will be satisfied
that in this case the power of the written word was clearly
demonstrated and that clearly it did corrupt the mind of that
young man, David Smith ...

William Mars-Jones QC, 'The Moors Murder' address
to the Medico-Legal Society, 9 November 1967

Myra described the months that elapsed between Lesley Ann Downey's
murder and the brutal killing of 17-year-old Edward Evans as 'the
most peaceful time of my life'.[1] Ian insists that Lesley's death marked
the end of their murder spree: 'Contrary to popular perception, the
so-called Moors Murders were merely an existential exercise of just
over a year, which was concluded in December 1964 ... The final
ten months of our freedom in 1965 were entirely preoccupied with
return to mercenary priorities, reorganising logistics and eradicating
liabilities.'[2] He offers the acquisition of the pistols, the sale of the
Tiger Cub and Myra's purchase of a new car as supporting evidence:
'All these facts testify that the Moors Murders ended in December
1964, and that throughout 1965 we were hurrying to make up for
wasted time, cutting reliance on others down to the bone, with Myra
doubling as driver and sole armed back-up. All we required was a
"mule" to pick up and carry during robberies.'[3]

The mule he had in mind was Dave Smith, but Ian's purpose
in befriending him went deeper than he is willing to admit. Dave
himself reflects on what he was unable to see at the time: 'Looking
back, I think Brady was trying to control me ... [Myra] had already
gone along with murder with him and I think he was almost
grooming me to become part of their sickening gang.'[4] Ian passed
him books to read, including those he had shared with Myra at

the start of their affair, and at his suggestion Dave duly took notes from his small library. During the trial, one of the extracts, from *The Life and Ideals of the Marquis de Sade*, was read to the court: 'Should murder be punished by murder? Undoubtedly not. The only punishment that a murderer should be condemned to is that which he risks from his friends or the family of the man he has killed. "I pardon him," said Louis XV to Charolais, "but I also pardon him who will kill you." All the bases of the law against murderers is contained in that sublime sentence ... In a word, murder is a horror, but a horror often necessary, never criminal, and essential to tolerate in a republic. Above all it should never be punished by murder.'[5] In his address to the Medico-Legal Society, William Mars-Jones QC commented on Dave Smith: 'It is clear that this was a lad of above average intelligence. He had the misfortune to be born illegitimate, as was Brady. It may well be that the fact that they were brought up by relatives gave them cause to have some grievance against society ... I hope that you will be satisfied that in this case the power of the written word was clearly demonstrated . . . I have no doubt that it contributed to producing the sadistic killer Ian Brady.'[6]

Although their evenings together were not as frequent nor as alcohol-fuelled since the birth of Angela Dawn, whenever the two couples met Ian would take the opportunity to air his views on politics to Dave. He bought a bottle of Drambuie to celebrate the death of Winston Churchill in January 1965 and referred to the former prime minister as 'that cigar-smoking twit', while Myra agreed, 'The best thing Churchill did for Britain was dying.'[7] Discussing politics led on to race and religion. 'I didn't think he was cracked,' Dave recalls of Ian. 'I thought he was intellectual. I thought he was impressive.'[8] Their corrosive friendship wasn't always intense; Dave would tease Ian for being 'a real square' in his musical tastes and Myra noted resentfully that Dave had the ability to make Ian laugh and relax in a way that she could not.[9]

In early 1965, Myra and Ian began planning their Whit holiday, hoping for company – not Dave and Maureen, but Patty Hodges. Myra asked Patty's mum Elsie if the girl could go with them to Scotland, explaining that while Ian stayed in Glasgow, she and Patty would camp in the van at Loch Lomond. Although the two households were still close (Myra spent hours training Patty's dog, Duke, not to bark constantly), Elsie declined the offer. Soon afterwards, when Elsie's son James invited Myra and Ian to his wedding to Anita, Myra turned him down flat: 'I'm not going to no bloody wedding.'[10] By the end of February, when Ian moved in permanently with Myra, Patty was no longer speaking to them, having made friends with twin sisters her own age who had recently moved into the neighbourhood: 'About three weeks after I stopped going around with Ian and Myra, I climbed over a wall at the side of their house – a lot of people do that. I remember meeting Ian. He said that Myra's gran had said that me and my friend Margaret had been in the garden. I said, "We weren't in the garden." He said, "You were." I said, "Only over the wall." He said, "Don't let me cop you in the garden again." He was telling me off. He said, "I'll break your back if I cop you in there again." I never spoke to Myra and Ian again after that.'[11]

On 5 April, Myra sold her Mini-Traveller to a garage in Stretford and bought a turquoise Mini-Countryman on hire purchase. In their new car, which had the same fold-flat rear seats, the couple travelled to Scotland mid-month for a long weekend ahead of their Whitsun holiday. The impromptu trip was funded by a sum of money Ian had recently won in a bet on the horses.

Lesley's mother was desperate for news of her daughter. A magazine paid Emile Croiset to visit the area in the hope that he might sense something useful. Accompanied by Ann, Alan and the local police, the Dutch parapsychologist walked about the deserted recreation ground, where all traces of the fair had gone. Eventually, he pointed in an easterly direction and muttered, 'There is a road . . . it divides at a fork . . . there is a cemetery . . . the people who have taken the little girl have gone on the low road.'[12] He referred vaguely to a motorbike and Lesley's body being either buried in a field with water nearby or burned in a factory furnace. He told Ann that four people were involved and that they had taken Lesley to Belle Vue before killing her in Philip's Park. Ann couldn't get his vision out of her head, but the police were unimpressed with Croiset.

On 25 April, Maureen and Dave's six-month-old baby, Angela Dawn, died of bronchitis. Dave was at work when he learned that Maureen was at Ancoats Hospital with the baby. His daughter, whom he had last seen that morning when he had played with her on the sofa in Wiles Street before leaving for work, was dead before he arrived at the hospital. Hysterical with grief, he destroyed the room in which he stood before returning to Wiles Street alone, where he packed a suitcase with her tiny clothes and threw it down the railway embankment. Myra remembered that she and Ian were watching *Richard III* on the BBC when her mother turned up with Maureen and Dave to tell her about the baby's death. Ian was so annoyed at having his viewing interrupted that Myra ushered the three of them out to the car. Dave could barely speak in his anguish, while Maureen lost her girlishness overnight and followed her husband about everywhere like a ghost. Neither of them could bear to be in the house on Wiles Street. Dave returned to his grandfather's house in Ardwick, while Maureen moved back in with her parents at Eaton Street.

On the day of Angela Dawn's funeral, Myra and Ian arrived at Dave's childhood home in Aked Street, where the baby was laid out in her small coffin in the front room. Ian remained in the car while Myra went inside. She looked down on the little girl, then turned away to write on the card for her wreath: 'Another flower in God's garden'.[13] Dave remembers: 'We showed her into the parlour, and it was an open coffin, and I think that she wasn't prepared for that, so – just for a few seconds – tears appeared in her eyes. That's all. I'm not over-elaborating – it was seconds, but it had smudged the make-up under her eyes. She wore very Dusty Springfield type make-up under the eyes, very heavy black mascara . . . She had to dry her eyes and clean her eyes before she returned to the car.'[14] Within days, she was telling her grieving sister to dry her own tears: 'Don't cry about it, buy yourself a dog.'[15]

After the funeral, Maureen returned to work as a part-time machinist alongside her mother at a factory in Gorton. The giddiness that Dave loved about her had gone forever, and he had changed too, barely speaking to anyone for days at a time. Looking back, he believes that this was the point at which Ian decided to take advantage of the situation. Two days after Angela Dawn's death, Ian and Myra called round. The foursome spent the day drinking morosely on the moor, then returned to Gorton, where Ian sulked after losing a game of cards. He suggested heading back to the moor. Myra parked the car by Hollin Brown Knoll in the usual spot and Ian asked Dave to take a stroll with him, leaving Myra and Maureen in the car. They had only gone a short distance when Ian suddenly pulled Dave to a standstill and told him to look at the moon shining on the reservoir. They remained there for ten minutes, Ian swaying slightly and silent, before returning to the car, where Myra and Maureen sat with the doors locked and the lights on. Six months later, when the body of John Kilbride was recovered from the moor, Dave realised that he had been standing directly on the child's grave that night.

Myra and Ian called on the couple frequently after that. 'We'd go up to the moors with cheap bottles of wine,' Dave remembers. 'We'd go shooting up there with guns they had through a gun club. Brady seemed very sophisticated to me then. He wore three-piece suits and drank wine and showed me how to play chess. With hindsight, I can see that I was impressed by him. It was a bad time for me, having lost Angela, and Brady seemed to be there for me as a friend.'[16] For target practice, they walked to the back of Hollin Brown Knoll, where Dave and Maureen unwittingly stood where Pauline and Lesley lay beneath the earth, and to another place opposite the Knoll, ten minutes from the road in a valley where an old railway sleeper rotted near an oil drum. Ian flew into a rage if he spotted hikers nearby; neither Dave nor Maureen could understand the possessiveness he and Myra felt towards the moor, but they were grateful to be able to escape their quiet house for a few hours. Their outings weren't restricted to Saddleworth: they often travelled to Whaley Bridge and Taxal, and to a pine forest in Derbyshire, where they would climb over a low stone wall and down an embankment, then head through the forest to a clearing to picnic. Every other Saturday, Myra and Ian had to work at Millwards, but after lunch they called for Dave and Maureen and went off for the day, usually returning mid-evening.

On one occasion, the four of them set out for Blackpool in the turquoise Mini-Countryman. As they travelled, they were overtaken by another car whose horn blew rudely as it passed, and from the rear window someone flicked them the V-sign. Ian's temper snapped. He recalls: 'I said, "Pass him." We were cruising along at about 50, at the most. [Myra] started to overtake and as we came abreast I rolled down the window. In the pocket of the car there was a wine bottle. As we came abreast I put my arm right out of the car. I don't know if they put the brake on, but the bottle missed them by an inch. I was astonished it didn't hit them. There were about six people packed in this little car.'[17] Temper spent, Ian realised that the occupants of the other car could have taken down the registration number of the Mini-Countryman and reported them to the police; he told Myra to forget about Blackpool and head back to Manchester instead.

Whenever they were on the moor, Dave noticed that Ian often appeared to look for a certain spot before they sat down to picnic. Sometimes he would leave them for a while, seeming tense, then return calm and smiling. Dave was curious, but dismissed both habits as another of Ian's many foibles. They picnicked mainly on Hollin Brown Knoll, where they could see across the jutting stones and heather thickets to the glass-like pool of Greenfield reservoir. Near the shore was Ashway Gap House, an abandoned Gothic mansion through whose empty rooms bats and owls flew.[18] Ian liked to stand on the rocks on the knoll, his long coat billowing in the breeze, gazing across the moor to the water. He told Dave it brought him peace to be there, in that vast, bleak landscape, away from the 'maggots' wasting their lives down in the city.

Myra was deeply distressed that summer when Puppet was run over. Ian sympathised; he loved the dog almost as much as she did and had wept when his own dog, Bruce, had died a while before. Kitty Roden from Wardle Brook Walk recalls: 'Myra came into our front room. Her dog had been knocked down and Tom took it to Mrs Maybury's. The next morning Myra came in here to say thank you and she gave our children money for sweets. Brady was outside on the path.'[19] Elsie Masterton, with whom Myra was still friendly but not on such close terms as before, remembered: 'Myra said to me, "I'd like to put my hands on that driver. I'd go to the police, but I've no dog licence." She kept looking over there at the place in the road where the van had knocked the dog down. He had a badly injured leg. After she had gone to work, Gran came knocking on our back door. She said that Myra had made up the settee with pillows and sheets like a bed for Puppet to lie on. He kept staggering out of bed on three legs, trying to lie on the rug. That night Myra said to me, "No sleep for me tonight. I won't go to bed. I'll be up with the dog." She gave it half of one of Gran's sleeping tablets to soothe it.'[20] Elsie knew how dedicated Myra and Ian were to their pets: 'They thought the world of these dogs. I had to stand up while the dogs sat down in chairs.'[21] When Myra took her weekly wash to the huge laundrette near Millwards and heard that a dog in Gorton had died of malnutrition, she seethed: 'I don't know how people can be so cruel. They ought to be arrested.'[22]

In June, Myra decided to decorate their front room. Dave helped Ian paint the walls a pale pink and pasted a wood-effect paper on one side of the room and a brick-effect paper on the chimney breast. Myra had the cigarette machine removed from the hall after the first anti-smoking campaign was launched amid reports linking tobacco to lung cancer in particular. She seemed to have a pronounced fear of dying: she gave up smoking instantly after the reports came out and panicked when a polio scare struck Manchester that summer; at the Plaza nightclub, DJ Jimmy Saville offered free polio inoculations with every entrance ticket and she was keen to ensure that she and Ian had their jabs at the local surgery in Hyde. When Ian and Dave had finished decorating, Gran invited Elsie and Patty in to see how it looked.[23] Elsie recalled that Myra encouraged Patty to go upstairs to play Gene Pitney's 'Twenty-four Hours from Tulsa', the record that 'commemorated' the killing of John Kilbride.[24] Elsie admired the garden as well as the house; the patch on the left side of the front gate belonged to Myra and Ian, who were both gardening enthusiasts, while the patch to the right was mostly Gran's, tended by her son Jim. Gran disliked Myra's giant nasturtiums and wanted to pull them up, preferring her own smaller nasturtiums and dahlias. Myra's garden was profuse with flowers nurtured on peat brought back from the moor.

On 11 June, Elsie gave birth to a daughter, Martine. When Myra looked in on her a few days later, she peeped at the new arrival and offered: 'Not bad, for a baby.'[25] She was less abrasive the following month, when Elsie's ten-year-old daughter Elsa was knocked down by a car and rushed into hospital. Myra expressed concern about the little girl and gave Elsie lifts into Hyde to visit Elsa, who soon recovered. Myra was then in so much debt that she told Gran she couldn't afford July's rent or food (Gran usually bought her own groceries, while Myra shopped for herself and Ian). The rent man came round on Wednesdays, much to the annoyance of most residents, who didn't get paid until Thursday. Gran paid him Myra's share that month. The neighbours had become accustomed to hearing her complain about Myra, whom she said was too bossy and no support. Gran asked friends to visit during the day, while Myra and Ian were at work, and told Lily Yates, one of her old neighbours from Gorton: 'These people are no good to me now. They never speak to me. I go to bed at seven o'clock to get out of the way. They seem unfeeling.'[26]

On 23 July 1965 – Myra's 23rd birthday – Maureen and Dave moved to Hattersley. Dave had refused to live at Wiles Street after his daughter's death but was upset at having to leave his beloved retriever, Peggy, behind with his father – dogs weren't permitted in Hattersley's tower blocks. He and Maureen were allocated the flat at 18 Underwood Court, on the third floor of a skyscraper facing Wardle Brook Avenue, 300 yards away. Myra observed how the friendship between Ian and Dave intensified following the move; Dave called in on Ian most days, and sometimes visited the Mastertons, making a fuss of Patty's dog, Duke. Myra often refused to let him in, claiming that Ian was busy, or else she would tell him to wait over the road while she checked with Ian and if he saw the landing light flick on and off, then he knew it was fine to return. Once, when the Smiths popped their heads around the front door, she and Ian rose in silence and walked out, remaining upstairs until their guests had gone. Maureen told the court that on a couple of occasions when they called unannounced, 'Myra would do a lot of moaning and shouting and Brady would go upstairs.'[27] She remembered another incident: 'I had been working on some cushion covers for my sister . . . I took them round to Wardle Brook Avenue. It was about 9 p.m. I knocked and could get no answer. As I began to walk away, Brady opened the door. I told him about the cushion covers and he barred the way. He put his arms around the door and said they had company. I gave the cushion cover to him and went home.'[28]

After work one evening, Ian wanted to go to the cinema and Myra drove into town, expecting to accompany him, but as they neared the city centre, Ian told her that he was going alone. Myra was angry but dropped him at the Queen's Hotel on London Road near Piccadilly Station as he asked, agreeing to collect him at eleven o'clock that night. She returned home and spent the evening with Maureen, who helped to set her hair in rollers. Realising she was going to be late collecting Ian, Myra quickly put on a headscarf and drove into Manchester. She parked in their usual meeting place – under a railway arch on Store Street – and waited. When Ian didn't arrive, she climbed out of the car and went up the steps to the station approach, but there was no sign of him. She returned swiftly to the car, embarrassed by the rollers poking out beneath the headscarf. For two hours, she sat in the dank, derelict underpass, growing increasingly angry. Ian was steaming drunk when he rolled up at one o'clock that morning and the two of them had a blazing row. Myra questioned him about his evening and he flashed back that it was none of her business, then lapsed into silence as he flopped into the passenger seat. Fuming, Myra accelerated down a quiet road then slammed her foot on the brake, nearly sending Ian through the windscreen. He turned and struck her so forcefully that she felt as if the rollers had gone through her skull. He laughed then and began talking normally, as if nothing had happened. She accused him of treating her 'just like a chauffeur. You arrange for me to pick you up and you're hours late', but Ian's temper had passed and, with it, her own. By the time they reached home, the argument was all but forgotten.[29]

'I felt old at 26. Everything was ashes. I felt there was nothing of interest – nothing to hook myself onto. I had experienced everything. You either strike inwards or you strike outwards,' Ian told journalist Fred Harrison by way of an explanation for the apparent departure from the known pattern of the murders.[30] In *The Gates of Janus*, Ian writes of a spurious, paradoxical feeling among serial killers in which the actual act of murder 'serves to slow down the cycle of homicidal compulsion . . . the killer yearns for a period of rest, wishing to enjoy the ordinary things of life like other people'.[31]

There was no known murder that summer. Ian claims to have been standing on the edge of a precipice: 'I felt that time was running out. Things kept coming into my mind that seemed exciting, they weren't when I carried them out, and I got more and more outrageous until I got sucked into a death dive and lost control, I lost sight of reality.'[32] Myra already suspected that the unwitting architect of his 'death dive' might be Dave Smith; and she knew that Ian's destruction meant her own, giving her another reason to secretly loathe her brother-in-law.

During their nights that August at Underwood Court, when Myra and Maureen sloped off to bed, Ian raised the subject of robbery again. In the past, Dave had ignored Ian's hints, but that month, while the news about the race riots in Los Angeles played in the background, he admits he 'got interested in it. We agreed on robbing a bank, the three of us.'[33] He agreed to keep watch on the Williams & Glyn's bank on Ashton Old Road: 'I had to take notes of certain things – of arrivals and departures for a good three hours – and then meet him again and tell him what I had taken down.'[34] Ian said he and Myra would carry loaded guns during the raid. Dave later explained to a packed courtroom: 'He called it a safeguard, an insurance, in case there was any obstruction, and then they would be used with the live ammunition in them . . . I did not object to the carrying of the guns, but I did object to the use of live ammunition. I said I preferred blanks. He waved it aside by just laughing.'[35]

On the Saturday following their first serious discussion about robbery, Myra drove Ian and Dave to the moor and remained in the car while the two men climbed out. Ian led the way past John Kilbride's grave, down into the valley where they had been before, to practise their aim on the old oil drum. They unloosed several rounds of shot before returning to the car. Afterwards, at the Waggon and Horses in Gorton, they quietly discussed their plans. 'We're going to use the guns,' Ian insisted, and Myra joked, 'I wonder what would happen if we took Maureen along with us.'[36] During their next conversation, Dave recalls: '[Ian] gave me instructions that whenever they decided to do the job at the bank, all writing materials, books and things like that, were to be moved; and if I had any, I was to let him have them so that he could dispose of them.'[37]

One evening, after Myra and Maureen had gone to bed, Ian suggested to Dave that they play Russian roulette. He knocked out all but one of the bullets from a pistol and spun the chamber, then pointed the gun at Dave and squeezed the trigger. There was a loud click, and Ian started to laugh: 'There would have been an awful mess behind you if the bullet had hit you.'[38] When Dave had recovered from the shock, Ian asked him if there was anyone whom he truly hated. After a while, Dave told him about some trouble he'd had earlier in the year with Sammy Jepson and Tony Latham. Jepson had been heard boasting that he had slept with Maureen; Dave twice attempted to confront him but then discovered that Latham, with whom he had fought at school, was spreading the same rumour. Although Dave didn't believe them, he was furious enough to question Maureen and threaten Jepson, though had forgotten everything when Angela Dawn died. Ian's question stoked his anger anew.

Ian was more interested in Latham than Jepson, and asked, 'Is it real? Has it got to you?'[39] Then he told Dave that he needed a photograph of Latham and proposed that Dave should take a Polaroid snap of him in his favourite pub, the Dolphin on Hyde Road: 'We'll take you down. Keep him talking, make him nice and friendly. Set him up good and proper . . .'[40] Dave's attempt at photographing Latham went wrong. Although Myra drove him to the pub and Dave found his old rival inside, he had forgotten to load the camera with film. To his surprise, Ian seemed to shrug off his mistake and dropped the idea of 'setting up' Latham. But to Myra, Ian admitted that, as far as he was concerned, Dave had screwed up and presented a risk. On the hills above Buxton, sipping from a bottle of wine, he debated with her whether or not to murder her brother-in-law. He was concerned about Dave's reliability and tired of his domestic problems, but Myra talked him round, albeit grudgingly, not wanting to hurt Maureen.

At the end of August, Ian's mother and stepfather moved from Westmoreland Street – which had also been earmarked for demolition – to a council flat in Heywood. Ian seemed unsettled by the change of address and appeared to suddenly want to cling to the past. On 18 September, he and Myra travelled up to Scotland, picnicking just south of Carlisle, and Myra was relieved when his mood brightened as they reached Gretna Green. They stayed in a hotel that night and he visited his foster family alone to tell them he had brought his girlfriend on the trip. Myra made a good impression on the Sloans, despite an attack of nerves that left her tongue-tied. She perked up when they asked about Puppet, and showed them the photographs she always carried of her dog.

From the Pollock estate, they travelled into central Glasgow, where Ian used a new camera to take endless snaps of his old childhood haunts. He found that he 'couldn't get enough of people, roaming the old bars and cafes, soaking up the atmosphere and delighting in overheard conversations. Each face I then observed seemed to radiate unique character. I felt truly *alive*, all criminal inclinations and ambitions forgotten . . .'[41] There was one instance when Myra was left with his foster family while he explored Glasgow alone, and he claims to have killed a tramp that night. Police subsequently found nothing to indicate that he had committed a murder on Scottish soil, and when Peter Topping questioned Myra about the matter, she told him it was unlikely, citing an incident that occurred when the two of them were driving beyond Loch Lomond to camp. She admits to having asked Ian, after spotting a child walking alone, 'Don't you want to do another one?' to which he replied – as he had once before – that he would never kill one of his own.[42]

On the final leg of their trip, they visited St Monans, leaving the car near the cemetery and walking to the castle, where Ian photographed Myra sitting beside an archway. From there, they travelled to Dunning, but Ian was frustrated by their inability to find the cottage he had stayed in with the Sloans as a boy. As they left the village, Maggie Wall's cross reared up at the roadside and they climbed out of the car to scrutinise it. Ian took his last photographs in Scotland there; he and Myra each took it in turns to sit on the witch's monument. They stole one of the small boulders for their garden from the foot of the cross, pushing it into the car boot before driving off, the white-painted inscription 'burnt . . . as a witch' fading into the pale blue distance.

15

Our Mo was a fool for ever marrying that David Smith . . .

Myra Hindley to Elsie Masterton, quoted in
Jean Ritchie, *Myra Hindley: Inside the Mind of a Murderess*

On the evening of 25 September 1965, Myra and Ian called at Underwood Court to find Dave lying in bed, white-faced from vomiting. He had been drinking heavily, agitated at the news that his father had arranged to have his dog, Peggy, put to sleep. 'Ian walked into the bedroom and he asked me if I was all right. Then he turned round and he said, "It's that bleeder who should have got the needle and not the dog" . . . Myra went out of her way to try and save the dog. She drove all the way down to the dogs' home . . . She was just too late. The dog was in the house on its own because my father was working in London.'[1] The four of them spent the evening together in the flat, and Dave momentarily forgot his troubles when Ian screamed hysterically for Myra to kill a daddy-long-legs that fluttered across the balcony to where he sat by the open door. Dave couldn't stop laughing; he remembered when a spider had scuttled across the sitting-room floor in Wardle Brook Avenue and Ian had dashed out, shouting for Myra to get it. On both occasions, she dealt calmly with the cause of his panic.

After the sisters had gone to bed, Ian began talking about the robbery. Dave recalled in court how Ian raised a new subject: 'What would happen if someone obstructed us . . . the guns would be used to move them, stop the obstruction . . . He asked me what my reaction would be if this was to happen. We had been drinking for a good four or five hours, and I thought it was the drink talking, and I looked at him and waited for him to carry on. He asked me if I was capable of using a gun or of murder . . .'[2]

Ian fixed Dave with his cool, grey eyes and gave the first broad intimation of the appalling secret he and Myra had kept to themselves for the past two years. 'He went on to say that he had killed three or four people,' Dave told the court. 'This just convinced me that it was the beer talking. He leaned back and he said, "You don't really believe me." I must have smiled at him. Getting a bit tired, I was. And then he said, "It will be done," and a matter of a quarter of an hour later we were both asleep.'[3]

Myra was absent again when Ian made the same claim to Dave a few nights later, in the flat and drinking into the early hours. This time, he went further, Dave recalls: 'He said the ages of the people were between 15 and 21, and the reason he gave was because when the police received missing person reports between those ages they did not pay all that much attention. And he went on to say that he waited in the car until somebody came along, and then he just got out and did it. And another way he mentioned, the way he preferred, was to go out in the car, wait in a place and pick somebody up, and take them back to the house and do it in the house. He preferred that way because any evidence against him was in the house and he could get rid of it in his own time . . . All his clothes would be brushed and cleaned and inspected, everything would be listed that he had on, and he said he took a drug, Pro-Plus, as a stimulant . . . He mentioned that he had photographic proof of his killings . . . He said they were buried on the moors.'[4] Ian's description of his 'method' failed to convince Dave that he was telling the truth. In the mundane surroundings of the Hattersley flat, with the two women asleep and Maureen's beloved cats curled up nearby, it seemed so implausible. Dave changed the subject, returning to the robbery, which they now agreed would centre on an Electricity Board showroom and settled on 8 October as the date for the crime.

Myra and Ian had to work on Saturday, 2 October. During a break, Myra bumped into Anne Murdoch, her former Ryder Brow rounders teammate. Anne recalls: 'I hadn't seen Myra for a long time. Then I heard from a lad she used to hang about with at school that she was working at Millwards. It was a rotten, scruffy-looking place near the big laundrette. On this particular Saturday, I put my two-year-old daughter Sharon in her pram and went shopping at Gorton Cross. I met up with two other lasses I knew from school, Mary and Marge. They had tots as well. When we were walking home, I spotted Myra coming out of Millwards, on the other side of the road. She saw the three of us with our toddlers and shouted sarcastically, "By God, you've all ended up with good jobs." I shouted back, "You've got an even better one there." She snorted at me, "You do my job then and I'll take the babies for a walk." I didn't answer. She went off, clicking down the street in her high heels. The following week I heard she'd been arrested.'[5]

That night, Myra and Ian walked over to Underwood Court, where Dave introduced them to Bobbie, the dog he had bought despite the tenancy rules. After the sisters had gone to bed, Ian's conversation again turned to murder. Dave played a tape recording of himself reciting from *The Last Days of Hermann Goering*, and Ian asked again why he didn't believe that he was capable of murder. Dave ignored him, even when Ian leaned over and said in his soft voice, 'I've killed three or four and I'll do another one, but I'm not due one for three months. But it will be done and it won't count.'[6]

On Tuesday evening, Dave called at Wardle Brook Avenue with a heavy parcel. Myra opened the door and mentioned that Gran was visiting friends nearby. She placed the parcel on the coffee table in the front room. 'Ian came downstairs,' Dave recalls. 'Myra told him that I had brought [the parcel] round and he just took it upstairs. After about two minutes he came down with two suitcases . . .'[7] The parcel contained the books Ian had asked him to return that afternoon: *Mein Kampf, Tropic of Cancer, Kiss of the Whip, The Life and Ideals of the Marquis de Sade, Justine, Orgies of Torture and Brutality* and *The Perfumed Garden*. Dave assumed Ian wanted the books as part of the process they had discussed leading up to the robbery. He watched Ian carrying the suitcases – one brown, one blue – outside. 'I picked one of them up,' Dave remembers, 'and as I handed it over the wall to Myra, Ian said, "Whatever you do, don't drop it, or it will blow us all up."'[8] Myra pushed the suitcases into the boot of the turquoise Mini-Countryman, then climbed into the seat next to Ian. Dave watched as they sped off, in the evening sunlight, towards the city.

Two suitcases, deposited for a shilling each, in the grey lockers of Central Station.

Little is known about the last victim of the Moors Murders. Edward Evans's parents never spoke to the press, devastated first and foremost by his horrifying death but also by the rumours surrounding their son.

Edward was 17 in the summer of 1965. Tall and slim, with light-brown hair and an engaging smile, he lived with his parents Edith and John, brother Allan and sister Edith. Their home at 55 Addison Street, Ardwick, was due to be swept away by bulldozers the following year. Edward's father worked as a lift attendant; Edward had found himself a better-paid job, employed since May as a junior machine operator at Associated Electrical Industries Limited on the vast Trafford Park industrial estate. He worked hard and liked to relax at night in the city bars with friends or at football – he supported Manchester United and was a regular face in the stands at Old Trafford. His friend Jeff Grimsdale described him as a sociable lad who dressed smartly. Whenever his parents expressed concern about his nights out, he reassured them with a smile, 'I can handle any trouble.'[9]

In the aftermath of Edward's murder, when Ian Brady was scratching around for a motive to throw detectives off the 'Moors' trail, he told police that he knew Edward vaguely from the homosexual bars on Canal Street. Ian hoped that would lend credence to his invention that the murder was the result of a fight that got out of hand following his and David Smith's plan to blackmail a homosexual for money. The term Ian used was 'rolling a queer'.[10] Homosexuality was not only illegal at that time, but also viewed as a perversion. Hostility intensified sharply in the 1950s as a reaction both to the Cambridge Five spy circle, three of whom were homosexual or bisexual, and as a result of the post-war emphasis on 'the health and sanctity of marriage and family life'.[11] A 1952 issue of the *Sunday Pictorial* ran a series on 'Evil Men', focusing on homosexuality and promising an end to the 'freaks and rarities', while the same newspaper, renamed the *Sunday Mirror*, published a guide for its readers in April 1963 entitled 'How to Spot a Homo', listing 'shifty glances', 'dropped eyes' and 'a fondness for the theatre' as 'unmistakable signs of dangerous and deviant intentions'.[12] Under these unenlightened circumstances, Edward's family were dealt a cruel blow by rumours surrounding their dead son's sexuality. The fact remains that Ian Brady was the only person to claim Edward was homosexual – and he did so merely as a means of deflecting police interest.

The morning of Wednesday, 6 October 1965 was crisply autumnal and slightly warmer than average. Sun slanted across the moor from the upper windows of the house on Wardle Brook Avenue. Over breakfast, Ian handed Myra a record to mark the murder that lay ahead: Joan Baez's single 'It's All Over Now, Baby Blue'.[13] The song was written by Dave's favourite musician, Bob Dylan, and concerns the replacement of one lover with another. Myra had faded into the background somewhat as the friendship between Ian and Dave had intensified; she told Peter Topping that it had crossed her mind to wonder in recent weeks whether it was her own life that hung in the balance. The last verse of the record Ian gave her that morning could be read as a direct salvo about Dave Smith replacing her as his partner in crime: 'Leave your stepping stones behind you, something calls for you/Forget the dead you've left, they will not follow you./The vagabond who's rapping at your door/Is standing in the clothes that you once wore./Strike another match, go start anew/And it's all over now, Baby Blue.'

The two of them departed for work at the usual hour and left Millwards that evening at five o'clock. The skies were a clear, brilliant blue as they drove back to Hattersley, where Ian walked the dogs before calling Myra out to have her photograph taken with Patty, Puppet and Lassie. The photographs – the last Ian would ever take – show Patty looking into the camera with a shuttered, inscrutable expression. Myra, wearing a red V-neck sweater and white beads, casts her gaze down and smiles faintly.

In Ardwick, Edward Evans returned home from work and told his parents he was meeting Mike Mahone at a pub in town, then going off to watch the match between Manchester United and Helsinki. He ate his tea, then went up to his bedroom to change into white shirt, best jeans and favourite jacket, and a pair of brown suede shoes. He came downstairs just after six o'clock and picked up his keys. 'Edward went out between 6.15 and 6.30 p.m.,' his mother remembered. 'I didn't see him alive again . . .'[14]

It was a beautiful Indian summer's evening; the last red Victorian buildings to survive the modernisation of Manchester seemed to glow a soft ruby. By half past seven, Edward was in sight of the familiar cream-coloured tiles and frosted windows of Aunty's Bar on Oxford Road. Inside were two rooms, both plainly furnished and with a telly.

Edward had a drink and chat with the landlord, George Smith, who recalled: 'It was very unusual for him to come in on his own. When I last saw him that night, he was on his own.'[15] Thirty-one-year-old Mike Mahone had no idea Edward was expecting him: 'On the previous Sunday, he was at our house for tea. His last words were, "I'll see you on Monday or Tuesday." As he never came, and therefore we had made no proper arrangements to go to the game, I never turned up to meet him. I wasn't feeling too well at the time – I had my leg in plaster – and wasn't sure that he would turn up anyway.'[16] Edward drank up and bid George goodnight, then headed outside into the blowsy air of the city night.

In Hattersley at eight o'clock, Dave knocked on the door of 16 Wardle Brook Avenue. Ian let him in and read the note left at Dave's flat by the rent man, Mr Johnson: 'Mr Smith, I want £14 12s 6d at the Town Hall on Saturday or I shall take legal proceedings. Mr Page is doing his job and if that dog is not out of the building by tonight I shall have you evicted. If there are any more complaints of Teddy boys and noise, I shall take further action.'[17] Ian studied the note for a while, then gave it back, shrugging, 'There's nothing you can do about it.'[18] Dave explained that he was less worried about the money – which he knew he could borrow from his father – than about the possibility of losing another dog, Bobbie. Ian fastened his cufflinks and straightened the waistcoat of his grey suit, saying nothing. Dave looked beyond him to where Myra stood, primping her blonde hair into a puffball in the mirror. Her make-up had been freshly applied and she wore a tight, leopard-skin dress. Ian told their visitor he'd have to go; they were on their way out for the evening. Dave followed them down the slope to the car and was still talking to Ian when Myra turned the keys in the ignition. After a minute or two, he took a step back and Myra put her foot down on the accelerator. He watched the car drive off towards Manchester, then took the short cut home, passing the back garden where the boulder stolen from the foot of Maggie Wall's cross sat among the stones in the little rockery.

Myra's and Ian's drive into town was cut short when the car in front of them hit a dog. The owners of the animal screamed and Myra pulled over the Mini-Countryman and leapt out. She ran along the street and found the dog whimpering in an alleyway. As far as she could tell, it seemed miraculously unharmed. When the couple reached her, breathless with shock, she offered to take the dog to the vet. They thanked her profoundly but told her there was no need – they would take care of it. She returned shakily to the car and drove on to Central Station but refused to pay the extortionate parking fees, so stopped on a double-yellow line instead. Ian got out, telling her he wouldn't be long. She glanced up at the huge clock on the arched facade of the station: it was almost half past ten. Then she jumped as a policeman tapped on her window. She rolled it down and explained that she was only waiting for her boyfriend to nip into the buffet; he told her that if she wasn't gone when he returned from his round, he'd have to book her. She nodded and watched him walk away.

Inside the station, Ian approached the buffet bar. It was shut. In his statement to the police, he recalled: 'Evans was standing at a milk vending machine. I knew Evans; I had met him on several occasions previously. As I went to try the [buffet] door, he said it was closed, but I tried the door anyway. Then we got into conversation. He kept saying there was no place to get a drink . . . I invited him back to the car.'[19] Ian promised Edward a drink at his home in Hattersley, where he said he lived with his sister – Myra. She said hello as Ian introduced 'Eddie' and mentioned the visit from the policeman as they drove back to Hattersley, parking the car in the amber glow of the streetlamp, below the house.

In her interview with Peter Topping, Myra said that Ian asked her to call on Dave as she was locking the car. Yet she didn't go straight to Underwood Court. She must have accompanied Ian and Edward into the house because when she did arrive at the flats, ringing the intercom sometime after eleven o'clock, she was wearing a different set of clothes. Maureen answered the buzzer, getting out of bed while Dave pulled on his jeans. When his wife opened the door, Dave was struck by the change in Myra's appearance. Earlier that evening, her make-up and hair had been immaculate and she had been wearing the leopard-skin dress, but now she was clad in an old jumper and skirt with the hem hanging down, a pair of shabby tartan pumps on her feet. Her make-up was smudged and her hair was tousled. Maureen told the courtroom: 'She said she wanted to give me a message to give to my mother. To tell her she would see her at the weekend and she could not get up there before . . . I asked her why she'd come round so late and she said it was because she'd forgotten earlier on and she had just remembered. I asked her why she had not got the car and she said because she had locked it up . . . She asked David would he walk her round to 16 Wardle Brook Avenue because all the lights were out . . . David said he would, and he got ready.'[20] Dave picked up what he called his dog-stick, a walking stick he had fashioned for himself with string wound tightly round the end as a grip. Myra asked him what he was bringing it for and when he told her he always carried it if he went out at night, she eyed him and said, 'You're in the frame, you are.'[21]

In his official statement given to the police the next day, Dave described what happened next: 'We got almost to Myra's house. I intended to leave her there, then she said, "Ian has some miniature wine bottles. Come and collect them now." As we got to the front door, Myra stopped walking and she said, "Wait over the road, watch for the landing light to flick twice." I didn't think this was unusual because I've had to do this before whilst she, Myra, went in to see if Ian would have me in. He's a very temperamental sort of fellow. I waited across the road as Myra told me to, and then the landing light flicked twice, so I walked up and knocked on the front door. Ian opened the front door and he said in a very loud voice for him, he normally speaks soft, "Do you want those miniatures?" I nodded my head to show "yes" and he led me into the kitchen, which is directly opposite the front door, and he gave me three miniature bottles of spirits and said: "Do you want the rest?"

'When I first walked into the house, the door to the living room – which was on my right, standing at the front door – was closed. After he put the three bottles down in the kitchen, Ian went into the living room and I waited in the kitchen. I waited about a minute or two, then suddenly I heard a hell of a scream; it sounded like a woman, really high-pitched. Then the screams carried on, one after another, really loud. Then I heard Myra shout, "Dave, help him", very loud . . .

'When I ran in, I just stood inside the living room and I saw a young lad, about 17 years old . . . He was lying with his head and shoulders on the couch, and his legs were on the floor. He was facing upwards. Ian was standing over him, facing him, with his legs on either side of the young lad's legs. The lad was still screaming. He didn't look injured then, but there was only a small television light on, the big light was off. Ian had a hatchet in his hand, I think it was his right hand, it was his right hand, he was holding it above his head, and then he hit the lad on the left side of the head with the hatchet, I heard the blow, it was a terrible hard blow, it sounded horrible.

'The young lad was still screaming, and the lad half-fell and half-wiggled off the couch, onto the floor, onto his stomach. He was still screaming. Ian went after him and stood over him and kept hacking away at the young lad with the hatchet. I don't know how many times he hit the lad with the hatchet, but it was a lot, about the head, about the neck, you know that region, the shoulders and that . . .

'I felt my stomach turn when I saw what Ian did, and some sick came up and then it went down again. I couldn't move. When he, Ian, that is, was hacking at the lad, they got close to me and one of the blows Ian did at the lad grazed my right leg. I remember Ian was swinging about with the hatchet, and one blow grazed the top of Myra's head . . .

'After Ian stopped hitting the lad, he was lying on his face, with his feet near the door. I could hear a gurgling noise in the lad's throat . . . Ian got a cover off one of the chairs and wrapped it round the lad's head. I was shaking, I was frightened to death of moving, and my stomach was twisting. There was blood all over the place, on the walls, fireplace, everywhere . . .

'Ian never spoke a word all this time, and he got a cord, I think it was electric wire, I don't know where he got it from, and he wrapped it round the lad's neck, one end of the cord in one hand, one end in the other, and he then crossed the cord and pulled and kept pulling until the gurgling stopped in the lad's throat. All the time Ian was doing this, strangling the lad, Ian was swearing, "You dirty bastard." He kept saying that over and over again.

'Myra was still there all this time, just looking. Then Ian looked up at Myra and said something like: "It's done. It's the messiest yet. It normally only takes one blow."'[22]

In those first moments after Edward's life was so violently ended, Dave felt himself grow very still: 'You think you would jump out of a window or run into the street shouting blue murder, but I knew if I did that I wouldn't even make it to the front door, that Evans's wouldn't be the only murder that night. It was an almost animal self-preservation that clicked in. I suddenly became very calm, knowing I couldn't put a foot wrong if I was to survive. I knew I had to show no emotion, no bad reaction to what he had done, or I wouldn't be going home. It frightens me to think I was even capable of that.'[23]

As the thick smell of death filled the room, turning it from a place where plastic chrysanthemums sat on a sideboard to a charnel house, the air was shrill with silence. Dave turned to his sister-in-law: 'Myra just looked at [Ian]. She didn't say anything at all. Ian got up then, the little light was still the only one on, and he lit himself a cigarette, after he'd wiped his hands on a piece of some material. Then Ian turned the big light on, and he told Myra to go into the kitchen and get a mop and bucket of warm water, and a bowl with soapy water in it and some rags.

'Myra did that and Ian turned to me then and said, "Your stick's a bit wet", and he grinned at me. The stick he meant was a stick I'd taken with me when I went with Myra from our place. It's like a walking stick, and the only thing I can think is that when I rushed into the living room at first I'd dropped it, because it was lying on the floor near the young lad . . .

'Then Myra came in with the bowls of water and that. She didn't appear upset, and she just stepped over the young lad's body and placed the bowls of water and that on the carpet in front of the fireplace.

'Then Ian looked at me like, and said: "Give us a lift with this mess." I was frightened and I did what he said and I helped to clean the mess up . . . No one spoke while this was going on, then after we'd cleaned most of it up, Ian – he was speaking to Myra – said, "Do you think anybody heard the screams?" Myra said, "Yes, me gran did. I told her I'd dropped something on my toe." Then Myra left the living room.[24]

'While she was out, Ian offered me a bottle of wine . . . The young lad was still lying on the floor. Myra came in with a white bedsheet. I think Ian had told her to get one. And a lot of pieces of polythene, fairly big they were, and a large blanket . . . Ian told me to get hold of the lad's legs, which I did, and Ian got hold of the lad's shoulders and we lifted him onto the sheets and blankets. The only reason I did this was out of sheer bloody fear. Then Ian came out with a joke. He said, "Eddie's a dead weight", and both Ian and Myra thought it was bloody hilarious. I didn't see anything to laugh about . . .

'On the stick I had, the one I mentioned to you, there is some bound string, and Ian took the stick and unwound the string. He cut it into lengths, about two or three foot in length, and he gave me one end, and he tied the lad's legs up in a funny way, so that the lad's legs were together and bent up into his stomach. Then Ian carried on tying the lad up; it was like a maze of bloody knots . . .

'I had to help him while he folded the corners of the sheet together, with the lad in the middle, and then he tied the corners together. Then he made me do the same with him with the polythene sheets, and last of all came the blanket. He didn't tie that – it was like a kind of cradle. Myra was mopping up all this time. Then Ian told Myra: "Go upstairs and hold your gran's door to", and he said to me: "Lift your end up", and between us we carried the young lad upstairs into Myra's bedroom and we put him down near the window.

'Then we came downstairs and I saw a wallet lying on the floor. Ian picked it up and pulled out a green sort of card and said, "That's his name. Do you know him?" I looked at the card and saw the name Edward Evans. I didn't know him. I saw a pair of shoes lying on the living room floor as well as the wallet, and Ian picked them up, and a couple of letters that were lying there, and put them in a shopping bag. He picked the hatchet up, gave it to me, and said something like: "Feel the weight of that. How did he take it?" I said nothing and gave it him back. I was frightened of him using it on me. He put the hatchet in with the rest of the things, and he took them upstairs. Myra was still cleaning up, and by this time the house was looking something like normal . . .'[25]

Questioned later about Myra's attitude that night, Dave said, 'She would pick bone and hair up off the floor and not have a problem with it. Just drop it in the bag. There was no, "Oh . . . would one of you pick that up . . ." No. Just straightforward.'[26] There was no doubt in his mind that she was a young woman used to witnessing murder; what she said next established that she must have been standing in front of Edward as Ian drew out the axe.

'Ian went on to describe how he'd done it,' Dave confirmed in his police statement. 'How, he said, he'd stood behind the settee looking for some miniatures for me, and the lad Eddie was sat on the settee. He said: "I held the axe with my two hands and brought it down on his head." Myra said: "His eyes registered astonishment when you hit him." Those are the exact words she said.'[27]

One of the blows had taken a piece out of the fireplace plaster; Ian put his finger into the gap.

Dave's statement continues: 'Ian was complaining because he'd hurt his ankle . . . they'd have to keep the lad's body upstairs all night and he wouldn't be able to carry the lad down to the car because of his ankle. Myra suggested that they use my wife's and my baby trolley to carry the lad's body into their car. Well, it's Myra's car. I agreed straight away. I'd have agreed to anything they said. We arranged to meet where Myra works in Manchester tonight, that's Thursday, at five o'clock . . .

'After we had cleaned up Evans's blood, Myra made a cup of tea, and she and Brady sat talking. She said, "Do you remember that time we were burying a body on the moors and a policeman came up?" Then she drew me into the conversation and said, "I was in the mini with a body in the back. It was partitioned off with a plastic sheet. Ian was digging a hole when a policeman came and asked me what the trouble was. I told him I was drying my sparking plugs and he drove off. I was praying that Ian wouldn't come back over the hill whilst he was there."'[28]

Shortly after three o'clock, Dave got up slowly and ventured that he should be going if he didn't want Maureen waking up and wondering where he was. Myra saw him to the door and smiled as they said goodnight. He recalls, 'I was terrified. I tried not to panic. I didn't run for the first two or three streets, thinking they might be watching me, ready with an axe.'[29] As soon as he was out of sight of Wardle Brook Avenue, he fled, racing through the dark streets to Underwood Court, whose lit stairwell was as welcome as a lighthouse beam to a lost sailor.

In the flat, he washed and undressed, then crawled into bed, his mind spinning: 'I couldn't get to sleep, I kept thinking about the lad, about the screams and the gurgling he was making.'[30] He realised why Edward Evans had been murdered: 'I believe Brady had planned to kill him, in a controlled way, with a single blow of the axe from behind . . . I think I was meant to come in and find the dead body and that would have been the ultimate test. He would have been looking for a reaction from me, to see if I could be trusted.'[31] After fidgeting in the pitch-blackness, he sat up and put on the light: 'Maureen was in bed, I got her out of bed. I went to the bathroom and I absolutely vomited. To the point where I was retching and in a bad state. Physically in a bad state. I then had to tell her what had happened. "I've just seen somebody killed." Didn't go into any great detail . . . just . . . "How do you mean?" . . . "Look, look at me. We've got to do something."'[32]

Maureen started to cry as she gazed at her husband: 'He was very white and shaky. He was sick.'[33] Although Myra was her sister, Maureen was adamant that they had to call the police. Dave was frightened of leaving the flat, knowing that Ian and Myra were only a few streets away: 'I still thought they might be outside, waiting.'[34]

In the last lines of his statement, he recalls that at six o'clock 'we decided it was the best time to go out, there were milkmen and that knocking about, so I armed myself with a carving knife and a screwdriver, in case I met Ian and Myra. Maureen came with me and we walked to the telephone kiosk in Hattersley Road West and telephoned the police. That's it . . .'[35]

The lights were on in the newspaper shop near Underwood Court. Dave and Maureen, two terrified teenagers looking bedraggled and thin and nothing like their normal fashionable selves, ran with their dog to the red telephone box on the corner of Hare Hill Road. Dave snatched up the receiver and dialled 999, the burr and clicks of the phone resounding inside the box with its strong smell of iron filings.

At 6.07 a.m., Police Constable Edwards, the duty policeman at Hyde station – a town described as 'an S-bend with chip shops' – took Dave's stammered call: 'There's been a m-murder . . .'[36] Edwards rang through to Police Constable Antrobus, who said he would drive out to Hattersley. Dave replaced the receiver, then picked it up and dialled again to ask if they were definitely sending someone. 'This is a matter of life and death,' he insisted. 'My life is being threatened!'[37] Reassured that a car was on its way, he and Maureen carried Bobbie over to an overgrown gateway and hid there. 'Before, the hours had seemed like minutes,' Dave recalls. 'Now the minutes it took the police to arrive seemed like hours and we hid in a bush nearby.'[38]

PC Antrobus pulled into the estate in his panda car: 'David Smith was carrying a carving knife in one hand and a large screwdriver in the other, and both he and his wife were clawing at the doors of the car before it stopped. Police cars are usually locked from the inside, so that they were not very successful in making an effort to get in. In fact, they could not get into that police car quickly enough . . .'[39] Dave tried to climb into the front seat in his panic. Eventually, PC Antrobus managed to calm the young couple down and prised the knife and screwdriver off Dave, who leapt into the passenger seat. Maureen sat trembling in the back with the dog on her knee, staring out of the window like Dave, gazing at the houses and shops as if they didn't recognise them, while the car rolled away from Hattersley and headed towards Hyde.

IV

The Shadow of the Rope:
6 October 1965 – 6 May 1966

16

On the day Brady and Hindley were arrested, Joe came in at night and told me this terrible tale about the phone call made by a young chap called David Smith and a body being found in a house in Hattersley. The story went through the force like a dose of salts. One of the Lancashire lads kept Joe briefed. It came out of the blue . . .

Margaret Mounsey, widow of Joe Mounsey,
interview with author, 2009

'The original files will not tell you the truth. If you look at the evidence . . . I'm not saying it's lies, but sometimes, because of expediency, facts get muddled. Who did what changes depending on certain factors, including who was there to give evidence at the time. Names have been changed. There's never been a single book on this case that's got the facts right. I've given interviews, but people still get it wrong because they'd sooner tap into old myths. I know the truth because I was there.'[1]

Scotsman Ian Fairley was Hyde's newest member of the CID in October 1965, a 21-year-old single man living in digs: 'A sergeant from Hyde, John Mosley, called me to go in, even though I'd been working all night. There were more people knocking about at the station than usual. Detective Sergeant Alex Carr, Superintendent Bob Talbot and another Detective Sergeant called Roy 'Dixie' Dean, who was based at Stalybridge. There was a buzz about the place. Dean was interviewing a young lad called Smith. I asked what was up and was told there had been a murder the night before.'[2]

Dave and Maureen were given cups of tea after being shown through to the inquiry office. At 7.20 a.m., PC Antrobus, who had taken Dave's telephone call, had rung his superior, Detective

Inspector Wills, at home in Hyde; he then called his boss, newly promoted Superintendent Robert Talbot, who was due to leave for 12 days' holiday that morning. Talbot was a plain-spoken, serious man, married with two grown children. When he arrived at the station, he found Wills had called in Detective Sergeant Alex 'Jock' Carr, who was also supposed to be enjoying a day off. Carr was the burly six-foot son of a Rosyth docker, a quiet man who got on with the job without fuss.[3] Talbot and Carr went into the inquiry office, where Dave and Maureen were sitting with Antrobus and Dean. Dave stammered out his story again; Talbot's eyebrows rose at mention of pistols and rifles hidden in a suburban semi.

Fairley recalls: 'Jock Carr came out of the inquiry room and said, "It looks like you and me are going up to Hattersley. Roy Dean is talking to the lad who said he witnessed the murder last night." Just then, Dean appeared and was . . . let's say, *disparaging* towards David Smith. He basically said the lad was talking a load of shit. I suppose it did sound a bit far-fetched at first, but it had to be looked into, so I ended up with Jock in his car, while Talbot sped up to Hattersley in his blue Hillman Minx.'[4] He dismisses the story reported in the past about Talbot deploying a veritable army of men in a circle around the estate: 'There was a traffic car put at Godley, near the railway arches, and a car put somewhere north up Mottram side. And that was it. We drove up to Hattersley and parked our cars on the road below the New Inn. Bob Talbot was in uniform. Jock and I were in plain clothes. Then Talbot took it into his head to disguise himself.'[5]

The estate was coming to life on that cloudy morning. People were running for buses and climbing into cars, children were walking to school and *Housewives' Choice* drifted from open kitchen windows. Just after eight, Elsie Masterton popped out of number 12 to empty her tea leaves into the dustbin and was seen by Fairley and Carr, who gesticulated for her to 'keep in the house'.[6] She stared, open-mouthed, then backed indoors, calling for Duke to stop barking. Among the mobile delivery vans going around the estate was Sunblest; Talbot stopped the driver and asked if he could borrow his coat and basket of bread. He pulled on the white jacket and approached number 16 from the back. It looked as neat as a new pin, with the cheery floral curtains at the bedroom window and the fern-filled rockery.

'It's good drama, that bread man's coat, isn't it?' Fairley reflects. 'But why did he do it, really? Because Brady might have had a gun? No. Seriously, I've no idea. Jock Carr and I just looked at each other in amazement. We went across the green, climbed the fence and stood to the side. Bob Talbot knocked at the back door.'[7] From inside the house came the sound of dogs barking, setting off Duke further down again.

The door opened.

Myra stared at her caller, then frowned. She was dressed for work in a skirt and blouse, with thick black eye make-up and her hair lacquered into a careful beehive. She eyed the Sunblest logo on the caller's white coat, wondering why he was bothering to knock when they always had Mothers Pride.

'Is your husband in?' Talbot asked.[8]

'I haven't got a husband.'

Talbot put down the basket of bread and awkwardly slipped off the white coat. 'I'm a police superintendent and I have reason to believe that there is a man in this house.'

If Myra was alarmed, she didn't show it. 'There's no man here,' she said.

Talbot stepped up into the pantry. 'I'm not satisfied. I want to come in.' He pushed past her into the dark little kitchen and Myra followed. 'He's in the other room,' she said.

Fairley and Carr entered through the front door. The three policemen converged in the sitting room, where the weak sunlight seeped in on Ian, who was sitting on the unmade sofa bed in his underwear, writing a letter with a green biro. He looked up.

Myra recalled: 'I'll never forget his face when I took the police into the living room the morning after the murder of Edward Evans. It was expressionless, as it often was, but I saw him almost shrink before my eyes, helpless and powerless . . . it was all over.'[9]

In a letter to Colin Wilson many years later, Ian recalled the strategy he and Myra had discussed: 'We planned to exit by gunshot if cornered beyond salvage. But the revolvers and rifle were upstairs and I was in bed downstairs when the police poured in through the back door.'[10] It had always been his intention to shoot the police who captured him, then turn the gun on himself and Myra. But he remembered that he had taken the revolver in its shoulder holster off the night before, when he and Dave had carried Edward's body upstairs.

Ian swung his legs over to sit on the edge of the sofa bed. He saw the policemen glance at the cloth wrapped around his ankle.

'I've received a report that an act of violence took place in this house last night and we're investigating it,' Talbot said. Ian glanced from Carr to Fairley and back to Talbot, but didn't respond.

'There's nothing wrong here,' Myra said.

Talbot turned to her. 'Who lives in this house?'

'My gran,' Myra replied. 'She's upstairs in bed. And myself and Ian.'

'I'm going to search the house. Have you any objection?'

Myra shook her head, 'No.'

Talbot went into the hallway and upstairs, followed by Myra. There were three doors on the small landing, all closed. He reached out for the handle of the one on the right. Myra hesitated, but he pushed it open and saw an elderly, frail lady sitting up in bed, the curtains not yet drawn. Her eyes widened at the sight of his uniform; Myra bobbed her head in and told Gran she wasn't to worry, she would bring her a cup of tea and explain later. Talbot looked at the doors to his left. One was just slightly ajar: a cold little bathroom lay beyond it, so he tried the other door. It was locked.

He looked over his shoulder at Myra. 'What's in here?'

Myra's reaction was swift: 'I keep my firearms in there and I keep the door locked for safety.'

Talbot realised that David Smith had been telling the truth about the guns at least. He asked, 'Can I have the key?'

'It's at work.'

They returned to the sitting room, where Ian was still sitting on the sofa bed under the watchful gaze of Carr and Fairley. 'There's a locked room upstairs,' Talbot said, addressing himself to Ian. 'I'll have to search it. Have you got a key here?'

Myra parroted, 'It's at *work*.'

Talbot turned to face her. 'Then get your coat on and we'll take you in the car to work and bring you back again.'

She raised her chin slightly. 'I don't want to. It's not convenient.'

Talbot spoke more firmly, 'I'm afraid you must get the key. I'm not leaving this house until I've searched that bedroom.'

Myra and Ian stared at each other in silence.

Talbot nodded his head at Fairley: 'You go to Manchester with her to fetch it.'[11]

The younger man looked at him incredulously. 'Just kick in the door.'

Talbot glanced at Ian, who remained silent.

'*Kick in the door,*' Fairley repeated.

Her eyes still locked on Ian, Myra said, 'You'd better tell him.'

Ian rose immediately from the sofa bed. 'There was a row last night. It's in the back bedroom.' He nodded at Myra. 'Give them the keys.' She was already feeling in her handbag and handed the keys to Talbot, who went quickly upstairs and unlocked the door. He later testified: 'The room was furnished with a single bed, wardrobe, table and chair. Underneath the window, on the floor, was a bundle wrapped in a dark-coloured blanket. I went to it and saw the shape of a human foot . . .'[12]

He straightened up again and stared at the bundle. On top of it was a pile of books and beside it a bulky Adesga carrier bag and a long stick. Carr appeared. The two men looked at each other and returned to the front room. Carr spoke first, to Ian: 'We've found a body in the back bedroom and I'm taking you to Hyde police station for further inquiries.'[13] He began to caution him, and Ian said impatiently, 'Yes, I know.'[14] Talbot quickly made arrangements for Dr Ellis of Hyde to examine the body: 'He arrived shortly afterwards and pronounced life extinct. I examined the bedroom and found two loaded revolvers; each gun was fully loaded.'[15]

Ian unwound the cloth from his ankle and dressed, declaring, 'Eddie and I had a row and the situation got out of hand.'[16] Myra hadn't been cautioned, but now she knew the story she had to build upon if they took her in. She insisted on going to the police station anyway, even though Talbot told her it was unnecessary. She didn't want to be parted from Ian, and Talbot sent for WPC Slater, who arrived promptly. Gran was sent round to the Hills', at Wardle Brook Walk, with Lassie. Myra lifted Puppet into her arms and followed Ian out. He managed to whisper to her that it was the two of them against the world now.

Several neighbours had gathered on the path outside and stared curiously as the small group left the house. Fairley borrowed a pair of handcuffs from another policeman who had arrived to stand guard outside and clapped them on Ian's wrists. Further along the road, another police car had drawn up. Inside sat David Smith. Ian and Myra passed directly by him; Ian inclined his head and smirked, while Myra fixed him with a glare.

'Is that them?' asked the officer with Dave, and he nodded.

Ian Fairley recalls, 'Jock drove the car back to the nick, and I sat with Brady. He was handcuffed to my left wrist. I didn't like the fact that I'd been told to handcuff him to myself – all right, cuff him, but not to me. He was quiet, though, no problem.'[17] Myra held Puppet on her knee throughout the journey into Hyde. She and her dog were shown through to the station canteen while Ian was ushered into the CID room. Until a suitable policewoman could be found to question her, Myra sat sipping endless cups of tea and cadging food for Puppet.

In the CID room, Fairley recalls, 'We sat Brady down. He wanted a fag, so I gave him a fag. I chatted to him and he was very easy, very calm. Jock Carr came back, sat down and said, "What happened last night?" Brady repeated the same thing, that it had just got out of hand, that's what he kept saying, it had just got out of hand. He was asked if he wanted to make a statement and he said he did.'[18] Ian's statement was taken that morning, formulated by him with two aims in mind: to absolve Myra and incriminate Dave.

'Last night I met Eddie in Manchester. We were drinking and then went home to Hattersley. We had an argument and we came to blows. After the first few blows, the situation was out of control. When the argument started, Dave Smith was at the front door and Myra called him in. Eddie was on the floor near the living-room door. Dave hit him with the stick and kicked him about three times. Eddie kicked me at the beginning on my ankle. There was a hatchet on the floor and I hit Eddie with it. After that the only noise Eddie made was gurgling. When Dave and I began cleaning up the floor, the gurgling stopped. Then we tied up the body, Dave and I. Nobody else helped. Dave and I carried it upstairs. Then we sat in the house until three or four in the morning. Then we decided to get rid of the body in the morning early next day or next night.'[19]

While Ian gave his statement, Talbot made a few telephone calls, including one to his boss, fifty-two-year-old rotund and balding bachelor Arthur Benfield, who had been appointed Detective Chief Superintendent of Cheshire six days earlier.

'If it had been left to Benfield, there would have been no Moors Murders inquiry,' Fairley asserts. 'I hesitate to criticise the dead, but if he was here I would say the same. By the time Benfield arrived that day – he was based in Chester and booked himself into the Queen's Hotel in Hyde – he'd already decided he could wrap everything up in a couple of days. He took charge because he was the senior investigating officer. Various other people came and went during the course of the day. But what I want you to understand is this: there were not a lot of troops, only a handful of us. To run a full murder inquiry takes 48 detectives. We had nothing like that, but initially what we were looking at was one body and a prisoner who admitted hitting the victim with an axe. Hindley wouldn't speak to anyone. Smith was our witness. He kept telling us, "She came and got me, this murder happened, and I helped them tidy up because I was bloody frightened."'[20]

At lunchtime, Talbot and Benfield visited 16 Wardle Brook Avenue with Home Office pathologist Dr Charles St Hill. Detective Constable Leighton from Cheadle Hulme was there, photographing the process of unwrapping Edward's body from its crude shroud. St Hill lifted the books that had been placed on the youth's ruined skull and Leighton's camera captured the titles: *The Red Brain* (*Tales of Horror*), *Among Women Only* (*La Dolce Vita – Love and Sensation in Post-war Italy*) and *The Road Ahead*, a volume of children's poetry. St Hill removed the blood-drenched cushion cover from Edward's head. His mild features had been distorted beyond all recognition. Wound tightly about his throat was the length of electrical flex. His knees had been pushed up under his chin and tied with the cord from the dog-stick. The pathologist made a note that Edward's trousers were unfastened; at the trial, forensic evidence would show that at some point his lower clothing had probably been removed, leading to speculation about what occurred before the murder. St Hill removed a bloodstained letter from Edward's pocket. It was from a girl called Wendy in north Wales and addressed to the dead youth: '. . . You know that girl from the farm shop, her name is Val, well, she wants to go out with Brian, will you ask him for her. When will you be coming down, I hope it will be soon, I miss you. The weather here is awful, it rains most of the time. I'm going to Liverpool on Sunday for the day to my aunty's. Well I can't think of much to say now. Love Wendy. PS. Write soon. Lots of kisses.'[21]

Despite Ian's and Myra's efforts, there was plenty of 'forensic' for the police to find in the sitting room and Myra's bedroom. Into a series of plastic bags went samples of hair, blood and clothing, two tape recorders and tapes, hundreds of photographs and negatives, a tartan-covered photo album, a photographic lightbulb, two revolvers and bullets from a cardboard box and the Adesga carrier bag containing the murder weapon. The letter Ian had been writing when Talbot knocked on his door was discovered under the sofa bed: 'Dear Tom, sorry I could not phone yesterday. My family are at Glasgow this week. I was crossing the road in town last night when someone on a bike came round a corner and knocked me down. Except for a few bruises I was all right until I got up this morning. I could not put my weight on my ankle. I must have weak ankles or something. If it is no better tomorrow, I will see the doctor. Ian.'[22]

By half past two, Benfield and Talbot were back at Hyde station, where Detective Policewoman Margaret Campion had been called in from another case to question Myra. Irish-born, one of only two detective policewomen in Cheshire, and with sixteen years of experience in the force, she was the ideal person to interview Myra, whom she suspected would be difficult. She began questioning her just after two o'clock: 'This morning a man's body was found in your house. Who is that person?'[23]

Myra replied: 'I don't know and I'm not saying anything. Ask Ian. My story's the same as Ian's.'

'Come on. What's the story of last night?'

Myra took Ian's initial statement at the house that morning as her brief: 'We came home from work about six o'clock, then went out about eight o'clock and then went to the outdoor [off-licence] in Stockport Road, Longsight, for some wine. We often go there. Then we went up to Glossop way near the moors and sat talking for ages. It was just a normal evening out before all this happened. It was the same as hundreds of other evenings out.'[24] She didn't realise that her version of events already differed from the one given by Ian; he told police that they'd spent the entire evening in Manchester prior to meeting Edward.

Campion didn't mention the discrepancy. 'Would you care to tell me what happened at your house last night?'

'All I'm saying is that I didn't do it and Ian didn't do it,' Myra responded. 'We are involved in something we didn't do. We never left each other. We never do. What happened last night was an accident. It should never have happened.'

'An accident? If what you say is true, it's in your interests to tell the truth of what did happen.'

Myra shook her head, 'No. Ask Ian. His story is the same as mine. We never left each other. Ian can't drive and that's that.' Then she asked urgently, 'What are they going to do with Ian, because what he has done I have done.'

Campion paused, then asked, 'Do you realise how serious this matter is?'

'Yes,' Myra shot back. 'And I also know David Smith told you all this and he's a liar.'

'David Smith alleges you cleaned up the mess in the living room after the murder of this man.'

'Yes, and I suppose he told you he sat on the chair benevolently looking on while I cleaned up.'

'Is it true that you went to David Smith's house last night and he walked home with you?'

'Yes.'

'What time did you go there?'

'I'm not saying. All this happened because there was an argument and that's that.'

'How did this man get to your house? Who brought him there?'

'I'm not saying how he got there or when. I've told you before, I'm not saying anything.'[25]

The interview was terminated. Myra would repeat the same words – 'I didn't do it, Ian didn't do it, ask David Smith' – like a mantra in the weeks ahead. Ian occasionally made a few minor blunders, but Myra refused to be drawn. She came close to blurting something out when the police suggested that she was a prostitute and Edward was killed because he'd refused to pay up, but she recovered herself.

Various people came and went that day. Dave and Maureen remained cloistered in one of the rooms, away from Myra. Nellie arrived, ferried in by the police with Myra's Uncle Bert, and pleaded with her daughter: 'Myra, they say you're in a lot of trouble because you won't talk to them. They're talking about bodies being buried on the moors.'[26] At this, Myra became upset. Nellie told her that Gran was staying with the Hills for the time being, but no one believed the story they'd concocted about Myra causing an accident by dangerous driving. At four o'clock, Nellie and Bert left, promising to return that evening.

Half an hour later, a small, stooped woman in spectacles and a pillbox hat arrived at the station. She was shown into a building across the yard. Alex Carr stood watching Myra as the sound of loud sobbing filtered through the window. Myra went on sipping her tea as Edward's mother, Edith, identified the savagely wounded body of her eldest son in the mortuary. Carr formed an opinion of Myra that didn't waver until his own death decades later: 'She was totally lacking in emotion. She never showed any remorse at any time when I spoke to her. She was hard and evil.'[27]

At half past six, Benfield returned to Hattersley for another poke around the house. Lights were on in almost every window across the estate, with families settling down for tea and telly. He walked down to where Myra's car was parked at the foot of the slope and found a dog-eared brown wallet on the dashboard. He felt inside and pulled out three sheets of paper.

First sheet

No. all List 1 up   1 + 2   Destroy
Note how many pages each

OB	DET	CARR	STN	END
HAT	Clean before wipe pts place in paper container which has been cleaned After use, replace in container	X		Burn shaft Bury head
CAR	Remove all moveable objects, clean cover floor and seat fresh Poly. at night Count all moveables, Keys, etc.		X	Destroy Poly. inspect car for spots
GN	Polish, Bulls Polish	X		Dave

TICK	Place P/B		X	
REC	Check periodically			W/H
	unmoved			
PRO P	STIMULATE			
CARR	For Hatch, paper bag			Destroy

Second sheet

OB	DET	CARR	STN	END
ALI	Period of		X	14 days.
WE HOME	termination?			Vague no
THEN	Dave Carr 7-8.30			memory after
HEYWOOD	Use bus, pick-up end			14
	CARR			
	Belle Vue, bus back			
	HATCH			
METH	Drop me off, pass		X	
	agreed Point			
	ever five mins			
Dump	Have container		X	
	Hatch for			
	Dave Carr Discuss			
CLOTH	Check & Polish all	X		
	buttons &			
KEYS	clasps.	10 BUT		
	Brush hairs, clean			
	shoes, wear glov			
	Packamac?			
	Delete key ngt.			

Third sheet, no columns: Reverse of third sheet, no columns:

2 GN	5 Bulls EA	money	IF I AP Store Gn &
MATCHES			Bulls where? New
CIGS		WALLET	Story
WATCH		10/- Note	
GLVES			
2 PR Shoes			Dist Why

He knew immediately that he was holding in his hands a blueprint for murder. Some of the abbreviations were immediately obvious – GN for gun, HAT for hatchet and so on – but others were more obscure. He tucked the papers into his pocket. At eight o'clock, he slid the notes across the desk in the CID room to Ian, who struck him as 'a normal fellow [who] looked a bit worried'.[28] Ian asked after Myra, but Benfield pressed him on the list. Ian admitted it was his but claimed to have written it *after* the murder.

'What does OB mean?'

'Object.'

'DET?'

'Details.'

'CARR?'

'Car.'

'STN?'

A slight pause, then Ian said, 'Stationery, paper.'

Benfield asked him why he had written about guns when the murder was committed with an axe.

'For if anybody had seen us burying the body,' Ian replied. 'The guns were for self-protection.' Then he offered: 'Pro-P, that's Pro-Plus, a stimulant. ALI means alibi. METH is method. CLOTH is clothing. BULLS, bullets.'

'And P/B?'

Another flicker of a pause. 'Penistone Burn.'

Benfield frowned. The reference was lost on him, though he knew Penistone was a town on the eastern side of the Pennines. He decided to leave it for the time being; he was still turning over the question of whether or not to arrest David Smith. Benfield's theory was that they had meant to dispose of the body that night, but Ian's sprained ankle prevented them from getting any further than the car, where he had left his wallet with the disposal plan inside, because however much Ian protested otherwise, Benfield was convinced that the plan had been written *prior* to death.[29]

He left Ian and decided not to charge David Smith. Fairley explains: 'The argument was this: if you're going to charge Hindley, you've got to charge Smith, because what you had at that time was Hindley helping clear up, no more than that. Who else helped to clear up? Smith. We took Smith's shoes off; there was blood on his shoes and Brady said

Smith had kicked Evans. He had this stick, too; and the stick wasn't as thick as your finger, bit of string tied on it, that had blood on it. Smith told Dixie Dean that he'd spent time with them on the moors and Brady had told him he'd killed more. I know Dixie Dean's view, because that came through loud and clear before he left to return to Stalybridge – he thought Smith was saying this to get himself out of a tight spot. He didn't believe him. But in those days you didn't lock people up easily.'[30]

Fairley's own views on David Smith were already solid: 'All right, he was a bit of a rum customer, but if it hadn't been for Smith, other children would have been killed. People were so vicious about that poor lad after it all came out, but he saved lives *and* he enabled us to bring home those children who had already been murdered so that their parents could give them proper funerals. Without him, we would never have known where to start. Smith was the one man more than anyone who brought the whole thing to justice. Albeit unknowingly in parts, but he did it and it wasn't an easy thing to do. Because if he hadn't come to us, Evans would have ended up on the moor and we would never have been any wiser. The men who mattered on that inquiry – Jock Carr and Joe Mounsey – they believed in David Smith completely. Unfortunately, mud sticks and he ended up an outcast. But it's about time people started realising he's a hero, not a villain.'[31]

Before detectives sent Dave and Maureen home, they asked him if he had any ideas for getting Myra and Ian to open up. Dave had two novel suggestions: kill Puppet to make Myra squeak, and stick a spider or daddy-long-legs in Ian's cell and watch him start crawling the walls.

Myra was still in the canteen with Puppet. Her mother returned with her lover, Bill Moulton. Myra slipped into the skirt and blouse Nellie had brought; the clothes she had worn earlier were taken away for tests. She was appalled when detectives told her they needed samples of her saliva, blood and pubic hair. The results showed that she and Edward Evans shared the same blood group and a medical examination revealed that she hadn't had sexual intercourse recently; she told the doctor it was two weeks since she and Ian had last been intimate.

At twenty past eight that evening, Ian was charged with the murder of Edward Evans. He responded, 'I stand on the statement made this morning.'[32] He wrote the same words on the charge form, signed it and was escorted to the basement cells for the night. At nine o'clock, Arthur Benfield strolled into the canteen where Myra was sitting with Puppet on her knee, next to her mother and Bill. She recalled, 'I was both terrified and reluctant to tell the police anything which could have harmed Ian in any way. I said such stupid things . . .'[33] In fact, she uttered very little. Benfield asked her if she wished to say anything about the events of the previous evening.

'No,' Myra shook her head. 'Not until you let me see Ian.'

'He's been charged and will be up in court in the morning.'

Myra stared back at Benfield. 'Then I'll be at court and I'll see you after I've seen Ian.'[34]

'You can go,' Benfield said shortly. 'But not to Wardle Brook Avenue.'

'And Ian?'

'He'll be spending the night in a cell.'

Myra's expression altered immediately; she looked crestfallen.

Nellie took her daughter home. Myra was silent for the rest of the evening, apart from a small cry of astonishment when she saw a column on the front page of the *Manchester Evening News*: 'Body Found in House – Murder?' She quickly scanned the article. There was a comment from Talbot about Ian, who was not named ('A man is helping us with our inquiries') and then, at the foot of the page, 'Mrs Ellen Maybury, aged 76, who has lived there for twelve months with her granddaughter Myra Hindley, aged 23 . . .'[35]

The path towards infamy had begun.

17

A piece of paper bearing the name of a person who vanished
two years ago has come into their possession . . .

Manchester Evening News, 'Police in Mystery
Dig on Moors', October 1965

On Friday, 8 October 1965, the *Manchester Evening News* ran a few
lines about that morning's activity at Hyde Magistrate's Court: 'At a
three-minute hearing at 10 a.m., a man was charged with the murder
of Edward Evans. As he left the dock, he nodded at a blonde woman
friend.'[1]

Standing outside the court in the autumn sun was Clive Entwistle,
a young journalist from Rochdale who had set up a freelance agency
with a colleague in Ashton-under-Lyne that September. Coming out
of the court was a detective whom he knew well, and after speaking to
him about the Evans case, Entwistle climbed into his car and drove up
to Hattersley. A policeman standing guard at Wardle Brook Avenue
told him the girlfriend of the murder suspect was in a neighbour's
house on the street behind. 'There was a policewoman on the door,'
Entwistle recalls. 'I was smartly dressed, in a suit, collar and tie, said
good afternoon and just walked straight past her, as if I was meant
to be there. I went into the kitchen. The owner of the house was
there with Myra's grandmother and another woman. I said that I was
looking for the young lady from the house at the front and one of the
women said, "Oh, Myra's in through there." I asked if it was all right
for me to talk to her and she said, "Would you like a cup of tea?" I
suppose she thought I was from the police. I said yes and she asked,
"Will you take one to Myra as well?" She poured two teas into fine
china cups, put a couple of biscuits on the saucers and I carried them
through to the front room. Sitting by the window to the left was

this young blonde woman. She wore a floral dress and a cardigan. She didn't have her hair in that familiar bouffant style, though. I sat down and said, "I've brought you a cup of tea." I told her who I was and what I knew. She just looked blankly at me, then turned to the window again. All I could get out of her was that her name was Myra and her boyfriend was Ian. That was it. I'd no idea of the volcano that was about to erupt.'[2]

After her first encounter with a journalist, Myra returned to Hyde police station with Puppet in tow and asked to see Ian. When she was told that was impossible, she asked if she could have her car back but was informed that it was undergoing forensic tests. Then she asked for her driving licence, which had also been seized. She wanted to hire a car instead of relying on buses but, after a short search, was told it couldn't be found. Finally, she said that she couldn't stay at her mother's house any more and would be staying with her uncle Bert and auntie Kath. The desk sergeant made a note and Myra left the station.

Talbot and Benfield ran through what they knew about the case. Edward's mother had given them the names of her son's friends; they contacted Jeff Grimsdale, who didn't recognise Ian when he was shown a photo of him. Nor did Mike Mahone: 'I blamed myself for a long time afterwards for what happened.'[3] He spent three weeks in hospital being treated for a perforated ulcer caused by stress.

Fairley recalls: 'I was at Millwards on the Friday. I spoke to staff and searched the place, then went on to Brady's mother's house in Heywood. She lived in a block of flats and was a well-mannered woman, quite timid, refined. I told her Ian had been arrested for murder and she couldn't believe it.'[4] In the afternoon, while Ian's ankle was examined by a doctor, Detective Chief Inspector John Tyrrell of Manchester City Police arrived at Hyde police station to talk about Lesley, Pauline and Keith.

Fairley recalls: 'There was a feeling they were linked, but no evidence. Lesley, Keith and Pauline fell under the jurisdiction of Manchester and John Kilbride, who was from Ashton-under-Lyne, was under Lancashire. We had more affinity as a force with Lancashire than we did with Manchester. That may seem strange when you're talking about seven miles, but you've got to go back to the '60s and see that people were very parochial. Lancashire Constabulary were a rich force because of the size of the county. We were Cheshire, a rural force, and our budget was tight. Manchester were a bit richer than us. Once it started to filter through that we'd got Brady for the murder of a 17-year-old boy, and that he'd boasted about other murders, other constabularies began to show an interest.'[5]

The following morning, when Myra arrived at the station, Benfield asked her into an office to answer a few questions. She still hadn't been able to see Ian and was in no mood to cooperate, repeating to Benfield, 'Ian didn't do it and I didn't do it.'

'Then who did?'

'I'm saying nothing till I've seen Ian's solicitor.'[6]

She was allowed to leave the station after agreeing to return on Monday, when she had a meeting with solicitor Robert Fitzpatrick, who was acting on behalf of Ian. From Hyde, she travelled to her mother's house and the two of them carried a large bag of washing to the laundrette near Millwards. Myra went on alone to her old workplace.[7] According to her confession, she opened a cupboard near the fireplace, where some old records were stacked, and found an envelope containing evidence of some kind. She burned the envelope.[8] Shortly afterwards, Tom Craig arrived. He had read about the murder in the *Manchester Evening News* and at first imagined it was Ian who had been killed. Having learned the truth, he told Myra that Ian was never to set foot in Millwards again, but that he would keep her job open – even though she asked him to sack her so that she could claim dole. He handed over their wages and she left to join her mother at the laundrette again.

A small item in the *Manchester Evening News* noted: 'A piece of paper bearing the name of a person who vanished two years ago has come into [police] possession.'[9] Just a short, innocuous sentence, but the piece of paper in question blew open the entire investigation.

Ian Fairley found the piece of paper, although Dixie Dean claimed the credit.

The items taken from the house on Wardle Brook Avenue were deposited at Hyde police station and it was while Fairley was sitting at his desk, idly flicking through an exercise book belonging to Ian Brady, that his attention was caught by a particular page. 'I found a list of names,' he recalls, 'scrawled absent-mindedly around two doodles, rough sketches of gangster types. Most were the names of film stars, but there were others too. Ian Brady, John Sloan, Jim Idiot, Alec Guineas, John Kilbride, J. Thompson, John Gilbert – John Kilbride! *John Kilbride.* The lad who had gone missing from Ashton market in November 1963.'[10]

A call was put through to Joe Mounsey at Ashton-under-Lyne police station. He arrived at Hyde with Detective Policewoman Pat Clayton and studied the notebook in silence. He spoke to David Smith and trusted what he was told. Then he asked for the photographs that had been found in the house on Wardle Brook Avenue. A few stood out because they were eerily devoid of purpose: landscapes shot as if the photographer was crouching down to include the ground rather than the scenery. Mounsey was intrigued by the picture of Myra's white car against molar-shaped black rocks. He remembered David Smith's statement about bodies buried on the moor and told his superiors, 'We'll do what Brady did. Bloody well dig.'[11] Harold Prescott, Mounsey's superior, agreed, but Benfield was less certain; it looked like a needle-in-a-haystack job to him.

Nonetheless, on Sunday, 10 October, a team of police headed up to the moor. The enormity of the task wasn't lost on anyone: 400 square miles of peat and bog and furze, with the steep streams known by the old Lancashire name 'clough' and green cliffs 2,000 feet high that fell away to deep, fathomless valleys and reservoirs. At half past one, Mounsey and Talbot collected Dave and Maureen from Underwood Court and drove, under Dave's direction, east along the Snake Pass towards Woodhead (a contender for the W/H of the disposal plan). Mounsey handed Dave several photographs and asked if he recognised any of the locations. Dave went through them carefully, passing them on to Maureen, but shook his head dismally, leaving the police to trudge around at random.

The Kilbrides had been informed about the notebook and Mounsey had no intention of letting them down.[12] Pat Clayton recalls: 'He spent hours and hours on the moor with Ray Gelder, Mike Massheder, various other officers, trying to trace the exact location of these photographs.'[13] Margaret Mounsey hardly saw her husband when the search began: 'He was off all day every day; I was busy with our children – our daughter was born in 1965 and our two sons were still very young. Nowadays if they sent a bunch of blokes up to the moors they'd be kitted up left, right and centre. Joe was up there in his suit and trilby hat. It looked like an impossible task at first. "Surface of the moon", Joe used to call it."[14]

On Sunday afternoon, Myra visited Gran, who still didn't know the truth behind Ian's arrest. Bert and Kath were there, and Jim Masterton and his wife Anita arrived shortly afterwards. Arrangements were made for Gran to move in with her daughter Annie, in Gorton's Railway View. Eventually, she ended up living with Nellie and Bill in Clayton, after Nellie split from Bob, who wanted nothing to do with either of his daughters, not because of Myra's crimes but because she and Maureen had kept him in the dark about their mother's affair. Lassie was given a permanent home with Myra's uncle Jim, and Myra asked Elsie Masterton if she would look after Puppet for the time being. Later that day, she took food and books into the police station for Ian. When he glimpsed her walking between two policewomen, he wrongly assumed that she'd been charged. A policeman made a record of his mistake and passed it on to his boss.

Those hours were Myra's last in freedom.

On Monday, 11 October, Myra met Ian's solicitor, Robert Fitzpatrick. She told him that she went along with whatever Ian had to say. The police tried to question her again, but she sat in stony silence. A short distance away, the inquest into Edward Evans's death was being held at Hyde town court. His mother spoke almost inaudibly to confirm that she had identified her son's body. The coroner, upon hearing that Ian had been charged with his murder, adjourned the inquest for three months.

On the moor, the police had begun to highlight areas of interest with circles of yellow dye. Mounsey was scrutinising five of the negatives: Ian on rocks with white vehicle below; Myra on rocks with white vehicle below; similar view without figures; white vehicle with rocks behind; and an empty moorland scene overlooking a road. Inspector John Chaddock of Uppermill, the largest village in the district of Saddleworth, was brought on board; he knew the area better than any other policeman. Plans were formulated for a mass search, integrating neighbouring police forces.

At quarter-past twelve that Monday, Detective Chief Inspector John Tyrrell joined Mounsey to question Ian about the disappearances of John Kilbride and Keith Bennett. In response to their queries about the missing Ashton schoolboy, Ian told them, 'I've read about him, I think, but don't know anything of him.'[15] When they pressed him about the disposal plan with regard to the reference 'periodically unmoved', asking, 'Is this a reminder to check that graves are still intact?', Ian shrugged, 'It's only to do with Evans.'[16] At three o'clock, he was given a break for half an hour.

At that same hour, in another room within the station, Arthur Benfield was standing in front of Myra, who sat between her mother and uncle Bert. He told her that they had all the evidence they needed to charge her. Detective Sergeant Carr read out the formal charge: an accessory to the murder of Edward Evans. Detective Policewoman Margaret Campion witnessed Myra's response: 'Nothing to say until I see Mr Fitzpatrick.'[17] She would never be free again.

With a policewoman on either side of her and a plain-clothes detective in front, Myra was led out of the room. In her autobiography, she recalls: 'I was tired and frightened. When we left the room, they led me down what seemed like endless flights of stone stairs, dimly lit with 60W bulbs. I thought I was being taken to a dungeon somewhere. Then we came to some doors and a policeman kicked one of them open. I immediately thought they were going to interrogate me, so I clenched my teeth, hard.'[18]

She was shown into a tiled cell. At one end stood an old-fashioned wooden camera on a tripod. Lights glared down from the ceiling. The photographer told her where to stand, then draped a black cloth over his head and adjusted the focus of the lens.[19] The lights flashed and an image of unparalleled British female notoriety was made.

Afterwards, as she was led upstairs, one of the policewomen tried to convince her to confess, telling her it wasn't worth sacrificing herself for a man. Myra said nothing. She had her fingerprints taken and was ushered back to her mother and Bert, unaware that the photograph she had posed for that afternoon would haunt her for the rest of her life.

Throughout the day, Ian's interrogation continued, with Benfield present in the evening. Questions were asked in court about the way in which the interview was conducted; Ian claimed that Mounsey, Tyrrell, Detective Inspector Norman Mattin and Detective Inspector Jeffrey Leach bawled at him incessantly and that he was never left alone: 'When Mounsey and Tyrrell stopped questioning, Mattin and Leach came in. They continued to question during the meals . . . The interview was Mounsey on one side, Tyrrell at the other, Mattin and Leach at the front . . . They were shouting a foot from each ear from both sides.'[20] He added: 'There were threats . . . At one point [Mounsey] said, "I don't think you have any feelings at all. The only feelings you have got are for your dog. We'll destroy your dog, and maybe you'll realise what it's like to lose something you love."'[21] At eight o'clock, the interview was terminated. Ian told the court: 'It ended with Mounsey grabbing hold of the door and saying, "Bastard", and banging the door shut . . .'[22]

Ian was driven back to Risley Remand Centre (known by its inmates as 'Grisly Risley') 30 miles away, near Warrington. It was Myra's first night there; she travelled in another car and was shown into the reception area. Asked her religion, she replied none, then submitted to the routine medical inspections. Her pubic hair was examined for lice. She was given a room on the hospital wing for her own protection because rumours were already circulating that she and Ian were involved in the deaths of several children; neither of them dared venture out for exercise.

Myra awoke early the following morning, her first in captivity. Her bladder was full, but she couldn't bear the thought of using the pot beneath her bed and hoped she could hang on for a proper toilet. A guard had left her a pile of shapeless clothes in shades of brown and grey. She put them on in disgust. Before breakfast an officer appeared and handed her an envelope containing Ian's reception letter. He told her that he was facing life imprisonment, which he wouldn't be able to bear. His allusion to suicide was cemented by his next line, urging her to be brave like Emmy Goering, the widow of Luftwaffe commander Hermann Goering, who killed himself the night before he was due to be hanged. He wrote that his influence on her would pall and she would be able to begin a new life. Myra focused on the last line instead, recalling later, 'In his first letter to me on remand he wrote at the end, in German, that he loved me and I poured all my love for him into my letters to him.'[23]

She asked the governor of Risley whether she and Ian might be permitted to see each other before their first joint court appearance. Consent was granted and they met in a room separated by a sheet of glass, with a guard standing nearby on either side. Ian wore a suit, and smiled at the sight of Myra in the clothes she had been given, telling her that she was free to wear what she liked until after sentencing. She explained that she was saving her own clothes for court. He advised her to keep herself occupied and not dwell on things, recommending a visit to Risley's library.[24] He asked her softly if she had managed to retrieve the receipt for the suitcases that still lay unclaimed at the left luggage office in Central Station. She shook her head and whispered that the house had been under police guard.[25]

Miles away, in the bitter air, a line of men moved across the land to the side of Penistone Road, near Woodhead. They carried sticks, pushing them into the earth continually, then sniffing the ends, resembling 'a frieze of wintry flautists playing music beyond the human ear'.[26] Detectives had managed to identify some of the locations in the photographs found at Wardle Brook Avenue: some were at Leek, others at Whaley Bridge and another, of Myra in front of a waterfall, was apparently taken at Shiny Brook Clough, six miles from the advancing line of police.

Detective Chief Superintendent Douglas Nimmo of Manchester City Police had unearthed a receipt, but not for left luggage. This one came from Warren's Autos on London Road and was for the twenty-four-hour hire of a Ford Anglia, registration number 9275ND, for 23 November 1963. The day that John Kilbride vanished.

Nimmo met with Benfield and Prescott to scrutinise the missing persons files under their jurisdiction. They began with twelve files and narrowed it down to a possible eight, including those of John Kilbride, Lesley Ann Downey, Pauline Reade and Keith Bennett.

That day, the press got wind of the search taking place at Woodhead. Clive Entwistle, who was the only reporter at that stage to have spoken to Myra, recalls, 'On Tuesday morning I was doing a shift on the *Daily Sketch* and Jim Stansfield, in the *Daily Mail*, broke the story that morning that there was a search taking place on the moors. That was the start of everything clicking into place. Myra had been arrested by then, too. I spent the next three or four weeks on the moors or chasing people for interviews. The story just exploded. We had the world's press coming to us; not just Britain, but everywhere – New Zealand, America, Japan, Paris. Every night we met at the Queen's Hotel in Hyde, where the police also congregated, to swap information. It was a colossal story.'[27]

The *Manchester Evening News* ran two major articles: 'Police in Mystery Dig on Moors' and 'Forensic Men Comb Terraced House of Secrets'.[28] Father Theodore, Myra's priest from St Francis' Monastery, wrote to her at Risley but received no reply. Reporters and detectives swooped on Millwards, where little work was done. Staff taking down the pictures above Myra's desk discovered her black scrawl across the cream paint: 'Money and food is all I want, all I want is money and food.'[29]

On Wednesday, 13 October, Mounsey visited Woodhead with three other detectives. They dug through the fern-rich bank of a ravine beside the road but found nothing, while forensic experts from the Home Office Laboratory in Preston went inch by inch through the house on Wardle Brook Avenue. Blood smears were found on the clothing Myra had worn on the night of Edward's murder, both on the sleeve of her coat and skirt, and spots of blood were found on her shoes. The *Manchester Evening News* covered both stories, adding that dossiers on eight missing people had been reopened and that among them were the files of Keith Bennett, Pauline Reade and Lesley Ann Downey. In Manchester, Edward Evans was quietly laid to rest in Southern Cemetery. His parents reserved places within the same grave.[30]

The following day, heavy rain and gales called off the search at Woodhead. At twenty-five past eleven, Mounsey and Tyrrell arrived at Risley to question Myra. Mounsey kicked off the interview: 'I've been told you visited Ashton market regularly for over two years, particularly on Saturday afternoons, and it was there that John Kilbride was last seen.'[31]

'I've never been to Ashton market.'

'I've been told by your sister that you visited the market regularly.'

'It's not true.'

Tyrrell questioned her about David Smith's accusation that following Edward's murder, she had mentioned being approached by the police on the moors while Ian was burying a body. 'That's rubbish,' she responded, replying in similar vein to Mounsey's queries about intended robberies, adding, 'Smith's an idiotic moron.'

Suddenly, Mounsey switched to a different line of questioning: 'A girl called Lesley Ann Downey, who is ten, has been missing from her home since Boxing Day last year. She was last seen on a fairground off Hulme Hall Lane in Manchester about half past five in the evening.'

Myra stared at him, then snapped, 'What are you suggesting?'

'I merely want to know if you know anything about her disappearance.'

'I don't know *anything* about her. I've never been near a fairground.'

At quarter past two, the interview ended and the detectives visited Ian in his cell, cautioning him before laying out photographs for identification. Ian looked at the photograph of himself on the rocks at Hollin Brown Knoll with the white car in the background and said, 'That's Whaley Bridge.' They questioned him about his boasts to David Smith but got very little out of him, and left at five past four.

Alone in her cell, Myra wrote to Elsie Masterton, asking her to take care of Puppet because 'we don't want him to have to be put to sleep as he's only a baby . . .'[32] She added that she had given her mother some money towards Puppet's upkeep and that Ian was going to give his pensions contributions money to her as well. Her letter ended, 'If you do write back, which I hope you do, don't mention anything of the case, etc., as I won't be allowed to read it. I hope the family are all right and if Pat's took Puppet for a walk, thank her for me. Love, Myra xxx'.[33] But Elsie had already given Puppet to the RSPCA's Gorsey Farm Kennels in Ashton after her son Peter had had an allergic reaction to the dog. Elsie also told police that her daughter Patty had gone to the moor with Myra and Ian on countless occasions. When detectives asked Patty if she thought she might remember where they'd been, she replied that she'd already seen it on telly. They arranged to collect her the following day after she explained that she didn't know the name of the place; Ian and Myra had always called it simply 'the moor'.

On the morning of Friday, 15 October, a press photographer took Lesley Ann Downey's mother to Woodhead, snapping her as she watched the search, which was resumed despite the gales and cold.[34] Shelia Kilbride refused a similar request. 'My mum never went up there while the search was on,' Danny Kilbride recalls, 'but my dad did, and I wanted to go too, but he locked me in my bedroom to stop me. I tried to get through the window, but it was too steep a drop. There was a feeling that John would be the first of Brady and Hindley's victims to be discovered.'[35]

At half past one, Detective Constable Peter Clegg and Policewoman Slater collected Patty from her school, Lakes Secondary, in Dukinfield. On Patty's instructions, they drove along the A635 rather than the A57 Snake Road. She guided them through Greenfield, past the Clarence pub at the foot of the steep, winding road known locally as the 'Isle of Skye'.[36] They rounded a bend and a sign came into sight: Holmfirth 7, Oldham 7¼. 'Stop here,' Pat announced. 'This is it.'[37] She pointed to the rocks of Hollin Brown Knoll. Clegg looked at his map and noticed an area two miles away called Wessenden Head. He remembered the W/H of the disposal plan and radioed through to Ashton police station.

Following Clegg's call, the search switched dramatically at three o'clock to Hollin Brown Knoll. Three buses filled with police lumbered up to the moor, tailed by four or five police cars. Areas were marked to be searched the next day. Patty told Detective Sergeant Leslie Eckersley that she and Myra had spent hours sitting in the van while Ian wandered about the moor with a spade, digging for peat. She also told him that she'd visited the spot with Myra and Ian on Christmas Day last year – 24 hours before Lesley Ann Downey had disappeared. As Patty was driven home, thrilled with the compliments she'd received from the police, Mounsey arrived at the Knoll and climbed out of his car, holding a sheaf of photographs. His face blanched as he turned to look at the jutting rocks. He held up the picture of Myra's white car on its own and shook his head in disbelief. The scene was identical.[38]

At Hyde, Jock Carr asked Ian Fairley to pick up plans of Hattersley and the house at Wardle Brook Avenue from Manchester Town Hall. He told him to call on David Smith and bring him back to the station. Fairley recalls, 'I got the plans, came back to Hyde nick, then drove out – at Jock's suggestion – to Hattersley, intending to go into Smith's flat. We got up there, a dog in the flat, electricity on a meter. None of us had a two bob bit for the meter. So we ended up interviewing him in the car park next to Underwood Court. We sat there all afternoon and it started going dark. I was in the driver's seat, Jock in the passenger seat and David in the back. And we ended up getting the biggest breakthrough in the entire case.'[39]

Fairley remembers the interview in the ill-lit car park of Underwood Court: 'Smith was cooperative. He never hid anything, and he never changed his story. But he was – well, not exactly belligerent, but I think he was fed up. During the course of the interview, Jock asked him where they spent their time. Smith said he'd already gone through all this: the moors, drinking, at home, drinking, plotting robberies. He mentioned the fact that Brady asked him to bring anything incriminating back to him. Like what? Dodgy books, mainly. We asked him what Brady had done with them. And he said, "Well, they put them in the suitcases." *What suitcases?* "I don't know," he said, "just suitcases packed with stuff, but I don't know what else apart from the books." We questioned him again about the places they'd gone and he said, in passing almost, that Brady had a thing about railway stations. And Jock said, "Right, that's it, you can go, David." He knew he was on to something.'

They returned to Hyde. Carr went ahead to the office, while Fairley parked the car. When he walked into the station, he heard Benfield shouting at Carr: 'When I say shouting, I mean *bawling*, telling Jock to get his arse in gear, wrap up the investigation. He turned on me and said, "Where have *you* been?" I said, "Manchester." "Oh aye. Well, don't go anywhere." I went into the CID office. Jock's on the telephone. He said, "Can you field the door for me? I've just got to make one or two calls. I'm trying to get them to check the left luggage offices in Manchester." So I go out and try to placate Benfield, act normal.'[40]

Later that evening, Benfield asked for the file on Edward Evans. Fairley recalls: 'He put the file, typed and finished, into his car. As far as Benfield was concerned, the inquiry was over. He buggered off. Talbot had washed his hands as well; he had other fish to fry. It was only Joe Mounsey who was interested, and because of him the search was due to last one more day – just one – and then the whole case would be closed. Jock said I could go home as well. I'd been in about an hour when the telephone rang. It was Jock Carr, asking if I could pick him up. I said, "What for?" and he replied, "Found the suitcases."'[41]

18

They used the technology available to them. Thank God it
wasn't as advanced then as it is today ...

Ian Fairley, interview with author, 20 July 2009

Detective Constable Dennis Barrow of the British Transport Police
located the suitcases when the regional crime squad failed to follow
up Carr's inquiry. Barrow's son-in-law happened to be reporter
Clive Entwistle: 'Dennis rang me when he got home from duty.
He said he'd been asked by the sergeant at Hyde, Alex Carr, to look
for a suitcase belonging to Ian Brady. He'd been through all five
stations and at the last one, Central Station, he found them. He
said, "I opened one. There were all sorts of things inside: German
books, pornographic magazines, a gun, a knife, a cosh. And there
was a tape, a reel-to-reel tape. We played a bit of it ... Clive, I don't
know what it was, but there was a little girl, crying for her mum. We
switched it off. It was terrible ..."'[1]

Carr, Fairley and their colleague Bill Edwards drove back to Hyde
station. Fairley recalls: 'Jock said, "Right, the situation is this: the
suitcases are in Manchester, but I don't trust Benfield and that lot to
deal with this properly, so stay here and answer the phone if it rings."
He went off and came back with these huge suitcases and heaved
them onto the desk. They were packed full, so we didn't go through
everything systematically, but we rummaged through and found some
photographs. Pictures of a little girl with a scarf pulled tight around
her face, wearing nothing but her shoes and socks, lying on a bed with
her head to one side, one of her praying, and another of her stood
with her back to the camera, her arms outstretched in a crucifixion
pose. I've got to confess we didn't recognise her. But the nature of
the photographs was enough. Jock said, "Right, OK, put them away.

We're not going through it all now. At least we've got them." So I locked them in the property cupboard and Jock told me to keep the key. On the way home, after we'd dropped Bill off, Jock invited me in for supper with him and his wife, June. We were sat eating and watching telly when a Granada programme called *Scene* came on. This particular edition linked in with the inquiry. And up on the screen flashed a photograph of Lesley Ann Downey. Jock and I looked at each other. We knew then that the girl in the photos was her.'[2]

The following morning, on Carr's orders, Fairley took the suitcases to another office in Stalybridge and deposited them in a cupboard there. He remembers: 'When I got back to Hyde, I found senior policemen from every area packed into the chief inspector's office because they'd got wind of the suitcases. They were arguing over who was going to run the inquiry. Benfield came back from Cheshire, Eric Cunningham – head of the Number One Regional Crime Squad and a detective chief superintendent who carried the authority of an assistant chief constable – turned up and there were any number of others, including Joe Mounsey. All demanding access to the suitcases. Cunningham was trying to use his rank to get hold of them and a big row was going on. Then Benfield spoke over the lot of them: "Look, the situation is this: *I'm* the only one with a substantive murder inquiry and *I* have the prisoners. The suitcases have been found as a result of *my* officers, therefore *I* will lead the murder inquiry and this will be a *Cheshire* inquiry. Of course I'll welcome any assistance." And that was why it became a Cheshire murder inquiry. It should have gone to Mounsey. He deserved it.'[3] The suitcases were brought in from Stalybridge. 'I wasn't there when they were opened and inspected,' he admits, 'but I heard that the office was full that day. Mounsey and everyone else crowded round to see what was in those cases.'[4]

Inside the blue suitcase was a stack of books: *The Anti-Sex*, *Sexual Anomalies and Perversions*, *Cradle of Erotica*, *The Sex Jungle*, *The Jewel in the Lotus*, *Confessions of a Mask*, *Death Rides a Camel*, *Werewolf in Paris*, *The Perfumed Garden*, *Sexus*, *Paris Vision 28*, *Satin Legs and Stilettos*, *High Heels and Stockings*, *The Life and Ideals of the Marquis de Sade* wrapped in the *Daily Mirror*, *The Kiss of the Whip*, *The Tropic of Cancer*, and a copy of *Mein Kampf* wrapped in the *News of the World*. There were several soft porn magazines – *Men's Digest*, *Penthouse*, *Swank*, *Cavalier*, *Wildcat* – and various other items: a 1965 pocketbook diary belonging to Ian, notes, papers and photographs, an insurance form and a tax form belonging to Ian, two library tickets in the name of Jack Smith (David's father), string, Sellotape, a bandolier belt for holding ammunition, bullets and a black wig.

Inside the brown suitcase were more pornographic books, including one called *Jailbait*, and a study of Jack the Ripper, fifty-four negatives and fifty-five photographic prints, key rings, a pamphlet on family planning addressed to Mrs A. Hope of 7 Bannock Street, a notebook belonging to Ian, his 1962 pocketbook diary, some papers, Myra's 1964 pocketbook diary, correspondence, an SS knife, a key on a shoelace, a sheaf knife, a key wrapped in cloth, Ian's birth certificate, small truncheons, pieces of soap, a cutlery box containing a cosh and a black mask, another cosh with 'EUREKA' on it, some pieces of cloth, a Halibut oil tin – and two tapes.

The red leader on one of the tapes was damaged; Talbot found a technician to replace it. Then a reel-to-reel machine was brought into the office and the first tape was loaded onto the spindle. An impenetrable silence fell as the detectives leaned forward to listen. '*Sieg Heil, Sieg Heil, Sieg Heil . . .*' Ian Brady's voice chanted as the tape segued into German marching music, then a *Goons* sketch, and Freddie Grisewood, presenter of the BBC's *Any Questions?* talking about the rise of Hitler. The last track hissed into play, and the silence in the office was rent apart by a little girl's scream.

'People wept when they heard that tape,' Fairley recalls quietly. 'I heard it a week or so later and I cannot describe how horrific it is. Not just the content, but the preparation that had gone into its creation. I wouldn't like to hear it again.'[5] Pat Clayton remembered, 'I heard the tape many, many times. And it was probably more horrendous the more you heard it . . . the more you could understand what was being said . . . It got worse. The horror of it.'[6] When Jock Carr returned home that night, his wife June was shocked to see him sit down and cry. Their own daughter was three years old at the time and Carr recalled, 'I thought about this little girl's voice on the tape and about how I would feel if that had been my daughter . . . Hindley was a willing partner in the atrocities that were taking place.'[7]

The search started early that day: Saturday, 16 October 1965. Young Scots Police Constable Robert Spiers was among the men moving in a slow line along the roadside at Hollin Brown Knoll. He recalls: 'All the forces had given in except for Mounsey. He said, "My boy's up there", and he got the bosses to organise a small group from Ashton division, about a dozen of us, and a few lads from Droylsden. I'd rolled up for the early shift but was told to go home, get some breakfast and get changed. About an hour later I was on the moor in a pair of wellies and a "submarine" sweater. We were armed with picks, shovels and rods. It was dry but cold. I was working not far off the road.'[8]

Probing around the protruding rocks, Spiers felt himself inexplicably drawn to the hill. He continues: 'I kept looking up there. It was the strangest thing. But I went on as I'd been told, prodding the peat, fumbling my way along. It was so quiet, grey and cold. All I could hear was the wind. It got to lunchtime. Mounsey and Mattin went back to Ashton. We went down to the Clarence for pie and chips and a pint. Then back in the Black Marias to the moor. The boss, Detective Sergeant Leslie Eckersley, said we'd give it till three. After that, the search was off.'

The light drizzle died out, the breeze dropped and a mist began to roll in from across the valley. 'We started wrapping up about half past two, bringing all the gear down,' Spiers recalls. 'I decided I was going over the hilltop before we left, so I climbed up and looked about. It was getting really cold by then and the mist had thickened. But I couldn't see anything, so I started heading back. And then I saw it: a sunken pool in the peat and what looked like a short length of white, withered stick. I peered at it, at this white thing pointing upward from the black water, and I found myself a proper stick and poked about in the hole. It was too dirty to see – just thick, peaty water that stank. But beneath the water, I could feel something.'

Not wanting to admit that he'd felt drawn to the hill, Spiers told his colleagues that he'd been for a pee and had found something over the rocks worth investigating. Detective Sergeant Leslie Eckersley was in charge; he looked quizzically at Spiers, who reached for a metal rod and went back up the hill. 'I wasn't going to leave it,' Spiers explains. 'There was something lying there, beneath the murky surface. The sky was getting darker now, and by this time everyone was shouting at me, but Eckersley started up the hill and they piled up after him, grumbling. I showed him the white withered thing poking out of the water and he nodded for it to be inspected.'

The 'white withered stick' was the mutilated forearm of a child, wasted to bare bone by the weather conditions on the moor. 'It was nothing like the media made out,' Spiers remembers. 'They described it as a beckoning arm: *find me, find me*. It was actually far more eerie than that. We drained the water by digging a trench, then began moving the peaty soil, bit by bit. I was getting a load of earache at this point from a certain Scots sergeant, who was telling me I was an idiot and we should have been on our way home, not standing there in the cold and dark next to this black mess. He said, "It's just a bloody sheep, that's all, just a bloody sheep." We stood there, arguing back and forth while the others kept carefully digging away, and then all at once I looked down and said, "Well, if it is a sheep it was wearing a dress." And he shut up straight away because there at our feet was a little tartan skirt and a pair of buckled shoes.'

The press presence on the moor had dwindled to a lone *News of the World* photographer. 'He came over to ask if we'd found something,' Spiers recalls. 'I told him no, I said it *was* a sheep. But he wouldn't leave and we had to give him the slip by heading down to Greenfield and splitting into two groups. Eckersley rang Mounsey from the phone box by the Clarence, then we hid in the van by some old gasworks and the photographer followed the other van back to Ashton.'

When they returned to the now pitch-black moor, where Mounsey and Mattin were waiting for them, Spiers remembers: 'Mounsey said, "Right. You, me, Mattin and nobody else. Take me back up to what you found. What did you see?" I told him I'd seen bones and a plaid skirt. And a skull. Once I'd explained everything to him, he got hold of the circus. They came up with lights, tents, pathologists and all that. I left at five, before they brought the body off the moor.'

Figures crowded onto the misty Knoll as canvas screens were placed around the grave and the huge, hissing arc lamps were switched on. The sodden peat was dug away to reveal the body of a small girl. Piled at her feet were her clothes: a blue coat, pink cardigan, tartan skirt, socks, shoes and the white plastic beads won at the fair by her brother. After Inspector Chaddock witnessed the remains, the pathologists – Professor Cyril Polson, head of forensic medicine at Leeds University, and his colleague, lecturer Dr Dave Gee – took over. Gee testified that the child lay in a shallow grave on her right side: 'The skeletal remains of the left arm were extended above the head, and the hand was missing. The right arm was beneath the body, the hand being near the right knee. Both legs were doubled up towards the abdomen, flexed at hips and knees. The head was in normal position. The body was naked. A number of articles of clothing were present in the soil near to the feet . . .'[9] Animals had caused two injuries to her chest and groin, and 'disappearance of the abdominal organs'.[10] Detective Constable Tom McVittie, part of Mounsey's team and husband of Pat Clayton, recalls, 'We could see that it was the body of a little girl, but where she had lain against the mud, that half of her was gone. It was destroyed, no features, nothing. But the other half had been perfectly preserved by the peat. Half of her face was intact.'[11]

Clive Entwistle was tipped off by the Granada newsroom and raced up to the moor: 'I blew the engine because I was going so fast. When I arrived, it was just like a scene from a Hitchcock film. It was pitch black, no moon. I parked the car and walked up to the Knoll. The arc lights were burning, there were shadowy figures standing about and there was thick, low cloud. The only other light came from the odd car passing by on the road below. I saw four officers lifting a tarpaulin sheet off the ground and start carrying it down to the van. I stood on the bumper of a black Maria, not realising that they were actually going to put the bundle into it. And as they came along, they drew back to lift it in and I saw the remains of Lesley Ann Downey. It was awful. Just awful.'[12]

Lesley's body was driven to the tiny mortuary at Uppermill. The screens were left on the Knoll, but the arc lamps were switched off. Two policemen were stationed on the moor for the night.

'I didn't know it was Lesley Ann Downey until I heard it on the news,' Robert Spiers recalls. 'I didn't sleep much that night. I couldn't get the sight of the hill and the protruding bone out of my mind. I couldn't forget the smell. Once we'd drained the hollow . . . Death has a smell, and on the moor it was distinct. You can't forget. That's why you'd see people lighting up cigarettes, just to try and get rid of the smell.'[13]

The post-mortem examination on Lesley's body, conducted by Dr Gee, Professor Polson and Home Office pathologist Dr Manning, casts doubt on Ian's accusation that Myra killed Lesley with a silk cord. Violent injury was ruled out, but Gee's examination of the body

Myra Hindley (back) as a teenager.
(ASSI84/430 National Archives, Kew)

Ian Brady (second from left) as a teenager.
(ASSI84/430 National Archives, Kew)

Ian Brady and Myra Hindley.
(ASSI84/430 National Archives, Kew)

Ian Brady, photographed by Myra Hindley.
(ASSI84/430 National Archives, Kew)

Maureen Hindley, Ian Brady and Myra Hindley. (ASSI84/430 National Archives, Kew)

Myra Hindley on the rocks at Hollin Brown Knoll. (ASSI84/430 National Archives, Kew)

Ian Brady on the rocks at Hollin Brown Knoll, May 1964. (ASSI84/430 National Archives, Kew)

Myra Hindley in the same spot on the same day. At that time, the grave of John Kilbride lay just beyond the van, while Pauline Reade was buried yards from where Myra Hindley stands. Seven months later, Lesley Ann Downey was buried in a shallow grave in the shadow of the rocks. (© Express Newspapers)

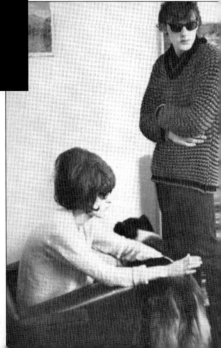

Patty Hodges with a ghostly Myra at 16 Wardle Brook Avenue, Hattersley. (ASSI84/430 National Archives, Kew)

David Smith, who witnessed the murder of Edward Evans and immediately informed the police, with his wife Maureen in their flat at 18 Underwood Court, Hattersley. (From David Marchbanks, *The Moor Murders*, London: Leslie Frewin Publishers, 1966)

Myra Hindley's mugshots, Hyde police station, October 1965.
(© Greater Manchester Police)

Ian Brady's mugshots, Hyde police station, October 1965.
(© Greater Manchester Police)

The discovery of Lesley Ann Downey's grave; Bob Spiers, the policeman who found her, is in the foreground. (© Mirrorpix)

Myra Hindley crouches with Puppet directly above the grave of John Kilbride, with the rocks of Hollin Brown Knoll visible on the horizon. Joe Mounsey used the photograph to find the boy his colleagues called 'Mounsey's Lad'.
(© Greater Manchester Police)

Mike Massheder's photograph of the same spot, taken minutes before the grave was uncovered. (© Greater Manchester Police)

The body of John Kilbride is carried from the moor. (© Mirrorpix)

The Trial of the Century: illegal photographs taken of Ian Brady and Myra Hindley in the dock at Chester Assizes, April–May 1966. Behind them (arrowed) sit Mary Hayley Bell and Emlyn Williams, both of whom intended to write books on the case. Williams' book, *Beyond Belief*, was published the following year. (Reprinted with kind permission of Horwitz Publications Pty Ltd from Anthony Syme, *Murder on the Moors*, Australia: Horwitz, 1966)

Myra Hindley in her graduation gown; she achieved a BA in Humanities in 1980. The photograph caused an uproar when it appeared in the press. (© Alamy)

'excluded strangulation by ligature [but not] other forms of mechanical asphyxia, notably smothering'.[14] None of that was any comfort to Lesley's mother, who arrived at Uppermill to identify her daughter's body. She had to endure the procedure alone; because he wasn't a blood relative, her partner Alan wasn't permitted into the mortuary. Inspector Chaddock was at her side as she identified Lesley's clothing and was 'led deeper into the place. There were more doors. There was a new smell to assault the senses, a smell of rubber and formaldehyde. The room was cold even for October . . . A green sheet covered the little body from stomach to feet. For some reason the sheet had been drawn up to hide the right-hand side of her torso and face . . . She looked beautiful. She seemed to be asleep. Her dark, curly hair spilled out over the protective sheet. I winced as I saw the swelling round her lips. It was as if she had bitten hard on them . . . Lesley lay so silently. She had always been a quiet girl, but this silent stillness was something I had not experienced before. This was the absolute and final stillness of death. My Lesley was dead. I knew it now. I knew it but could not accept it.'[15] Ann was not allowed to touch her daughter or take a lock of her hair. When she returned home, her house was under siege from the press.

'Anonymity is a luxury much undervalued until you lose it,' Ian Brady wrote years later.[16] On the morning of Monday, 18 October, he and Myra made separate remand appearances before magistrates. The driver of the van ferrying Myra to the courtroom didn't address a single word to her, but, as they neared the town, the accompanying prison officer advised her to put a scarf over her hair. Myra was puzzled by the suggestion, until they arrived at the back entrance of the court, where yelling crowds jostled the van and flashbulbs exploded in bursts of blinding light. She stooped to avoid the distorted faces at the glass, pushed her chin into the collar of her cherry-red coat and kept close to the guards as they shuffled her into the building.

Ian appeared first, in his grey suit, charged with Edward's murder. He said nothing as he was remanded for a further three days. Then Myra entered the dock, charged with 'well knowing' that Ian Brady had murdered Edward Evans on 6 October and had thereafter received, comforted, harboured, assisted and maintained him. She and Ian met in the canteen of Hyde police station immediately afterwards with solicitor Robert Fitzpatrick. After a brief discussion about legal visits and their defence, Fitzpatrick left them alone in the canteen. In her autobiography, Myra records that she told Ian she loved him and he replied that he loved her too.

In the afternoon, they were each taken in for questioning. At half past two, Benfield threw Lesley's shoes and socks and the soiled plastic beads on the desk in front of Ian. 'These garments were recovered from the moor near Greenfield late Saturday night,' he said. 'This clothing has been identified as Lesley Ann Downey's, whose body was recovered at the same time and place. I've reason to believe that the photographs of the naked girl which were found in your suitcase are of Lesley Ann Downey. Would you like to say anything about these photographs?'[17]

'Not at present.'

Benfield glanced at Talbot, then said, 'I'd like you now to listen to a tape recording. Two tapes were found in the blue suitcase belonging to you—'

'—I know the tape,' Ian interrupted, but the tape had already begun to play. He bowed his head and sat with his face averted until it finished.

'You say you know the tape,' Benfield said. 'The voices appear to be those of yourself and Myra and Lesley Ann Downey.'

Ian raised his head: 'She didn't give the name Downey. It was something else.'

Benfield and Talbot were taken aback by his flat response. Ian admitted he had photographed Lesley but claimed that she was brought to his house by two men who dropped her at Belle Vue afterwards, matching the press reports of parapsychologist Emile Croiset's 'vision' of Lesley. When the interview ended at five past eight, Ian refused to sign the deposition notes.

Benfield and Talbot moved on to Myra, questioning her in the presence of Margaret Campion and Detective Chief Inspector Clifford Haigh of Manchester Police.

Benfield threw the black wig on the table. 'What's this?'

Myra stared and said nothing.

He pushed the photographs Ian had taken of Lesley across the table. A muscle moved in Myra's jaw. Then she bent her head.

Benfield dropped the discoloured beads onto the table, together with Lesley's socks and shoes. Myra raised her hands and pressed them against her skull. She put her elbows on the edge of the table, holding a handkerchief to her face.

'This little girl was reported missing from home on Boxing Day last year and these photographs were taken on the same day.' Benfield paused to give Myra the opportunity to speak, but she went on staring down at her lap. 'Brady told us the girl was brought to your home by two men. One of them came into the house and remained downstairs while Brady took the photographs in your presence.'

'I'm saying nothing.'

'There's a tape recording, too. I believe the voices are those of yourself, Brady and Lesley Ann Downey.' He paused again. 'I'm going to play it.'[18]

He flicked the switch on the machine and the spools began to revolve.

Myra took her elbows off the table. She kept her head bowed and shut her eyes. A pulse throbbed rapidly in her throat. As the tape played on, she began to sob. When the music faded and the footsteps died away, Benfield turned off the machine.

'Did you hear that?' he asked.

She nodded, then whispered, 'I'm ashamed.'

But if the detectives were hoping Myra's tears marked a change in her demeanour, they were mistaken. DCI Haigh later testified that her weeping 'lasted for a very short time. And then she said again, "I'm saying nothing."'[19] The interview ended at quarter to ten. Myra told Peter Topping that she had been terrified of the police, whose methods 'left a lot to be desired . . . they frightened me to death'.[20] She claimed that her silence was a defence mechanism and that she 'took refuge behind the mists that swirled in my mind . . . my instinctive reaction to escape the unbearable reality was construed as arrogance and hard defiance'.[21] She used the same phrase in her parole plea, maintaining her ignorance of everything but the photographing of Lesley and the murder of Edward, insisting that during the police interrogation her mind was fogged with fear and shame, leading her to construct a front behind which she could hide. The veneer, she insisted, had enabled her to bear the condemnation that came her way during the trial, and in time became second nature to her: 'Such is how one part of my reputation evolved.'[22]

19

Joe was always convinced Brady and Hindley had taken photographs of where they'd buried their victims . . .

Margaret Mounsey, author interview, 2009

Hyde police station was transformed following the discovery of Lesley's body on the Knoll – the canteen became the press room and was inundated with inquiries – while over 200 journalists descended on the moor itself. A press conference was given daily, filmed by Granada – the first of its kind to be televised. The case was permanently in the headlines, and the *Manchester Evening News* frequently referred to the disappearances of John Kilbride, Keith Bennett, Pauline Reade and a 16-year-old girl named Susan Ormrod who had 'vanished 15 weeks earlier from her home in Gibbon Avenue, Woodhouse Park, Wythenshawe'.[1] But with nothing specific to link Myra and Ian to those cases, there was very little the police could do to gain information from them.

In the days following Lesley's discovery, searchers swarmed over Hollin Brown Knoll on Mounsey's instructions. He paced about the place, marking sites of interest on his map, wearing what was known as his 'Dunkirk look' beneath the tilted trilby. Several members of the public had come forward with sightings of Ian and Myra, ranging from Saddleworth to Thurlston Moor; some were highly detailed, others less so. Mounsey wanted each one investigated, with a view to linking them with the photographs found at Wardle Brook Avenue. Detective Constable Ray Gelder, a police photographer, took comparison shots on Hollin Brown Knoll and was satisfied that four of Ian's pictures were taken within fifty yards of Lesley's grave.

Mounsey gave a bundle of negatives to Mike Massheder and told him: 'Get more enlargements. Are we absolutely sure it's the same rock outcrop as in the album – there must be dozens like it. We're concentrating on this north side of the road. But could it be on the other side?'[2]

Massheder recalls, 'I was handed them in a big envelope and told, "There you are, get cracking on that." They were all 2¼ sq. negatives. When you printed them off, the problem was that they were square and the format of a photo is oblong, so the skyline and other details would be missing. There were other people working on the photos and they cropped bits off at will under the impression that the middle section was the point of interest. But they missed vital clues by doing that . . .'[3]

Massheder's enlargements were passed to the CID, who searched a spot Patty Hodges had pointed out below Hollin Brown Knoll on the other side of the road. Ordnance survey maps identified it as Sail Bark Moss. Massheder recalls: 'They were out by about a hundred yards. And by this point, the assistant chief constable, Harold Prescott, had begun to waver in his support for Joe's mission. Four days after Lesley was found, Prescott rang Joe and said, "What you doing buggering about on the moors? Come on, it's time you got back to work." The search took a large amount of manpower and a lot of money. It wasn't looking very productive.' In a press conference on 20 October, Benfield was similarly dour, telling reporters, 'I don't believe there are any more bodies on the moor.'[4]

Even as he spoke, searchers were spreading out across the moor in the bitter wind. Their method had been improved with the use of a new probing rod to which particles of earth stuck; it was the invention of local mill engineer Victor Hird, developed with the cooperation of the War Graves Commission years before. The *Manchester Evening News* ran a front-page article: 'Boys Take Police to Moors Spot', which described how Mounsey and another senior detective had been taken by two hikers to a spot two miles from Hollin Brown Knoll: 'A police car stopped at Shiny Brook, Wessenden Head . . .'[5] Mounsey and the detective followed the hikers down a small valley to a bluff beneath a rock face about a mile from the road. They returned some time later, with Mounsey 'perspiring and with shoes muddy after the long walk'. He told the press, 'The two hikers have given us certain information and we have been making a survey of the spot.'[6] The newspaper also mentioned Susan Ormrod and highlighted public interest in the case under the headline 'Hundreds Flock to Watch Moor Hunt': '. . . in small family cars and executive limousines . . . sensation seekers have rolled up in their hundreds . . . Some stayed for only a few minutes. Others parked their cars by the roadside and settled down with vacuum flasks and sandwiches.'[7] A policeman called it 'morbid curiosity at its worst. All we needed was a hotdog vendor.'[8]

Later that day, Tyrrell decided to have another stroll about the house on Wardle Brook Avenue. Home Office pathologist Dr Manning was there, and the curtains had been drawn against the crowds outside. Tyrrell ran his fingers along the bookshelf and pulled out a few books, fanning the pages of *Forever Amber*, *Goldfinger*, *Return to Peyton Place*, *Frankenstein* and *Fanny Hill*. He came to one book smaller than the rest and held it in his hands for a moment. A white prayer book, it was inscribed on the flyleaf: 'To Myra from Auntie Kath and Uncle Bert, 16 Nov 1958, souvenir of your first Holy Communion'. He flicked through the pages, and the spine gave a small creak. He lifted the book and saw that something had been pushed inside the spine: a tightly rolled slip of paper. He unfolded it carefully: counterfoil number 74843 – two suitcases, deposited at Manchester Central Station on 5 October 1965 for one shilling each. The disposal plan flashed before his eyes: P/B and TICK. *Prayer Book* and *Ticket*. He drew in his breath.[9]

Myra was charged with the murder of Lesley Ann Downey, at 9.40 a.m. on Thursday, 21 October 1965. Fifteen minutes later, Ian was charged with the same offence. At Hyde Magistrate's Court, the couple appeared separately to face the charges laid before them. Myra, in her cherry-red coat, passed Ian on the steps into the dock. Like Ian, she pleaded not guilty and was granted Legal Aid, then returned to Risley.

On the moor, in the watery sunshine, Mounsey strode up and down Sail Bark Moss with Detective Sergeant Clancy, holding a photograph that he hadn't been able to put out of his mind. It was the one taken by Ian of Myra and Puppet crouching on the grave of John Kilbride, although no one else knew the intent behind it or where it was shot. Mounsey had given it to Massheder, who recalls: 'The photograph had been cropped to print on normal paper, which meant that the skyline was gone. But I printed it again including the skyline, which was very faint. I used a common enough technique of two seconds' exposure for the foreground, then covered the foreground and burnt in the horizon for another four or five seconds. Overexposure brought up the background and I saw these jagged rocks . . .'[10] He showed it to Mounsey, who recognised the rocks from Hollin Brown Knoll.

That morning Mounsey and Clancy tried to pinpoint the spot where the photograph had been taken. 'I don't know how Joe did it,' Massheder recalls, 'but lo and behold, he lined it up. He called me and said, "Bring yourself and your camera up to Hollin Brown Knoll and don't let the bloody press follow you." So I knew there was something going on. I got to the moor and nonchalantly strolled down to him. He gave me the photograph and said, "Right, stand there and look at that." As soon as I saw it, I said, "It's got to be." I took a photograph to match the two scenes up and we knew we'd got it.'[11] Mounsey, Clancy and Massheder were joined by John Chaddock, who recalled that shortly before midday, 'I pushed my stick a short distance into the ground at that spot. Upon withdrawing my stick, there was a strong smell of putrefaction on the end of it. We removed the topsoil to a depth of about nine inches and uncovered a boy's left black shoe. Underneath the shoe I saw some socks and what appeared to be part of a heel.'[12]

Massheder remembers, 'You could smell the putrefaction straight away. I looked at Joe as John's black shoe was unearthed. The policeman in him was quietly euphoric. But I'll never forget the sight of him leaning over the grave, smoking his cigarette and the look on his face. It affected him very deeply. My reaction was on a professional level. As a photographer, it was an achievement and as a detective, my first thought was, "We've found him. John Kilbride. Bloody hell."'[13]

Detective Constable Ray Gelder arrived and Mounsey said, with some measure of satisfaction, 'One of you lads go back to headquarters and get on the phone to Harold Prescott. Tell him: we've found John Kilbride.'[14] Massheder, who was Gelder's superior, sent him down to make the call: 'Polson and Gee were sent for and a canvas screen put up to shield the grave. Of course, that alerted the press and soon a whole crowd of journalists were standing on the roadside.'[15] The police arrived in droves, too: Benfield, Prescott, Nimmo and Cunningham. At half past three, Gee and Polson began to excavate the body.

Ian had buried John 370 yards from Lesley, less than 18 inches below the surface of the soil, face down against the earth. The boy's feet were towards the road, his body twisted slightly to the left, right forearm under his chest and left arm straight down at his side. He was fully clothed except for his trousers and underpants, which were rolled down with the underpants knotted at the back, leaving the detectives in little doubt of the sexual cruelty that had been inflicted upon him prior to death. The young boy whose whistle and grin had made him a familiar figure about the streets where he lived was gone; buried close to a stream bed, his body was so severely decomposed that only bones, teeth and a tuft of brown hair remained. Only one of John's shoes was found with him; Ian had thrown the other on the fire at Bannock Street. About a dozen bones were missing from John's hands, but Polson was certain that his body was intact when he was buried.

Late afternoon brought a glorious sunset, bathing the moor in pale red light. The pathologists 'undercut' John's remains in order not to disturb what was left of him, digging down on both sides of the grave. Shortly before five o'clock, two stretcher-bearers arrived with a West Riding pathologist. Half an hour later, John's body on its earthen bed was gently lifted onto a stretcher and covered in plastic sheeting. As dusk fell, the scent of putrefaction kept even the most forceful journalists at bay as John's body was carried away from the moor to Uppermill mortuary. No one envied the policemen who were assigned to guard duty on the moor that night.

Margaret Mounsey recalls: 'When Joe came home that night, he was very quiet and terribly upset. In all the time I knew him, that was the most distressed I ever saw him from his job. He was usually very good at zonking out anywhere because he was always exhausted, as policemen generally are, but he didn't sleep that night. Our children were very little at the time and, of course, you immediately think how you would feel if it was one of your own.'[16]

The post-mortem at Uppermill mortuary was conducted by Polson and Gee, who couldn't establish a cause of death. Mounsey called on the Kilbride family at their home in Smallshaw Lane, carrying John's small black shoe. Danny recalls: 'My mum identified it straight away. I was there, I'd insisted that I wasn't going to be pushed into the kitchen with my brothers and sisters. We all knew then, what had happened to him. Although . . . I didn't know about the sexual abuse. That was kept from me until I was about 18. I was told that he'd been strangled, but no more than that. I can't say it was a relief that he'd been found. Everybody imagines it must have been. I know it meant we were able to have a burial and had somewhere to lay flowers for him. But I didn't want my brother to be found dead, and I'm positive my mum and dad felt the same way. Relief was the last thing any of us felt.'[17]

'I had to go up to the mortuary,' Shelia Kilbride remembered. 'They'd cleaned [the clothing] up as best they could, but . . . I'll never forget it, that. I'd altered his jacket, I'd altered his underwear – his father's underwear, because I wasn't rich, I couldn't always buy him new. I knew it was him. The buttons on the jacket, footballs, I'd stitched on myself. There was no doubt at all.'[18] There was nothing left of her son himself; only those few strands of hair, which she confirmed looked the same as John's hair.

Policewoman Pat Clayton was with her: 'She was upset. We were all upset. We just hung to her in the back of the car. It was terrible. It was her child that was being identified, but there was no child to identify. Only clothing. It was horrendous, that murder. And particularly when you see pictures of a woman, which you later learn is a picture of a woman standing over the grave of a child that's just been buried, dumped like a bag of rubbish on the moors. It's horrific . . .'[19] Mounsey helped arrange a special Mass to be said for John at St Christopher's Roman Catholic Church in Ashton on 24 October, led by Father William Kelly, who had known John well.

The police concentrated on building up their case against Myra and Ian. Detective Sergeant Roy Jarvis was given the task of proving that the headboard seen on the pornographic photographs of Lesley was the one in Myra's bedroom; he matched marks on the wall and the headboard with marks on the photographs, and experts were able to prove that Ian's old Ensign camera had been used for the photographs. The Fujica was the only one found in the house, but the owner of the shop where Myra had bought the camera using the Ensign as a deposit remembered her and was able to trace the Ensign to its new owner. The forensic team, led by Dr Manning, finished searching the house in Hattersley on 25 October and moved on to David Smith's old home at 13 Wiles Street, where they stripped wallpaper, removed floorboards and labelled samples with 'the grubby curtains pulled tightly across the windows all day'.[20] Traces of blood were discovered, but Dave explained to the police that the blood was his from when he cut his wrist while installing a new pane of glass in the window. The incident occurred two months after Pauline Reade vanished; it was Joan Reade who had bandaged the wound for him, as she confirmed to the police. From Wiles Street, detectives moved on to 18 Westmoreland Street, Ian's old home.[21] His mother was in Glasgow, staying with the Sloans; her husband Pat insisted she get away from the ever-present reporters and ghouls. She collapsed after learning her son and his girlfriend had murdered children; however, she returned to Manchester to stand by Ian. Detectives also traced Myra's first car to a farm on the outskirts of Nottingham, where it was being used to accommodate broody hens.

The moor search, having yielded the graves of Lesley and John, was allowed to continue, with Benfield back-pedalling and declaring that he was now certain there were more bodies to be found. Ian's landscape photos were distributed to rambling, cycling and hiking clubs in the hope that they might help. Police probed the Knoll and returned to Woodhead, where over 100 volunteers searched around the Snake Pass. The weather was starting to close in, with night frosts, thick mists and gale-force winds. At Wardle Brook Avenue, the police had turned over the garden but found nothing except large quantities of peat.

On 26 October, the *Gorton & Openshaw Reporter* covered the funeral of Lesley Ann Downey at Trinity Methodist Church in Ancoats, where she had been a member of the Girls' Guildry. A silent crowd of 2,000 people lined the rain-swept streets as Lesley's small coffin covered by a huge cross of red roses was carried into the church. The £100 reward offered by local people for Lesley's safe return went towards her funeral instead. The Reverend Harold Ford began the service with 'One of our flock is not with us today . . .'[22] He quoted from the Bible: 'Woe be unto you that cause one of these, my little ones, to stumble. It were better for that person that a millstone were hung around his neck and thrown in the depths of the sea.'[23] After Lesley's favourite hymns – 'The Lord Is My Shepherd' and 'There's a Friend for Little Children' – were sung by the 300-strong congregation, the coffin was borne to Southern Cemetery. A white headstone was erected soon afterwards bearing the inscription: 'A little flower lent, not given/To bud on Earth/And blossom in heaven'.

Two days later, on Thursday, 28 October, Myra and Ian were driven in separate vehicles to their remand hearing in Hyde. Myra was stunned by the volume and ferocity of the crowd that had gathered in the heavy, slanting rain on Water Street. The public gallery inside the court was packed with women, who had also brought their children along. Terence and Patrick Downey, Lesley's father and uncle, were among the few male faces. The *Gorton & Openshaw Reporter* announced: 'Brady, a bushy-haired man wearing a grey suit and a white open-necked shirt was brought into the dock first . . . After a few moments, Hindley was brought up, between Detective Policewoman Margaret Campion and Policewoman Hazel Simpson. Hindley, wearing a cherry red coat, appeared to have had her blonde hair freshly set.'[24] The public gallery rumbled with anger and shouts of 'Shame!' and 'Monsters!' Kenneth Pickup, the magistrates clerk, read out the charges in less than two minutes, but Terence and Patrick Downey had used the time to try to loosen a wooden floor block with their feet. Terence recalled, 'I would have smashed their heads in if only I could have snatched it up in time. But I daren't reach down. The police were watching everywhere.'[25] By the time he'd prised it free, the couple were being led out of the dock.

Outside, the crowd had swollen to twice its earlier number. Lesley's relatives thought they spotted Myra and Ian being driven away and made a dart for the car. Terence managed to wrench open the door before being roughly tackled by the police, who had used Margaret Campion and a young male colleague as decoys.[26] Myra and Ian were safely inside the red-brick building, waiting until the crowd had dispersed. Overhead they could hear the whine of a Canberra jet heading to the moor for aerial shots.

Thwarted by the police, the crowd turned on another couple in their midst. The *North Cheshire Herald* reported: 'A young couple who had been spectators in the public gallery were later chased across Hyde market by a group of shouting women. As cameramen's flashbulbs popped, the couple dodged in and out of the stalls. The girl, in high heels and a grey suit, had difficulty keeping up with the man accompanying her.'[27] Dave and Maureen, who was pregnant at the time, were targeted for public abuse.

At half past twelve, Ian arrived at Ashton-under-Lyne police station. Mounsey explained that the switch from Hyde to Ashton for the interviews that day was due to 'an irate crowd', but he had an unconventional plan in mind which he hoped would cause both Myra and Ian to crack.

Mounsey and Detective Inspector Leach began by questioning Ian about John Kilbride again, asking him to look at various landscape photographs, including ones taken at Hollin Brown Knoll. Ian denied they had been taken to indicate a grave. Mounsey slapped down the photographs of Myra and Puppet on Sail Bark Moss: 'This photograph was taken by you showing your girlfriend crouching over John Kilbride's grave. How can you possibly say you know nothing about his death?'[28]

'I've only got your word that it's a grave.'

'Do you imagine for one moment I would tell you lies about a matter as serious as this?'

'If my solicitor gets another photograph from somewhere . . .' Ian began, then broke off.

Mounsey frowned at him. 'What do you mean?'

Ian fell silent and the two detectives could get no further response from him. Mounsey left the room shortly after two o'clock, leaving Leach with Ian.

In another room at the station, Myra had been brought in from Risley to answer a barrage of questions from Tyrrell and Mattin. Tyrrell began by asking her about her childhood and her relationship with David Smith. Myra was sweating; she wore a mohair coat and had Ian's letters tucked into the waistband of her skirt, under her clothes.

Tyrrell wanted to know where she thought the photograph taken on John Kilbride's grave had been taken.

'I don't know,' Myra said.

'Who took it?'

'Ian, I suppose.'

'How old was the dog then?'

'He was only a pup,' Myra said. 'He's two years old in January. That will make him 20 months old now. It's my other dog's pup.'

'What are you looking at there on the photograph?' Tyrrell asked.

'The dog.'

'You're looking at the ground.'

Myra fell silent.

'According to the photograph,' Tyrrell said, 'it appears to have been snowing.'

'It looks like it,' she conceded.

'Who chose the place where you would kneel?'

'No one. We just took a photograph where we felt like it.'

'Did Ian take all the photographs of you?'

'Not all, but quite a lot.'

'Who else would take photographs of you?'

'Just depends who I was with.'

Tyrrell asked, 'Who else has taken a photograph of you on the moors?'

Myra stared at him. 'What do you mean?'

'Who else has taken a photograph of you on the moors other than Brady?'

'What do you mean?' she repeated.

'It's quite simple. Who else has taken a photograph of you on the moors?'

Myra said slowly, 'You say these are on the moors, do you?'

'Yes,' Tyrrell said. 'They were taken on Saddleworth Moor above Greenfield.'

'Possible.'

Tyrrell repeated, 'Who else took photographs of you on the moor?'

'Well, Smith could have taken this. I can't remember.'

Tyrrell placed a photograph taken by Ian near Lesley's grave next to the one of Myra with Puppet on the moor. 'The ground in the area of both photographs was dug up and immediately beneath where you are crouching the body of John Kilbride was found.'

Myra responded sarcastically, 'So there could be bodies all over where I've stood then.' Tyrrell continued the discussion about the photographs, despite Myra's constant parrying. At one point he told her: 'I suggest to you that the purpose of these photographs was to locate the graves again and satisfy yourselves that the ground hadn't been disturbed.'

'They have no significance for me,' she said categorically.

'Are you suggesting—'

Myra interrupted: 'I'm not suggesting anything. I can't remember when it was taken. We've taken photographs all over the place.'

At half past four, Tyrrell left and Myra was offered tea. Mattin wanted to discuss Maureen's statement, in which she said Myra had been a different person before she had met Ian. Myra bristled: 'I made all my own decisions. People go through several stages in their lives. After discussions, they change their minds. Ian never made me do anything I didn't want to do. All that about killing is bloody rubbish.' Then she asked, 'What time did Smith say he left our house that night?'

'I don't know,' Mattin said, 'but it was very late.'

'It was about 3 a.m. or just after,' Myra told him. 'And what time did he go to the police? They tell me it was sometime after he left our house. Well, obviously he was getting his story straight.'

'If you say he's responsible for these deaths, let's be knowing just what it is that you know.'

'I'm not saying any more, except that he brought her to the house with another man and Smith took her away with the other man,' Myra said, repeating Ian's story about Lesley Ann Downey. The interview continued until quarter past six. A plate of ham sandwiches and more tea were brought in for Myra.

Twenty minutes later, Mounsey began questioning Ian about John Kilbride again but could get nothing out of him and ended the interview at ten to seven, fuming at Ian's silence.

At twenty past seven, Tyrrell resumed his questioning of Myra, asking her about visits to Ashton market and what she knew about John Kilbride.[29] She interrupted him: 'Ian didn't kill Kilbride and I didn't kill Kilbride. I never set eyes on Kilbride before.'

'Since you and Brady have been together, has he, so far as you know, ever been out on his own?'

'Never,' Myra said. 'Wherever he has gone, I have gone.'

And that was the end of the interview. Myra sat back and refused to answer any further questions. She was taken to a waiting room and left with two police guards while detectives converged to discuss what would happen next. At one point, Myra and Ian were brought into an interview room together, where other detectives were able to view them without being seen. A microphone was plugged into a wall socket with a wire leading back into the viewing room. But neither of them said anything incriminating and they were separated again before the final stage of the strategy was put into place.

Mike Massheder recalls, 'The night before I'd been up till about two o'clock in the morning under Joe's instructions. "Make up a book of photographs," he said, "of all these moorland scenes, and in among them I want Lesley's grave and the photographs of Lesley's body being exhumed, I want John's grave and the photos of John's body being exhumed. Muddle them up, so we don't know what's coming when we turn the pages." Now, I frightened myself to bits making this book up. It shook me, and there's not a lot I haven't seen. But the idea was to present them with one of their landscape photos and ask, "Do you recognise this scene?", then on the next page present them with a grisly photograph of the victim in order to get Myra, especially, to break down. Even just a look of revulsion would have been something.'[30]

At ten to eight, Myra was taken into the interview room, where Massheder watched her covertly from behind a glass. Mounsey entered the room with Detective Inspector Leach and dropped the book of photographs on the desk. He began turning the pages – one, then another and another, presenting her with the terrible images of the dead children.

Myra jerked her head away and said, 'I don't want to see any more.'[31] Mounsey turned another page and pushed the book further towards her.

Myra shouted, 'Take them away! I'm not looking at them.'

Mounsey stepped back from the desk and began pacing up and down the room, chanting, 'Suffer the little children to come unto me . . .'

Myra bent her head, but she did not break down. She set her mouth in a firm line and said nothing. At ten past eight, Mounsey left the room, exhausted.

'It didn't work,' Massheder admits. 'They tried the same thing on Ian, but it was just a complete waste of time. I was in the viewing room, minding the tape recorder. It wasn't really cricket to set up a stunt like that, but we were desperate. They were just blank, the pair of them. Not willing to answer anything, not willing to engage in any way. Blank. Was it self-protection or arrogance? Arrogance certainly with Brady. With Myra . . . I don't know. She came across as very cold and heartless.'[32]

Myra had withstood the interrogation better than her lover. The police had the photograph of her stooping over John Kilbride's grave but couldn't prove that she knew the boy was buried there; they knew she had hired a car for the day of his abduction but couldn't prove where she had driven it; the police had the tape recording, but that didn't prove she was present at Lesley's murder; and she was present when Edward Evans was killed but did not participate in his death.[33] Ian, on the other hand, had told police that he'd taken the photograph of Myra on John Kilbride's grave knowingly; he confessed to taking the photographs of Lesley and knowing where she was buried; he admitted hitting Edward with the axe; he conceded to having written the found disposal plan; and he agreed he had discussed burying bodies on the moor with David Smith. Despite his years of careful study and his obsession with eliminating all signs of 'forensic', Ian had failed. The police were able to draw more from him than from Myra.

Pat Clayton, who spent endless hours with Myra during the investigation, recalled: 'Myra was a hard, arrogant woman. She had no compassion for children, she had nothing. She would not say anything . . . During the interview someone put on the table in the interview room a poster of John Kilbride. And her lunch was brought in, on a tray . . . That didn't have any effect on Myra. She was just an emotionless female.'[34] Pat's husband, Tom McVittie, remembers: 'Pat hated Hindley. The case really upset her, even though she was very experienced and one of the first detective policewomen in Lancashire county. When she came home at night after interviewing Hindley, she would cry with rage and frustration. She was full of anger, and pity for the families. She'd say, "That bitch. Sitting there and not saying a word. The *bitch*." It affected Pat very deeply.'[35]

On 29 October, Nellie, Bert and Kath visited Myra at the police station. The two women wept and pleaded, while Bert urged her to make a clean breast of everything. Myra recalled that she almost broke down, but glimpsed Dave Smith being escorted from the station and her resolve was strengthened anew.

The *Gorton & Openshaw Reporter* ran a front-page article about RAF jets sweeping the moor using infrared equipment to search for graves. Benfield told a press conference that he wasn't investigating black magic 'practices'; the search focused on a gully running at an angle away from the road, towards John's grave. The following day, however, gale-force winds and heavy rain swept over the moor, bringing the search to a halt. The side of the road where John had lain was only partially investigated, and though the search was resumed, from then on it was sporadic. Police concentrated their inquiries in Hattersley, where over 5,000 households completed a questionnaire about suspicious activities in the area.

On 31 October, at twenty to ten in the morning, Myra was cautioned and charged with the murder of Lesley Ann Downey. She responded, 'It's not true.'[36] Fifteen minutes later, Ian was charged with the same offence and replied, 'Not guilty.'[37] In a letter written many years later, Myra recalled, 'When Brady and I were on remand in Risley, we had weekly visits from our solicitor, who always gave us around 15 minutes to speak together privately. He also did this when we appeared in Hyde court weekly to be remanded for another week. We had our solicitor's visits in the police canteen and, again, he would sit as far away as possible from us, pretending to sift through some paperwork.'[38] They wrote to each other regularly, in letters that displayed macabre humour. In one letter to Ian, Myra wrote, 'Hope your cold's disappeared – if it has, get out your spade, Benfield!'[39]

John Kilbride's funeral was held on 1 November 1965. The service was conducted at St Christopher's Church, where St Damian's school choir sang from the gallery. Crowds lined the streets, as they had for Lesley's funeral. Danny Kilbride remembers: 'You couldn't move in the streets for people. That *was* a comfort, to see that people wanted to pay their respects and show they were sorry for what had happened. But I remember having to stand outside the headmaster's office for a week afterwards because I'd battered a lad who laughed at me and called me a sissy because he'd seen me crying at the funeral. So I went for him. I wouldn't tell the headmaster why and this lad wouldn't either. We were both stood outside the headmaster's office for a week until they brought the priest to me. I told him and he explained the situation to the headmaster. My punishment stopped then.'[40] John was buried at Hurst cemetery, where the inscription on his headstone reads simply: 'Kilbride/In memory of John, eldest child of Shelia and Patrick. Missing: November 1963. Buried: November 1965. Aged 12 years. At rest with God.'

During the ongoing police investigation, Margaret Campion collected Puppet from where he was being kept at the RSPCA kennels and took him to vet James Gourley in order to confirm the dog's age, thereby establishing when the photograph of Puppet with Myra on John's grave was taken. At the trial, Campion admitted she hadn't obtained permission from Myra but had acted on Benfield's orders. Gourley administered the anaesthetic on Puppet and X-rayed the dog's teeth, estimating him to be between eighteen months and three years old. When he tried to revive Puppet following the examination, however, the dog remained still. For 45 minutes, Gourley persisted in trying to rouse Puppet but without success; he later discovered that the dog suffered from a serious illness that had caused his heart to fail during the anaesthetic.

At the trial, Ian raised the subject of Mounsey allegedly taunting him that they would destroy Puppet to see how it felt for his owners to lose something they loved. Ian told the court: 'And [Puppet] was destroyed one week later.'[41] The Attorney General rebuked him sternly: 'It is a wicked suggestion that the dog was deliberately put to death, Brady, and you know it.' Ian replied mildly, 'It's a funny coincidence.'[42] Myra was hysterical when she was given the news. She screamed out one word at the police who had accidentally killed Puppet: 'Murderers!'

20

Dear Mam, as you know, the trial begins three weeks on Tuesday … Could you bring me a bottle of make-up, it's Pond's Angel Face, shade Golden Rose. If you can't get Golden Rose, Tawny will do.

> Myra Hindley, letter to her mother,
> 27 March 1966

When Myra and Ian appeared for their remand hearing in Hyde on 4 November 1965, competition for seats in the public gallery was fierce. Security barriers and extra police were drafted in to deal with an unprecedented outpouring of public condemnation. Those who had known Myra in Gorton were stunned by her crimes. Anne Murdoch remembers: 'I never liked her sense of superiority or how, if she took a dislike to someone, they'd know it. But it was still a terrible shock when the news came out. To think I'd gone to school with her and played games with her … I only saw her with Ian once, and he was walking along behind while she marched ahead. I always thought, afterwards, that she must have dominated him, not the other way around. It was awful in Gorton – the press wouldn't leave us alone. I used to dash home from the shops in case one of them accosted me.'[1] Allan Grafton echoes Anne: 'We just couldn't believe it. She went from the girl who helped out at football to a sadist who buried kids on the moor. We'd all grown up together, so it was just an overwhelming shock.'[2]

In her first letter to Nellie after being arrested, Myra asked, 'If you could send to the station a decent pair of high heels, I'd feel a lot better than I do in these mules. I feel like a tramp in your clothes (only because they don't fit me properly).'[3] Grieving for her dog – 'I feel as though my heart's been torn to pieces. I don't think anything else could harm me more than this has. The only consolation is that some moron might have got hold of Puppet and hurt him' – she asked for Puppet's nametag to be kept for her, then added: 'This letter will probably be censored. If you should write at all, <u>do not mention anything regarding the cases</u>.'[4]

During her meetings with Ian, they remarked on each other's appearance; she thought he looked gorgeous, while he teased her about her prison clothes. They discussed the books they borrowed from the library; Myra complained about the prevalence of religious books to Risley's governor, who explained that many prisoners found them a comfort. She plucked Spike Milligan's *Puckoon* and Joseph Heller's *Catch-22* from the shelves, instinctively knowing they would be suitable topics to include in her letters to Ian.

On Wednesday, 10 November, the moor was searched for the last time. Benfield made inquiries about excavating Hollin Brown Knoll but was told it would entail diverting the gas supply at a cost of £10 million. Ian Fairley recalls, 'Why did it stop in 1966? Money. That's what it came down to. I couldn't come to terms with the search being stopped when we were sure there were other victims up there. I call it dereliction of duty. I blame Benfield and the Chief Constable, Henry Watson. The men who made the most meaningful contribution were Joe Mounsey, Alex Carr and Mike Massheder, but they received no recognition. Once the case came to trial, dates were fudged to make everything easier for the jury to understand, such as implying that the ticket stub was found before the suitcases. It disgusted me, and I know it disgusted Alex Carr, too.'[5]

Margaret Mounsey recalls: 'Joe didn't want the search to end. He felt sure that they would find the other missing children. He never forgot – he often went up to the moors, even many years later, just to stand at the roadside. I've been with him. We'd go and he'd say quietly, "This is it." He knew – we *all* knew – that there were other victims up there. Unfound.'[6]

On Monday, 6 December 1965, committal proceedings against Myra Hindley and Ian Brady opened at Hyde Magistrate's Court.[7] For a fortnight, the entire country was gripped by the case. The world's media converged on the town, packing out the hotels, cafes and bars. The Queen's Hotel, close to the police station, became a hive of journalistic activity, with reporters downing pints and wolfing down the hotpots cooked by the proprietor, Nellie Bebbington, and her daughter, Derry. The magistrates – former Mayoress Mrs Dorothy Adamson, Harry Taylor and Sam Redfern – briefly became celebrities; Mrs Adamson's fondness for quirky headwear was pored over in the press.

Myra's hair was bleached and set, her make-up immaculate. She wore a monochrome flecked suit and yellow blouse, and sat with Ian, jotting down observations in a ring-bound notepad or laughing quietly over their doodles of Mrs Adamson and her natty little hat. Travelling back to Risley on the first day, she and Ian sat together, talking about dogs. Their conversation was overheard by an accompanying policeman. 'When you're driving, you must always run over a dog to avoid running over an individual,' Ian said, to which Myra responded, 'Oh, I couldn't do that.'[8]

The prosecution presented their case the following day. On the journey back to Risley, Ian told Myra that he might kill himself. She recalled: 'To Ian, [prison] symbolised a living death: something he told me he couldn't endure. He had a jar of jam brought in with other things on a visit from his mother and he intended killing himself with the glass. I begged him not to, not to leave me, he was all I had lived for. He said I couldn't be found guilty if I went on trial without him, that his influence would pall and I'd be able to rebuild my life. But he said he would wait and see what happened at the trial. I felt then that he needed me even more than I'd ever needed him . . .'[9]

On 8 December, David Smith took the stand, giving his evidence in a voice so low and halting that microphones were brought in. His evidence was crucial to the prosecution; although there were widespread rumblings of discontent that he had been granted immunity in exchange for his cooperation, his evidence was the linchpin. As he stepped down from the dock, Ian caught his eye and nodded and smiled at him.

Maureen took the stand, noticeably pregnant. She declined an offer to be seated and spoke with more assurance than her husband. Afterwards Myra wrote to her mother, who had disowned her younger daughter for 'betraying' the family: 'Did you read the lies Maureen told in court, about me hating babies and children? She wouldn't look at me in the dock, Mam. She couldn't. She kept her face turned away.'[10] In a reference to rumours circulating that David Smith had been offered cash by the press in return for his story, Myra wrote bitterly, 'I noticed she was wearing a new coat and boots, and that Smith had a new watch on and a new overcoat and suit. I suppose he's had an advance on his dirt money.'[11]

On 10 December, Edith and John Evans were photographed entering the court. Edward's mother, her face a study in bewildered sorrow, was described in a local newspaper as 'a small, frail woman dressed completely in black, and wearing glasses'.[12] Edward's 15-year-old brother, Allan, was photographed outside the family home in Ardwick, crying. After the evidence was heard in relation to Edward's murder, the photographs discovered at Wardle Brook Avenue were discussed. Myra wrote to her mother, imagining that the slides, negatives and tartan album had been returned, 'Keep all the photos for us, <u>for reasons</u>, the ones of dogs, scenery, etc.'[13] On 13 December, Myra's solicitors, Bostock, Yates & Connell, applied on her behalf for a hairdressing appointment because 'her dark roots are becoming very obvious. This fact has been the subject of press comment, which is naturally a source of irritation to our client.'[14] The request was refused.

The following day, Lesley Ann Downey's mother took the stand. Dressed in black with a chiffon scarf over her hair, she stumbled over her words as she described the events of Boxing Day 1964, then clutched the sides of the witness box as her voice spiralled: 'I'll kill you, I'll kill you!'[15] She screamed at Myra: 'She can sit staring at me and she took a little baby's life, the beast.'[16] Detective Constable Frank Fitchett, sitting just below the witness box, spun round and grabbed the water carafe just as Ann's hands reached out for it. She carried on screaming at Myra, calling her a tramp, then broke down, sobbing. Myra recalled that she had whispered to Ian that she wasn't a tramp; he had squeezed her hand and reassured her, 'No, I know you're not.'[17] The policeman who'd found Lesley's body, Robert Spiers, was there that day: 'It was the first time I saw Brady and Hindley and they were truly faces of evil. All the goody-two-shoes who complained later that the mugshot of Myra was the only photo ever shown, it was nonsense. That's how she looked.'[18]

The evidence about Lesley's murder continued the following day. The court was emptied of press and public as the tape recording of Lesley's last moments was played. Rain beat against the long windows as Ian's voice snapped through the silence: '*This is track four*

. . .' Lesley's mother had already listened to part of the tape and had looked at two of the pornographic photographs in order to identify her daughter. The quality of the tape recording had been improved by BBC Manchester technician John Weekes so that every sound was appallingly clear.

The prosecution case then turned to John Kilbride. The jacket he had worn on the day of his murder was unwrapped from its polythene cover and shown to the court. The stench of putrefaction clung to it. Ian had tried to pin John's murder and Lesley's abduction on David Smith and another man, increasing public suspicion against Myra's brother-in-law.

On 16 December, the weather was so atrocious that Myra and Ian spent the night in separate cells below the courtroom. Myra sat huddled under a blanket, shivering and unable to sleep. When she asked for her make-up bag the next morning, the guard ignored her, and she was given a cup of tea laced with salt, not sugar. She lodged a complaint with the station commander. Later, she wrote to her mother, 'Nothing matters in the world as long as Ian is all right. If you'd drop a short note and a box of Maltesers, I'd be glad. He says he doesn't want anything sending in, even from his mam, but I know he'll be glad you sent them.'[19]

The committal proceedings came to an end on Monday, 20 December 1965. The couple pleaded not guilty to all charges and headed back to Risley. The *Gorton & Openshaw Reporter* announced that they were committed in custody awaiting a decision on 11 January to decide where, and when, the trial should take place.

Shortly before Christmas, Robert Fitzpatrick visited Myra and Ian in Risley, bringing them a volume of poetry each: Wordsworth for Myra and Ovid for Ian. During their few minutes alone together, Ian surreptitiously handed Myra a notebook. In her cell, she read its coded stories of sexual cruelty towards children. Using the key Ian had provided, she deciphered the stories and camouflaged them as poems in an exercise book. She also invented similar stories of her own, which she confessed afterwards were written as 'stimulation'.[20]

Many years later, she admitted the stories spilled over into their correspondence: 'Over the seven months we were on remand, Brady compiled a notebook in which he wrote dozens of messages that I was to respond to in a code he'd devised. If the date on which either of us wrote a letter to each other was underlined, it meant there was a message in the letter.'[21] The code began six lines into the letter, taking the seventh and eighth words as the start of the message. There was no code in the next line, but the seventh and eighth words of the following line continued the message. Myra explained: 'It carried on in this way every other line until the message was over [and] was written in such a way as to make complete sense as a normal letter to whoever read it – the censor, etc. – whilst containing [secret] messages.'[22] She gave an example of one message she had sent Ian before the trial (the coded words are in italics):

> I've been thinking for a while, *why don't* you ask if you can go/to church on Sundays so we can at least see each other there?/*You get* someone to help with this./See the Governor if necessary. There are places in the chapel for people/ in your situation Ian, so ask *someone to* look into it for you. There's/ someone here who goes with two officers. She's in here for killing her own/children and also for attempting to *throw acid* in her boyfriend's face. No one/likes her; she's on Rule 43, of course. Re; your mention of facial expressions in your last letter, I too, wish/I could have seen the one *on Brett*. His face was a picture when you stared him out!

The decoded message read: 'Why don't you get someone to throw acid on Brett?' Myra disclosed: 'Brett was at that time the youngest son, aged about four or six, of Ann West. This was in the papers at the time of Lesley Ann's disappearance; details of the family as part of the reporting of the disappearance. That's not the whole message, but those ten words were the crux, so to speak . . .'[23] Through the letters, detectives discovered that Myra and Ian hoped to marry; it was their only hope of seeing each other if they were sent to prison. Myra later claimed that Ian had proposed because a wife couldn't be forced to testify against her husband, but she filled in the necessary application forms for the Home Office nonetheless. Permission was refused.

The couple read avidly while on remand, sharing quotations with each other. Myra copied out bits of narrative: 'To you, my alter ego, what is there left to say? The charm of our minds is beyond the token of tongues . . .'[24] and poetry by Housman, Tennyson, Wordsworth, 'AC' Clough (Arthur Hughes Clough), Kahlil Gibran and Charlotte Mew. She invoked the spirit of the moor through Wordsworth ('Do I behold these steep and lofty cliffs,/That on a wild and secluded scene impress/Thoughts of more deep seclusion; and connect/The landscape with the quiet of the sky') and used Shakespeare to instil strength ('I am determined to prove a villain,/And hate the idle pleasures of these days').[25] Ian quoted from *King Lear*: 'I grow, I prosper:/Now, gods, stand up for bastards.'[26] They both loved *Richard III*; Ian later opened his own book with a quotation from it: 'Let us to it pell-mell; if not to Heaven,/then hand in hand to Hell!'[27]

In a pre-Christmas letter to her mother, Myra asked her to take care of whatever had been left at Wardle Brook Avenue and to have items moved to Peggy Brady's flat for safekeeping. Fitzpatrick attempted to have their 'non-exhibit' property, including the tartan album, returned. Myra and Ian were able to look through all their photographs and pick out those they particularly wanted to keep. They indicated a handful and Fitzpatrick promised to do his best to have the photographs returned to them.

Myra and Ian were able to spend Christmas Eve together. She described it in a letter to her mother: 'Mrs Brady brought a meal in. We had half a chicken each, turkey sandwiches, half a bottle of Sandiman's port wine, chocolate biscuits and Swiss rolls. I really enjoyed it, it was almost like being free again. My counsel, Mr Curtis, has written here asking permission to have my hair bleached because the dark roots are very much in evidence. But permission has been refused, so I'll appear at the trial with streaky, lifeless hair. I can't even have it trimmed or thinned. It's a constant source of irritation.'[28]

They were each seen frequently by Dr Neustatter, a forensic psychiatrist whose notes on Ian were summarised by William Mars-Jones QC: 'Brady had been extremely cagey and would give nothing away during a three-hour interview. Perhaps the most interesting feature had been his negative attitude. Brady had not been particularly suave, but he chatted away . . . Brady had admitted that he was illegitimate; this had seemed to cause him some embarrassment in that he had been embarrassed about giving the names of his parents. Asked whether he had any inferiority feelings, Brady said that everyone had them. Anything he felt afraid of doing, he said, made him feel inferior. If you were short-changed on a bus, even by only 4d, and you did not make a fuss about it, you felt weak . . . possibly Brady had the slight irrelevance that one found in a schizophrenic . . . The long letters he had written to Myra Hindley showed that in fact there was no difficulty in his thought processes normally . . . abnormality of mind could not be assumed.'[29] Myra quite liked Neustatter until he commented how eloquent and well read she was. 'What, for a murderess?' she retorted, adding, 'I don't like being taken for a working-class idiot.'[30] She refused to submit to an EEG to pick up any abnormalities in the brain.

Myra had no contact with Maureen or her father during her time on remand, but remained close – protesting her innocence – to her mother, aunts and Gran. Kath attempted to revive her interest in religion, but Myra told her mother: 'I suppose she means well, but it means nothing to me.'[31] Nana Hindley visited her in Risley; much later, when they met again, Myra asked, 'Do you remember how we both thought I'd be out on probation in no time?'[32] Before the trial, May Hill came forward to tell the police about the letter Myra had written about her fear of Ian. When the neighbours found out, a hate campaign was mounted against May until she withdrew her statement. The vitriol aimed at Dave and Maureen was ferocious. Dave's temper snapped in March 1966, when he was on the balcony of a friend's house in Hattersley and a group of teenagers goaded him for being 'the third Moors Murderer'. One of the lads yelled, 'You're no bleedin' good without that axe, Smith', and Dave pelted down the stairwell and attacked him with a chain.[33] Police, having witnessed the harassment he and Maureen had faced without respite, took no action.

At the end of March, Myra's request to have her hair bleached was granted. She had her make-up sent in from her mother and borrowed a pair of size five stilettos from her, although her own feet were a seven. She set out everything in her cell: grey suit with dark piping, one yellow blouse and one blue. Then she sat down to write to her mother before the event every newspaper had dubbed the 'Trial of the Century': 'Dear Mam, This is just a few lines before the "off" in case I don't have any time during the week to drop you a line. I had my hair done on Saturday. It looks so nice that I'm sorry that I'm all dressed up and nowhere to go (joke).'[34]

21

Put her down.

Mr Justice Fenton Atkinson, sentencing
at the 'Moors trial', 6 May 1966

'We are in danger of creating an Affectless Society, in which nobody cares for anyone but himself, or for anything but instant self-gratification. We demand sex without love, violence for "kicks". We are encouraging the blunting of sensibility: and this, let us remember, was not the way to an Earthly Paradise, but the way to Auschwitz. When the Nazis took on the government of Poland, they flooded the Polish bookstalls with pornography . . .'[1]

Of the many volumes written about the Moors case, Pamela Hansford Johnson's *On Iniquity* (1967) may not have aged well, but it tapped succinctly into one of the much-discussed issues arising from the trial. Johnson covered the trial for the *Daily Telegraph* and out of that came her book, in which she investigated the correlation between the murders and the reading matter of the two accused. Simultaneously condemning pornography and the British Realist Theatre of Shelagh Delaney, Brendan Behan and Harold Pinter, she speculated that certain types of literature should not be accessible to 'minds educationally and emotionally unprepared'.[2] Her argument echoed the *Lady Chatterley* trial of 1960, when prosecuting counsel Mervyn Griffith-Jones asked the jury, 'Is this a book you would want your wife or servants to read?' The influence of literature on malleable minds had also been raised by Richard Hoggart. In *The Uses of Literacy* (1957), he posited the theory that 'sex-and-violence' novels and films 'give the working classes cheap, sensationalist entertainment, enervating, dulling and eventually destroying their sense of taste'.[3]

The idea that specific books could prove damaging to the newly affluent young – even contributing to rising crime rates – was given serious consideration. As Britain moved forward into a very different age, the press picked up on the collective fear that society as a whole was becoming more violent in the aftermath of the Second World War. Crime rates *were* escalating: from 6,000 major incidents in 1955 to 12,000 in 1960, and four years after the Moors trial that figure had leapt to 21,000. Analysing the reasons behind the increase, one commentator lists the 'wider anxieties [of] the decline of traditional authority, the instability of the family, the break-up of settled communities, the uneasiness of class identities . . . the impact of affluence, education and mobility on traditional customs and communities'.[4] At a time when so many advances were being made, some of which seemed to threaten the future of mankind, crime became a natural focus of anxiety, and none more so than the 'beyond belief' crimes of the Moors Murderers.[5]

The issue of literature's pernicious influence was raised immediately at the trial when, before the jury was sworn in, Mr Justice Fenton Atkinson asked whether the books read by Myra and Ian might be used as evidence. The Attorney General replied that they were evidence only insofar that Brady had told David Smith to return the books before Edward Evans's murder; he added that he intended to read aloud an extract from de Sade, to which Fenton Atkinson responded, 'You are not asking the jury to read *Justine*?' The Attorney General replied dryly, 'No, my Lord, I have suffered the agony of having to read that myself.'[6] But inevitably, just as the *Chatterley* trial sent sales of D.H. Lawrence's novel soaring, so the Moors trial provoked a surge of interest in de Sade; when William Mars-Jones QC and a colleague arrived afterwards at Brompton Air Terminal in London, they were amazed to find Marquis de Sade novels prominently on sale.

The trial opened on Tuesday, 19 April 1966 at Chester Assizes. The oak-panelled Castle Courtroom had been adapted to accommodate the particular needs of such a highly charged case under the glare of the media spotlight. Microphones were fitted in the witness box, carpet had been laid to reduce noise and press rooms were set up with telephones installed for those reporters who couldn't get a seat in court. Otherwise, as Pamela Hansford Johnson commented, 'it is clean, bright, has been newly decorated. Canopy and curtains of red velvet, braided with gold, frame the judge's seat. The benches of the public auditorium and of the Distinguished Visitors' gallery are upholstered in scarlet leather. Above the galleries are royal portraits . . . the dock has been shut in, on three sides, with splinter-proof glass.'[7] The other noticeable security feature was the police presence: 300 officers had been drafted in.

One hundred and fifty journalists arrived in Chester, bringing with them camera crews and technicians who largely ignored the Queen when she visited the races. The BBC originally intended to cover the trial, having accumulated more than 25,000 feet of filmed interviews, but on the second day of the hearing it was decided that the details of the case were too shocking for television – only the verdicts were given airtime. A number of authors turned up, including Mary Hayley Bell, the wife of actor John Mills, and Emlyn Williams, who had begun his book about the case at the end of 1965. In the courtyard, those wishing to enter the public gallery were carefully screened. Only 60 seats were available, and the queue of mostly women forming at dawn each day was never less than hundreds-strong. They were greeted by a downpour on the first day, followed later by a freak heatwave. The courtroom remained cool, but the odour of damp plastic mackintoshes hung about the wood-panelled walls.

The judge, Mr Justice Fenton Atkinson, presided over the court coolly and unobtrusively. Myra's solicitor, Manchester-born Godfrey Heilpern QC, discovered on the first day of the trial that his sister-in-law, the manageress of a Salford dress shop, had been murdered (her death was not related to the case); in his absence, Philip Curtis took over. Ian was represented by Emlyn Hoosen QC, Liberal MP for Montgomeryshire. Sir Frederick Elwyn Jones QC, appointed Attorney General two years earlier, led the case against Myra and Ian; he had been a prosecution counsel at the Nuremberg War Trials.[8] His presence underlined the enormity of the case, since the Attorney General only prosecutes in the most serious murder cases and those involving national security. His occasional absences (due to the opening of Parliament and Cabinet discussions on the Rhodesia crisis) were filled by William Mars-Jones QC.

Before the trial began, despite the submission by the defence counsels, Fenton Atkinson decided that the two accused should be tried together. Ian had no doubt that he was facing a lengthy prison sentence but hoped to achieve an acquittal for Myra. She was now charged with all three murders, together with the secondary charge of harbouring Ian after the murder of John Kilbride. 'I wanted to help the girl,' Ian said in retrospect. 'All my evidence was to get her off . . . I was reinforcing some things by saying, "Yes, that's right", and on other things I was going out of my way to be destructive with the prosecution.'[9] He clarified: 'I also told her to adopt a distancing strategy when she went into the witness box, admitting to minor crimes whilst denying major.'[10]

The couple arrived each day from Risley, sitting in separate compartments in the back of the van. As they entered court that first day, every member of the press and public craned their necks to stare. Myra was the one whom the women queuing for seats in the public gallery wanted 'to get their hands on' – *she* was the focus of national disbelief, hatred and curiosity, and there was a media scrum each day to snap her as she arrived and left Chester. How she looked became an obsession; for many, the concept of evil had put on a face and walked into a courtroom. Her freshly bleached blonde hair was tinted lilac and she wore her make-up like a mask. She dressed in a neat suit that first day, with a blue blouse. Pamela Hansford Johnson described her: 'Hair styled into a huge puff-ball, with a fringe across her brows . . . the lines of this porcelained face are extraordinary. Brows, eyes, mouth are all quite straight, precisely parallel. The fine nose is straight too, except for a very faint downward turn at the tip, just as the chin turns very faintly upward. She will have a nutcracker face one day.'[11] Ian, in his smart grey suit, white shirt and blue tie, looked 'like a cross between Joseph Goebbels and a bird', but Myra resembled Clytemnestra or 'one of Fuseli's nightmare women', with the authority one expected to find 'in a woman guard of a concentration camp'.[12]

There exist two photographs of Myra and Ian, taken illegally at the trial, shot from the bench where the dignitaries sat. Clive Entwistle recalls: 'Allegedly, it was a *Paris Match* photographer who managed it. He flew into an airstrip near Chester, was chauffeur-driven to town, slipped into court with a James Bond-type camera that clicked sideways, but was spotted by a court usher who started beckoning security, so dashed from the room, back to the waiting car, and off to the airstrip back to France.'[13]

In response to the charges read out to them, Myra and Ian answered 'Not guilty' to each one. As the jury were sworn in, their solicitors objected to four women, resulting in a men-only jury. Proceedings were opened by the Attorney General, who outlined the crimes and their background. He warned those in court that they would have to listen to a harrowing tape recording and examine distressing photographs. After completing his speech, he presented the photographs Ian had taken of Lesley. Among the victims' relatives who didn't attend the trial was Winnie Johnson: 'My mother wouldn't let me, she knew it would be too much for me. We had come so close to solving Keith's death, but we still didn't know where his body was. I couldn't have faced seeing the killers in the flesh.'[14] John Kilbride's parents did not attend either, Danny recalls: 'They stayed away, but I wanted to go. My dad wouldn't let me though, no matter how hard I pleaded. I was an old 13, but I had to be. I was getting a lot of tormenting – "You'll end up on the moors like your brother" – all that. Then you'd get some people who would cross the street so they didn't have to speak. Perhaps it was embarrassment. But my dad flatly refused to let me go to the trial.'[15]

The second day of the trial opened the evidence for the prosecution. The first witness proper to take the stand was Myra's sister, Maureen. She was called earlier than planned because her baby had been due on the first day of the trial; arrangements were in place to whisk her off to hospital if necessary.[16] Wearing a black polo-neck jumper and maternity smock, she described the relationship between her sister and Ian, the friendship that had sprung up between her husband and Ian, and confirmed Myra had shopped at Ashton-under-Lyne market. Maureen's relatively calm exterior belied her fear of reprisal; a few days earlier she had been viciously attacked in the lift at Underwood Court and the flat she shared with Dave was daubed with foul graffiti, while every post brought a new pile of hate mail. Despite Myra's claims of being rejected in favour of Maureen during childhood, Nellie continued to disown her younger daughter in order to give her full support to Myra. Maureen was also still estranged from her father, who had become a recluse from the wrath of the public.

That afternoon, a dense fog crept across the city, causing traffic chaos. Myra and Ian were kept in the cells at Hyde police station overnight. The Police Ball was held that evening, and while Myra and Ian sat alone in their cells with a blanket and a cup of tea, above them the police entertained local dignitaries – big band music and the sound of hundreds of foxtrotting feet reverberated through the ceiling.

The following day, Maureen took the stand again and described the night of Edward's murder. She admitted that Dave was receiving a regular income from a national newspaper in relation to the case and that they stood to receive a large sum for syndication rights if Myra and Ian were convicted. When Dave was called to the stand, it emerged that not only were the couple receiving £20 a week from the *News of the World*, but they had also taken a holiday in France at the newspaper's expense and Dave had been promised £1,000 for his post-trial story. The Press Council later condemned the newspaper's interference in the case, while Fenton Atkinson declared that the *News of the World* had given the defence 'a stick with which to beat Smith'.[17] Dave's background caused a few eyebrows to be raised in court, and some of his comments ('I love having money, it's gorgeous stuff') and use of journalistic phrases did him few favours.[18] Nonetheless, he remained calm, despite his habit of fiddling with the microphone, and answered every question directly.

On the fourth day, Carr and Campion were among those to give evidence.[19] The court then adjourned for the weekend. When it reconvened on Monday, 25 April, the evidence moved away from Edward Evans to the murder of Lesley Ann Downey. Most of the witness statements were read to court, but Patty Hodges gave her evidence in a rapid clip and remained unfazed during her brief cross-examination. On 28 April, evidence concerning the abduction and murder of John Kilbride was presented. Throughout it all, Myra's face remained a blank disc, except to share a smile with Ian or whisper with him. They played noughts and crosses in her notepad and passed each other mints. On one journey from Risley to Chester they shared a Quality Street Easter egg and felt sick as they climbed the stairs to court. Only once did Myra's impassive public facade drop: when she stuck her tongue out at reporters as she left court.

On 29 April, Emlyn Hoosen opened the case for the defence by reminding the jury, 'It is terribly, terribly important that you dispose from your minds all the natural revulsion one has in reading or hearing evidence connected with the death of children', and that 'the very least or meanest person of this country is entitled to a fair and dispassionate trial and a proper assessment of the evidence for and against'.[20] He then stood aside and Ian Brady stepped into the dock. He stuck to his story of bringing Edward to the house for the purpose of blackmail, and that Lesley had left the house safely in the presence of David Smith and another man. But he made two significant slips during his account of what happened while Lesley was at Wardle Brook Avenue.

He told the court that after the nude photographing session, he had put the handkerchief in Lesley's mouth, then covered the lower half of her face with a scarf 'just before the end'.[21] Fenton Atkinson leaned forward: '"Just before the end" – what do you mean by "the end"?' Ian stuttered, 'The end of – just before the – or it could be just after the tripod being opened.'

The matter was allowed to pass, but, only a minute later, after Hoosen prompted him to explain what followed the taking of the photographs, Ian declared, 'After completion, we all got dressed and went downstairs.'[22] The blunder went unnoticed until after the weekend, when the court reconvened and Ian entered the witness box to be cross-examined by the Attorney General, who asked him about the slip. Ian refused to admit he had said it, and Hoosen backed him up, but a note of it had been made and one of the jurors piped up, 'He said that, sir.'[23] Ian insisted, 'I didn't say that. I said *the girl* got dressed and we all went downstairs. *The girl. The girl.*' Later, in his summing up, Fenton Atkinson referred back to the error on Ian's part, telling the jury, 'It possibly casts a flood of light on the nature of the activities that were going on.'[24]

The Attorney General questioned Ian about the 'landscape' shots, asking, 'Those are photographs of this cemetery of your making on that moorland, are they not?'[25] Ian replied that they were snapshots, but the Attorney General insisted that the photographs served a dual purpose: both as markers 'for future reconnaissance' and as 'morbid enjoyment of the trophies of murders'.[26] Asked whether he read 'dirty books', Ian responded, 'It depends on the dirty mind. It depends on your mind.'[27] The Attorney General pressed him: 'This is the atmosphere of your mind. A sink of pornography, was it not?'[28] Ian delivered a pithy reply, 'No. There are better collections in lords' manors all over the country.'[29]

Whenever an opportunity presented itself for him to protect Myra, Ian did so. He stated that during Edward's murder, 'She wasn't in the room. I told Myra, Evans was dead and she became overwrought, hysterical.'[30] He asserted that Myra hadn't wanted to be present when Lesley was photographed, but he'd insisted. He said that Myra had asked him to destroy the tape recordings and that she had never been involved in any plans for robbery. He deliberately belittled her in order to give weight to his argument that she was a dupe: 'She was my typist in the office. I dictated to her in the office and this tended to wrap over.'[31] Myra kept her eyes fixed on Ian throughout his time in the dock, except for brief moments when she rested her forehead on the wooden bench in front. She wrote to her mother during the trial, 'He's not concerned about his future, just mine. It's the same with me: I'm not interested in my future, just him. However, we'll have to wait and see what happens. I believe in one thing though, that no matter how black things look, some day we can begin together again. I know what we've done and what we haven't done. You know too, no matter what happens.'[32]

The two of them had banked on Myra receiving a minimal sentence; after her release she would travel and share her experiences with Ian through letters until his release. Years later, she told Peter Topping a quite different tale, proclaiming that Ian had tried to exonerate her only within the boundaries of what he was willing to admit. 'Beyond that,' she said, 'he was prepared to sacrifice me to my fate.'[33] But in court, she was keen to see that the stories they had agreed upon were put across accurately and passed a note to her solicitor, Godfrey Heilpern, with a distinctly peremptory tone: 'I told you, no cross-examination that damages Ian.'[34]

Ian's testimony ended on 3 May; he was followed into the dock by Nellie Hindley, who told the court that Myra was not in the habit of shopping at Ashton market, whatever Maureen said. When she had finished giving her evidence, Myra stepped into the dock, with every eye in the courtroom turned upon her. A glint came from the public gallery, where someone was watching her through opera glasses.

Asked if she wished to take the oath or affirm, Myra replied, 'I want to affirm.'[35] Fenton Atkinson said, 'That is because you have no religious beliefs?'

'Yes.'[36]

Her defence counsel's first question concerned her relationship with Ian: 'Could you tell us, Miss Hindley, what were your feelings for Ian Brady?'

In a low voice, she responded, 'I became very fond of him. I loved him. I still – I love him.'[37]

She was in the witness box for almost six hours; Ian had been there for a little under nine. He kept his gaze averted while she stood there, either sitting with his chin resting in his left hand or glancing about the court. Questioned that day and the next, Myra gave little away. She declared that she was ashamed of the tape recording of Lesley and that her attitude towards the child had been 'brusque and cruel' because she was worried someone might hear.[38] She said that she had drawn the curtains and was only there as 'insurance' that Lesley left the house safely: 'I was in the room, but I was looking out of the window because I was embarrassed at what was going on . . . I was on the other side of the curtains, looking out of the window, which was wide open. I didn't want to be there in the first place, but Ian asked me to. She started getting undressed and I went in there.'[39] The Attorney General retorted, 'A pretty rotten witness you would have been, looking out of the window.'[40] She claimed not to know who told Lesley how to pose, to which the Attorney General responded with more sarcasm, 'It isn't the Albert Hall; it's a small room and you were there.'[41] Inexplicably, she claimed that the woman's voice clearly heard at the beginning of the tape recording was not hers but in fact Ian's. Asked about the threats she had made to Lesley, Myra responded, 'I wouldn't have hit her much. I never touched her. I never harmed her . . . when she started crying and shouting and screaming I just wanted her to be quiet.'[42] The Attorney General thundered, 'The screams of a little girl of ten – of your sex, madam', and demanded to know why she hadn't removed the child from the room and 'treated [her] as a woman should treat a female child, or any other child'.[43]

'I should have done, but I didn't.' She paused. 'I have no defence to that.'[44]

Grimly, he told her, 'Your shame is a *counterfeit* shame, Miss Hindley.'[45]

Myra answered a torrent of questions about the 'landscape' photographs and denied knowing that any were taken on or near graves. She never slipped up, as Ian had, and threw off the question about his blunder over the three of them getting dressed after Lesley was photographed. Junior Prosecuting Counsel was the now-retired High Court Judge Sir Ronald Waterhouse, who recalls: 'She was an intelligent woman – that, I think, everybody recognises – and she had a rather statuesque appearance. She seemed to be really rather unblinking and certainly, for most of the time, quite emotionless.'[46] Myra said later that the icy mask she presented to the courtroom hid her terror and sickness; she didn't want to add fuel to a fire that was already raging by showing her emotions: 'I needed that veneer . . . I could not express my ravaged self.'[47]

Godfrey Heilpern, Myra's own lawyer, put to her the one question that everyone wanted to ask: why she had done what she did.

'I would go along with him,' she replied, referring to Ian.[48]

'Miss Hindley, why?'

'Because I just did.'

'Can you help us with the reason?'

She shook her head. 'I cannot.'

The grilling ended with a number of questions from the Attorney General about John Kilbride, finishing with, 'It was from Ashton market that you and Brady picked up this little boy. It was from there that, ultimately, with your assistance, his body ended up in that lonely grave on the moors.'[49]

Myra uttered her last line in public: 'No, I was nowhere near Ashton at all.'[50]

Her solicitor stood up. 'I have no re-examination. That is the case for the accused, my Lord.'[51]

The closing speech for the Crown followed, in which the Attorney General conceded that the main witness for the prosecution, David Smith, was 'certainly no angel' but had told his story 'frankly . . . and exactly'.[52] The two accused formed 'an evil partnership together and co-operated together in all they did', while Myra was 'a calculated, pretty cool operator'.[53] He ended: 'My submission is that the same pairs of hands killed all three of these victims, Evans, Downey and Kilbride, and these are the pairs of hands of the two accused in the dock.'[54]

Over the next couple of days, Hoosen and Heilpern gave their closing speeches on behalf of Ian and Myra; Heilpern described the evidence against her as flimsy and intimated that her relationship with Ian was one of master and servant. Fenton Atkinson then began his summing up, describing it as 'a truly horrible case'. He told the jury, 'From first to last, there has not been the smallest suggestion that either of these two was in any way mentally abnormal or not fully responsible for his or her actions. That leads on to this – that if the prosecution is right, you are dealing here with two killers of the utmost depravity . . . they are entitled to the unusual incredulity which such terrible offences must raise in the mind of any normal person. Could anybody be as wicked as that?'[55]

On the morning of Friday, 6 May 1966, Myra tried to compose a letter to her mother. She knew that the day ahead would determine the rest of her life: 'Dear Mam . . . I don't know what the verdict will be yet, but I do know that I will be convicted of something, like harbouring Ian after he and Smith killed Evans. Once you know what the verdicts and sentences are you must not let them affect your life as they will mine. I've just started crying and don't want anyone to see me . . .'[56]

In Chester, the van carrying the two accused swept through the vast crowds and blinding flash of camera guns to the back of the courthouse. Myra climbed the stone steps to the dock, and Fenton Atkinson finished his summing up by referring to her as being 'very closely in Brady's confidence . . . Brady was quite dependent on her for transport.'[57] He described the Downey case as the 'really crucial' one against her and told the jury that if they were convinced she was guilty in that instance, then they might think similarly about the Kilbride case, and thus conclude that she was a willing participant in the Evans murder. Nonetheless, he advised, 'The first thing to remember in considering Hindley is this: that a great deal of the evidence against Brady is not evidence against her; and in particular Brady's statement to Smith about killing people and burying them on the moors. That is something said behind her back and that is not evidence against her. Anything that Brady may have said to the police by way of an apparent admission is not evidence against her. The plan to dispose of Evans's body is only evidence if you think that from the whole of the evidence she must have seen it and known its contents. It is very important to remember this . . .' He paused: 'There it is. You have listened long and very patiently to all the evidence in the case and you must now go and consider your verdict.'[58]

At twenty to three, the jury retired. Two and a half hours later, they filed back into the courtroom and took their seats. Myra and Ian stood side by side in the dock, staring resolutely ahead. The clerk asked the foreman of the jury to stand and give their verdict: Ian Brady was found guilty of all three murders; Myra Hindley was found guilty of the murder of Edward Evans, guilty of the murder of Lesley Ann Downey, not guilty of the murder of John Kilbride, but guilty of the charge that she 'well knowing that Ian Brady had murdered John Kilbride did receive, comfort, harbour, assist and maintain the said Ian Brady'.[59]

Myra's hands tightened on the wooden edge of the dock.

'Are those the verdicts of you all?' asked the clerk, to which the foreman responded, 'Yes, my Lord.'[60]

'Call upon them,' Fenton Atkinson declared.

The clerk proclaimed: 'Ian Brady and Myra Hindley, you have been convicted of a felony on the verdict of the jury. Have you anything to say why the court should not pass sentence upon you according to law? Have you, Ian Brady?'[61]

Ian responded, 'No – except the revolvers were bought in July 1964.'[62]

'And you, Myra Hindley?'[63]

Myra shook her head. 'No,' she said quietly.

The judge looked down at them. 'Ian Brady, these were three calculated, cruel, cold-blooded murders. In your case, I pass the only sentence the law now allows, which is three concurrent sentences of life imprisonment. Put him down.'[64]

Ian was led from the dock without a glance at Myra, whose grip remained taut on the wooden frame. A feeling of numbness seeped through her, though when she'd heard Ian sentenced to life, 'I prayed that I would get the same because the world outside meant nothing to me as long as he wasn't in it . . .'[65]

The judge turned to her: 'In your case, Hindley, you have been found guilty of two equally horrible murders and, in the third, as an accessory after the fact. On the two murders, the sentence is two concurrent sentences of life imprisonment, and on the charge of being an accessory after the fact to the death of John Kilbride a concurrent sentence of seven years' imprisonment.' He gave a brief nod: 'Put her down.'[66]

Myra swayed forward and the female prison officer sitting behind her grasped her arm, steadying her. Catching sight of Myra's ashen face, one observer commented: '. . . we were reminded that here, after all, was a woman'.[67] The *Gorton & Openshaw Reporter* noted: 'Hindley, still sucking on a mint as sentence upon her was passed, turned and was escorted quickly from the dock. The click-click of her high-heeled shoes could be heard on the steps as she was taken down to the cells.'[68]

A crowd of over 250 people milled in the twilight outside the court. Circled around them were the media, boom and camera held high, waiting for the couple to emerge. The anger surrounding Chester Castle that evening was palpable; Pamela Hansford Johnson described the mood: 'When the Moors trial ended, we did feel a lack of catharsis: something violent should have happened to put an end to violence. Throughout, *we were missing the shadow of the rope.*'[69]

MP Sydney Silverman's Murder (Abolition of the Death Penalty) Act had been passed on the day of Myra Hindley's arrest. Since then, John Kilbride's aunt and uncle, Elsie and Frank Doran, had organised a petition to reinstate it for child murder and had sent more than 10,000 signatures to the Home Secretary. Lesley Ann Downey's uncle stood as a pro-hanging candidate in the general election against Sydney Silverman and polled 5,000 votes; he also urged Emlyn Williams to make his next book a call for the return of hanging. Detective Chief Superintendent Arthur Benfield felt that Myra and Ian might have said more had that terrible threat still been in place: 'There was no question of capital punishment in the Moors case. Brady and Hindley were not fools, so why should they admit any more? If they did, there might be no possibility of release in the future.'[70]

Francis Wyndham, writing in the *Sunday Times*, declared that what was missing was not the rope but the souls of Brady and Hindley themselves: 'This "sensational" trial seemed to have a hollow centre, where the accused should have been. It was almost as though they were being tried by proxy, ghostly presences in an empty dock, as dead as their victims on the moors.'[71]

In the corridor below the courtroom, Myra and Ian met briefly in the presence of their solicitor. Myra recalled, 'The first thing I asked [Ian] was not to kill himself, as he'd said he would do.'[72] Within minutes, guards stepped up and led them separately to the prison van, where they remained in different compartments. It was dark as the van swept out of the yard behind Chester Castle, but the crowds had waited for that moment and Myra could feel fists pounding the sides of the vehicle and hear the screams and jeers. Blinding lights flashed outside the tinted windows as the van veered away, taking her back to Risley for one night before she was driven south, hundreds of miles from the man with whom her name would be forever linked, towards the forbidding gates of Holloway Prison.

In Hattersley, 16 Wardle Brook Avenue lay in pitch darkness, every one of its windows shattered, the curtains billowing in the winds that came down from the moor to blow through the still and silent house.

V

God Has Forgiven Me:
7 May 1966 – 15 November 2002

I could feel no pity for her at the trial; now I can feel some pity for what her life is to be. I shouldn't be surprised, though it seems an improbability now, if she eventually returns to the Roman Catholic Church.

Pamela Hansford Johnson, *On Iniquity*

'My first impression of London was of trees ... mercifully I didn't see the yawning gates of Holloway until we were locked inside them.'[1] Myra's arrival at Britain's largest prison for women left her bewildered. Built in north London in 1852, Holloway was home to half the country's 950 female inmates. Myra was told to strip and bathe under guard and her hair and pubic hair were inspected for lice, which 'appalled and affronted' her, since she had already endured the process in Risley.[2] The prison uniform – blue shirt, grey skirt and thick black shoes – was handed to her, and she was shown into the hospital clinic, where the elderly female doctor instructed her to take her underwear off for a VD test. Myra burst into tears, insisting that she had only had one sexual partner (which wasn't true) and that she'd never heard of VD. After dressing again, she was provided with bedding, medicated soap and the tin of green tooth powder that was used by inmates instead of toothpaste. Prisoner 964055 was then taken to her cell in the hospital wing, C Wing, where she was held until it was deemed safe to move her into the prison proper.

Myra was a 'nonce', a sex offender (the term literally means 'nothing'). Shortly after her arrival on D wing, the whispering began: 'Suffer the little children to come unto me, suffer the little children to come unto me ...' Then the attacks: she was struck with a broom by one prisoner cleaning the stairs, while a group of ten women asked her to join them for a game of cards, then beat her badly before hurling her on the wire mesh that hung between each landing. She didn't fight back and refused to name her attackers, asking instead to be put on solitary confinement, Rule 43. The doctor and an assistant governor advised her to stick it out because she faced a long stretch inside. An officer was temporarily assigned to escort her whenever she left her cell.

A week after arriving in prison, Myra appealed against her conviction on the grounds that it had been detrimental to have been tried with Ian. In October, *The Times* discussed the failure of the appeal. A report dated 21 September 1966 demonstrated that the Attorney General found 'eleven points of similarity in each of these cases . . . a formidable common pattern of killing' and that Myra 'exhibited good general health, good general intelligence, above average powers of expression, and gave no indication either of mental or psychopathic disorder or that there was any diminution in her responsibility for her actions.'[3] The Lord Chief Justice stated that Ian sought at all times to exonerate her and therefore, on that basis, a joint trial had proved beneficial.

She remained in close contact with Ian, who was placed on Rule 43 after being scalded by another prisoner. His cell in Durham was in E Wing, where he ate his meals alone and took walks in the yard with three guards while the other prisoners were locked in their cells. He spent his time reading, absorbing all the classical works in the prison library, choosing *War and Peace* on his first visit. He shared his cell with a mouse, feeding it crumbs from his own meals and on one occasion left it half a chip. He wrote to inform Myra that, much to his surprise, the mouse had eaten that too. A month passed and he received a letter from his mother, telling him that his stepfather was dead. At the age of 48, Patrick Brady had collapsed and died in the street. Ian remained close to Peggy and his foster family in Glasgow, who refused to talk to the press.

Myra's lengthy letters to Ian were filled with private jokes and references. One read: 'Dearest Ian, hello my little hairy Girklechin. It was with profound relief I received your letter today . . . It was a lovely, soothing, nostalgic letter which comforted me almost as much as if you were here yourself. I had a beautifully tender dream about you last night and awoke feeling safe and secure, thinking I was in the harbour of your arms . . . I pictured your face and said your name to myself over and over again and imagined the arms of the chair I was clenching to be your hands, lovely strong "insurance" hands (remember?). Freedom without you means nothing. I've got one interest in life and that's you. We had six short but precious years together, six years of memories to sustain us until we're together again, to make dreams realities.'[4] In another she referred to the collective name by which the rest of the world knew them: 'I didn't murder any moors, did you?'[5] They both studied O level German; Ian wrote to congratulate her when she passed with an A grade.

'I still had feelings for him as I began my sentence,' Myra declared. 'I was prepared to die for him and that strength of emotion doesn't go away easily.'[6] At Ian's suggestion, she asked her mother to take out an insurance policy for her at half a crown a week. He encouraged her to believe that she would one day be released. Nellie visited as often as she could. At the end of 1966, she divorced Myra's father and married Bill Moulton. Bob Hindley never visited Myra, who recalled, 'It devastated him that his daughter could possibly have done the things I did and he disowned me.'[7] But she wrote weekly to her mother, including a letter in bold capitals for Gran, who had initially been told that Myra had moved to Scotland. When she learned the truth, she showered Myra with knitted clothes to demonstrate that nothing had changed between them.

Maureen read in the press about one of the attacks on Myra and wrote to her but received no reply. She and Dave were parents to a son, Paul Anthony, one of the few joys in their life: it was impossible for Dave to find work – when he managed to secure a job in a factory, the other employees threatened to walk out unless he was sacked. Every day brought hate mail, and Maureen recalled later how she would open the letters and scream with horror. Not long after the trial, Lesley Ann Downey's mother, her partner Alan West and another man called at Underwood Court one evening. A violent fight ensued between them. Ann recalled, 'I beat Maureen Smith's head against the wall and screamed incoherently at her. I tore at her and for a moment it was as if I had her foul sister in my hands . . .'[8] The next day the police called on the Wests, carrying a bag filled with Maureen's hair. No action was taken, but the police warned them not to make any further calls.

Myra enlisted her mother's help in trying to obtain visiting rights to Ian. She put in a request to the governor of Holloway and Ian pressed the assistant governor of his wing for the same, but inter-prison visits were refused. Myra wrote to her mother, telling her to contact Lord Stonham of the Home Office, with whom Myra had become friendly during one of his regular visits to Holloway. He described Myra as 'very calm and collected . . . She was studying for her O levels. Apparently she was more concerned about the fact that she was not recognised as Brady's common-law wife than about anything else.'[9]

A number of titled individuals called upon Myra regularly during the course of their prison work, and some became friends. One who visited but did not cross the boundary from philanthropic caller to ally was forty-year-old Lady Anne Tree, daughter of the 10th Duke of Devonshire, whose family home was Chatsworth.[10] At the request of the prison governor, she began visiting Myra, whom she found 'a dull figure. I did find it rather difficult until we got on to books. I used to look very carefully on Saturdays at the book reviews to have things to talk about, to say, "Myra, have you seen this is coming out?" I'd take the books in sometime, or she'd get them through the prison library.'[11] She dismisses Myra's reputation for being extremely intelligent: 'No, I don't think that was true at all. Or else she wouldn't have done it, would she? They were both monsters actually. I think they had no pity, just were lacking it. And I don't think she ever thought about her victims. She passionately loved animals, but I once saw her kicking a pigeon that was lurking about in the prison. It was horrid.'[12] Although they didn't discuss her crimes, Myra talked often about Ian: 'She was absolutely obsessed with him. She was mad about the moors, of course. She had a definite calling to nature to that part of the world. And to animals, in spite of kicking one.'[13] Lady Tree admits, 'I didn't like Myra. I felt outraged, really, because she was so blaming of other people. She really wanted to prove herself fit for release from the start. She never expressed remorse with me, but I have to say we kept pretty well off it. I think she saw everyone as a saviour. She definitely regarded herself as a heroine.'[14]

Despite her firm attachment to Ian, Myra embarked on her first lesbian affair. Prison officers largely ignored relationships between inmates, with a view that if it kept them quiet, then it was fine. Myra's prison counsellor feels that her many affairs with other inmates were largely due to her situation rather than being indicative of her true sexuality: 'She told me she was a lesbian only because of circumstance, though I'm sure she'd say different about Nina and Tricia, two later relationships. I felt that she was very confused about her sexuality. She loved Brady and fancied him like mad, and she was naturally heterosexual, but this happens with women in prison. Not as much with men. I think women want touch and comfort more. But I know lesbians who are sure of their sexuality and she definitely wasn't.'[15] Myra's first affair was with a pretty, bespectacled girl with cropped blonde hair called Rita whom she met on D Wing. This was followed by a fling with a gangster's wife, and another with a woman in her forties called Norma who was in prison for stabbing her girlfriend to death with scissors. Myra and Norma spent hours closeted together in Myra's cell. In the prison kitchen, Myra worked with an ex-lover of Norma's called Bernadette, who exploded with anger when she discovered the affair, attacking Myra, throwing urine on her clothes and defecating in her bed.

Despite these affairs, Myra remained in constant touch with Ian, who wrote to her just before Christmas to say that he was ill and confined to bed. Myra found herself reminiscing about the previous Christmas, which they had spent together in Risley on remand. Peggy Brady sent her some chocolate liqueurs as a substitute for the port wine of the year before. By this stage, Myra had been moved to Holloway's newly upgraded maximum-security wing, E Wing. There, two members of the Portland Spy Ring, Helen Kroger and Ethel Gee – who loathed each other – were being held, together with a small group of other long-term prisoners. She was allowed to cook her own food and sunbathe in the garden when the weather was fine. There was no work for the inmates when the wing was initially opened, so she was woken at 7 a.m. to the strains of Tony Blackburn's Radio 1 show and spent her time having her hair done by another prisoner, cooking, reading or strolling in the garden. Myra was in cell 11; next to her, in cell 12, was Ethel Gee, whom Myra said she felt sorry for because she'd become embroiled in crime after falling for the wrong man. Myra was attacked by Ethel's fellow spy one day in the kitchen: Helen Kroger hit her on the head with a teapot, then pummelled her to the ground, screaming, until officers ran in to intervene.

Soon after her arrival in Holloway, Myra was questioned by police about other murders. The *Gorton & Openshaw Reporter* ran an article on 12 May 1966, with the headline 'Moors Search Plan: Belief that There May Be Other Bodies in Secret Graves'. Keith Bennett and Pauline Reade were specifically mentioned. Although the search had been called off, there were plans to resume it if incontrovertible evidence of other murders was found and, with that in mind, detectives visited Myra in Holloway on 27 January 1967. At first, she had refused to see them. It was Ian who persuaded her otherwise, having received the same request himself. He told her that a snub implied they had something to conceal. In a letter to her mother, Myra declared, 'Once the police have been, I'm not going to see them again. They can leave us alone for the rest of our sentence and I'll tell them that when they come down.'[16] In the same letter, she asked Nellie to send her a copy of Joan Baez's 'It's All Over Now, Baby Blue', the record Ian had given her for the last murder.[17]

Myra spoke to Detective Chief Superintendent Douglas Nimmo and Detective Chief Inspector Tom Butcher but told them that she couldn't help with their inquiries about Keith or Pauline, or any other victims. She repeated her pre-trial mantra that they should question David Smith.

The first books about the case appeared in late 1966 and 1967. A group of university students tried to stage a play based on the murders, but their script was banned by the Lord Chancellor's office.[18] Myra asked for a copy of John Deane Potter's factual account, *The Monsters of the Moors*, which was sent via her solicitor and the prison governor, and in 1967 came the publication of Emlyn Williams' bestseller, *Beyond Belief*. A combination of fact and fiction, Williams' book received largely favourable reviews, with comparisons made to Truman Capote's seminal *In Cold Blood*.[19] Myra and Ian were outraged by the book – or, rather, its success. Myra called it 'the most obnoxious piece of lies and fabrications that I have ever read'.[20] She wrote to Benfield, wanting to know how Williams had managed to obtain a copy of her diary, sending the detective into a tailspin. In another letter, she fumed: 'This diary was amongst property which was taken from my house by the police upon my arrest and was in their possession for two years, until it was obtained for me by the solicitor who acts for us in this case.'[21] She was further angered by plans to turn *Beyond Belief* into a film, with William Friedkin mooted as director, and disgusted when she received a draft contract to give her written consent. She instructed her solicitor to block the film because of the 'harrowing' effect it would have on her and Ian's relatives.[22] The film was eventually shelved when the victims' families stepped in to protest.

In February 1968, Myra left Holloway to spend a week in Risley, a special privilege granted on compassionate grounds to allow Gran to visit her. Ellen Maybury died in March. The press reported the temporary transfer and the ensuing public outcry led to Myra's reclassification as a Category A prisoner, branding her an inmate whose escape would be extremely dangerous to the public, police or national security.

She was still desperate to see Ian and recruited the help of another visitor, Frank Pakenham, 7th Earl of Longford, to whom she was introduced via Lady Tree. A Labour Cabinet minister and staunch Catholic, Longford was a passionate campaigner for penal reform and an indefatigable prison visitor. Happily married to Elizabeth Harman, with whom he had eight children, his visits to Myra coincided with the dwindling of her appointments with Lady Tree, who recalls: 'I went off her and [Myra] went off me. I was having a minor change of lifestyle, my children were growing up. I said I don't think I shall have time. We'd come to the end of the road.'[23]

Longford was immediately drawn to Myra and blamed Ian unequivocally for her downfall: 'She was totally unlike that picture of her with blonde hair and staring eyes that appears in all the papers. She was a quiet, dark woman . . . Many people have done terrible things. The point about Myra is that she was a good Catholic girl before she met Brady . . . She fell under his spell . . .'[24] He gave her a few of the books he had written, published by Sidgwick & Jackson, of which he was chairman. Their subsequent friendship might have begun and ended on Myra's part with less than charitable intent, but for many years they remained loyal to each other, until she came to realise that his stalwart vocal support was damaging her bid for freedom.

Soon after their introduction, he visited Ian and announced that he had no doubt that the couple could be paroled 'in a good many years'.[25] He urged Myra to consider returning to Catholicism; she wrote to her mother: 'I doubt I'll "see the light" again, but who knows?'[26]

Myra began to form friendships with other inmates, her closest during her early days in Holloway with twenty-two-year-old Carole Callaghan, who was serving a six-year sentence for attempted armed robbery. She nicknamed Carole 'Eccles' after Spike Milligan's *Goons* character. They shared a love of philosophy and English literature, listened to classical music together and studied French. At night they stood at the windows of their adjoining cells, talking for hours and looking out at Holloway Road, where lit buses rattled by and revellers spilled from Holloway Castle pub. They shared a similar sense of humour; Carole recalls laughing as she caught sight of Myra one day, balancing a dish in each hand as she went down the stairs singing 'Swanee River' at the top of her voice. Carole was married, but also had lesbian relationships in prison. She viewed Myra's girlfriends as minions: 'Not only would [the girlfriend] be useful sexually but she would also preen and polish Myra's cell, wash and iron her clothes, and generally be servile.'[27] The two of them occasionally peeped in at cell 18, the old execution chamber where five women, including Edith Thompson and Ruth Ellis, were hanged. The scaffold had gone, but the drop was there.

In June 1968, as part of a government experiment, Holloway inmates were allowed to wear their own clothes, which eventually led to the abolition of prison uniform for women. Myra's interest in fashion resurfaced; she asked her visitors to bring her clothes, using what she and Carole termed her 'Baby Jane' voice. Her weight had gone up by three stone to a size sixteen since her imprisonment. She didn't smoke – although she did try cannabis, which was stitched into the bellies of dead pigeons thrown over the wall to inmates from associates outside – but spent most of her earnings on sweets. Unlike the majority of prisoners, who depended on medication, Myra survived without pills, other than the ones she took for chronic insomnia, which plagued her until the end of her life (she was unable to sleep in the dark and permission was granted for her to leave the light on in her cell). She learned tapestry from a Royal College of Needlework tutor and discovered a latent gift for it. With two other inmates, she created an intricate carpet, working to a commission from the Polish Embassy, and recalled secretly slipping a Rizla paper inside the hem, reading, 'Myra Hindley made this carpet.'

In January 1969, the prison authorities discussed resentment among staff towards Longford's visits to Myra. One memo observed:

'The already existing feelings of superiority in this very dominating woman are being augmented by his encouragement.'[28] Another memo echoed: 'Myra is a forceful, dominating woman at any time and is adept at manipulating any circumstance to her advantage.'[29] Longford's request for private visits with her was refused, although he continued to see her at three-monthly intervals.

Myra begged her mother for family news, although she and Maureen were not yet reconciled, despite her sister sending letters and photos of her three small sons: Paul, David and John. That summer, Dave was sentenced to three years' imprisonment for knifing a neighbour, William Lees, who had twice attacked him, once with a gang of people and again alone. The judge accepted that since the Moors trial he had been 'subjected to a great deal of open and sustained hostility'.[30] In prison, Dave opted for Rule 43; still only 21 years old, he slashed his wrists soon after his arrival.

Afterwards, he began to think about his life and the father he wanted to be. Maureen left him, unable to cope, and asked the social services to take their sons into care while she tried to find herself a home and work. A job in a department store ended because the other staff refused to work with Myra Hindley's sister. Maureen recalled: 'I learned to stick my nose in the air and close my ears to them. You've got to make up your mind that you are going to stay firm, no matter what you feel inside. You must act hard on the outside and say, "Look, I don't care what you say, I'm not budging."'[31] She wrote again to Myra, and asked for a visiting order, but was informed that her sister didn't wish to see her.

Myra still hoped to be reunited with Ian, writing to her mother: 'I've been in prison for three years now, Mam, and I haven't seen Neddy for two and a half of them, which I think is awful, thinking how many other prisoners have been granted this privilege.'[32] In Durham, following the refusal of his petition to see her, Ian's anger exploded. He flung scalding tea at fellow child-murderer Raymond Morris, which resulted in the loss of 28 days' privileges, including cigarettes. He then went on hunger strike, and there followed further fights with Morris. In a calmer period, Ian declared, 'I realised that, in a way, I was attacking myself. I could see a reflection of me in the Cannock Chase killer.'[33]

When the maximum-security status of Holloway's E Wing was

relaxed in autumn 1969, more prisoners arrived on the wing, although there were never more than 20 inmates at a time. Myra was nervous of the influx but worked quietly in the tapestry room and had her meals in her cell. She wrote to Longford that November: 'I have completely accepted the possibility that I may never be released. Or at least if I am, I will be much older than I am now.'[34] She began thinking about Catholicism and spoke to the prison chaplain, Father William Kahle, whose parents had emigrated to Britain to escape Nazi persecution. He recalls, 'I was asked to see her because I was a Roman Catholic and a German with a lot of knowledge of a cruel people.'[35]

Dorothy Wing, Holloway's governor since 1967, strongly supported Myra's renewed interest in religion, feeling that she would either kill herself or become irreparably hardened to prison life otherwise. Wing bonded with Myra over a passion for nineteenth-century poetry. She believed in giving prisoners as much freedom as possible and allowed them to furnish their cells as they wished. Encouraged by Wing, Myra told Father William that she would like to attend Mass and wrote to Longford: 'I'm still desperately trying to make my peace with God and to prove myself worthy of being a Christian . . .'[36] Her friend Carole told her that a burst of religious fervour would boost her parole chances; Ian wrote that he hoped she wouldn't be disillusioned by the process.

Their relationship was under strain, not only from their separation and her leanings towards Catholicism, but also from the thinly veiled threats in his letters concerning the 'scenic' photographs. An issue ever since their imprisonment, their desperation to retrieve the photographs first surfaced in Myra's letters to her mother in June 1966. She wrote that Fitzpatrick, their solicitor, had a list of photographs to send on when he managed to reclaim them. Three months later she wrote again to her mother, asking her to phone Fitzpatrick to ensure the photographs were returned. A year later, she complained that their solicitor was still trying to get the photographs – and tapes – sent back and had written to the Director of Public Prosecutions. In August 1968, Fitzpatrick finally succeeded in gaining possession of the photographs, negatives, slides and tartan album and passed them on to Nellie. The police took copies of everything before handing it back.

Although there was a great quantity of material, Myra asked her mother to have three specific slides developed and sent on to Ian. A week later, she wrote again about the slides, but Nellie hadn't sent them, her suspicions roused by the insistent tone of Myra's requests. Fitzpatrick informed Myra and Ian that he had been offered a large fee for the tartan album from the press; Myra was against the publicity that would arise from the sale, while Ian suggested that the money might prove useful upon her release. He was unconcerned about the album – the photographs that held special significance were the three slides of Myra that he knew Nellie had. But he grew agitated when the slides didn't arrive. By the end of 1969, Myra wrote to her mother: 'He keeps asking why he hasn't received them yet. In his last letter he said he'll have to send someone round for them . . .'[37]

23

What is life for? To die? Then why not kill myself at once? No, I am afraid. To wait for death until it comes, I fear that even more. Then I must live. But what for? In order to die. I cannot escape that circle . . .

Myra Hindley, personal essay, 'The Intimate Revelations of Myra Hindley in Prison for Life', 1975

The photographs still occupied Myra's thoughts at the beginning of the year. She wrote to her mother, demanding to know why they hadn't been sent, adding that she was having to ward off Ian's threats. Eventually, Nellie did send the slides, but Ian continued to pester Myra for other photographs. Months later she admitted to her mother that she was sick of the whole thing and just wanted them all sent on to Ian, telling Nellie not to make things difficult for her, adding that she was 'sorry (in more ways than one) to have to mention the slides and photos yet again'.[1] But still Nellie didn't send the rest of the collection: her suspicions remained strong enough for her to take a rare stance against her daughter.

In January 1970, Myra attended Mass for the first time since she'd been a teenager and wrote to Longford: 'I wish I could put complete trust in God, but I'm frightened to do so, for my faith is full of doubt and despair that I'll never be good enough to merit complete forgiveness. I don't think I could adequately express just how much it means to me to have been to confession and to have received holy communion. It is a terrifyingly beautiful thing – terrifying because I have taken a step which has taken me onto the threshold of a completely new way of life which demands much more from me than my previous one, and beautiful because I feel spiritually reborn. I made such a mess of my old life and I thank God for this second chance.'[2] She reassured Ian that she hadn't revealed anything of substance in her confession. He became openly scornful of her return to the Church, asking, 'What colour hair-shirt are you wearing?'[3] She reflected, 'Ian, like so many other people, considered my returning to the Church simply as a means of "working my ticket"... I realise it is something I will always have to contend with, but as long as God knows, it matters little what anyone else thinks.'[4]

That summer Myra sank into a deep depression as her last birthday in her twenties approached. She grew nostalgic, listening to the music she and Ian loved, and pressed a fellow Mancunian inmate to ask relatives for photographs of the house on Wardle Brook Avenue. When they arrived, she grew maudlin, appalled at the neglected state of the house, which the council were finding difficult to rent out. To lift her spirits, she began searching for a new crush. Her friend Carole told her about a new officer, small and slim, with short, dark hair. Tricia Cairns was the officer in question; like Myra, she had been brought up in Gorton. During the months of the Moors investigation and trial, she had been a Carmelite nun in Salford but left the convent following a crisis of faith and joined the Prison Service, working in Bullwood Hall, where she met her partner, a fellow prison officer, before they were transferred to Holloway. Due to a shortage of staff accommodation at Holloway, they lived in a subsidised flat in Earls Court. Myra enlisted Carole's help in writing a letter to Tricia; her friend recalls a few lines: 'Is it too much to hope that one day we may sit in the sunshine together enjoying a glass of wine ... it gives me hope just being able to see you, and when you're not on duty the day drags by ...'[5] On Myra's 29th birthday, Tricia presented her with a Rachmaninov record and their affair began; she remained part of Myra's life until the end. Discovering that Tricia hailed from Gorton cemented the relationship between them. Carole loitered outside Myra's door to allow the two women to conduct their relationship in private, while Myra's then favourite song, 'We've Only Just Begun', played. If anyone approached, Carole started singing 'To Be a Pilgrim' loudly; she also wrote poems, which Myra then handed to her lover, pretending they were her own.

Myra's love for Ian had died. Not wanting to reply to his letters any more, she asked Carole to write, pretending to be her; the ruse worked. The strain of wanting to cut the ties with Ian and conducting a secret affair with a prison officer told on her own mental health, and in December 1970 she wrote to Longford that she was having difficulty 'keeping my head above the waterline . . . I have rampant "gate fever" . . . my spirit has left me and is hovering restlessly on the other side of the wall.'[6] Her friends rallied round, among them Dr Rachel Pinney, a Quaker doctor in her sixties who had lived in a commune and was serving time for kidnapping a fourteen-year-old boy whom she had judged at risk from his troubled mother. She recalled how her friendship with Myra began: 'Myra was sitting in the corridor with her head in her hands. I went up to her and said, "I'm your friend, do you mind if I talk to you?" She said, "No, of course not. I wish you had approached me the last time you were here. I never speak to people first in case they spit at me." So then we sat and talked for half an hour.'[7]

All the women in Myra's circle believed she had acted under the spell of a wicked man; after her release, Rachel set about trying to prove Myra's innocence by spending a year in Manchester, researching a book about her until Myra got word to her to stop. The law then forbade ex-prisoners from writing to their old inmates, but Rachel maintained contact with Myra through Honor Butlin, a wealthy Quaker widow who often visited Myra and sent her bouquets. It was Rachel who brought Myra back into touch with her paternal grandmother, Nana Hindley, who visited her in Holloway. By then, Myra's mother had been reconciled with Maureen, who recalled, 'It was just as if we'd never been parted. After all, your mum's your mum! We talked about everything.'[8] She moved in with Nellie and Bill but lost custody of her sons to Dave, who was working hard at building a new life for himself and his children. He lived with his cancer-ridden father but found lasting happiness with a feisty, kind-hearted teenager named Mary, the daughter of his father's best friend.

Although Myra wanted nothing to do with Maureen, her thoughts dwelled increasingly on the past; she wrote to her cousin Glenys about Michael Higgins and places she had known in Gorton. Glenys was aware of the relationship with Tricia and acted as a go-between for the two women. Myra sent long coded letters to Tricia via Glenys; when Carole left Holloway in early 1971, Glenys then forwarded the letters on to her. Tricia visited Carole's flat to decipher the letters away from the home she shared with her partner. The same process worked in reverse.[9] Pat Ali, an illiterate prisoner, acted as a local messenger between Myra and Tricia but complained about them to a board of visiting magistrates. She was disbelieved and lost six months' remission for 'malicious allegations'. Despite the intensity of their relationship, neither Myra nor Tricia were faithful; both had several lovers. After falling for Tricia, Myra's weight dropped from twelve stone to eight, largely due to the cigarettes she bought in order to bribe fellow inmates to pass messages to Tricia. She also worried about eating the prison food, which was often contaminated with urine from the prisoners who prepared it.

When Carole left Holloway, Myra was forced to write to Ian herself again. He sent her a coded message to ask if she wanted to end their relationship. Myra later claimed that she found it difficult to do so because she didn't want him to feel alone.[10] She recalled, 'He wrote back to me and said he had waited for my letter to arrive so he would know where his fate lay, because if my answer had been yes, that I wanted to finish with him, he would do what he had originally planned.'[11] Hinting that her feelings for him had changed nonetheless, she sent him a poem about the maturation of love by Wordsworth.

Ian continued to write to Myra every week following his transfer from Durham to Albany and then to Parkhurst, where he learned Braille and transcribed books for the blind. But on 13 March 1972, Myra wrote to Longford that she had found the courage to end the relationship after all: 'The decision was an agonising one, which cost me dearly. It shattered me because previously I had deemed it impossible that my feelings for him could ever change and this, coupled with my long religious struggle, which took place before my complete reconciliation with God, convinces me for, at the moment, some inexplicable reason, that I am doing the right thing, however much it may cost.'[12] Myra told Ian not to bother writing again; she would simply pass any future letters on to the prison governor. As a final gesture, Ian returned a bookmark that Myra had given him the previous Christmas via the prison staff. Myra's mother was so relieved by the end of the relationship that she immediately dispatched five of Ian's sought-after photographs to him. When Myra wrote again to Longford, she used a phrase that she would resurrect in future prose: ' . . . Flaubert once said we should never touch our idols because some of the gilt rubbed off on our fingers and this is all too true . . . I wish to put him out of my life as totally as I do all the unhappy, destructive and godless aspects of my past life with him, and I must admit that I rarely ever think of him now . . . had it not been for him, I would never have been involved in any of the things that brought me to prison . . .'[13]

Myra's friendship with Lord Longford was made public in 1972. He was lambasted that same year for his anti-pornography campaign, which saw him dubbed 'Lord Porn' by the tabloids. The juxtaposition of the two – his call for censorship and his insistence that Myra was a changed woman – brought criticism and ridicule upon him. Father William, who had left Holloway and was living in Belgium, made a prophetic comment: 'Lord Longford said to me when he had seen Myra on one occasion, "Has she not changed a great deal? Hasn't her personality changed?" I told him, "I don't think so" . . . I must stress that the publicity will not do Myra any good and will only be worse for her, possibly set her release date back many years.'[14] Lesley Ann Downey's mother was sickened by Longford's comments; her revulsion only increased after meeting Myra's champion at his Sidgwick & Jackson offices. Her fury spread like flame in the interviews she gave to counteract the publicity heaped upon Longford, whom she called a 'most dangerous and woolly minded buffoon'.[15]

The widespread disgust that greeted Longford's defence of Myra acted as tinder to the news that broke in September's press. Myra's categorisation status had been lowered from A to B, which gave her more freedom within Holloway and meant that the governor, if she chose, could escort her beyond the walls for a certain length of time.[16] She had already visited Dorothy Wing's house within the prison perimeter to discuss poetry, and in early September Mrs Wing decided to take her out to Hampstead Heath, where they were accompanied by a friend of Mrs Wing and her cairn terrier, Piper.[17] Myra was exhilarated: 'It was as though I had never been inside. Everything came back to me. It was the smells – of grass and trees, and throwing a ball for the governor's dog. There were children playing.'[18] They were seen returning to the prison and the ensuing firestorm provoked deep anger in television and radio debates, and questions were asked in the House of Commons. The Home Office released a statement declaring that the outing was not an attempt to prepare Myra for release and that the Home Secretary [Robert Carr] considered it 'an error of judgement [and] not to be repeated'.[19]

Following an internal inquiry, Mrs Wing – who was about to retire – issued her own statement: 'I took Myra out because I thought it would do her some good to see some grass and trees and have a breath of fresh air. Bless her heart, she enjoyed it very much. She said, "Doesn't the grass smell beautiful?" . . . I now realise that it was an error of judgement because Mr Carr has said that it was.'[20] Journalist Norman Luck tracked Mrs Wing down to her sister's home in Wales where, after a chat about flowers and a few glasses of Glenfiddich, she told him it hadn't been Myra's first outing: 'One day we took Myra to the Tutankhamen exhibition [held at the British Museum in spring, 1972]. We queued up for a while but couldn't wait, so we took her for tea at a store in Oxford Street, where she was recognised by a member of the public who thought she'd escaped from prison. The police arrived and the incident was hushed up when we explained the outing was a compassionate visit under strict supervision of prison staff designed to start Myra's rehabilitation programme.'[21]

The outcry left Myra in little doubt over public feeling. She realised that she was unlikely to be granted her freedom in the immediate future and began to fantasise wildly instead about escaping to Brazil with Tricia to work as a missionary. The two women decided to put their pipe dreams into action: Tricia asked Carole if she knew of a gang who could spring Myra from prison and offered the £4,000 she had in her savings account as payment. Her friend laughed, telling her the people she knew would expect about five times that and would probably kill Myra in the process. They then turned to 22-year-old Maxine Croft, who was serving time on Myra's wing for handling counterfeit cash. She was a 'green band', a more trusted prisoner who had access to the officers' sitting room as part of her cleaning duties. Myra became friendly with her and enlisted her in the escape plot. Maxine, intimidated and aware that the last woman to speak to the authorities about the couple hadn't been believed, took photographs of Myra for the passport she would need to fake and made impressions of keys from modelling plaster, which she then sent in a package to her friend, a garage owner. Immediately suspicious, he handed the parcel over to the police, just as Maxine plucked up the courage to confess to the prison authorities. Under questioning, Myra and Tricia denied the plot, despite the authorities having taken possession of a driver's licence found in the name of Myra Spencer. The press had a field day with the story.

The case was heard at the Old Bailey in April 1974. One of the reporters present was amazed at the difference in Myra's appearance: 'She looked softer, prettier, and feminine.'[22] All three women pleaded guilty to the charges laid before them. Maxine's solicitor defended her client as a much younger, naive woman intimidated by two older women, while Tricia's defence counsel insisted that the relationship between her client and Myra was merely platonic; when Tricia took the stand she told the court that Myra was sorry for her crimes and had been 'purified in the crucible of suffering', a phrase that Myra picked up on and used herself in the future. Lord Longford appeared as a defence witness. Maxine was sentenced to eighteen months' imprisonment, while Tricia was given a six-year sentence and had her Prison Service pension frozen until she was sixty. Myra was sentenced to another 12 months' imprisonment to be served consecutively with her other sentences.[23]

Myra tried to retain contact with Tricia, who was sent first to Durham, then to Styal, where she was singled out for harsh treatment by prison officers. Myra smuggled letters to her via other prisoners moving between Holloway and Styal, ignoring Tricia's warning that she was going to hand in her letters to the authorities. Myra was furious when Tricia carried out her threat and vowed to have nothing more to do with her. Upon her release, Tricia returned to her family in Manchester and found a job as a bus driver. Danny Kilbride recalls: 'I got on the bus one weekend to go to Ashton and *she* was the driver. I just stood there and said, "Oh my God." I turned round and told everyone on the bus who she was, and she had a tough time of it. I never saw her again after that – she obviously asked for a transfer.'[24]

Myra wrote to Lord Longford in the wake of the trial: 'I have forfeited every right to be trusted in here and I am not trusted an inch. Looking at this objectively, on the whole I agree, but with several reservations.'[25] She told him how sick she was of the authorities taking into account public opinion every time they made a decision about her, citing her recent application to study with the Open University as an example. She had written to her mother, 'I'll be the first woman in prison to do it, right from scratch. So to speak. It'll be nice to make "history" in a more pleasant way.'[26] The press and public disagreed, and the prison had another outcry on their hands when the news leaked that Myra was taking a course in humanities.

Transferred to F wing, where she was permitted to have a small black-and-white television in her cell, Myra was surrounded by photographs of family and friends, and books and records. Prison staff felt she was suffering from genuine depression, however, and heard her 'weeping and wailing' in her cell.[27] Her weight had dropped again; she was now seven stone and painfully thin, even though she joined in with a cookery club and paid (with cigarettes) a West Indian woman to cook her a meal once a week. She wrote despondent letters to her high-profile supporters, including actor Robert Speaight and the former Secretary of the British Board of Film Censors, John Trevelyan, who was an old school friend of Lord Longford. She told Trevelyan: 'Something is slowly dying inside me, and it's the will to live . . . I just want to drag myself into a corner in the dark, as does an animal when it knows it is dying, and if I had no moral responsibilities and didn't owe so much to so many people I think I could quite easily do so now . . .'[28]

A new affair cheered her, but when the authorities heard about the relationship, the girl in question was moved to another prison. Myra was flattered to be chosen for the prison's Nativity play that Christmas, but the entire remand wing filed out in protest when she walked onto the stage as Mary.

She became hopelessly maudlin as the new year began, writing an essay, 'The Intimate Revelations of Myra Hindley in Prison for Life', in which she queried why her hair had not turned white 'under the intolerable burden of my thoughts'. She described the escape plan in excessively florid terms: 'I told [Tricia] the way is suspicious, the result uncertain, perhaps destructive. "You would have to give up all else. I alone would need to be your sole and exclusive standard. Your motivation would even then be long and exhausting. The whole past theory of your life and all conformity to those around you would have to be abandoned."'[29] In letters that would have appalled her victims' families, she began to think about motherhood: 'I would like a child, perhaps even two. I would like to have a child before I reach forty, but I'd like to have a couple of years free in order to cram in as much living as possible to make up for the years of merely existing.'[30] The authorities wondered whether she was again planning to escape; internal memos refer to Myra having been given an official warning about her ability to mimic the voices of prison staff, which they feared might enable her to open the electronic door locks.[31]

In an effort to convince people that she was a reformed woman, Longford, Trevelyan and Speaight released her letters to the *Sunday Times*, which resulted in more contempt being heaped upon themselves, while Myra was branded a hypocrite. John Trevelyan asked his daughter Sara to visit Myra, thinking it might lift her spirits. Sara, then training to become a psychotherapist and sharing her father's campaigning zeal, agreed. She recalls, 'Dad felt it would be good for Myra to be visited by someone her own age, instead of all these elderly men. Because I'd been living on the other side of the world when Myra was tried, I didn't have any preconceived ideas about her. She spoke quietly but was very easy to talk to and highly intelligent. She had started smoking again, as a way of coping with a completely monotonous routine. We didn't speak much about the past, but I was very much under the impression that Ian had dominated her and that it was his fault that she'd got into these "situations". I was always quite sensitive about not wanting to push her and let her talk about whatever she wanted. She told me a lot about her immediate family, and about Maureen especially.'[32] After ten years apart, Myra had been reconciled with her sister.

Maureen and Dave divorced in 1973.[33] She had a new relationship with lorry driver Bill Scott; on their first date, she blurted out why she hadn't gone out with him earlier when he'd asked: 'I'm Myra Hindley's sister.' But he was interested in her, not her family, and recalled later, 'We'd had some good fun and a few laughs and she told me later it was the first time she'd laughed since 1965.'[34] He eventually divorced his wife – his children were grown up – and found a place to live in Manchester with Maureen, where he witnessed the constant abuse to which she was subject. She travelled with him up and down the country in his lorry and began to enjoy life again. When she fell pregnant with her daughter Sharon, the two of them were delighted; Maureen still saw her sons from her marriage to Dave, but they were settled with their father and had come to regard Mary, who was a constant presence in their lives, as their mother.

Six weeks after Sharon was born, Maureen and Bill took their daughter to visit Myra in Holloway. Maureen recalled: 'I was really nervous the first time. I think, honestly, in the back of my mind, I still had a repulsion for what she'd done, what she'd got herself involved in . . . I didn't know whether I'd be able to act normally. I went in and there she was. She was nothing like she was when she first went in. Actually, at first I didn't realise it was her. She'd really changed.'[35] They hugged and wept and talked about old times; Myra called Sharon her queen and 'my little ray of sunshine', inundating her with gifts and cards.[36] She decorated the walls of her cell with photographs of Sharon and urged her sister to ask her ex-husband for pictures of their three sons. Maureen had also been reunited with her father, who had suffered several strokes and was confined to bed in the council maisonette where he lived alone, visited by nurses. Although Bob's speech was afflicted by the strokes, he was overwhelmed to meet his tiny granddaughter and remained in close touch with Maureen and Bill. The couple married 18 months after Sharon's birth; she travelled with her parents and Maureen's dog, Rusty, in the lorry until starting nursery school.

Maureen always planned on telling Sharon about Myra's crimes before she heard it from anyone else, insisting, 'When she is old enough for it to sink in and intelligent enough for her to understand, I'll take her to the newspaper section of the library and let her read all about it for herself. She'll then have to make up her own mind about it.'[37]

Despite, or perhaps because of, their renewed closeness, Maureen questioned Myra twice about other missing children; she wanted to know about her friend, Pauline Reade, especially. Myra shook her head vehemently and said she didn't know anything about them.

An internal report, dated 26 March 1976, on Myra's progress noted that she caused trouble for herself and others by asking inmates to carry letters for her. She had also 'earnestly requested' that Lord Longford and his friends stop their campaign on her behalf. She looked 'thin and haggard . . . On rare occasions she chooses to talk about the past, but there is absolutely nothing new to report on her revelations about her offences and there probably never will be.'[38]

'Vice-queen' Janie Jones was among Myra's newer circle of friends; blonde and glamorous, she denies that her friendship with

Myra ever developed into a sexual relationship but admits that Myra bombarded her with attention when she arrived. Even after their friendship began in earnest, Myra would shower Janie with extravagant poems and letters, which Janie shared with another inmate, laughing hysterically at lines such as: 'I wish I could tell you how much and how deeply I love you, but I can't. Words have not yet been invented to describe such feelings of such capacity and depth in such a short space of time. (Yet I feel it has been written across the face of fate even before the concept of time evolved) . . .'[39] Janie also believed that Myra had fallen under the spell of a murderous Svengali. Apart from Myra's tendency to sulk or shout when she didn't get her way, Janie regarded her as a kind and gentle woman who adored children and would spend many hours in the prison's mother and baby unit, cuddling the children and treating them to sweets.[40] Several inmates asked Myra to be godmother to their children, and she accepted.

On Sunday, 26 September 1976, Myra asked to see the *News of the World*, after a fellow inmate told her that *The Sun* was running a tenth anniversary feature about the Moors trial. She was horrified to find that the article partially quoted the transcript of the tape recording, and told an officer, 'I'm so uptight, I'm going to freak out.'[41] She was assured that the newspaper would not be available to inmates on her wing. At the same time, 19-year-old Josie O'Dwyer, who had been in and out of custody since the age of 14, was primed to attack Myra. She recalls how she knew nothing of the case until two officers took her into a room, 'sat me behind the door, opened out this two-page spread and said, "Read that" . . . and because what I read had made me shake and tremble with horror, they took me for a walk round the prison grounds. When I got back it was dinner time, so I went up to the recess to the loo, came out and was washing my hands when I heard someone coming up the stairs. It was Myra. I thought, "I'll just stay here until she goes by." But she didn't go by, she came on across the bridge. Apparently, she had been talking to the officers and she had actually been kept in the office until they knew I was in the recess . . . I went for her.'[42]

According to an internal memo: 'O'Dwyer states that Hindley hissed at her, whilst Hindley states that she "tut-tutted" at O'Dwyer when the latter called her a "child-murdering bastard". From staff statements it would appear that O'Dwyer's version is probably correct.'[43] Josie launched herself on Myra, punching and kicking her to the ground. Janie Jones heard the commotion and rushed to the scene: 'Myra did nothing. Absolutely nothing. Her blood was squirting all over the place, she was being kicked and punched senseless, but she simply swayed around limply as she took every blow . . . She didn't lift a finger to help herself. So in I charged . . . Josie released Myra – but not before she'd broken her nose and kicked out the cartilage in her leg. There was blood everywhere . . . The alarm bells were sounding but no officers came. Josie was kicking Myra full in the face . . . Then she picked her up and seemed to be trying to throw her over the rail. Myra did not scream or cry out, but she clung limply to the rail.'[44]

Officers eventually went to Myra's aid. She was taken to an outside hospital and booked in under the name 'Susan Gibb'. Surgeons discovered her nose was broken, her lip and one ear had been split, her eyes blackened, front teeth loosened and the cartilage in one of her knees damaged. She had to eat liquid food through a straw for six weeks. Josie also ended up in hospital because the stitches from the tattoos she had recently had removed had burst open as she tackled Myra. She recalls, 'The officers treated me like a celebrity. It was: "Here's half an ounce of tobacco, Josie"; "Let me shake your hand"; "Well done, Josie, I've waited 12 years for someone to do that," etc.'[45] Myra wrote a private letter to the authorities, sensing what had happened: 'It is my opinion, which I feel at liberty to express to you, confidentially, that Josie O'Dwyer was in some way used as a pawn, however willingly a pawn, in a most unhealthy and, to me, frightening game. If anything I have said here can be used as mitigating circumstances at the adjudication which Josie O'Dwyer faces, then I hope it can do so, even though I still feel a natural antipathy for what she did to me.'[46] To other inmates, she was less charitable about Josie. Carole Callaghan claimed that Myra had asked her to 'find that cow and break her arms and legs' and an internal memo alleges that she and Lord Longford 'both laughed' when he informed Myra that Josie had been placed in the punishment block.[47]

Myra's facial injuries were such that in December she wrote to inform her mother that she didn't want Sharon to visit in case she was frightened by her appearance. She was also depressed by the news that her friend Robert Speaight had died unexpectedly, but she welcomed a visit by Elizabeth Longford. Initially opposed to her husband's friendship with Myra, Lady Longford decided she should meet her and recorded in her diary: 'Myra, very slim, was dressed in a long skirt and white blouse, her long brown hair loosely combed – very pale complexion and dark blue eyes – black lashes and regular eyebrows . . . The impression she now gives is of deep sadness. Her voice is low and rather husky . . . She showed us her bandaged and swollen leg and knee and the marks of her two black eyes were still visible . . .'[48] After persuading Myra to let them renew the campaign for her, Lady Longford recalled that Myra 'kissed me goodbye, putting one hand at the back of my fur hat. I responded, feeling deeply moved and unhappy at the whole ghastly tragedy.'[49]

For Myra, 1977 began auspiciously. On 23 January, she sent her mother a birthday card and enclosed £3 from the money she had won after coming first in the Koestler Prize for prison arts – she sang three Joan Baez songs while playing the guitar. But that same month, due to renovation work in Holloway, Myra was transferred without warning to Durham, where the routine was far stricter and the place itself uniformly dismal. Myra was put on H wing, within the men's prison, where women had to eat their meals watched from a glass observation box. Every morning the inmates emptied their toilet pails into a sluice room whose stench hung over the breakfast table. Prisoners were not allowed to socialise behind closed doors, cameras were everywhere and even the toilets had half-doors.

Anne Maguire arrived in Durham after being wrongly convicted of running an IRA bomb-making factory. Her husband and two sons were imprisoned for their alleged part in the Guildford bombings, despite the complete lack of evidence against them. Anne's strong Catholic beliefs, and her knowledge that she was innocent and would eventually be reunited with her family, sustained her, together with the friendships she made in prison. She vividly remembers Durham's bleakness, its poor and often contaminated food, and the cold gym. She recalls: 'When Myra arrived, we were all locked in. There were girls already there from Holloway who knew her and didn't want anything to do with her. They were called into the office about that. They wouldn't go to church either, if she was there. I said to the priest, "Well, Father, it's like this: the devil himself won't keep me out of

Mass. I don't have to sit beside her, I have my own seat that I had before she ever came into the building." He asked me to have a word with the other girls because I got on with them all – they called me Mother. So I did and the following Sunday they went to church as usual.'[50]

Anne kept her distance from Myra, determined not to get involved in anything that would affect her own sentence. 'I just passed the time of day with her. But then when I was sat in my cell, a knock came on the door and I heard Myra say, "It's me, Anne." Well, I just froze, I did. I'm telling the truth, I didn't know what to do. I said, "Yes. What do you want, Myra?" And she said, "I know you don't believe that I'm innocent of this." I said back, "Look, Myra, please, I don't want to know. Really, I just don't want to know. I've enough to get on with. I don't want you to talk to me about anything. But I'll tell you this: at the time, when it all came out, if I could have got into Holloway I'd have smacked your face, so I would. What you've done is horrible." And Myra said, "If you'd just read the court papers—" "No," I said, "I couldn't and I don't see any purpose in it. I'm not a judge. The only judge who'll judge us rightly is the Man above us." She agreed with me, "I believe that too, Anne. That's my belief." So I said, "Well, you live with that, then. But I know I'm totally innocent." She said straight back, "And what are people thinking about you today, Anne?" I said, "Yes, I'm sure there are mothers thinking I'm a horrible woman, but I *am* innocent."'[51]

Myra hated Durham, where exercise was taken in the concrete yard overlooked by male prisoners who chanted 'Hang Mad Myra' every time she appeared. When Longford visited her in February, bringing her repaired record player, she told him, 'I'm all right, but I've gone back ten years and I've started my sentence all over again from square one. I've had to become a cleaner again. My pay has gone down 70p and I think it's terrible to start again after ten years of it.'[52] Sara Trevelyan also visited Myra in Durham: 'The conditions were horrendous and had a profound effect on her. She was dosed up with Valium. Myra described the place as "a concrete submarine". She got very depressed and her voice would become very low. Her handwriting, too, was infinitesimal, the microscopic handwriting of a deeply depressed and disturbed woman.'[53] Myra had to give her small personal library to friends, keeping only those books that were essential for her OU course.

The lack of fresh air and greenery turned her skin grey and her eyesight deteriorated. Her movements were shuffling; one prisoner described her as a zombie because she took so many tranquillisers, which also contributed to her weight gain. She smoked heavily, and the only thing that really cheered her was an affair with a married Scots woman. She liked the Roman Catholic chaplain, Father Algy Shearwater, and at his instigation began practising *The Spiritual Exercises*, a Jesuit book of prayers and reflections about the Bible.

Anne Maguire recalls: 'Myra was depressed, but so were all of us. I will say that she did a lot of good concerning prisoners' rights, helping people write petitions and telling us what we were allowed. She arranged for us the right to offer refreshments to our visitors, because before then we hadn't been able to give them so much as a glass of water. When she first tried approaching us, some of the girls didn't want to know, but she said, "You either listen or you don't. But I'm going to have a tray with a teapot, biscuits, you name it, I will have it on that tray and I will take it out with me on visits. Because I know my rights." The first time I took a tray out, Myra was near the hot water boiler. This officer in spectacles came up to me – she was nice, we used to be able to have a laugh with her – she said, "Right, Maguire, I have to check everything on your tray." I said, "Aye, all right then." She said, "Right, teapot," and I took the lid off the teapot and all the steam blew out and misted up her glasses. Myra went into fits of laughter, absolute fits of laughter. The officer said, "I should have known I could leave it to you to do that, Maguire." I said, "Well, you asked to see the teapot, didn't you?!" But Myra sorted that out, and it was really a blessing for us. She did a lot in that respect.'[54]

Myra's attention was deflected in May to putting a stop to *Our Kid*, a play about her crimes.[55] She asked for an injunction to be taken out against it on her behalf, writing to a correspondent: 'Whilst it would be a change for something constructive to be written about me, as opposed to the usual unedifying rubbish, I don't want it to be at the expense of people to whom it would cause any kind of distress, including Mrs West, who seems to think I condone and even encourage this kind of thing, or to my own mother, who has suffered also in her own way.'[56]

On 6 July 1977, the BBC discussion programme *Brass Tacks* devoted an episode to Myra's bid for parole. Representing her were

Lord Longford, Janie Jones (recently released from prison), Maureen (in silhouette) and Sara Trevelyan. Among those speaking against her was Ann West, whose grief and fury lent eloquence to her delivery: 'When does *my* parole begin? I am serving a life sentence because of that monster. I had to listen to those tapes of my daughter begging for mercy. If Myra Hindley comes out, *I'll* be up for murder. I've said this to Lord Longford once and I'll say it again: she will be *one dead woman*. I want *justice*.'[57] Patrick Kilbride, John's father, telephoned the studio to echo her words: 'I'll wait outside the jail for her and I'll kill her.'[58] Afterwards, the BBC switchboard was inundated with calls supporting the victims' families; while those who had defended Myra were quickly ushered out of the back doors of the studio.[59] An opinion poll taken in the wake of the show revealed that 84 per cent of those approached believed that Myra should never be freed.

Writing to Maureen afterwards, Myra spoke of her desperation at the diminishing prospect of parole and the effect of her notoriety on her mother Nellie: 'I often feel it would be better for her if I were dead, for although it would be terrible for her at first, eventually she would find peace of mind . . . I think of Ann West, her natural grief curdled and made rancid by hatred and bitterness, perpetually robed in almost manic fanaticism, and my heart aches for her, about the state she's allowed herself to get into. But then I think of her constant harping about mothers and children, and think of my own mother, whom she never gives a thought to; my mother who is as innocent as that child was (whose innocence I was partly responsible for taking away, but whose life I was <u>not</u>) and some of her hatred and bitterness rubs off on me . . .'[60] When Longford visited Myra, he found her in low spirits and wrote to *The Times*: 'No one who knows her seriously supposes that she would be a public menace if she were released. Her state of remorse is such that she will be haunted by it all her life.'[61]

In January 1978, Ian Brady resurfaced in the public eye with a letter in the *Daily Mirror*, declaring that Longford didn't represent his views on parole; he wrote that he no longer allowed Longford to visit him because of his 'Free Myra' campaign, adding from his cell in Wormwood Scrubs: 'I have always accepted that the weight of the crimes both Myra and I were convicted of justifies permanent imprisonment, regardless of expressed personal remorse and verifiable change.'[62]

Myra was briefly cheered by another development: 'On a recent TV programme, David Smith, chief prosecution witness, admitted to planning a murder with Ian Brady. Things could be changing, rapidly ...'[63] But no further action was taken, since Dave had told the police everything during his original interview at Hyde.

In October, an internal memo noted: 'Hindley ... gives the impression that she is complying willingly with the system but beneath the surface she is continually trying to beat the system. She is most selective in her choice of associates and opts to mix with the brighter and financially endowed individuals . . . In addition, her correspondence is full of innuendos and these are written to people who she feels can be of help during her sentence.'[64] The memo referred to John Trevelyan asking Myra to let him have a list of complaints that he might take up on her behalf; Myra had done so 'with alacrity'.[65] Although the memo ended more positively: 'She maintains high personal standards, works hard in her studies and creates few problems', a follow-up memo two months later describes her as 'a devious and difficult prisoner'.[66]

Since her arrival in Durham, Myra had worked tirelessly on her parole plea, penning 21,000 words over 36 pages, which was then sent on to Labour Home Secretary Merlyn Rees. In it, she presented herself as the girlish victim of her love for a cruel older man and innocent of the crimes for which she was convicted: 'To me, [the Moors] have represented nothing more and nothing less than a peaceful solitude which I cherish. Of the bodies and graves I know nothing ...' Repeating her earlier declaration to Lord Longford, she went on: 'I had placed Ian Brady on a pedestal, where he had always been, aloof and out of reach, and I had loved him blindly . . . Flaubert said we should never touch our idols, for the gilt always rubbed off on our fingers. One day I gained the courage to reach up and touch, and the gilt did rub off. He crashed from his pedestal and the dust and ashes of a dead love flaked around my feet. But it was unbearably painful, it always is when one is prepared to face reality squarely.'[67] She described her part in the photographing of Lesley as an 'unsavoury business' that 'bad as it was, was a far cry from what it has been alleged to be'.[68] She ended her plea: 'I feel that Society owes me a living . . . I have served Society in good stead as scapegoat and whipping boy for far too many years . . . Is my life going to be sacrificed? . . . Hope springs eternal, but I'm afraid the spring is drying up.'[69]

Her petition was rejected. On the recommendation of a joint Home Office/Parole Board committee, Rees stated that Myra's case wouldn't be considered again for another three years. She described the outcome as 'the latest piece of infamy connected with my fate' in a letter to Longford.[70] To John Trevelyan she wrote that she would only recover from the shock 'when my spirit has wept its last weary tear'.[71] At the same time, an internal memo discussed Myra's attempt to change her name surreptitiously and concluded that she had 'the intelligence to manipulate and subvert both situations and individuals without resorting to actual untruths but merely by quietly and persistently putting her case in a seductive and disarming manner and leaving it to others to carry through the inappropriate and untoward activities'.[72]

Ian Brady was furious when he read in the press about the picture Myra presented in her parole plea. At Wormwood Scrubs, he received psychological help, worked as a cleaner in the hospital wing and used his literary skills to help other prisoners fill out parole forms. He played chess expertly with an array of infamous characters, including the disgraced former Labour Cabinet Minister John Stonehouse and poisoner Graham Young, who favoured the black chess pieces every time, even though he never won a match against Ian. He also had long conversations with Peter Sutcliffe, the Yorkshire Ripper. Lord Longford visited to ask Ian to confirm the account he had given at the trial of Myra's role in the crimes. The answer was a definite no; from then on, Ian intended to do whatever he could to establish her guilt without incriminating himself further – or revealing the truth about their other murders.

24

I really am haunted by that missing child and his poor mother:
I've been haunted for years and years but more so now that I've
been able to confront the nightmare.

Myra Hindley, letter to David Astor, 28 March 1988

In January 1980, Myra received her Bachelor of Arts degree in
Humanities, despite having had the beginnings of pleurisy when she
sat her final exam. She declared: 'I do feel an amount of pride. It
was a challenge.'[1] She aimed to continue with her studies, intending
to convert her achievement into a BA (Hons) degree, but took a
break for the remainder of the year when her sister Maureen died
unexpectedly.

During a night out that summer with Bill, Maureen complained
of a headache and the following morning he woke to the sound of
her retching. He called the doctor, who rushed her into hospital. A
brain haemorrhage was diagnosed, but after an emergency operation,
Maureen seemed to rally and Myra sent a get well card for her to
Nellie, with £5 to cover her mother's travel costs to the hospital and
back. Then she heard that Maureen had suffered a relapse and was in
a coma. Myra was hysterical; the Home Office granted her permission
to visit her sister, but when she arrived at Crumpsall Hospital – where
she herself had been born 38 years earlier – she was told that the life
support machine had been switched off an hour earlier.[2] Maureen
died on the morning of 9 July 1980, at the age of 34.

Three years later, Myra described the pain she felt at her sister's
death as almost unendurable, but if it gave her cause to consider the
anguish felt by her victims' families, then she never mentioned it; she
untruthfully told another reporter that when she visited Maureen's
coffin in the hospital chapel, 'It was the first time I had ever seen a

dead person.'[3] She wrote to her mother afterwards, telling her that however painful it was for her, as a sister, she knew it must be worse for a parent to lose a child.[4]

Her fellow inmates were in no doubt that her grief was genuine. Anne Maguire recalls: 'Maureen was such a lovely girl. When we passed through on our way to the exercise yard – you had to pass through the visiting room by the door – she would be waving and smiling at us. The day after she died, Myra asked if we would do a rosary for Maureen, and we did; you don't refuse to pray for anybody. Myra thanked us all. She was broken by her sister's death.'[5]

On 11 July, Myra wrote to the authorities: 'I do want to attend the funeral and share my family's sorrow, but I feel I would only add to it if the press or other media are present, which I'm sure they will be. So I have decided not to ask to go for that reason – to protect my family and my sister's dignity.'[6] The press were indeed out in force at Blackley crematorium; the night before, Patrick Kilbride and Ann West were anonymously tipped off about the funeral and went, expecting to see Myra there. Patrick mistook Bill's daughter for Myra and made a rush at her. He was tackled to the ground and the police charged in as Ann West started to scream. After everyone had gone, Lesley's mother shredded the wreath Myra had sent and its card – 'There are no words to express how I miss you. I love you – Myra.'[7]

It fell to Bill to inform Bob Hindley that Maureen was dead. He took the news badly and four months later, on 7 November 1980, died of a heart attack. His son-in-law felt it was for the best; the elderly man had been plagued by gangs of teenagers who knew that he was Myra Hindley's father and threw bricks at his windows and shouted abuse through his letter box. Again, Myra informed the prison authorities that she had no wish to attend the funeral, although her reasons were different, since she had never been reconciled with her father. It was another 14 years before she began to make her peace with him, telling her prison therapist: 'I've only recently understood why he was the way he was. His experiences in the war produced violence in many men; my dad was no different.'[8]

Although Bill continued to visit, bringing Sharon with him, and her relationship with her mother grew even stronger, Myra sank into a deep depression towards the end of the year. At the start of 1981, she wrote to Lord Longford that she had asked to be placed on Rule 43 (solitary confinement), which was refused: 'These feelings have been building up inside me for a long time now. I can trace them back clearly to when Maureen died, because – personal grief apart – I was beginning to realise that someone whom youth and health guaranteed to be around when they finally let me out wouldn't be after all ... Maureen's death ... crippled me with grief.'[9] She brightened when, following a relaxation of British law, ex-prisoners were granted the right to correspond with and visit inmates, resulting in a torrent of letters for her from Rachel Pinney, Janie Jones and Carole Callaghan, among others.[10] She also sought solace in affairs; an internal memo dated 1 September 1981 states that Myra had been found in a compromising position with another inmate and lost 14 days' privileges as a result. In protest, she went on hunger strike. A report on her progress two months later observed: 'She does possess a strong will and character, but has always shown a feeling for others which would appear genuine and not entirely self-centred in character. I think in particular this relates to her own family and to one or two close friendships she has struck up with other inmates. Whilst the nature of her inmate relationships has, on occasions, been questioned, I think they simply reflect the constraints and experiences imposed by long-term imprisonment.'[11]

Myra had passed another Open University course and began her next, Man's Religious Quest, which she was forced to drop after breaking a heel in the prison gym. She set her academic ambitions to one side, but told friends she hoped to complete an external MA in English Literature either at Durham or London university in the future. In letters, she scoffed at the idea that her studies would have any influence on her chances of parole: 'After all, what will it matter to the decision-makers that I've obtained a degree, when I wasn't sent to prison because I was illiterate? The public are only concerned with the myth they've been saturated in.'[12]

Two new and hugely influential people entered her life: Peter Timms and David Astor. Timms began his career in the Prison Service as an officer at Wakefield Prison in 1952 and after various promotions became governor of Maidstone, where he met Lord Longford during one of his regular visits to East End gangster Charlie Richardson. Through Longford, Timms met former *Observer* editor David Astor, who used his name and connections to lobby for various causes, including the early anti-apartheid campaign. At

Astor's request, Timms became a trustee of the prison arts charity, the Koestler Trust. Longford pressed both men to help Myra. 'He wasn't getting anywhere,' Timms recalls. 'Not in terms of getting her case thought about seriously. He said to David, "You're a press baron, what can we do?" So David and I went to the House of Lords and had a cup of tea with Frank. I said there was really no point in being involved unless Frank shut up. Frank was one of the world's angels, really, but every time he opened his mouth about Myra it was a disaster. He said, "But you can't expect me to stop saying things altogether", and I said, "Well, just shut up a lot then." And, in fairness, he did, and when he couldn't stop himself, he told us about it.'[13] David Astor's widow, Bridget, recalls: 'David and Frank were very good friends; Frank was a contemporary of David's older brother, Bill. Frank and David discovered they had various social concerns in common, though they quarrelled violently on other issues, but neither of them really minded and they were extremely close. David was particularly interested in prisoners because he had a half-brother who was jailed for homosexuality in the 1940s for about six months.'[14]

Timms is at pains to point out that he never argued for Myra's release: 'That's not why I got involved. I know people think I said that, but I didn't. All that concerned me was that she shouldn't be treated differently to any other prisoner because of her name, her crime or her gender. She was entitled to justice like every other prisoner.'[15] His first attempt at intervention concerned Pope John Paul's visit to Britain: 'I rang the chaplain to the Archbishop of Westminster beforehand and said, "Look, I think that if the Pope were to ask to see Myra Hindley, that would be enormously liberating for this country. People are locked in a vicious cycle of bitterness fuelled by the press. I think the Pope could create a whole new climate of the way in which we approach people who've done awful things." He said no. I said, "Well, get the Pope to at least ask about her then. On the record if possible." But he didn't.'[16] In the meantime, Astor wrote to Myra – they corresponded for several months before meeting – explaining why he thought people in general were so staunchly opposed to her and Longford's efforts on her behalf: 'The public associates both of you with something which they are frightened of in themselves. It is generally admitted that violence towards children is much more prevalent than people generally like to admit. My wife and I think that every parent instinctively knows that the possibility of this happening is present in all parent–child relationships. But of course this is something of which most people are very much afraid and about which they feel very ashamed.'[17]

Myra gained a new solicitor through another long-time friend, Sara Trevelyan, who introduced her to Michael Fisher: 'Myra liked him. He was a wonderful solicitor, quite radical, and at that point I felt hopeful that we might be able to help her.'[18] Fisher shared Astor's opinion that Myra had been obsessed with, and intimidated by, Ian Brady, and believed that if they could convince people that she had changed radically since her conviction, then she might have a chance of freedom. But an early attempt to rehabilitate her in the public eye rebounded, when Fisher persuaded Myra and her friends and family to meet two journalists, Linda Melvern and Peter Gillman. Myra gave her first prison interview to Melvern and wrote 6,000 words in response to her questions. The subsequent article appeared in the *Sunday Times* under the headline 'The Woman Who Cannot Face the Truth'. Myra was horror-struck at the unfavourable piece, as were Fisher and her other supporters. It was many years before Myra believed any journalist could be trusted at all. She warned friends who mentioned talking to the press: 'Remember Linda.'[19] She was further agitated when she heard that Ian had been visited at his own request by the police. Ian told them nothing but knew the news of the meeting would rattle her.

Myra had petitioned to return to Holloway and was transferred in 1983 – but to somewhere far superior. Cookham Wood in Kent was built in the 1970s and originally housed only young men, but was adapted to accommodate the rising number of women prisoners. When Myra arrived on South Wing, she remained in her cell for two days until other inmates had absorbed the fact that she was there. When she ventured out, the attacks were harsh but few and she was ecstatic about the relaxed atmosphere in comparison to Durham and Holloway. She was allowed to study every afternoon, limiting her prison work to the mornings, although she was delighted to be assigned to garden duty, and could furnish her cell with her own choice of curtains, bed linen, rugs, plants and pictures, as well as toiletries, records and books. She was able to sit in her cell chatting with friends and wrote to Carole that her new billet was 'as different from Durham in every respect as a Matabele Zulu warrior is to yer average Wall Street executive . . . I've just looked at the calendar to see what date it is . . . the 19th [April]. A shattering alarm bell reverberated around my whole head. Seventeen years ago today I was climbing up the steps to the dock in Chester Castle. And the judge and jury are *still* sitting in condemnation . . .'[20]

Ann West was photographed standing outside the prison gates in protest against the move. In the previous three years, she had twice taken an overdose of the tranquillisers she relied upon, and voluntarily admitted herself to a psychiatric hospital; she had also become close to spiritualist Doris Stokes, who she believed was able to communicate with Lesley. She would have been incensed to discover the effect Cookham Wood had on Myra. Sara Trevelyan, who was married then to Jimmy Boyle, a former gangster who had served time in Glasgow's Barlinnie Prison for a murder he claimed he hadn't committed, recalls: 'She really blossomed. She grew tanned and slim, healthy-looking again. At Cookham Wood there were trees and gardens, lighter buildings and more pleasantness generally. I didn't see her often because it was much further away for me to visit, plus my children were very young. The challenging part was that Jimmy always said, "she isn't telling the full truth". He had much more street sense than me and challenged her about it, but she didn't say anything.'[21]

Myra was happier than she had been for a long time. She had several short-lived affairs in Cookham Wood, which crime writer Val McDermid, then a journalist, highlighted in an article in the *Sunday People*.

Shortly before her first visit from David Astor, Myra wrote to him about the 'scurrilous' press, quoting from *Jane Eyre*: 'I envy you your peace of mind, your clean conscience, your unpolluted memory. A memory without blot or contamination must be an exquisite treasure.'[22] Sounding very much like a pupil trying to impress a teacher, she asked: 'Would you agree with what Charlotte Brontë says a few pages earlier, that remorse is the poison of life, repentance its cure or antidote? I think that remorse can be poisonous if one tortures oneself with it; it can wear one's soul away if not tempered by sincere repentance and a desire for forgiveness . . . It's not that I will not but that I cannot express remorse for something I haven't done.'[23]

In September 1983, Astor visited her with Peter Timms (now Revd). On another occasion, and several times afterwards, they were joined by Bridget Astor, who recalls her first impression of Myra: 'Have you seen the *Longford* film? Well, she was *nothing* like that. There was nothing of Myra in that portrayal; that was a little mouse, but Myra was *self-assured* – she knew who she was, had a good sense of humour and was relaxed. She had great dignity and you could feel that she was nicely amused that David and I were there. She was calm, very well-read, clued-up on politics and highly intelligent. I found her incredibly easy to talk to. I saw her quite often after that, I should think on average about every six to eight weeks. She knew her rights, too; she could have been a lawyer if she'd wanted to be. I think she could have done anything with her life, really.'[24]

Nonetheless, Myra's studies faltered without the assistance she had grown accustomed to from an Oxford University graduate who had helped her in the past. At the end of the year, she failed her exam for the honours degree and temporarily set aside her studies. She was angry that a letter had reached her from Patrick Downey, Lesley's uncle, which included the line: 'I would still be prepared to kill you and stand trial for my crime.'[25] An internal memo notes that her primary concern was 'the possible influence the Downey family may exercise upon her release'.[26] When she didn't respond to his letter, Patrick wrote again and contacted the press. On 20 May 1984, Myra asked the prison governor to intervene, declaring that although she was worried about seeming 'callous' for not replying to his letters, 'I've always felt threatened by this family ... I really do feel very threatened,' and declared herself 'equally as haunted [as the Downeys] and hunted, not just by my own past actions but by their increasingly threatening campaign'.[27] There were no more letters from Patrick Downey.

A few weeks later, Myra was attacked in her cell. An inmate sneaked in and dragged her from her bed to the floor, beating Myra about the head with a shoe. Her recovery was slow; she was also experiencing chronic hot flushes as she went through the menopause and worried perpetually about her 'parasite' stepfather, whom she feared was spending all her mother's money on beer.[28] She grew despondent in the wake of the attack and shelved her Open University course. On 23 July, she was transferred to the prison hospital, where she remained for two months. One of her most pressing anxieties was the thought of her niece learning the truth about her; Sharon was then approaching double figures and knew only that her auntie Myra had done 'something bad' in the past. Myra was unable to sleep, even with medication – cannabis was her only weapon in the struggle against stress-related insomnia.

When her despondency lifted sufficiently for her to be sent back to the wing, Myra swapped jobs, working in the library and on reception, and prepared tea for senior officers. She spent hours knitting in her cell for the children of other prisoners and their families and friends. In a letter, she reflected: 'That's what I've missed . . . I'll never be able to have a baby now and I would have liked one so much. I'd have loved to have been a mother but I've no chance now. *If* I got out tomorrow, I'd still be too old.'[29] Although through circumstance her affairs were restricted to women, she was excited by the visit of a group of firemen to Cookham Wood, and tickled when she prepared tea and none of them recognised her. A prison officer – who, like all the other officers, called her Harry 'because it goes with Hindley' – told her that the men had asked about her and were puzzled when they learned she had been in their company. She began to take pride in her appearance again, buying expensive shampoo to wash her auburn hair, and asked another inmate to apply her make-up and nail varnish.[30] She was interested in politics and supported the Labour Party; she watched the news twice a day and read *The Guardian*. Her rediscovery of Catholicism didn't deter her from exploring other religions and mysticism: she enjoyed reading horoscopes and delving into the I Ching. She wrote a lot of spiritual nonsense in letters to her friends: '. . . feel me slowly around you – I'm weaving a green and gold web of mystical, magical strands, I'm spinning a calming cocoon of quiet sanity, an oasis of tranquillity . . .'[31] Unknown to her, Ian was weaving a web of his own, and aiming to trap her within it.

Ian's cell in Gartree Prison was bare but for a bed, bucket, table and chair, and the view beyond the window was too bleak even for him. He declared that his crimes 'were the acts of a madman. I don't deserve any sympathy and I would never seek it. I want to spend the rest of my life inside. I want to die in jail.'[32] Towards the end of 1984, he allowed journalist Fred Harrison to visit him; they had been exchanging letters for a year, after Lord Longford had telephoned Harrison to commend him on the accuracy of an article he had written about Ian for the *Sunday People*. No one else had visited Ian for years; he couldn't bear the idea of his mother seeing him on the hospital wing, where he had begun to imagine voices emerging from the radiators, questioning him about his crimes. At night the prison staff heard him cursing in his cell, where he slept on the chair rather than in bed; he often required sedation. He spent his canteen money on anything sweet and refused to exercise but left crumbs for birds on the window sill, shrinking back from the view of the misty marshland at night: 'I expect a 1930s Dracula to come out of the dark.'[33] Harrison sensed that Ian was readying himself to talk about the past and bided his time.

In Cookham Wood, Myra wished Anne Maguire luck when she gained her release after being transferred there for the last year of her sentence: 'She knew I was going to fight what had happened to my family and she got Lord Longford involved. When I won my case, Myra sent a message through him to say that she was happy we'd proved our innocence.'[34] She said a different goodbye to Carole Callaghan when her former fellow inmate sold her letters to the *Daily Star*. She accused Carole of having 'syphilis of the brain'.[35]

Her spirits soared when she learned that a Prison Review Committee had recommended her for parole. When the news broke in the press, Danny Kilbride told *The Sun* that he would kill her if she were released. He recalls: 'I was arrested on Hindley's instructions through her solicitor. The police wanted me to retract what I'd said, but I wouldn't. Her supporters never gave a thought to what *we* went through, as a family. It tore my mum apart and it affected my parents' relationship with us – we couldn't move because they were so protective. I had to take one of my mates with me when I did my paper-round, otherwise my dad wouldn't let me do it. I remember the first time I asked my mother if I could go all-night fishing. She said no and I said, "Well, I'm going." Typical teenager. But I couldn't do that to her. Then three weeks later, when my mates asked me again, she said, "Go then, but be careful." It used to break my heart, watching her trying to play with the young ones while she was crying for our John. When I became a dad, and my kids wanted to go out, I'd be right there. They'd be playing with a football or a cricket bat and I'd be watching every move. I realise that in a lot of ways that was unfair, but I couldn't help it. What happened to us affects you in ways you can't imagine. Life would definitely have been easier for my family if she'd have just accepted her punishment.'[36]

In May 1985, Home Secretary Leon Brittan announced that the Parole Board had recommended that Myra Hindley should spend at least another five years in prison before being considered for release. Myra was shattered by the news. She poured her resentment into a long-winded letter to Brittan, telling him that her religious beliefs were the only thing preventing her from taking her own life. She labelled him her 'mental executioner' and ended with her favourite quote from *Jane Eyre*. Nellie was moved to give a rare interview: 'It's better she dies there than comes out of prison and gets killed out here. Myra's been in prison all these years, so what difference could it make if she stays there forever? If Myra came out, she couldn't come here. I don't know where she would go. People wouldn't let her alone. She might as well die in prison. Poor Myra. Life means life for Myra. For others it means just a few years. When they call her a beast or a devil, they don't know what they're talking about. They don't know her. She's still my daughter. I love her just like I always have done.'[37]

If Myra thought her position could not get any worse, she was mistaken. On 23 June 1985, Fred Harrison broke the story that Ian had confessed to the murders of Pauline Reade and Keith Bennett. Myra was so distraught that she ended up in prison hospital, swallowing tranquillisers and rejecting food. Her solicitor, Michael Fisher, promised to take her case to the European Court of Human Rights, but she saw little reason to be optimistic. Detective Chief Superintendent Peter Topping, head of Greater Manchester CID, visited Ian in Gartree. Originally from Gorton, he had been a uniformed policeman in the mid 1960s and had called on Pauline's mother during the months before the Moors trial. After his promotion to head of the CID in early 1985, Topping's thoughts turned to the unsolved murders and that summer he and two other senior detectives attempted to interview Ian but found him in no fit state to speak to anyone.

Fuming and panicked by the stories unfurling in the press almost daily, Myra wrote to her mother: 'Mrs "pain in the neck" West got back on her bandwagon and threatened to dig up the moor herself . . .'[38] Ian had achieved his aim of being transferred from prison to hospital; diagnosed with acute paranoia and schizophrenia, he was moved to a high-security psychiatric unit, Liverpool's Park Lane. His mother, with whom he had always corresponded, travelled from her flat in Manchester to see him for the first time in many years. She recalled: 'It was lovely to be with him and actually talk face to face again after so long. It was a visit I had been longing for and one I shall remember for a long time.'[39] Two young women also visited him: one was a student at Edinburgh University who wrote to him about literature and philosophy; the other was Christine Hart, who went on to write a book about her mistaken obsession that he was her real father. She painted a strange, vivid picture of a disturbed but quietly spoken man in black sweater and jeans, wearing dark glasses and Hai Karate aftershave, his breath smelling of mints and tea. Among his many other correspondents was author Colin Wilson, to whom Ian sent a tape of extracts from his favourite films, including *A Christmas Carol* and *Carousel*.

Perhaps inevitably, David Astor and the Revd Peter Timms encouraged Myra to consider writing her autobiography. In November, they approached a woman they felt might be a suitable co-author, but Myra decided to tackle the task herself and a literary agent was found. She advised Myra to read Jan Morris's books for tips on style. A sum of £100,000 was mooted; her agent suggested 70 per cent should go to charity, with the remaining 30 per cent to be divided between Myra's mother and her brother-in-law (to be held in trust for her niece). The NSPCC was Myra's first choice for the funds, but she was advised against it and went instead for the National Council for Civil Liberties. The Home Office granted her permission to begin work on the book, which she delivered in instalments to David Astor.

In early 1986, Ann West announced that she had written to Ian, suggesting they meet. She hoped to convince him to tell the full truth about the murders and to reveal the gravesites of the missing victims, but the idea was vetoed by the authorities. To another correspondent, Ian admitted that he hadn't read Ann's letter, nor one he had recently received from Winnie Johnson: 'Re: letters from Mrs West and the mother of Keith Bennett. Although I have been given them I have not been able to bring myself to read them. I have been afraid to read them ... I have to keep mental blocks tightly shut ... I can't say how it would have worked out if the meeting had taken place. Remorse for my part in this and other matters is axiomatic, painfully deep.'[40] But in April he wrote to Ann, telling her that he would never seek parole and hoped to assure her personally 'of the remorse I feel, but I prefer actions to words. I have spent the last 18 years doing Braille work. I know I can't balance the past, of course, but at least I can do something positive and useful.'[41] To Winnie Johnson, Ian wrote not a word.

Winnie had also written to Myra. Renowned journalist Ian Smith had helped her to compose the letter, in which she implored: 'Please, I beg of you, tell me what happened to Keith. My heart tells me you know and I am on bended knees begging you to end this torture and finally put my mind at rest . . . Please, Miss Hindley, help me.'[42] A memo from staff at Cookham Wood describes Myra's reaction: 'She became extremely upset and tearful whilst reading it and it took a very long time for her to compose herself sufficiently to talk (this is most unusual as Myra is normally very controlled).'[43] But the memo also discloses that despite her tears, Myra declared: 'I wish I did know something – I could at least then put the poor woman out of her misery.'[44] On 3 November, she wrote to the Revd Peter Timms about the letter, declaring that she had nothing to hide nor harboured 'any guilty secrets' and wondered whether she should ask her solicitor to reply on her behalf. She asked Timms to visit not for her sake 'but for the sake of this poor, demented woman. The awful tragedy is that I cannot help her in any way – if I could, I would, I swear this as God is my judge. I'd even be willing to contact the police and ask them to take me to those awful moors [but] those moors are so vast, I wouldn't know where to start or even what I was looking for . . .'[45] Timms felt that it was in Myra's best interests *not* to reply: 'Yes, I tried to persuade Myra not to answer her. Then Winnie wanted to meet her, and out of good motives Myra wanted to do that too, but I said no. Myra still had that bit of belief that people would be all right with her.'[46]

On 17 November, Timms visited Myra and, while they were discussing Winnie's letter, Myra received another visitor: Peter Topping. Unbeknown to anyone but Topping and his team, the preliminary stage of the moor search – basically one man and his well-trained dog – had already begun. Topping approached the investigation working on the premise that all the victims had been killed elsewhere and then driven to the moor for burial, making it likely that the graves would lie within a couple of hundred yards of the road. Topping had already pinpointed two areas to search: Hollin Brown Knoll, because it was the logical place to look, and Hoe Grain (two miles from the Knoll), for reasons which have never publicly been disclosed, leading to speculation that Topping settled on the second location because of the 'W/H' on Ian's disposal plan following the murder of Edward Evans. Ian and Myra both insisted it referred to Woodhead, but police suspected it might mean Wessenden Head, the area in which Hoe Grain lay.[47] Myra agreed to talk to Topping, but only with Timms present. Topping asked if she would be willing to look at maps and photographs, and Myra agreed, drawn to his quiet approach and his Gorton background.

Topping recalls: 'Hindley listened very intently to everything I said. Her face was pale and she chain-smoked. She paused and thought deeply before she spoke, obviously evaluating everything she said in her well-spoken, very precise and meticulous way . . . If anything was to come out of our meeting, it would be only when she believed it was in her interest.'[48] On 18 November, Topping returned to Cookham Wood, armed with maps and photos. He felt that she showed particular interest in photographs believed to be of Hollin Brown Knoll and Shiny Brook, the stream at Wessenden Head. Through Michael Fisher, Myra issued an adroitly worded statement that she had agreed to help Manchester Police search the moor for further victims and had 'identified from photographs and maps places that I know were of particular interest to Ian Brady, some of which I visited with him . . .'[49] Ian immediately contacted the press about the letters he and Myra had exchanged during their first years in prison, which he hinted would prove her guilt. On 20 November, while Topping's team began searching the rain-lashed moor in earnest, David Astor wrote to Myra that he, Timms and Longford had discussed her case and 'we all agree that your problems are not with the Law – but with public opinion'.[50] He suggested that Timms should act as her spokesperson.

Not having yet received a reply, Winnie wrote again to Myra, requesting a meeting, but Timms and Fisher advised Myra against it. Myra invited Topping to visit her again but told him that she would require Timms' support before, during and after any formal statement she might make. No one knew then that she had already confessed to Timms, who had promised not to break her confidence. Some months earlier, Timms had qualified as a Methodist minister and was a trained therapist. He counselled Myra once a week at Longford's request, in the office of Cookham Wood's Roman Catholic priest: 'She went through what I'd call the sheer routine practicalities of what happened. But I was more interested in why and I knew eventually that would come if I was patient. She told me about how Brady threatened to put her in the grave with Pauline and so on and that was very difficult for her to articulate. There was something psycho-sexual about what had happened, but there was an element in Myra that couldn't admit it – that's what I hoped to unlock. Unfortunately our sessions ended too soon, when another priest took over and the Home Office refused to let us continue. But she was talking to me long before she spoke to Topping.'[51] Ian was also approached by Topping again, but, although his psychological state had improved vastly since their last meeting, he refused to help.[52]

Home Secretary Douglas Hurd granted Topping permission to take Myra back to the moor if necessary; the media had already speculated about a visit, and a clear photo of Myra on the moor was reputed to be worth as much as £20,000. But Myra was given no warning about the visit until she was woken on the morning of 16 December and driven to Kent police headquarters in Maidstone, where she boarded a waiting helicopter with her solicitor Michael Fisher and two police officers. The 250-mile flight took Myra back to the landscape she hadn't seen for over 20 years. They touched down on the violet-hued, snow-dusted moor shortly after half past eight. Dressed almost identically to everyone else, in balaclava and donkey jacket, she was given sandwiches and a hot drink before being driven down to the Water Board track at Shiny Brook. MP David Mellor had leaked the news of her visit on Radio 4's *Today* programme and so the route Myra had to take as a result of his security lapse was unfamiliar to her; the track had been built after she and Ian were arrested. She told Topping, who was with her then, that she was unable to get her bearings. After lunch they approached from the lay-by, as Myra had suggested, following the deep banks of Hoe Grain valley towards Shiny Brook. The media were slowly edging their way across the moor and circling above in hired helicopters, which filled the skies with an insistent drone. Fisher recalled: 'She was confused and frightened. She was particularly worried about the helicopters overhead. She was asking, "Who are they?" . . . At one point about six helicopters were hovering above and she broke down in tears.'[53] Myra pointed out a couple of spots that she said might be worth investigating and mentioned a plateau but struggled to say more. They drove on to Hollin Brown Knoll, but any progress was stifled by her unwillingness to admit that she knew where the graves of John and Lesley had been. At three o'clock she was airlifted from the moor and arrived at Cookham Wood after seven, driven through a media cordon.[54]

The press were venomous in their condemnation of Topping's search of the moor, but for the most part he managed to ignore them.[55] On 27 January 1987, he visited Myra again with Detective Inspector Geoff Knupfer. In the presence of her solicitor, Myra told him that David Smith was not involved in the murder of Pauline Reade, that none of the killings had been committed in her house on Bannock Street and that the police should focus on searching Shiny Brook and Hollin Brown Knoll. Myra's advisors held an emergency meeting to discuss whether she should make a full confession to the police. Together with solicitor Lord Goodman, they decided it was in her best interests to do so. Fisher defended Myra to the press in acutely contentious terms: 'The heroine in this story is my client. She has been very, very brave.'[56] There was an unsubstantiated rumour that he leaked the news of the meeting with Lord Goodman to the press, giving Astor and Timms the incentive they needed to convince Myra to ditch him, although she did so reluctantly. Topping arranged for Timms to resume his counselling sessions with Myra.

On 5 February, Myra sent a curious letter to Astor in which she wrote: 'I seem to have unwittingly put myself into a dilemma, having told Mr Topping and Mike [Fisher] what I hoped to do, but thinking about it, I still intend to do the right thing, the only thing I can do, but from a different angle. And no doubt with the help and advice from a more objective solicitor, *everything will be resolved with satisfaction all round*, so to speak.'[57] She then mentioned her autobiography, writing that as far as its content was concerned, 'the only drawback is that it will be read, both here and at P4 at the Home Office, which means the things I want to tell the police, *things they have to know to clear this case up*, will be known to prison officials first'.[58] Astor immediately wrote to Timms, questioning the meaning behind her words, which seem to indicate that she may have been prepared to make a much fuller and franker confession than the one she gave to Topping a couple of weeks later. What might have prevented her from doing so isn't clear.

Nonetheless, on 19 February 1987, with Timms at her side, Myra admitted to Topping and Knupfer that she had helped Ian to kill Keith Bennett and Pauline Reade. Her confession was made without caution but was recorded. Topping recalls, 'She spoke very intensely, very emotionally, and was occasionally very distressed. Peter Timms comforted her often, holding her hand and encouraging her. At times the medical staff brought her doses of medicine.'[59] After the weekend, which Myra spent heavily sedated, she spoke to the detectives again on Monday and Tuesday, giving them her life story as well as more information about the murders. She cried copiously and swallowed tranquillisers, particularly when discussing the killings of Lesley and Pauline. She quoted often from the speech given in 1967 by William Mars-Jones to the Medico-Legal Society in which he declared she had been an ordinary girl prior to the relationship with Ian. Knupfer shared his view: 'Had she not met Ian Brady and fallen in love with him, she would have fallen in love and got married and had a family and been like any other member of the public.'[60] He felt that she was 'absolutely besotted by this man. I guess like many other women I've met in the course of my career, they do all sorts of things for the love and respect of their partner.'[61] Topping was less impressed: 'Whilst I accepted these points, her reference to this document made me realise that her confession was being carefully controlled.'[62] When he asked her if photographs were used as grave-markers, she said no, even though she admitted in her autobiography that 'photographs and not headstones' would record their victims' graves.[63] She emphatically denied any knowledge of other murders and ended her confession: 'I just hope to God that the case can be concluded and finally laid to rest, and I just hope that some day, in some way, I can be forgiven for making those families wait 22 years.'[64]

When Topping mulled over her confession, he felt that she truly wanted to help but was at pains to make her behaviour understandable: 'She showed tremendous emotion at times, very deep emotion – but it was coupled with complete control.'[65] He couldn't forget the starkly objective phrase she had used after telling them about Pauline's death: 'Well, that, as far as I remember, concludes the first murder, which was Pauline Reade.'[66] Ultimately, Topping felt he had witnessed 'a great performance rather than a genuine confession'.[67]

Afterwards, Myra returned to her cell, but called Timms to say that she was ready to go on the record. 'I said, "Myra, please don't. Give yourself time to reflect and think before doing that,"' he remembers. 'But she said, "No, I should have done this 20 years ago." Not that I didn't want her to do it – that was up to her. I rang Peter Topping that evening. And then we started all over again for another two days. This time under caution . . . Topping, of course, took those tapes and wrote his book.'[68]

The Home Office ended Timms' counselling sessions in the aftermath of her confession. Timms lobbied furiously against the decision, but memos and letters from the prison authorities show that they regarded him as a nuisance in his doggedness about the counselling he was promised. Myra also complained about the loss of their meetings, writing to the Home Office that she was 'burdened with the aftermath' of her confession. The letter had no effect, except possibly to perplex its recipient with the line: 'I believe suicide to be a mortal sin, and one that cannot be forgiven, unlike the mortal sins I recently confessed to and received absolution from.'[69]

Ian was clearly agitated when Topping visited him with the news that Myra had confessed. But he was lucid and polite, and said that he was willing to do the same provided he was given the means to kill himself afterwards, which he knew was out of the question.

On 23 March, Myra returned to the moor again, travelling by car in an unmarked convoy and evading the press. She spent the night at a flat in Sedgely Park Greater Manchester Police Training School before being taken, in the pre-dawn darkness, to the chill moor, where Topping had arranged for her to visit Hoe Grain first. She seemed keen to concentrate on the area he'd suggested, then after lunch travelled the two miles to Hollin Brown Knoll, where the mist clung to the crags above the reservoir. She told Topping that he was looking in the right places, but other than that had little to add – except to say that she and Ian had buried a metal box of some significance on the moor. She wouldn't say what it contained and police were unable to find it.

On 15 April, Myra wrote to inform the authorities that she didn't want to be considered for parole in 1990 and was focusing on her autobiography: 'I hope that in some way what I am able to relate will enable a wiser understanding of the awful complexities surrounding the abuse of children . . .'[70] The news of her confession broke in the press that month, causing another media storm. Winnie Johnson wrote again to Myra, who responded, thanking her for the letters and stating that if she had only written to her 14 years before (when Myra ended her relationship with Ian), she would have tried to help them then. The possibility of a trial was raised by the victims' families and Myra said she was willing to stand, but Topping informed her that it wouldn't be necessary. Her friends and family were stunned by the news. Sara Trevelyan recalls: 'I felt very confused. I'd really put myself on the line to support her and that whole '70s thing, I instigated a lot of that, and got these people involved, a solicitor and so on, working on her behalf. In a sense I felt very betrayed by her and I didn't feel that we were able to resolve that. It didn't stop me supporting her, but our contact became pretty infrequent. I would always want to acknowledge her and wish her well. But it was never properly repaired.'[71]

Myra's ex-fellow inmate and friend Janie Jones immediately began writing her own book about how she had been 'duped' by her; other ex-inmates similarly gave interviews to the press about their feeling of having been hoodwinked. Nellie's life was altered immeasurably by the news of her daughter's confession; she resigned from her work and became a recluse, sitting indoors with the curtains closed, leaving the grocery shopping to her husband, who wanted no more to do with Myra. Bill Scott, Maureen's widow, stopped taking Sharon to visit her aunt and grandmother until the furore had abated. The house at 16 Wardle Brook Avenue, which the council had long ago abandoned attempting to rent out and used as an on-site office, was demolished in an effort to discourage visits from ghoulish sightseers.

Myra was psychiatrically assessed following the confession and found to be of sound mind, although she declared that confessing had 'unleashed a thousand demons and they have not left me alone'. She felt 'like a walking time bomb' and was 'haunted by not talking earlier'.[72] The psychiatrists concluded that her revelations 'might have been partly motivated by a wish to remain a centre of interest to acquaintances, if not in the public mind as a whole'.[73] Myra's subsequent 'open letter' to Ian gave some credence to their analysis; via the BBC, she urged Ian to assist the police as she had done. Ian had already spoken to detectives again, but in return for his full cooperation, he asked for a 'human week' of being allowed to eat and drink whatever he pleased and permission to watch old films such as *Gone with the Wind*. He told Topping that Myra knew perfectly well where the graves were and could have taken him straight to them if she had wished.

After six weeks, torrential rain flooded the excavated areas at Hoe Grain and Shiny Brook and the search moved to the higher ground at Hollin Brown Knoll, in the immediate vicinity of Lesley's grave, out of sight of the road. During her confession, Myra had remarked on Pauline's body lying on the grass, which seemed to suggest the search should be concentrated deeper onto the moor, away from the road. On 17 June, Topping questioned Myra again by telephone; prompted by him, she recalled that Pauline was buried further back than Lesley and not in the gas pipeline trench. Almost in passing, she mentioned that when she had stood next to the dying girl she could clearly see the rocks of Hollin Brown Knoll outlined against the sky.

On 1 July 1987, the body of Pauline Reade was unearthed from the moor. The discovery came towards the end of the afternoon. Topping was with Ian at Park Lane when Knupfer rang to inform him that they had noticed a change in the vegetation and after a few minutes of careful digging, a white shoe had poked out of the soil.

The search team left the moor as usual in order not to alert the press and returned to the site that evening, with Topping. In the copper sunlight, the grave revealed Pauline's almost perfectly preserved body; like Lesley, she lay on her side, but on her left, facing the road 150 yards away, and 100 yards from where Lesley had been found. Her left arm was crossed over her front and her right lay along her side; her knees were bent up towards her abdomen. The injury to her throat was evident, and the disarray of her clothing left detectives in no doubt that she had been sexually assaulted. One shoe had fallen off; the exposed foot was better preserved than the other. As police lifted the shoes from the grave, the manufacturer's gold lettering glinted brightly.

Topping visited Amos Reade. Pauline's father received the news quietly, expressing deep regret that his wife Joan was in psychiatric care. Topping then had the equally painful task of informing Winnie Johnson that a body had been found but it wasn't Keith. She wept on the telephone as he assured her the search would continue. The media tide finally turned in the police's favour; Myra read about the discovery the following day. Visiting Ian, Topping was angered by his gloating comment about how close police had been to Pauline's grave for so long without finding it.

On 3 July, Ian returned to the moor, visiting Hoe Grain, where Topping hoped he would now lead them to Keith's grave. The visit was a fiasco; often Ian would stride off purposefully, then suddenly become confused and stumble about. At the junction of Hoe Grain and Shiny Brook, he pointed to an exposed slope and told police he had hidden a spade there, but excavations revealed nothing. He insisted on climbing a high rock formation; Topping scrambled after him, worried that he planned to throw himself off, but he only wanted to look at the view. Afterwards, Topping realised that the visit had been of little benefit to anyone but Keith's murderer.[74]

Ian's inability – deliberate or otherwise – to assist the search gave Myra a curious satisfaction. Her relationship with Topping had deteriorated, Fisher recalled: 'She was terribly hurt when he didn't ring her, didn't come to see her ... she was annoyed with him that he took so long finding Pauline's body ... On the other body, she gave him a clue that he thought he could crack – information about something, not a body buried on the moors. He preferred to go after that first, and he failed to find it. We believe he would have been better going for Pauline Reade's body first.'[75] Topping remained in talks with Ian and during one visit: 'He told me that he was ashamed of what he'd done. He said it very simply, his head down ... He said when he tried to recall the details of what had happened, "blocks" came down in his mind. He was struggling to explain himself; he said he did not want to discuss how he had killed the children. He got very disturbed and agitated whenever the subject was mentioned, saying he was frightened of losing control if the blocks were removed.'[76] Topping also spoke to Ian's mother: 'She seemed a very sensitive person, very keen to help ... both she and her home were very clean and tidy ... she felt responsible for her son's behaviour and was always trying to work out what had gone wrong ... She had obviously lived with a sense of guilt and distress for many years.'[77] On 4 August, he and Knupfer visited Myra to show her a video of Ian's photographs superimposed on footage of the moor. She pinpointed different areas, some over a mile apart, leading to further confusion.

On 7 August, Pauline Reade was laid to rest in Gorton cemetery. Her mother left the hospital under heavy sedation, accompanied by two nurses. Rain pattered down as a requiem Mass was said for Pauline at St Francis' Monastery before the internment. Hundreds of people lined the roads as the cortège passed by; among the mourners at the graveside were Ann West, Winnie Johnson, Patrick Kilbride, Danny Kilbride and his wife Ann, and Pat Kilbride. The funeral marked a breakthrough in Joan's mental health; although she remained hospitalised for some time, eventually she was able to return home.

The search was called off on 24 August. Topping promised a shattered Winnie Johnson that he would return to the moor if significant information came to light. He remained in contact with Myra and Ian for some time afterwards; in December, following positive discussions, Ian returned to the moor again, but the visit proved as futile as the first. Ian's suggestion that he and Myra should meet to discuss the location of Keith's grave was refused outright. Topping reflects: 'Despite the fact that he was at times very critical of her, and despite the fact that she had not hesitated to outline his crimes, I felt they both still had a lingering regard for each other. Neither seemed to want to hurt the other.'[78]

Myra returned to her autobiography, opening it with the 'unpolluted minds' quote from *Jane Eyre*. Elizabeth Longford offered to help with the manuscript, but both Timms and Astor felt that any connection with the Longfords would prove damaging to both parties. Myra worried that the public would assume she was writing for financial gain; Benedict Birnberg, a widely respected solicitor who also happened to represent Ian Brady, drew up the deed of trust for the charity that would administer the funds raised from sales of her book. The objectives of the Open Hand Trust were 'to alleviate the suffering experienced by children and young persons resulting from sexual and other abuse and violence and to promote their well-being' and 'to promote research into and the study of the cause, nature and effects of such abuse and violence and to publish the useful results of such research and study'.[79]

Public condemnation followed the release of a long, introspective letter Myra had written to Ann West. Her maladroit attempt to express sorrow ('the remorse I feel is agonising – the wounds have reopened again and are raw-edged and festering') backfired spectacularly due to one particular sentence, which drew censure from almost every quarter: 'I now want to say to you, and I implore you to believe me, because it is the truth, that your child was not physically tortured, as is widely believed.'[80] Her words were abysmally inept; intending to refute the rumours that Lesley was not mutilated prior to her death, Myra failed to grasp that the ordeal to which the little girl was subjected before her murder was precisely that – physical and psychological torture.

Few journalists were willing to be magnanimous toward Myra. A rare exception was Peter Stanford, with whom she had corresponded since the beginning of the year. A reporter and then editor of the *Catholic Herald*, Stanford had become interested in Myra's case through his friendship with Lord Longford. He began corresponding with her; Myra's first letter to him largely concerns her loathing of the media, who 'accuse me of never showing any remorse, as though I should put out a daily bulletin informing the unforgiving public of the particular degree of remorse on any given day ... I find a great comfort in knowing that Christ, for very different reasons, was also maligned and reviled . . . It helps a very great deal to know that some small part of the media isn't hell-bent on crucifixion but instead suggests a resurrection. The tabloids would no doubt vilify me for using such analogies as I have, but what better analogy to use?'[81] She enclosed £5 for the *Catholic Herald*'s leprosy appeal: 'that's something I can all too easily identify with mentally'.[82] Stanford visited her in Cookham Wood, wincing as he stood up when her name was called out in the antechamber to the visitor's room and unsure which of the inmates was Myra: 'I didn't like to go up to someone and say, "Hello, are you Myra Hindley?" But then I caught the eye of this mousy-looking woman sitting at a table, her hair dyed purplish and cut in an unflattering style. She had a very red face, lots of broken veins, and was quite small, quite slight, and sitting at the table with her arms crossed. We talked mostly about three things: religion, Frank Longford and about her case. She was very witty and an acute observer of the world. We had a long conversation about Margaret Thatcher, by whom she felt very let down, and women's rights. She was straightforward, articulate and warm. Having said that,

I was never wholly won over by her. I could always think of a caveat to anything positive that she did, which was awkward. I supported her bid for freedom, but that was another matter.'[83]

He didn't doubt that her Catholicism was genuine: 'I spend a lot of time around religious people and there didn't seem any dissemblance there. In one of our chats she told me that she listened to *Thought for the Day* on Radio 4. She said, "I'd be very good on that programme." I said, "You should do it," and she replied, "I would if they'd let me." I approached Reverend Ernie Ray, head of religious broadcasting at the time, but he said it was more than his job was worth. But there again, I suppose our letters and conversations were very religious because she thought that's what I was interested in. She played the part with whoever was her latest saviour. Frank Longford was 50 years out of date with public opinion; David Astor was 20 years out of date. Basically, Frank believed that if you said it often enough people would agree with you in the end and David thought that you could drip feed these things and change opinions that way. Dear old Frank didn't do her cause any good in the end, and he didn't do himself any good either. It's true what the victims' families suspected: Frank *wasn't* interested in victims. That's the bottom line.'[84]

He discussed her crimes with her but not in great depth: 'I didn't want to know. She talked a lot about her remorse, but it's difficult to reconcile with her not telling the truth about the other two children for so long, although I can understand how she got herself into that fix. Frank started visiting her in the late 1960s, and very soon was talking about parole and release and she got carried away with that, and she believed it was going to happen. I don't excuse her in any way at all, and if I was the parent of those children I would hate her for it. And it was a strange thing between her and Ian Brady, even then. Whenever he came up in conversation, she was very hostile towards him, but in an oddly competitive way. In relation to that, there was a very uncomfortable moment when I was visiting her at Cookham Wood. I'd bought Myra a bar of chocolate. Children were running round the table where we were sitting, and she picked up the chocolate bar, smiled at this little boy and waved the chocolate bar at him. I just sat there and thought, "Oh God . . . *this* is how you did it." It was extremely sinister. The overtones . . . I sat there horrified, and she must have picked up on that, but it didn't stop her, she went on waving this chocolate bar at the little boy. There was something in the way she did it that made me think there was a knowingness in it. There *were* things that made me uneasy. In the early days I took everything more at face value, but perhaps when you have children you look at things differently.'[85]

On one occasion, Stanford was accompanied on a visit to Myra by Bernard Black, who had written to her at the request of his friend John Trevelyan. Myra described Black, who was also Catholic, as 'kind and caring and with such integrity and a first-class brain'.[86] He recalls: 'I saw her several times, always with other people, and most of the conversations were about trying to get her case heard again. I never got involved with that but nothing I saw or read from her indicated she might be a danger to the public. I found it hard to understand how the person I got to know could have been responsible for the crimes she had committed. Her letters were exceptionally lucid, but in person she was rather miserable, which you might expect from someone who had been all that time in prison. I felt sorry for her, but she didn't help herself by keeping quiet for so many years about the extent of her involvement.'[87] Bernard Black's wife, Margaret, never met her: 'No, I didn't want to. I'm a mum and perhaps we have slightly different feelings to men.'[88]

Writing was Myra's main concern for much of 1988; she was scathing when she heard that Ian had asked Lord Longford to edit his prison letters, writing to Astor that it was 'rather a coincidence that Elizabeth is advising me, and Brady wants Frank to edit the letters he urged Frank to destroy after he'd sent them'.[89] On 2 June, she sent a delighted letter to the Revd Peter Timms about having been approached by barrister Helena Kennedy (who acted as junior counsel for Myra during her 1974 trial) to write an afterword for a book Kennedy was planning to edit about the role of women in child-connected crimes.[90] In addition, André Deutsch had agreed to publish Myra's autobiography and she was writing assiduously, mostly about her relationship with Ian, which gave her 'a succession of most unpleasant dreams, which I really can't handle'.[91]

She was distressed the following month when she learned that her stepfather had died of a heart attack; although she had disliked him, she worried about the effect on her mother: 'He died on July 8, the day before my sister's anniversary, and I felt so sorry for my mother because she, like me, has never got over Maureen's death. He was buried on the 14th, the day before Maureen's funeral.'[92] Her immediate concern was her mother's precarious financial situation and she queried whether her publisher might advance her some funds, but David Astor came to the rescue with money from his own pocket.

Plans for Myra's autobiography continued apace. Diana Athill, one of Britain's finest literary editors and writers, was approached to work on the book, but wanted to meet Myra before she would commit to the project. Athill visited her with Peter Timms, and found her 'intelligent, responsive, human, dignified. And if someone had then informed me that this unknown woman had been in prison for twenty-two years I would have been amazed: how could a person of whom that was true appear to have been so little institutionalised?'[93] Myra discussed her OU degree, Catholicism and the press. Athill recalls: 'She was flippant rather than grateful about what she called "my old men" – Lord Longford, David Astor and Timms.'[94] Ultimately, Athill turned down the role of editor for Myra's autobiography, doubting its worth both for the public and as a means of purging Myra of her own past: 'When she did what she did she was not mad – as Brady was – and although she was young, she was an adult, and an intelligent one. It seems to me that there are strands of moral deformity which cannot be pardoned: that Stangl was right when, having faced the truth about himself, he said, "I ought to be dead."'[95]

A new solicitor was secured for Myra: Andrew McCooey, who also happened to be a close friend of Lord Longford. 'Peter Timms asked me if I would be willing to act for her,' McCooey recalls. 'I discussed it with my wife and she said that if I felt I should do it, then to go ahead. I never regretted it, although there were some family members who thought I was mad to take this particular case on – my brother, for instance. Of course Myra came with a huge amount of baggage and was a Medusa figure as far as the press were concerned. The tabloids would ring me at midnight and ask the most preposterous questions: "Is it true that Myra's getting married?" I would respond wearily, "Do you know what time it is?" "Yes, but now you're awake, can you just reply to the question?" And I would say sarcastically, "Well, of course it's true. She has *so* much choice in an all-female prison." They would then report that the next day as my having confirmed the rumour. My phone lines were constantly engaged and journalists and photographers were always at my door. John Kay of *The Sun* said to me, "Anything you can give us about Myra, I will guarantee you a front-page spread." She was as lucrative to them as Princess Diana.

'I was lambasted too, of course, as her solicitor; they said she was manipulating me and so forth. I certainly don't think she manipulated me and I saw her more often than anyone. She was an extremely quietly spoken woman and very genuine in her desire to help the victims' families achieve resolution. She did her absolute utmost to aid the police during the 1980s search of the moor and her remorse was deep-seated and true. I certainly had far worse clients than her. She believed that God had forgiven her and she drew comfort from that, but men wouldn't extend her the same compassion. Despite all the hassle, working with Myra brought me many rewards in the way of wonderful friendships and learning a great deal. I never worried about the controversy; you have to be true to what you think is the right thing or else live your life looking over your shoulder the entire time.'[96]

If Myra was upset that Athill had withdrawn from her literary project, she didn't allow it to discourage her from writing, confiding in Peter Stanford that she was thoroughly absorbed by the process, and admitted to the Revd Peter Timms: 'I'm glad I'm not publishing this year, with the Krays' book coming out, and the film about the Great Train Robbers – I don't want to be part of a bunch of '60s East End villains!'[97] On 4 November 1988 she reported her progress to David Astor, buoyed by a recent visit from a friend and one of her many godchildren: 'I've written 640-odd pages, and have just reached the third crime [Keith Bennett], but when I get to the actual crime itself, as opposed to how it came about, I'll do as I did with the first two and say that reference to this offence is to be made later.'[98] Later that month, another book occupied her thoughts; she was outraged by the publication of Jean Ritchie's 'diabolical' biography, *Inside the Mind of a Murderess*.[99] Ritchie, an ex-*Sun* journalist, had approached Myra to ask her whether she would be willing to cooperate with the book. Myra forwarded Ritchie's letter to David Astor, with a few comments of her own; she was sure Ritchie meant well, and appreciated being informed about the book, but had no wish to be interviewed, and hoped the same was true of her family and friends.

Inside the Mind of a Murderess was serialised in *The Sun*, with television adverts featuring the arrest photograph and the tagline 'Sex

Romps with an Ex-Nun on E Wing'. If Myra could take comfort from Ritchie's blanket assertion that had she not met Ian, 'Myra might have done anything with her life . . . she would not have killed children,' there was little else to hearten her; Ritchie's incisive research was lost under the volume of stories about Myra's prison lesbianism.[100] 'I want to sue both *The Sun* and especially Jean Ritchie,' Myra raged in a long letter on the subject to David Astor. 'She has no integrity, no scruples and, in the case of the book, no moral conscience. David, I <u>must</u> do something about all this.'[101] In another letter, she described her battle with *The Sun* as 'like a Sherman tank bristling with modern weapons confronting a civilian with a plastic water pistol!'[102] Her anger deepened when she discovered that Ritchie had ghostwritten another book – Peter Topping's autobiography, which revolved almost entirely around his interviews with Myra and Ian. He had retired before starting work on the book, but was issued with a writ by Greater Manchester Police for breach of confidentiality. David Astor financed Myra's legal action against Topping, which she abandoned upon learning that GMP had begun theirs. Her supporters were appalled by the book and Keith Bennett's family were deeply distressed by details that hadn't been revealed to them beforehand by Topping or his team.

There was more upset for Myra in December. She had joined the lay Franciscans in May, but seven months later her membership was revoked. Peter Stanford recalls: 'Myra was distraught. She had been the ultimate outcast and that feeling of acceptance meant the world to her. They rescinded on the grounds that a lay Franciscan should be a person in good standing with the community – I think that's the exact wording they used.'[103] He and Longford spoke to the head of the Franciscan Order in London, but without success; Stanford then approached Cardinal Hume: 'He agreed with me and said he would write to the head of the Franciscan Order himself. I thought, "That's sorted then, they'll have to give in if the Cardinal tells them," but they ignored him as well.'[104] Myra attempted to console herself, writing to Stanford: 'I believe this is God's way of saying that my salvation – which I'm convinced is secured – lies in other directions to fulfilment . . . I feel very close to God – heaven is within us all.'[105] She hoped writing would distract her but found it difficult to continue: 'The sequence I was writing about reopened wounds and made me even more painfully aware that there are some memories which will never heal and I don't mean just my own. Those of the people I was partly responsible for cause me just as much pain. I've decided to go on to a totally different subject . . . the first 500 pages just flowed and felt fulfilled and productive; it was excellent therapy, and I know that when I finally manage to confront the traumatic subjects, however painful it will be at the time, it will, in the end, be a tremendous catharsis.'[106] She wrote in similar vein to David Astor about the sections that dealt with her relationship with Ian: 'Not one memory had healed at all. I knew they never would, but the scabs on the wounds were more fragile than I thought they were . . .'[107] She declared that she hated herself for having 'encouraged [Ian], motivated him even'.[108]

In April 1989, Myra wrote to David Astor about Keith Bennett's brother Alan, with whom she had been corresponding since the end of the official moor search; he had written to ask her if she could help his family in their own explorations of the area where Keith was said to be buried. Realising that he had no intention of publishing her letters in the media and was acting purely out of desperation to find his brother, she invited him to meet her. He accepted, finding the courage and strength to quell his own emotions in order to discuss the maps and photographs of the moor with her. He then contacted Professor John Hunter, founder of the Forensic Search Advisory Group, who agreed to assist free of charge. Myra informed Astor that she had received a letter from another member of the Bennett family's team, asking her if she would look at other maps. She remained in contact with Detective Inspector Geoff Knupfer, who was present both during her confession and the exhumation of Pauline Reade, and Myra claimed he advised her not to reply to the letter, 'saying it would be unwise of me to do so myself, and adding that these amateur searchers are only going over ground that the police have already searched'.[109] She told Astor that Knupfer had promised to 'have a word' with Alan about ending the search.[110] Despite having informed the authorities that she did not wish to be considered for parole, she confided in Astor that Knupfer had agreed to write positively to the prison governor about her conduct, honouring a promise made during her interviews with him and Topping. 'This can only help in the future,' she wrote. 'It will be the first time there'll be anything favourable on my record from the police. So really, there's no justification at all for them to refuse parole now.'[111]

Astor was troubled by her conviction that she had written a saleable book. Having read the manuscript, he realised that it was nothing short of a calamity, and wrote to Peter Timms that she had failed to confront the 'serious troubles in her life'; those sections were 'wholly inadequate', while the reams of pages about her childhood and teenage years made for 'very wearisome and wordy reading'. He had no doubt that the manuscript gave 'the impression of evasion . . . if it was offered as a book, it would be a disaster'.[112] Among Astor's papers is an undated, unsigned report on Myra's first draft that criticises her childhood recollections as overly nostalgic and not dramatic enough; they should be 'balanced by a franker treatment of whatever were the chief strains of her childhood. For instance, her father's violence.'[113] The report also warned Myra against making psychological interpretations about Lesley Ann Downey's mother and the general public.

Unaware that her manuscript had received a critical mauling, Myra contacted journalist Yvonne Roberts via Chris Tchaikovsky, a former inmate of Holloway who, together with criminologist Pat Carlen, had established the organisation Women in Prison. Roberts had written several incisive articles on miscarriages of justice, helped by Tchaikovsky, with whom she was good friends. Roberts recalls: 'Myra had invited me to meet her before. I worked in television and did a lot on the Cleveland affair and, of course, knew Chris very well. She was extremely ambivalent about Myra. She retained contact with her mainly because she felt sorry for Myra's mother, whom she used to drive down to prison for visits. Chris was very good at spotting someone who was vulnerable from someone who wasn't – there are lots of very vulnerable women in British prisons – and she was wary of Myra. Chris had counselling during the time she visited Myra because she knew Myra was highly manipulative and Chris didn't want to get drawn in. She left it up to me to decide whether to visit Myra or not.'

The meeting didn't go as Myra had planned. 'It was like a game of chess,' Roberts remembers. 'She looked nothing like any of the images I had seen of her. She wore a smart lilac trouser suit, pink nail varnish and pink lipstick. She had brown hair and her eyebrows were heavily plucked. She was friendly at first, much cooler later in the visit. She shook my hand, sat down, and made small talk. Then she said, "I really feel that I've done my time." She asked me what I'd like to know. I told her that I had a few questions, having read about the case. I asked her how she could take a ten year old off the streets. And she said, "She shouldn't have been out so late at night." I said – and she got quite cross – "It doesn't matter if it was three o'clock in the morning." She became less convivial after that, and I think she knew that both Chris and I thought that was a response that had revealed more about Myra than she would wish to reveal. I continued to question her – not about the case, but about why she had waited so long to divulge the second lot of murders. Her replies didn't add up to much. I just wanted to leave.

'I think she was a psychopath. She was a narcissist, too, and had very grandiose ideas about herself. I wrote to her and said I didn't think I could help her. I didn't want to help her because I felt instinctively that she had played a much stronger role in the murders, she had not fallen under Ian Brady's spell and there was more she could have done in terms of setting the record straight for the victims' families. I also suspect that she would rather have gone down in history as "Myra Hindley, Child Murderer" than not go down at all. As for the idea of remorse – first of all, you need to acknowledge the depth of your crimes, and the remorse that comes from that gives you a certain sincerity. Without it, you have to simulate sincerity and end up acting inappropriately, which is what Myra did. She was like a switchboard with the wires linked up all wrong.'[115]

At the end of September, David Astor's instincts about Myra's manuscript were confirmed when André Deutsch decided not to publish. Undeterred, Myra began work on another draft, using the guidelines in the reader's report: amplifying the troubles in her childhood was easy, writing honestly about the murders far less so.

She was still in touch with Alan Bennett, but uncertain of how much she wanted to become involved in the search for Keith. In letters to Astor and Timms, she vowed to do 'anything remotely possible . . . I'm not deliberately concealing anything, it's just locked somewhere in my memory,' then vacillated: 'I really have done all I can and have nothing to add to what Ian Brady has told him, except that he was more likely to remember where the grave is or was, since

I wasn't present when he killed and buried his brother. So I hope I don't receive any more letters now and will be glad when you're able to see Mrs Johnson.'[116]

The 1980s ended on a disastrous note for Myra. Having been presented with her Open University degree in a special prison ceremony, she was dismayed by the uproar that greeted the publication of a photograph of her wearing the black graduation gown. 'That was my idea,' Timms admits ruefully. 'Those photos were supposed to be for Myra and her family. But I went to the Camera Press in the hope that it would be seen for what it was. The OU were furious with me too, because they didn't want to be "besmirched". I said to them, "Let me understand what you're saying: that it's OK for her to study with you, as long as the public don't find out?" And that *was* it. Myra was proud of herself and rightly so. I thought the photograph would demonstrate how far she had come. Myra knew the photograph was going to be published, but it backfired, horribly. That's the power of the tabloid press in a nutshell.'[117]

By now, Tricia Cairns was again part of Myra's life. Although she never really left it, gradually the two of them drew closer again, and Tricia became a regular visitor to Myra's mother, helping her with practicalities such as shopping, and installing a telephone at her new home. In a letter to Timms, Myra admitted: 'Jean Ritchie got at least one thing right when she referred to Tricia as the love of my life.'[118] But her thoughts were focused on the loss of her sister, who had been dead for ten years: 'Tricia is taking [Mam] to the crematorium to "visit" Maureen; her ashes are scattered near a cherry tree, from which Tricia sent me a leaf to put in my Bible ...'[119] As she sank into a miasma of depression, Ian Brady emerged again with a new and compelling threat to the parole she was certain would be hers in the near future.

25

To confront and contemplate one's naked self, warts and
all, through the eye of truth, unlimbered by deliberate self-
deception, and to scrutinise the mind, the memory, purged
of selective amnesia and moral cowardice, is the work of a
lifetime.

Myra Hindley, 'My Life, My Guilt, My Weakness',

The Guardian, 18 December 1995

Myra was deeply unnerved when Ian sent an open letter to the press in
January 1990 warning her supporters that they were labouring under
a severe misapprehension and that he could prove she had revelled in
the murders: 'I have the written words of Myra Hindley herself, in
the shape of <u>six and a half years</u> of her letters written to me <u>after</u> our
imprisonment. In these she writes nostalgically and lyrically of the
murders, which she regarded as a substitute marriage ritual but which
I saw as products of an existentialist philosophy in tandem with the
spiritualism of Death itself. I have only given you a brief glimpse of
what occurred twenty-five years ago . . .'[1]

The letters had never been alluded to publicly before, and Myra
knew she could do nothing but hope that his threat to publish them
remained no more than that. Her fears subsided temporarily with the
news that a group of warders had barged into Ian's cell to investigate
claims that he was suicidal, strip-searched him, then removed him
to a psychotic ward. In protest, Ian began an extensive hunger strike,
which resulted in force-feeding and heavy supervision.

As her depression lifted, Myra focused on trying to win over
journalists and broadcasters to her campaign for parole, which had
failed again, although she wasn't informed then that the Home
Secretary had recommended she serve a whole life tariff. On 12
June 1991, Andrew McCooey informed David Astor that Myra

had mooted the idea of being interviewed in some capacity by Sue Lawley, who refused, thinking it 'unwise'. McCooey did say, however, that at the right time she would be pleased to visit Myra.[2] Her former campaign leader, Lord Longford, yearned to speak out on her behalf, but there came a period when Myra asked him to refrain from visiting her, dreading that the press would find out.[3]

Myra's relationship with Tricia strengthened considerably, aided by the Astors' support. Tricia resigned from her job in Manchester, hoping to be pensioned off due to illness, and moved to London, where she was given a room at the Astor home on Cavendish Avenue. She bought a liver and white spaniel, which she named Jake, ostensibly sharing ownership of the dog with Myra, and visited her regularly, planning their future. Myra's prison therapist recalls: 'Tricia thought David Astor might be able to do something to help Myra's chances of parole. She would turn up at the prison with furniture catalogues and wallpaper samples, pictures of carpets, building up this idea that she and Myra would have this cosy little life. I don't think Tricia really believed it would happen, but she got carried along with the fantasy.'[4] Bridget Astor confirms: 'Tricia came to us because she and Myra hoped to have a home together when she came out of prison. That was the idea.'[5] Myra thanked the Astors repeatedly for their hospitality, adding in one letter: '[Tricia] said how different our lives would have been, or rather, what different people we would be if we had had someone like you, David, as a father.'[6]

The Astors fought the most effective campaign for Myra and provided her with the staunchest practical assistance. In April 1993, *The Sun* picked up on David Astor's footing of Myra's legal bills and giving occasional financial assistance to her mother, denouncing his support as 'an insult to the children who wept and begged for mercy before they were butchered'.[7] The article coincided with another in *The Independent*, in which Geraldine Bedell wrote that 'higher standards are expected of women when it comes to the care of children: Myra betrayed her sex and exploited her sex so that children could be sexually assaulted, tortured and killed. Her sex may also explain why she has become such an object of concern to ageing aristocrats . . .'[8]

The negative publicity caused her supporters to close ranks, determined that anyone recruited to Myra's freedom campaign had to prove themselves trustworthy. One of the few people to gain admittance to Myra's inner circle was Joe Chapman. Employed in the Prison Service since 1977 as a therapist for deeply disturbed, violent prisoners and sex offenders, he was invited to counsel Myra at Cookham Wood. He recalls: 'I was brought in because Myra's tariff was going to be announced at the end of 1994 and it was my job to support her through it. I got on well with Chris Ellis, the governor at Cookham Wood, but had to take on another six clients to draw attention away from the fact that I was there specifically for Myra. I remember Chris telling me, "You've bought a Myra ticket now", and I soon realised what she meant. Myra set me a test to see if I could be trusted by getting me to send out a letter for her after the post had been and gone. Then I was summonsed to meet David and the campaign group in London. I found myself involved in something very calculated, run along the lines of a military campaign. I was introduced to television companies and very influential people. They were all focused on protecting Myra's interests.'[9]

Every week for a year, Chapman counselled Myra for an hour in a private room: 'I didn't know much about her case, but she was astonishingly open. We talked about her childhood first. She'd sort of made her peace with her dad since his death. She talked about his service in the war and the injury he'd sustained. She used to attack him when she was old enough to do so without worrying he could beat her, and it was his war wound she went for, knowing it made him vulnerable – they were serious physical assaults. She was always much closer to her mum and spoke about the guilt she felt towards her because of what had happened. Nellie wasn't stupid; when I met her she told me, "Myra would have ended up as she did no matter what. If it hadn't been Brady, it would have been somebody else." She didn't believe that Myra went into it with her eyes shut, and said, "She could have told someone within the family what was going on, before the crimes. There was always someone for her to talk to."

'And Myra told me about her sister, Maureen, whom she still missed dreadfully. She hated Ann West for causing trouble at Maureen's funeral, even though *she* had done far, far worse to Lesley. For all Myra's intelligence, that was the one thing that she wasn't able to grasp: that people grieve for years and years and had the right to feel the way they did. Nobody should be expected to put away their grief after a certain length of time when they lose their children to murder. But Myra just couldn't understand that.'[10]

They discussed the murders in some depth as part of the therapy: 'She showed the most emotion when she talked about Lesley, but again, I wasn't sure where that emotion was coming from – pity for herself because that was the murder that sealed the case against her, or for the little girl herself. I think she did realise how horrific it was, but she had trapped herself in certain stories and didn't want her supporters to discover the truth about it. She cried when she talked about Lesley, but there was no sign of any upset over Pauline – she spoke about her murder, and those of Keith and John, as if she was reading from a book. Edward, too. Some of Brady's power and feeling of control over lives appealed to her as well. But I think until the night of Pauline's murder she never really believed Brady was going to kill. One thing she and I argued about was the word "excitement" in relation to the crimes. When I wrote my report on her, she was very insistent that I should change that. I wouldn't, because it was entirely relevant. I don't think she was sexually interested in the children, but I know she got a kick out of the control element. It excited her to be involved in something that was so horrific and which was on everyone's lips.'[11]

Chapman believes that far from hating the media spotlight, Myra actually craved it: 'The fight for her freedom kept her in the public eye, which was what she wanted. She didn't want to be forgotten. Not that there was any way that was going to happen. John Kay from *The Sun* made it his mission to produce something at least once a month, if not more, which was ironic, given his history [John Kay was convicted of the manslaughter of his wife in 1977 on the grounds of diminished responsibility]. That's why Myra had such a problem with *The Sun* – she knew that John Kay had taken a life and yet he sat in judgement of her and stayed on the payroll of the paper that led the battle against her.'[12] He recalls that any press resulted in a mountain of mail, some of it from well-wishers, and in the early days of their work together, he helped her devise a standard response followed by a butterfly logo to symbolise freedom.

Chapman also became close to Tricia, at a time when her relationship with Myra was beginning to sour again: 'Myra referred to her as her partner and Tricia really loved her. She used to say prayers before our counselling sessions so that Myra would find it a positive process.

She'd phone afterwards to see if Myra was OK. But twice Myra took Tricia's life and turned it upside down. Yet Tricia remained loyal to her, even when another woman came into Myra's life.'[13]

The woman was Dutch criminology student Nina Wilde, who arrived at Cookham Wood as part of a placement scheme. When news of their affair broke in the press, Nina told a journalist how she and Myra would have long conversations 'about philosophy, religion, French and English literature. [Myra] has a very sharp mind and a great wit. She is sensible and sensitive and very good company. She always gets on well with everybody. I felt immediately at ease with her . . . We've talked about what happened. It was difficult at first, but Myra has been completely frank with me . . . the person I see now is a different person to the one Brady knew . . . We are both hopeful that one day she will be released.'[14]

Nina became Myra's 'mentor' in prison and was assigned to teaching her German and Dutch; she was also given the keys to the prison. The two women began planning their future and Myra made an official application to live abroad upon her release but was informed that she would have to demonstrate she had successfully adjusted to living in a British community before consideration would be given to her request to live elsewhere – Amsterdam was the place she had in mind.

Anticipating a favourable parole result, the *Sunday Mirror* ran an article in which Ian threatened to reveal other murders. Chapman witnessed Myra's shock and anger first hand and asked her outright if there were other victims. She replied ('stone-faced'): 'On my mother's life, which I hold the dearest, there are no others. Not to my knowledge, and certainly none that I have taken a part in, but that's not to say there aren't any.'[15] When Nina was suspended from work pending an investigation into her relationship with Myra, the press were swift to report the 'sacking of Myra's jail lover'.[16] Myra cried throughout the counselling sessions with Chapman, insisting she should have the right to see Nina. He recalls: 'It struck me that aspects of Myra's relationship with Nina had echoes of the past with Brady, in that it was all-consuming. Myra was obsessive over Nina.'[17] Myra pressed David Astor for financial assistance for Nina while she was suspended; he hesitated, explaining to Myra that his position was awkward, more so since Tricia was still living in his house. But when

Joe Chapman accused Myra of behaving selfishly, Astor sprang loyally to her defence.

Myra's supporters were keen to secure television time for her campaign; Astor spearheaded plans that led to a slot on *Heart of the Matter*, presented by Joan Bakewell. Astor, Longford, Timms, McCooey, Chapman and Father Bert White – the Roman Catholic chaplain at Cookham Wood to whom Myra had become very close – were all anxious to speak on Myra's behalf. The show's producers were quick to notice the absence of any volunteers from Myra's small circle of female friends and expressed their concern about the preponderance of 'old men in suits'.[18] Tricia refused to participate publicly, although she was involved in the decision-making, and Astor realised that Nina Wilde's presence would provoke nothing but antipathy. Further difficulties arose when Myra's solicitors informed the producers that they were against Ann West appearing: 'Her inclusion in this programme will not allow a proper reasoned debate to occur.'[19] A follow-up list of pointers from some of Myra's supporters referred to Lesley's mother as 'the most active and vicious ally of *The Sun* newspaper (and other tabloids). She gives extreme interviews.' In a codicil, they asserted, 'nobody in journalism doubts that Mrs West and all these other interviewees are well-paid', reiterating again that she was 'a paid propagandist and therefore unsuitable for engaging in an honest discussion' in response to the producers' explanation of why Mrs West had been invited to appear.[20] In a letter to the director general of the BBC, Myra's team asked that no other victims' relatives should be allowed to take part because 'this might later be held to mean that we had agreed to Mrs Johnson, who is apparently an imitator of Mrs West'.[21] The letter stated the withdrawal from the programme of most of Myra's supporters. *Heart of the Matter: Can We Forgive Myra Hindley?* went ahead but was not the auspicious showcase Myra's supporters had envisaged.

On 7 December 1994, Myra wrote to Astor in low spirits, stating that she had 'as much freedom as a battery hen'.[22] She was angry that Nina had been excluded from her list of approved visitors and had appealed for permission to travel to New Hall Prison in Wakefield to allow her mother to visit: 'It's been left so long that she's now incapable of even walking unassisted in the garden of the sheltered accommodation in which she's lived since June.'[23] Fearing a security breach with the media, the authorities vetoed the idea.

Myra's spirits plummeted completely when she was given the news that her tariff had been fixed as whole life. Chapman recalls: 'She had hoped that somewhere, sometime, there would be a Home Secretary robust enough to put her out there secretly, if not openly. She firmly believed that she could be given a new identity – she referred to the two boys who killed James Bulger and very often to Mary Bell. She felt very strongly that what was good enough for Mary Bell was good enough for her.'[24]

At their next meeting that month, Myra read aloud from 'Revenger's Tragedy', a recently published article written by Germaine Greer for *The Guardian*, which she described as 'a breath of fresh air in an atmosphere that has begun to choke me'.[25] Greer's article suggests, 'Perhaps Myra asks for freedom because she has no choice' and uses an analogy between two field mice that she kept in a bottle until she could resettle them with the rest of their family: the mice 'would rather run the gauntlet of their predators than stay in their warm newspaper nest surrounded by food'.[26] Greer was sympathetic to Myra but appeared less so towards the victims' families: 'The evil that flowed out of the Moors Murders spawns anew every time that the people whose lives were blighted by the original acts parade their undimmed vindictiveness . . . May God have mercy on you, Myra Hindley, for ungodly men will have none.'[27] Encouraged by the article, Myra arranged for an interview with a *Sunday Times* journalist. Mimicking Greer's field mice analogy, Myra described the escape of a bird from the prison aviary: 'Whatever fate awaited the budgie, it had done what it was created to do – to spread its wings and fly . . . I envied it and still do, whatever became of it.'[28]

The interview rebounded; the authorities rapped Myra's knuckles for instigating additional press coverage, infuriating her. Her resentment increased when she was told that there was no possibility of a visit from Nina because the authorities feared it would 'resurrect the allegations of last year and with them further adverse publicity'.[29] Myra's legal team attempted to intervene, warning the area manager of Kent's prisons that if the ruling wasn't relaxed they might 'be obliged to write to the Home Secretary informing him that Ms Hindley was now no longer willing to be hypnotised in an attempt to recall the burial place of one of her victims'.[30] This bargaining tool referred to a possibility first raised by Peter Topping; Myra had agreed to the proposal then, but Home Secretary Douglas Hurd was against the use of hypnosis in criminal proceedings and permission was refused in 1988.[31] Keith's family had never given up hope that the decision might be reversed under another Home Secretary and, by 1994, as a result of Myra's compliance, steps were taken towards finding a suitable hypnotherapist.[32]

Myra wrote to the authorities herself, insisting that Nina's visits were a prerequisite if she were to be mentally, psychologically, emotionally and physically fit enough 'to be able to honour my promise and commitment to the family of Keith Bennett to undergo hypnosis'.[33] Resenting the helplessness of her supporters to realise her wish of being reunited with Nina, Myra was fast becoming isolated from the people who had worked hardest on her behalf. Following a report in the *Daily Star* that her solicitor had requested psychiatric assistance for her to come to terms with the tariff, Myra was placed on suicide watch in January 1995. Afterwards, she remained for some time under permanent observation. Having previously told the authorities that she wanted a transfer from Cookham Wood, but not to Durham, Myra then got it into her head that Durham might offer the best chance of a meeting with Nina Wilde. Her counselling sessions with Joe Chapman came to an end, largely because of internal politics, but she thanked him for all he had done, promised to keep in touch and said he would always be her rock.

On 1 February, Myra informed the Home Office that due to her treatment in prison she no longer felt mentally or physically capable of undergoing hypnosis. The following month she wrote again, this time to assert that she couldn't contemplate hypnosis unless she was moved to another prison. Myra was then transferred to Durham. A month after her arrival, she wrote to Chapman that she had fallen in the exercise yard and her left leg had been operated on: 'I fractured the femur in several places – on Easter Monday. I am now in the male hospital, in considerable pain, having daily physiotherapy. Torture sessions.'[34] Nonetheless, she liked the other people in the hospital and was looking forward to a visit from former Middle East envoy Terry Waite, who had been to see her on several occasions.[35] She badgered Chapman and David Astor to speed through a grant that

Nina needed and persuaded Astor to help Nina out until the money arrived.

On 30 May, Myra wrote to Astor that she had asked Andrew McCooey to contact Winnie Johnson's solicitors concerning her 'regular outbursts' in the press: 'She's become as bad as Mrs West. If she's so constantly disgusted with or about me, why doesn't she ask Ian Brady to jeopardise his mental health with hypnosis. Please express my disgust with her in as discreet a way as possible.'[36] She was pleased by a letter from Geoff Knupfer in June, wishing her a speedy recovery from her fall and assuring her that he would honour his promise to provide a statement about the part she had played in their investigation. That same month, Joe Chapman sent Myra a copy of his report to accompany the review of her tariff. Although it was very much in her favour, she was adamant that he should remove references to her anger. He was equally unprepared to do so, assuring her that the Parole Board would be more inclined towards a positive response if they could see that she was working through certain issues. He had also argued with Nina Wilde about a remark she had passed about Myra's 'old men' taking up too much of her time. Chapman shared some of his concerns about Myra and Nina with Astor, who advised him that it would be 'inappropriate to continue to challenge Myra in her difficult circumstances, particularly with an appeal process continuing'.[37] He suggested that Chapman should concentrate his efforts on the development of his own charity instead.

An internal memo dated 26 July 1995 refers again to the issue of hypnosis; the authorities were suspicious of Myra's 'delaying tactics . . . it could also be that she is trying to delay hypnosis until nearer the time that her tariff will be reconsidered by ministers in the hope that her co-operation will be taken into account'.[38] The memo accused her of 'attention seeking' and concluded: 'We are always aware of Myra Hindley's ability to manipulate a situation for her own ends.'[39] Perhaps in an effort to transform her public profile, Myra agreed to a meeting with former prison inmate Mark Leech, editor of *The Prisons Handbook*, to discuss his plans for a biography of her. The subsequent press condemnation led to the proposal being swiftly dropped.

David Astor was beginning to worry that Myra was moving further into new and unpalatable territory; on 12 October, he wrote to her solicitors: 'I quite understand that Myra is in a phase when she wishes to contest everything said against her and is wishing to do so herself when she has a chance. While sympathising with her feelings, I am worried that she might appear as a quarrelsome and even self-righteous woman, rather than the reformed and dignified person who has become the victim of a grotesque campaign of abuse. However, that is for her to decide.'[40] Nevertheless, he remained active on her behalf.

On 14 November 1995, Myra drafted her appeal petition. She had little new to add, except: 'All my years in prison have reinforced my belief that crimes of any kind are totally destructive, not least for the victims, but also for the perpetrators . . . All I would want to do is lead a quiet life; keep out of the public eye, perhaps if possible do something quietly useful, and end my days in relative obscurity.'[41] The following month, outraged by an article that labelled her a psychopath, she penned a 5,000-word autobiography for *The Guardian*, declaring that she was a very different woman to the one who had abducted children from the streets of Manchester. She turned on her accusers, who 'want to burn all the facets of their own natures which they can't or won't confront or deal with'.[42] She had become 'bad by a slow process of corruption' but insisted that without Ian 'there would have been no murders, no crime at all. I would have probably got married, had children and by now be a grandmother.'[43]

On 29 August 1996, Myra's solicitors wrote to David Astor to inform him that Myra had received a letter from Winnie Johnson but was no longer willing to undergo hypnosis and 'is obviously anxious to stop the letters'.[44] Plans were put into place to find a doctor who would back Myra's decision with medical reasons as to why hypnosis was being shelved. She had repaired her friendship with Astor; the following month he responded to her letter about the courage of Auschwitz survivor and broadcaster Rabbi Hugo Gryn, who had recently died: 'You are quite right about [him]. It is amazing that anyone should go through all that was done to him and to remain as balanced and sane as he did. You ought to know, as you have gone through something of a similar achievement.'[45] Although Myra was in poor physical health, her spirits had revived and she wrote a whimsical letter to her solicitor in November, giving her address as 'M Hindley, "Howard's End", 2nd On The Right, Straight On Til Morning, Neverland.'[46]

Undeterred by *The Sun's* 1997 declaration that she was 'the most evil woman of all time', Myra decided to redraft her autobiography, giving it the provisional title *A Model Prisoner*. On 20 February, she wrote to Astor, railing against her 'medieval' punishment: 'confinement for 32 years, with ever-declining hope throughout, because of what I did when I was a daft and besotted girl . . . I seem to have been turned into a sort of real-life Countess of Monte Cristo in the closing years of this century . . .'[47] Astor remained troubled by Myra's alliance with Nina Wilde; he told barrister Edward Fitzgerald QC that he was still prepared to help her if she were released, 'but only via a charitable institution willing to be responsible for her care. She never liked the idea of protection by an institution, but I see no other possibility.'[48]

Fitzgerald was preparing to put Myra's case to a Judicial Review. Married to one of Lord Longford's granddaughters, his hugely successful legal career gave Myra renewed hope of overturning her tariff. Astor had absolute faith in Fitzgerald, but fretted about the loopholes the Home Secretary might exploit to keep Myra imprisoned, even if the review went in her favour: 'An objection to her release on the grounds that this would invite crimes against her is expected. As things stand, this would mean holding her, after over 30 years, for perhaps another 20 years.'[49] He viewed it as 'the moral equivalent of a woman who had been turned into a witch, being put in an "oubliette".'[50] Joe Chapman, on the other hand, no longer believed that Myra would ever set foot outside prison and abandoned the campaign. As the review approached, the media was saturated with articles and television programmes about Myra. Danny Kilbride resigned from his job to petition against her and collected 140,000 signatures in Ashton-under-Lyne alone from people who felt she should die in prison.

On the eve of the appeal, the *Bolton Evening News* reported the death of Joe Mounsey, whose dogged determination helped bring Myra Hindley and Ian Brady to justice. His widow, Margaret, recalls, 'He was "demobilised" at the age of 64 and had a grand retirement, really. We did talk about Hindley when she was making her bid for freedom. Joe always said, "They can do what they bloody like with her, as long as they don't stick her next door to me."'[51]

On 18 December 1997, the Divisional Court dismissed Myra's appeal.

26

I wonder if that horrible young woman would have managed
life all right if she hadn't met him. Not so badly, anyway, I
think. Indeed, if I can raise a glimmer of sympathy for her
at all, it isn't exactly for her – but for the kind of blinding
passion that drove her. In another context it could have
seemed classic and wonderful. Not in this one ...

Pamela Hansford Johnson,
letter to Emlyn Williams, 5 June 1967

In early 1998, Myra was moved to Highpoint, a medium-security
prison in Suffolk whose rules were so relaxed in comparison to other
prisons that it was known as 'High-de-hi-Point'. On 2 March, she
wrote to David Astor that she was delighted with the place, and
especially with her room in the segregation wing: 'The walls are a pale
restful green with a lovely papered frieze across the centre of each wall,
and a brown fitted carpet ... a TV, which to me is magical – it's also
got video facilities ... I also have a job as the segregation unit library
orderly ... so far as anyone can be content in prison, I am.'[1] She wrote to
Bernard Black in similarly joyful terms, describing how her visits were
to be held away from the other prisoners in the adjudication room,
'unsupervised but with the door open, of course'. She explained that
she was 'considered to be a Category D inmate, as in 1995, the Parole
Board recommended that I go to an open prison for two years to be
prepared for release – which [Michael] Howard the Coward vetoed
immediately, with the aid of Doris Karloff [Anne Widdecombe].' She
was astonished to be given her own garden, 'a large, square weed and
rubble-filled mess', which she planned to split, turning half into a
Japanese herbal rockery and the other into an English cottage garden,
inspired by the creaking garden door that 'reminds me of the secret

garden in that lovely book of the same name'.[2] She was so buoyed by the changes in her life that she intended to alter her image with a different hairstyle and new clothes.

She began taking communion in her cell, where Father Michael Teader visited her every week to hear her confession and hold a Eucharistic service. Despite 20 years' experience in the Prison Service, he admits to 'a certain apprehension when I first went to see her. The photo of her in the press was that young, hard-faced mugshot. But I met this elderly woman who was using sticks, had arthritis and wasn't well. She was very quiet, polite and cautious because everything she said and did ended up in the press. It took some time for her to trust me. Father Bert White provided the bridge between us, then when he withdrew I became more trusted. Because of her isolation, services were always in her room with Sister Carmel. She was in a little wing off the segregation unit. It wasn't a cell, although it was very small. She did everything in her room, from washing to going to the toilet, from having her meals to sleeping there. The room next to hers was for vulnerable prisoners. Myra would chat to the person there and help them if she could.'[3] Myra joined a number of charities that year, including Amnesty, Greenpeace, Common Ground and the Worldwide Society for the Protection of Animals. Father Michael recalls: 'When we took services together, she would pray for different things that had happened in the world. God became very strong in her life. She often talked about the church she had known in her childhood and became very wistful about its beauty. She was a spiritual woman. Spiritual more than religious – also because of the way we practise our religion in a community, gathering with others to pray and sing. Hers was only with myself and Sister Carmel. I was very aware that Sister Carmel and myself were probably her only true friends.'[4]

Occasionally, they discussed her past and her crimes: 'I wouldn't have said she was a psychopath because she empathised with people and was capable of deep love. I think Brady was the psychopath. She did have an obsessive streak, I will say that, she got these interests and would just focus, focus, focus on something. There would be a trigger and then it would be all or nothing. She was a very strong woman and could be manipulative, but that's also part of being in prison – it's survival. But the lies in the press hurt her. She'd created victims, but in the end she became a victim too – of the press and politics. I don't think the media understood the conflict she had within herself. She had gone through denial, self-loathing and fear. Redemption is the right word because redemption is a process; there are very few people for whom it is a flash of light. She was redeemed *and* rehabilitated. If she'd been released and housed next door to you, there would have been no problem. You would have seen her as a nice old lady and the next thing you would have been offering to help her with her shopping. Before much longer she would have had you running all sorts of errands because that's who she was, but I don't know that Myra would have had any knowledge of the reality of life outside. Prison doesn't rehabilitate in that sense. She would have been no danger to the public, but I'm not certain how she would have coped going out into a world she hadn't known for 30-odd years.'[5]

Journalists were among the people Myra trusted least of all, although she had been corresponding with *The Independent*'s Steve Boggan and reporter Alan Watkins since he had written to her concerning a detail of European law. In one letter to Watkins, Myra deliberated: 'I do not think you understand killing, although you may mean to try to. I don't think anyone who has not killed can understand killing.'[6] In 1998, she began working with Duncan Staff, who had contacted her a few months earlier about a possible *World in Action* special. She agreed to cooperate with the programme, writing to David Astor: 'In exchange for my participation in a way to be discussed at a later date, I asked for a written guarantee that Nina would not feature in any way in the programme.'[7] The *World in Action* feature fell through when Duncan Staff left Granada, but he remained interested in her case and intended to produce his own programme. In April 1998, he wrote back to Myra, agreeing to her terms and reassuring her that he had no intention of interviewing the victims' relatives since he felt that their emotional involvement made an intelligent assessment of the case impossible. Myra and her supporters were won over by his premise.

All year, her legal team prepared new evidence for the Court of Appeal which they hoped would prove Myra had been coerced into the crimes by Ian's systematic abuse and threats to her family. To that end, she wrote a tangled, seven-page statement detailing his alleged violence towards her and asserting that the pornographic photographs in which they both appeared were taken under duress. The new material would be presented alongside reports about her progress in prison. Aware of Ian's threat to release her post-arrest letters to him, Myra decided on a high-risk strategy; she told journalist Steve Boggan about the letters herself, explaining how the code worked and citing the line about throwing acid on toddler Brett Downey as an example, adding: 'Won't the media love that; that I could have been so utterly callous as to write messages like that to Brady, not knowing the facts behind it or what was coded in his messages to me.'[8] She declared: 'I'm pissed off with [Brady's] half-raving but very lucid threats made so often over the years. I'm not prepared to have a public slanging match with him; that's beneath my dignity and certainly my contempt, but as I said earlier in this letter, I will fight the bastard in public.'[9] Myra insisted to Boggan: 'People think I am the arch-villain in this, the instigator, the perpetrator . . . Brady made me do it . . . He dominated me completely.'[10] She claimed that guilt had prevented her from speaking out before about the 'dreadful abuse' to which Ian subjected her.[11]

Boggan published the information she gave him. Ian's reaction was immediate; in an open letter, he sneered: 'Hindley, in her usual Barbara Cartland prose, has created a Victorian melodrama . . . the 33 years of duplicity, taking advantage of others to achieve her impossible aims, has apparently exacted its toll . . . driving her into the realms of psychotic delusion and absurdity.'[12] Joe Chapman waded in with a statement of his own: 'Myra had a responsibility in the crimes that had nothing to do with the beatings from Brady. Myra has omitted to go into the details of her crimes openly. Perhaps the main reason is she does not want to turn people away from her by coming out with what she has done. She has to own up to that responsibility.'[13] Myra raged about Boggan's 'betrayal' but was equally livid at Ian's comparison of her with Barbara Cartland: 'The bastard, how dare he compare me to that old painted clown! I've never read a single one of her books; he obviously has.'[14]

In the same letter she expressed concern for Alan Bennett. A *Sun* reporter had confronted him as he left prison after visiting Myra to discuss the location of Keith's grave; the newspaper ran an article on the front page under the headline: 'Evil Myra Murdered His Little Brother . . . Yet He's Gone to Jail to Give Her *a Hug*'. The article had several repercussions, causing problems between Alan and his mother, Winnie, until she understood the reason behind his association with

Myra. In a letter to Astor, Myra wrote spitefully about Winnie: 'The hypocritical old bag . . . she got her solicitor to send me a letter from her, in which she said I must undergo hypnosis. I felt like writing back saying I would do, after she'd undergone a brain implant.'[15]

In September, Myra's legal team – Edward Fitzgerald QC and solicitor Jim Nichol – advised her to cease communication with Duncan Staff, worried that his documentary might be seen as an attempt to influence public opinion, which in turn might adversely affect her court case. She assured her supporters, 'I just know that [Staff] will never betray me and will help me wherever I've asked him to.'[16] Following concerned letters from Staff to her solicitor, Myra wrote to Astor that she hoped they could find a compromise, since she wanted the documentary to go ahead but was very anxious not to attract the 'wrong' sort of exposure. She had been angry with Lord Longford on a recent visit with his wife because 'he absolutely monopolises the conversation by talking about publicity . . . there is no way I'll ever shut him up'.[17] She was upset again when the Save the Children Fund returned two private donations she had made; David Astor and Terry Waite wrote to the director of the fund, explaining that his letter of refusal had 'reduced her to tears'.[18] But the director stood firm; the fund would not accept donations from Myra Hindley.

In January 1999, Myra wrote in a more optimistic mood to David Astor about a visit she had received from Geoff Knupfer, 'with whom I've maintained contact, whom I trust implicitly and who has been very helpful and supportive by writing letters to the Parole Board and to my legal team for use at the courts, etc.'.[19] That same month she informed Bernard Black that she had been granted Legal Aid for her appeal: 'My legal team are cautiously optimistic . . . but personally I think we'll have to go to the European Court of Human Rights, so have "set" seven to eight years aside until the whole process is finished.'[20] She outlined her plans to upgrade her Honours degree from a lower to an upper second and perhaps an MA; she had provisionally settled on studying Charlotte Mew, a much-underrated poet whose work she had quoted in her remand letters to Ian. The following month, the *Daily Mirror* ran a front-page article on a story that was already five years old but which caused ructions nonetheless: 'Jailed Moors Murderer Myra Hindley spent three hours looking after an eight-year-old girl with only her lesbian lover supervising the astonishing visit'.[21] Joe Chapman recalls: 'Prison staff are encouraged to bring their children in on occasion, under supervision, obviously. On that day, I'd taken Sophie into the healthcare centre, where she did some crayoning with Myra and spent some time doing forward rolls and so on in the gym, while Myra and Nina applauded. I don't regret what happened, only the way it was reported, which was my fault. I was telling a journalist how Myra had changed and he said, "Ah, yes, but would you trust your *own* children with her?" Stupid me, I said, "Well, I have done." And out it came.'[22] An internal investigation was launched and a statement was issued, reassuring the public that measures were in place to prevent similar incidents. David Astor was infuriated by the negative publicity; his accountant informed Joe Chapman that he was withdrawing his financial support for the Replay Trust, Chapman's charity. Several other donors followed his lead.

In February 1999, Myra's most formidable opponent, Ann West, died of cancer. In one of her last interviews, she described how Lesley's grave had been repeatedly damaged; *Let Myra Go* had been scratched across the marble headstone, and eventually Ann and her husband decided to have her daughter re-interred at a secret spot. Shortly before her death, Ann had visited the moor and presented retired policeman Robert Spiers with a plaque thanking him for bringing her daughter home. She told a journalist to pass a message on to Myra: 'If there is such a thing as haunting and ghosts, I'll be on her shoulder morning, noon and night. She'll not get rid of me.'[23] As part of her posthumous battle against Myra's bid for parole, she gave permission to journalist and producer Clive Entwistle to include one of Ian Brady's photographs of ten-year-old Lesley, bound and gagged, in his documentary about the Moors Murders. The tape recording was deemed too harrowing for broadcast.

Myra's supporters continued to work ceaselessly on her behalf. Astor considered purchasing a property in the Chatham area to rent out to Myra and Tricia, who continued to be part of her life. He also made enquiries about the possibility of Myra's release into a religious community, one of which was Turvey Abbey in Bedfordshire, recommended by the Roman Catholic Bishop of Norwich, who had visited Myra. Astor's emotional and fiscal support was extensive: since May 1998, when he declared himself 'shocked by the smallness of your spending money', he had instructed his lawyers to provide Myra with the sum of £200 a month, and for a six-month period increased it to £250.[24] In addition to her allowance, he paid her legal and medical bills, and her monthly expenses, which included items such as books, videos, bouquets for her cell, Moonberry Musk body spray, presents for relatives, Jungian analysis and a Filofax in response to her request to be as 'normal' as possible, as well as fleecy bedsocks, a featherbed topper, quilted bedspread and bottles of whisky for her mother. His widow, Bridget, confirms: 'He certainly did fund Myra's legal campaign and so on, because he believed in it. Myra asked for financial help for her mother, but I'm not sure how often. We have a benevolent fund and I don't know if he used that money or not, but neither of them cringed. They had a lot of dignity, Myra and her mother.'[25] Bridget wasn't involved in the parole campaign but visited Myra regularly: 'She had her own room in Highpoint and was surrounded by her belongings and pictures of her family. We could have been visiting someone down the road, just having a cup of tea. She talked about her family a great deal. She loved her niece very much – that was completely genuine. We visited her mother, who was a very pleasant woman, angular, tall, calm and, as I said, extremely dignified. Myra was someone I would be pleased to welcome after her release, to meet up with for tea and so on. I liked her very much. One does tend to like people who've gone through things and come out the other side.'[26]

At the end of the year, Myra had a living will drawn up in addition to her actual will, in which she named Tricia, Astor and McCooey as executors. In December 1999, her close friend Father Bert White died in a car crash, a few months after visiting his native India to celebrate his 50th birthday. Father Michael recalls: 'Myra was truly devastated by his death. I went to the funeral and took photographs of the grave and coffin and so on, so that it would become a reality for her.'[27] Shortly afterwards, Myra collapsed in her cell. She was admitted to Addenbrooke's Hospital in Cambridge under the name Christine Charlton. Diagnosed with a cerebral aneurysm (a swollen artery at the base of the brain), she informed her solicitor that she didn't want to be kept alive if she slipped into a coma. Surgery repaired the aneurysm and she returned to prison, ignoring doctors' advice to quit smoking. She applied again for permission to visit her mother but conceded that it was better for them to remain apart rather than prejudice her mother's anonymity. Tricia still visited Nellie regularly and kept Myra informed about her.

In March 2000, the BBC aired Duncan Staff's documentary *Myra Hindley* as part of their Modern Times series. David Astor was delighted by it, but the programme met with a more cautious response from her legal team. Staff and Myra met a few months before the documentary was televised. He recalls: 'Her appearance was extremely smart, she'd put effort into it and made sure she looked right for the meeting. Perfect trouser suit, perfect shirt, nice jewellery, manicured nails. Everything laid out properly for a tea. There was a sense of planning and control there and she looked very together. She was easy to talk to and she could be amusing. Did I like her? I always had in the back of my mind the knowledge that I was doing a job. That sounds cold, but it's how I approached it. She was an incredibly socially skilled person, but I was there for a reason.'[28]

On 30 March, Myra lost her fight for freedom in the English courts; her lawyers announced their intention to challenge the decision in the European Court of Human Rights. Andrew McCooey reflects: 'The parole provisions of the Criminal Justice Act are bound to two elements: serving a sufficient period and not being a danger to the public. The tariff from the judge was open to revision, but she served the tariff he set out originally for her and then Michael Howard added another stipulation of his own to the conditions for parole: that of whether or not the public would wear it. All tied up inextricably with the need for being seen to be reactive to law and order, for the purpose of winning votes. That third one is very obviously a political assessment and in her case it was applied . . . Nowadays, the Home Secretary has no part in that decision; it's been removed and Article 6 of the Convention states that as regards release, all criminal cases should be determined by an independent tribunal.'[29] In September, Myra's application was lodged at the courts in Strasbourg. Three months later she renewed her request to be granted a 'compassionate visit to her mother', this time informing the authorities that a refusal 'would make her extremely cross'.[30] But the visit did not take place.

When Myra was hospitalised again the following March (an internal memo outlines security concerns: 'limited risk of impulsive dash, as she is not mobile but there is a possibility of abduction'), some newspapers erroneously claimed that she was suffering from cancer and had weeks to live.[31] Upon her return to Highpoint, she received a letter from author Brian Masters, enquiring if she would consider working with him on an exhaustive book about her life. Masters' previous biographical subjects included Sartre and Camus, although his best-known work was *Killing for Company*, a study of serial killer Dennis Nilsen, written with Nilsen's cooperation and widely regarded as a masterpiece of its kind. Myra intended to discuss his idea, which she liked, with her solicitor, but shortly afterwards it seems that Duncan Staff highlighted the fact to Myra that working with Masters might bracket her amongst serial killers in general. He proposed that he would write a book himself, which would offer a true understanding of the case and would provoke the public into seriously questioning the role of the Home Secretary in her continued imprisonment. On 20 August, Myra wrote to Astor, agreeing with Staff that it wouldn't serve her well to be grouped with the likes of Nilsen and Jeffrey Dahmer, adding that she was confident a book by Staff would be 'no doubt more sympathetic' to her.[32] Even so, she questioned whether any book would aid her cause: 'The thing is, I really don't want the inevitable publicity, etc., of such a book being published; enough is enough, and Duncan's one is really part of his own agenda. Please let me know what you think, as I always value your advice.'[33]

Astor's reply is not among his papers, but shortly afterwards Myra began corresponding with Staff over the whereabouts of Keith Bennett's grave. A planned meeting between Myra and Alan Bennett with detectives in attendance had been shelved twice due to unforeseen circumstances and was never rescheduled due to her deteriorating health. Father Michael recalls: 'Alan Bennett approached Myra differently to everyone else. He was willing to speak to her, to work with her soberly, in order to see if Keith could be found. She did her best. We had photos of the moors to sift through – I think they were sent via a solicitor – which we looked at together. I asked her various questions, hoping to draw memories out of her, such as where she had sat, what she could see and hear, that sort of thing. Anything, really, to jog her memory. And from what she told me I drew a map, the one that was published everywhere,

Myra's map. But if you look at the handwriting you'll see that it's mine, not hers. I drew it to her instructions because she wasn't able to do so herself. There was no question of Myra returning to the moor again – she needed a walking frame to get about, so it would have been physically impossible. She did what she could.'[34]

In August 2001, Lord Longford died at the age of 95. Though the frequency of their contact had lessened since the late 1980s, he and Myra continued to correspond and meet occasionally, although she admitted to Astor on one occasion that she was 'forcing' herself to send Longford a visiting order.[35] Peter Stanford recalls: 'The problem was that every time he visited her, the tabloids would find out, mainly because he told them, and afterwards he would give them an update on her case, having just spoken to Myra about it. He couldn't help himself. But she retained affection for him, though having said that, the way she treated him was a bit disappointing. He mortgaged his good name in her cause. He'd been visiting prisons since 1930, and obscure inmates at that, and continued to do a great deal, but all that's been forgotten. I lost touch with Myra as well, partly because of that, and also because in the last Christmas card I received from her she said that she was making a collage on her cell wall of her friends' children and could I send photos of mine. My wife said she would leave me if I did. So that was the end of that.'[36]

Four months later, on 7 December 2001, David Astor died. Described as 'the gentleman editor' of Fleet Street in the obituaries, his association with Myra was not mentioned, although almost every obituary of Lord Longford referred to her. The man whom Myra regarded as her adopted father died at the age of 89, working until the end on finding somewhere for her to live upon her release; the last place he secured for her was a convent in New York, whose management cancelled their offer in the wake of tabloid interest.

Following the loss of the two men who had provided her with staunch public and private support, Myra became reclusive, shuffling out of her room only to make herself a cup of tea or receive one of her few visitors. Bridget Astor recalls: 'I saw her a couple of times after David died. She definitely wasn't well. She smoked a lot and gained a great deal of weight and then lost it again . . . She wasn't herself any more.'[37] In May 2002, the House of Lords ruled that the Home Secretary should not have the power to increase tariffs such as hers.

'Edward Fitzgerald fought for Myra so eloquently that the Law Lords had no choice but to agree with every word he said on her behalf,' Andrew McCooey remembers. 'He also represented Mary Bell and Maxine Carr, so he's no stranger to female notoriety. He always says that women are not forgiven for their crimes. Myra knew that if the ruling was upheld – a decision was due within months – she would be free. Of course, David Blunkett, who was Home Secretary then, directed Greater Manchester Police to come up with fresh charges to keep her imprisoned.'[38]

In autumn, Myra conducted an interview in her cell with crime writer Kate Kray. She spoke of her wish not to die in prison, then added, 'Over the years I wished many times that I had been hanged. It would have solved a lot of problems – for everybody . . .'[39] Weeks later, she was admitted to hospital with unstable angina, then returned to prison, where she caught a cold that left her struggling to breathe. She was habitually on a cocktail of medication for angina, asthma, bronchitis, osteoporosis, osteoarthritis, raised cholesterol, insomnia, depression, menopausal symptoms and psychological problems; on 10 November she was also given antibiotics for a chest infection. Two days later, on the evening of 12 November, she was admitted to Ward G2 of West Suffolk Hospital, Bury St Edmunds.

Barely able to breathe, she asked doctors not to resuscitate her in the event of cardiac or respiratory failure. She was given morphine as her condition deteriorated. On the morning of 16 November 2002, she began pulling at her oxygen mask and grew increasingly distressed. Nurses had to restrain her as she fought against them, finding it too painful to lie down. She drifted in and out of consciousness as Father Michael administered the last rites. Sister Bridget, a nun to whom Myra had grown close, held her hand. Then she seemed to rally, 'and we spoke about general things', Father Michael recalls, 'and she mentioned her mother in passing before she closed her eyes again'.[40]

At 4.55 p.m., Myra Hindley died in hospital of bronchial pneumonia. 'She slipped quietly from a world still raging against her,' Father Michael reflects. 'She wasn't frightened of death. It held no fears for her. Why should it? God doesn't have any favourites: he doesn't say, I'll forgive that sin but not that one, and I'll forgive you but not you. That's my belief and I tried to instil that in Myra before she died.'[41]

Following her death, the governor of Highpoint Prison wrote to the hospital administration: 'Would you please pass on my most sincere thanks to all of your staff who helped to keep the dignity and decency of a very sick woman.'[42] A document lists the property Myra left behind in her cell, including: photographs, cards, clothes, jewellery, a Westlife CD and a CD player, a plastic rosary and a pink baseball cap. Most of it, together with the bedding and furnishings in the room where she died, was consigned to an incinerator.

27

'Miss Hindley, why?'

Cross-examination of Myra Hindley,
'Moors trial', Chester Assizes, 3 May 1966

In their coverage of her death, the press reported how close Myra had come to freedom, highlighting that she had died 'within weeks of a decision by the House of Lords, which is likely to have led to her release . . . She was one of 70 prisoners who had already served longer than the recommended sentence . . .'[1] Personal reactions abounded: Nina Wilde told reporters that she had been struck by Myra's 'sharp mind and great wit'.[2] Peter Stanford penned her obituary in *The Guardian*, insisting that 'in middle age, Hindley was warm, funny and blunt, unrecognisable as the Gorgon who haunted parents' imaginations . . .'[3] There were a surprising number of cautiously sympathetic articles in the press, as well as the vituperative; *News of the World* announced triumphantly: 'Myra Hindley Went to Hell this Weekend'. Sara Trevelyan recalls: 'I felt very angry at the media exploitation of her death, the ghastly things that were written. If we cannot be respectful of death, what does that say about us as a society? I felt sad about the waste of her life, the lost potential of it. I felt very sad for her family and very sad for the victims' families. But the media had always demonised her. Always.'[4]

The families of her victims responded to the news with mixed feelings; glad that their struggle against her parole was over but despairing that she had died without leading them to Keith Bennett. Winnie Johnson, a widow since 1991, wept when she heard: 'At every opportunity, I begged Hindley to tell me exactly where Keith's grave was but, in my heart, I knew she was a wicked sadist who would never tell and would take her terrible secret to the grave.'[5] Pauline Reade's father died six years before Myra; Joan Reade died in 2001, but in a last interview spoke movingly of her daughter's discovery: 'She's not suffering now. No one can hurt her now. I feel her that close, you see. That seems to buck me up a lot. I feel her so close to me. I miss her so much. I still do. She's my little girl.'[6]

Danny Kilbride spoke for his family in the aftermath of Myra's death; his mother had also passed away by then. Today, he reflects: 'I didn't believe Hindley was dead at first. I told the authorities I thought they were lying – I was certain she'd been secretly released. I phoned the police chief constable of Manchester and said I wanted to attend her funeral, but he told me that if I, or any member of my family, did that we'd be arrested on sight. I know she's dead now. I'm just glad she's not still pestering for parole.'[7] When he heard the news, Alan West visited the grave where his wife Ann was buried with Lesley: 'I just sat there and told them about what had happened. I've placed my flowers on the grave again and I'll be going to see them every Wednesday, just like I've always done . . . Somehow, the spirits seemed to have lifted a little now that Hindley's gone.'[8] Edward Evans's surviving relatives have never spoken to the press; they retreated from the intense media glare following the trial in 1966. David Smith refused to speak to journalists but admitted later that the news came as a relief. Myra's brother-in-law, Bill Scott, told reporters that he and his daughter had absolutely no comment to make.

In the sheltered housing where Myra's mother lived, no one knew how deeply personal the news was to one of the residents. Nellie managed to retain her anonymity until her own death. Father Michael recalls, 'I stayed in touch with Myra's mother until the end. After Myra died, she became rather confused and would still ring me to ask how her daughter was. Sometimes I would gently remind her that Myra wasn't with us any more; at other times I would go along with it because her frame of mind seemed so disturbed. She lived in a state of abject terror – she'd suffered so much over the years, as a result of people discovering she was Myra Hindley's mother. She didn't socialise at all where she lived and wouldn't even go into the communal lounge because she was so frightened of getting into a conversation that might lead to the truth about her identity. She died within about a year of Myra's death.'[9]

There was no response from the man with whom Myra Hindley's name would be eternally joined.[10] In Ashworth Hospital, Ian Brady watched the news footage without a word, his face expressionless.

Duncan Staff, one of the last people to interview Myra, recalls, 'When she talked to me about Ian, I got the feeling there was still a very strong connection between them, that she knew exactly what he'd be thinking and how he'd react to anything. It was as if she hadn't left him behind. The connection was very, very alive. He was still a very real presence to her. And all the time they were in prison, even though they weren't physically together any more and didn't have any contact, that bond wasn't broken. I'd say, "What would Ian think?" and she would laugh, as if she had total understanding of him at any given point. There was a very powerful bond and understanding between them and that never went away.'[11]

Seven years after Myra Hindley's death, the Moors Murders remain part of our collective consciousness. There are a number of reasons why this is so. The victims were children abducted at random from streets regarded as safe and the killers were an upwardly mobile young couple. The murders occurred in the 1960s, a period viewed with particular nostalgia but which also seemed to usher in a new dawn of violence, from the Kennedy assassination in 1963 to the Manson Family murders in 1969. The crimes occurred in the working-class North at a time when it was the geographical focus of contemporary books, films and theatre, and were sadistic acts that tapped into people's fears of the progress of society. Capital punishment had been abolished shortly before the Moors trial, leaving many people feeling that resolution was lacking and justice had not been served. The searing impact of the mugshots has never lessened, despite the years that have passed since their taking. Lord Longford's involvement in Myra's persistent lobbying for freedom brought the case back into the headlines and kept it there. And above all, at least one victim remains unfound on the moors that gave the crimes their epithet and the case its chilling setting. The moors hold a distinct resonance in British literature and folklore, invoking the girl who is frightened of the brooding landscape in Myra Hindley's favourite book, *The Secret Garden*; Dewer, the huntsman, in *The Hound of the Baskervilles*, throwing a bag to a man walking on the moor, who finds the body of his own child inside; and the ghost of young Cathy Earnshaw scratching wretchedly at the window in *Wuthering Heights*. Hindley and Brady will continue to haunt us after their deaths, a demon Cathy and Heathcliffe condemned to stalk the moor for eternity.

The murders tap into our deepest fears; Myra Hindley's involvement serves to echo the fairy tales of our childhood where boys and girls are lured away by evildoers – usually women, as Helena Kennedy QC points out in *Eve Was Framed*: 'Wicked witches, old crones, evil stepmothers and ugly sisters leap from the pages in greater numbers even than the giants and ogres. Terror is a man, but wickedness is a woman. These women, who either have a cruel beauty like the stepmother of Snow White or are as ugly as sin, insinuate themselves into positions of power over children and grown men, luring them to danger . . .'[12] The public war waged between Myra Hindley and Ann West reflected the age-old fight between the evil, barren female who stole the child of a virtuous, devoted mother: 'I believe that *The Sun* newspaper has a note on my file which instructs whichever journalist intends to put their name to yet another scandalous, sensational and fabricated article not to forget to prefix my name with the now hackneyed adjective "evil",' Myra wrote in a 1987 letter.[13] Evil is not a psychiatric term but a moral and religious one; it is a void, a dearth of goodness. In the absence of madness, evil is the only answer if we are to make sense of the crimes. Ian Brady's diagnosis as psychotic is both a motive of sorts and a punishment in itself, although he, too, was deemed sane at the time of the trial. Myra's prison therapist declared some years before her death: 'Myra was evil then, but is not evil now.'[14] His opinion, echoed by several of her supporters, implies that evil is not predetermined and fixed, as we like to believe, but is something that shifts, transmutes, even fades. Diane Athill, who was approached to edit Myra's autobiography, took a different view: 'It seems to me that there are strands of moral deformity which cannot be pardoned.'[15]

Moral deformity implies a monster, another term frequently applied to Myra; it was the title of a 2003 documentary by Michael Attwell, *Myra: The Making of a Monster*. On old, nautical maps, unexplored oceans were inscribed with the legend 'Here Be Monsters' and often supplemented with images of gigantic and fearsome beasts of the deep. The unknown is still regarded as threatening; in our fears that which is strange and unfamiliar becomes monstrous, ugly. Yvonne Roberts explains: 'In Myra, it was as if the public could see the dark side of all women. That mugshot of Hindley from the 1960s is the symbolic incarnation of woman as witch, woman as monster. She looked a certain way and played into our nightmares.'[16] Peter Stanford agrees: 'It's a picture of the twentieth-century devil. That's all the devil was – a face that we put to the intangible reality of evil, a religious construct. Now we find that rather medieval and foolish, but continue to create our own devils through the media, and that picture became the icon of evil.'[17] In 1997, Marcus Harvey's vast canvas of the mugshot, recreated using children's handprints, was unveiled at the Sensation exhibition at London's Royal Academy. Winnie Johnson led the protests by Mothers Against Murder and Aggression, academicians resigned and the painting had to be reinstalled behind Perspex after someone threw eggs and ink at it. Myra herself asked for the work to be removed, writing in a letter to *The Guardian* that the idea that art was meant to be challenging was 'a lame and unacceptable excuse'.[18] The artist defended it as a critique of the media's exploitation of the original photograph. It was also 'a classic example of a *pittura infamante* – a painting intended to defame. The handprints of the child . . . literally brand Hindley with her crimes.'[19]

An article published in *The People* two months before Myra's death in 2002 epitomises the tendency to equate physical ugliness with moral deformity. It reads in part: 'These are Myra Hindley's twelve faces of evil . . . she is always marked out by her: STARING, close-set eyes, TIGHT, cruel thin lips, UGLY, bulbous nose, and SQUARE, masculine jaw . . . 1965: She is just 23 – but looks years older when arrested for the Moors Murders . . . a chilling stare sends shivers down the spines of parents everywhere . . . 1966: her jaw is defiantly set . . . 1967: the unblinking darkness of her staring eyes . . . 1969: the smile never reaches those evil eyes . . . 1973: even with long hair curling around her neck it's impossible to soften those hard-edged features . . . 1976: there is no mistaking that glare . . . 1977: nothing can ever add sparkle to a face so blank and dead . . . 1978: The years are beginning to take their toll on the ageing monster . . . 1980: The soulless eyes are tired and narrow . . . 1982: Any attempt at femininity has gone . . . 1996: The change is dramatic. Bloated and puffy . . . 2002: Her bulbous nose could be reshaped, her square jaw softened and lines reduced with collagen. But could even the most skilled surgeon ever hope to hide the Hindley Mask of Evil?'[20]

Female criminals are portrayed either as treacherously beautiful or hideously repulsive; their appearance is regarded as uniquely relevant to their deeds. Vanessa George, the nursery worker charged in 2009 with abusing toddlers in her care and taking indecent photographs of them, is habitually referred to as '18 stone Vanessa George', hinting at the uncontrollable appetites beneath her skin. The media demonisation of women who harm is to no one's advantage. Such descriptions serve to remove them from humanity and place them firmly in 'Here Be Monsters' territory, thereby cloaking the unpalatable and largely unspoken fact that 'ordinary' women both collude in and instigate the abuse of children. Such imagery builds on the stereotypes established by Caesar Lombroso and William Ferrero in their 1895 study *The Female Offender*, in which the woman criminal was characterised as biologically abnormal; her sexuality is always suspect, whatever her offence – she is essentially more male than female. Now, as then, a woman who behaves cruelly is seen as betraying her nature. 'Rarely is a woman wicked,' wrote Caesar Lombroso, 'but when she is she surpasses the male.'[21] A woman who deliberately harms a child commits 'the sin for which there is no forgiveness . . . a boundary which we cannot imagine ourselves crossing'.[22] Because of her gender we either banish her completely or find excuses for her; if she acts in conjunction with a man, she is either handmaiden to a master or a dominant female who enslaves her partner. Past prejudices complicate our view: we find it impossible to believe that she might simply be equally culpable, equally inclined to abusing and murdering children.

Myra's defenders – very few of whom were women willing to state their support of her publicly – believe that she was coerced and browbeaten into the crimes. Her solicitor, Andrew McCooey states: 'She was intimidated and threatened, entirely in Brady's thrall, in fear of her own life and frightened for those she loved. It should also be borne in mind that she didn't physically harm the children herself, except maybe to slap them once or twice to get them to do as they were being told.'[23] David Astor was of the opinion that Myra was brainwashed by Ian Brady and described her state of mind as similar to the German nation under Nazi rule. Helena Kennedy QC writes that 'while her role was criminal and appalling, she was not the prime mover in the murders'.[24] If that were true, should it minimise her culpability? Were the guards at Auschwitz and Belsen less blameworthy than the architects of the Holocaust, asserting that they were merely carrying out the duties demanded of them by their superiors? Myra wept as she discussed the issue with her prison therapist: 'Could they be so forgiving if they knew the whole story? I have said that I became as evil as Ian, but if they knew how deep that went everything would be spoiled.'[25]

The roots of her iniquity are regarded as an enigma. The primary explanation offered publicly by Myra herself – that she acted under duress – is upheld by her supporters. In a curious adjunct, Myra offered another justification. In the first draft of her autobiography, she ended her introduction with a question: 'If the sins of the father cause the child to be born with congenital syphilis, does it follow that the sins of the child should cause the innocent mother to become infected by that sin, and to be persecuted and harassed almost beyond endurance? I hope not; I pray not.'[26] Her implication – which is unconfirmed and may simply have been another attempt to find a pretext for her crimes – was that her father had at some point contracted syphilis and infected her mother who, when pregnant, had passed it on to her daughter. On 28 July 1987, Myra's then solicitor, Michael Fisher, wrote to David Astor after a conversation he had had with Dr Betty Tylden, a psychiatrist often called in as an expert on child abuse cases. Tylden had expressed the opinion that Myra's state of mind at the time of her crimes could have been affected by her apparent congenital syphilis. Fisher felt that Myra might take some small comfort from the idea that her actions had perhaps been influenced by an inherited illness and he wondered whether it might be worthwhile investigating further.[27] The following month David Astor replied tersely to Michael Fisher, advising him to drop the subject: he was in little doubt that a doctor's reference underlining Myra's congenital syphilis would be detrimental to her morale.

More commonly, in an effort to convince her detractors that she hadn't suffered 'moral deformity' she asked women to empathise with her and men to pity her: 'I challenge any woman who loved a man as deeply and as blindly as I loved Ian Brady to look into her heart and say under similar circumstances she would have gone to the police.'[28] When that failed, she drew on the psychoanalytic staple of vindication for her actions – a brutal childhood. And it *was* brutal in parts, but perhaps its deepest injury to her was the inconsistency of her upbringing: spoiled and indulged by Gran, flitting home daily to her warring parents. She learned to embellish the hardships, especially after submitting the first draft of her manuscript to her advisors, who encouraged her to amplify 'whatever were the chief strains of childhood'.[29] Her father became an unredeemable ogre in her subsequent memoirs, yet there are hints in her private correspondence that the truth was more complex. In a 1999 letter to Myra, David Astor praises her inner strength, remarking that her 'emotional warmth' probably came from her mother or grandmother, and her 'courage and daring from your dad'.[30] After a visit to Nellie, the Revd Peter Timms wrote to Myra: 'I showed her the pictures [of the Open University ceremony] and her comment immediately was how proud your dad would have been of you and of your achievements.'[31] Despite Myra's protestations that she was the cuckoo in the nest as a child, when her sister Maureen went to the police about her crimes, the family rallied around Myra, ousting Maureen for several years until finally they were reconciled. Danny Kilbride is angered by psychologists who cite Myra's childhood experiences as a factor in her crimes: 'Look what happened to me when I was a kid. Why didn't *I* become a maniac? Millions of people have had her childhood, and much worse, but they don't then go on to murder children. There is *nothing* in her childhood that can account in any way for what she did.'[32]

Myra and Ian each blamed the other for their crimes; in a letter to a regular correspondent, Ian wrote: 'It was my bad luck to meet Myra.'[33] But they were surprisingly similar in many respects. Each felt ostracised by their parents in some way – Ian by his mother and Myra by her father. There are glimpses of excessive temper as children in both, and intimations of taking satisfaction in the violence they meted out. They shared a sense of being an outsider among their peers, although both were able to form friendships in the schoolyard. There were very minor acts of criminality in their childhoods; Ian continued that through to his teens and ended up in borstal before he met Myra. They were ambitious beyond the confines of their upbringing, and intelligent, though not the geniuses they liked to believe; the education they received in prison was viewed by them both as the only compensation for their loss of freedom. They both had a strong competitive streak that occasionally ended in outbursts of temper – Myra in sports, Ian in games and betting. They had an innate sense of superiority and a tendency towards grandiosity

– Ian's love of long words, Myra's habit of comparing herself to literary characters. They openly admitted to having little respect for people but were excessively devoted to their pets and attacked those suspected of harming animals. When they met, their shared excessive public prudery concealed an interest in sadomasochism, use of pornography and role play in private. In place of religion, they followed the doctrines of Nazism and nihilism, and, bored with their environment, developed an existential view of the world. Power and control were important to them. 'We became our own gods,' Myra declared. They became hopelessly disconnected from normal life, and that sense of disconnection remained, with Ian seemingly failing to comprehend how discordant his remarks about drawing 'energy, spiritual stimulation and delight from the relative innocence and spontaneity of the young' are when juxtaposed with his crimes.[34] Myra's response to Yvonne Roberts's question about her cruelty towards Lesley Ann Downey ('That girl shouldn't have been out so late at night') betrays a similar detachment. In 1997, Myra wrote to David Astor about the difficulty of dealing with Lesley's abduction in her autobiography, displaying the same lack of understanding: 'I could reiterate that I didn't know a tape recording was being made and say that *had* I known, I would have been careful what I said, given that people now think that I was the evil genius. I could also point out . . . that the child wasn't pleading for her life but pleading to go home . . .'[35] Such an inappropriate and inanely egocentric phrase: '*I would have been careful what I said.*'

Myra insisted that before the murders she was in thrall to Ian, spellbound by his 'powerful personality [and] magnet-like charisma'.[36] She tried to convince the Parole Board that her crimes had their source in the 'virginal, vulnerable, young and inexperienced heart' that she gave to Ian: 'Within months, he had convinced me that there was no God at all (he could have told me the earth was flat, the moon made of green cheese, that the sun rose in the west and I would have believed him). He became my god, my idol, my object of worship and I worshipped him blindly, more blindly than the congenitally blind.'[37] Years later, she reiterated: 'He was God . . . I just couldn't say "no" to him.'[38] But she couldn't say no to Norman Sutton either, the married policeman with whom she had an affair in the aftermath of Pauline Reade's murder, which suggests that her obsession with Ian wasn't as all-encompassing as she claimed. Her character was robust enough to withstand the fears of discovery that were attached to the affair – of PC Sutton finding out about the murder, and of his wife and Ian learning about the clandestine relationship. Sutton himself provided the perfect opportunity to unburden herself of 'the terrible secret' she and Ian shared; if she truly felt unable to confess the murder plot to the police prior to its conclusion, afterwards she had absolute proof to present to a policeman with whom she spent many intimate hours alone. Turning Ian in to the authorities was surely a safer alternative to living with a psychopath whose alleged threat to kill her – and her family – would persist until his capture. She might have faced prison for her part in the conspiracy to murder Pauline Reade, but the charges against her would have been far less than they were two years hence.

'Curse all goddamned *bad* men,' she wrote to a friend from prison, 'and curse the bad luck we women have – and the bad judgement – when we meet them and fall for them and lose our sense of perspective and just about everything else we have to lose.'[39] No doubt most of us have been fools for love in one form or another, but Myra's loss of perspective went much further than mere stupidity. 'I knew what we were doing was wrong,' she admitted. 'But I can't explain it.'[40] The real depth of her involvement will never now be known, but over the years fragments of her participation in the crimes emerged from Myra herself. We know from what she was willing to admit that she and Ian fantasised about abusing and murdering children as part of their sex lives. Before the murders, she drove about Manchester with Ian at her side, tailing children, while he told her what he would like to do to a victim, and they sat together outside her old school, Ryder Brow, taking surreptitious photographs of children at play. She admitted that having the power of life and death in her own hands excited her and that their best performances sexually as a couple occurred in the immediate aftermath of a murder. She abducted the children. We don't know whether she was present at the first four murders: predictably, she insisted she wasn't, and equally predictably, Ian asserts that she was, but she *was* standing in front of Edward Evans when he was killed, passing the comment an hour or so later: 'His eyes registered astonishment when you hit him.'[41] Ian Fairley, who arrested Ian Brady the following morning, proclaims: 'How she acted afterwards reveals that she had seen other killings. Evans's death was particularly bloody. There aren't many women who could stand in front of a young man as an axe was brought down upon his head, help clear up the mess and then dress for work the next day as if nothing had happened. I've been a policeman long enough to recognise the difference between someone who's just witnessed their first murder and someone who is used to it. She was the latter.'[42]

We know that she was present at the tape recording and photographing of Lesley Ann Downey, helping to gag and restrain the girl, and threatening to hit her when she cried. The weird restraint of the tape recording and photographs – Lesley's rape and murder were not documented on either, when they could so easily have been – demonstrates that their creators were connoisseurs of cruelty. Despite Myra's pleading with Ann West to believe that Lesley was not tortured prior to her death, *all* the children were made to suffer. The blood on Lesley and Keith that Myra conceded to having seen came not from their fatal wounds but from the rapes to which her lover subjected them. Their murders were uniformly brutal: Pauline's throat was slit; Ian tried to kill John the same way, but the knife was too blunt and he strangled him instead; Keith was strangled; Lesley was either smothered or strangled; Edward was struck 14 times with an axe but survived long enough for Ian to decide to strangle him. We know that she looked at the photographs of Lesley and Keith after their deaths because she admitted it to Peter Topping, and her fingerprints were found on the photographs of Lesley.

Then there was the preparation of it all: she conferred with Ian about the lure held out to the victim to entice them into the vehicle; she discussed with him where she should drive and what she should do; she accepted a record on the morning of each murder, knowing its significance; she ventured into a department store to buy a black wig to disguise herself, and stood at a till to hand over the murder weapons for John Kilbride's death – a knife, rope and spade; she hired the abduction vehicles; she bought the tape recorder that would document Lesley's last hours and Patty Hodges talking about the little girl's disappearance; she bought the camera Ian used to take photographs of the victims and their graves.

And afterwards: she crouched on John Kilbride's grave, staring down at the ground with that strange half-smile on her lips; she stood grinning on the rocks overlooking at least three graves, while Ian snapped away with his camera; she enjoyed picnicking on the moor beside the graves with her sister and children from the neighbourhood. After her arrest, she exchanged coded letters with her lover in which they continued to fantasise about child rape and murder. In prison, she listened to the songs that Ian had bought her to commemorate the killings and asked her mother for a fresh copy of 'It's All Over Now, Baby Blue', the record that marked the last murder. It was six years before she broke off her relationship with Ian. Even then, she couldn't bring herself to be honest about the other murders until Ian forced her hand; her ex-partner, Tricia Cairns, asserts that Myra only told the truth because she had no choice. And she used a promise to be hypnotised in the effort to find Keith Bennett's grave as a bargaining tool to receive visits from another lover.

None of this is surmise; it is all by her own admission. Afterwards, she spoke eloquently of remorse and her supporters have no doubt that she was genuinely a changed woman who regretted with every ounce of her being what she had done. But what troubled those of us who didn't know her personally was summed up in an article by Nicci Gerrard, when she asked: 'How could the pleasant-looking woman peaceful in the garden, the smiling woman receiving her Open University degree, be the one who had tortured and killed children, who had posed laughing on the moors beside a grave? Can you change so much that you are someone else entirely, struggling free from the ghastly wreckage of your past?'[43] Yvonne Roberts, who did meet Myra very briefly, is convinced that she was psychotic. Is it possible, then, to enter a psychotic state in which such crimes are committed and then to return – and be allowed to return – to a normal life? Father Michael tells us that she wasn't psychotic at all because she was capable of empathising with others and feeling deep love for people. Yet even as she professed remorse and offered heartfelt prayers for those afflicted by leprosy, starvation or homelessness, she wrote spiteful letters about the mothers of her victims, suggesting one required a 'brain implant' and the other was a 'pain in the neck'.[44]

Andrew McCooey believes that religion saved her from insanity, but redemption on Earth proved impossible. 'What happens to us in a world which has no rituals for recognising repentance, atonement and forgiveness?' one commentary asked.[45] But the public heard the resoundingly hollow ring in Myra's expressions of remorse, while her desperation for freedom seemed to further undermine the repentance she assured us was sincere. In prison terms, she was a 'nonce', but she refused to cave in to being a 'nothing'. It was this determination to fly in the face of public revulsion by not bowing under the weight of hatred that set her apart from other once-notorious women such as Carol Hanson and Marie Therese Kouao. She was a gift to politicians, certainly; while other female killers served their sentences and were released, keeping Myra Hindley imprisoned provided successive Labour and Conservative governments with a spurious example of how tough they really were on crime.

Throughout her incarceration, as she became more Girton than Gorton, Myra attracted the support of many high-profile individuals. Sara Trevelyan, who campaigned for Myra's release during the 1970s and was shocked by her confession ten years later, believes there are lessons to be learned: 'We know that these kind of crimes happen, and that men *and* women are responsible for them. I think we need a collective willingness to look more deeply at them, to ask what kind of light this sheds on us as a society. Children are becoming increasingly sexualised, and pornography is no longer something people look at in private. Alcohol and drugs play a part in dulling people's senses and allowing things to happen. We have to look not just at the individual but also take a broader view. Some of it goes back to childhood, which we can see clearly in the life of someone like Ian Brady. But Myra's childhood wasn't unremittingly awful; there were some good bits, it wasn't all bad. We need to look at how we create the conditions where these crimes happen, but I also think that the roots go further into our history, national history even. Think of someone like Josef Fritzl; his crimes have their roots in the collective consciousness of Austria after the war – the wall of silence that built up then, generational dysfunction. There's always a cause, no matter how terrible the crime, *always*. And I think we have to be willing to go into that darkness in order to achieve some kind of resolution.'[46]

Not all of Myra's prison visitors were in favour of parole. Lady Anne Tree, who introduced Myra to Lord Longford, reflects: 'I kept well clear of his campaign. How could you be safe if you had this strange urge to kill someone? I still don't have the faintest concept. Think of going out to kill someone. Think of leaving their body on the moor. Think of capturing a little boy. It is actually unthinkable and I don't think you should embark on this without thinking of what unhappiness this has led to. Dreadful unhappiness.'[47]

Danny Kilbride confirms: 'No one has any idea of what our family – and the other victims' families – have undergone. People say they understand, but they don't. There is no excuse for what she and Brady did, and no amount of talking about causes and resolutions can help *us* come to terms with it. Unless you've gone through something like this, you haven't got a clue what you're talking about. Where's the resolution for Keith Bennett's family? There's none for any of us. One of my sisters says now, "I can't remember our John and I feel *awful*." But, God, she was only four years old when it happened. I've still got very strong memories of John. I can see him. I remember him. But it shouldn't be about memories. He should be here.'[48]

Ian Brady's philosophies made sense to Myra Hindley; together they indulged in paedophilic fantasies that led to the horrifying deaths of at least five young people. They acted in tandem. 'She had no judgement', one obituary in *The Independent* read.[49] But judgement was precisely what Myra Hindley had – in a sense, it is all any of us have – and she chose to use it with the most wicked of intent.

APPENDIX:
HE KEPT THEM CLOSE

> There is little intellectual or spiritual inducement for the
> captured serial killer to cooperate in any way. To all intents
> and purposes, his real life is over and done with, as he knows
> he shall never be free again, so why should he volunteer
> information . . .
>
> Ian Brady, *The Gates of Janus*

The official search for Keith Bennett ended on 1 July 2009. Detective
Chief Superintendent Steve Heywood, head of Greater Manchester
Police's serious crime division, told the press: 'As a force, there is
nothing we would have liked more than to draw a close to this dark
chapter, and we are very disappointed that we have not located Keith's
remains, but we will never close this case and remain open to any
new lines of inquiry which may come about as a result of significant
scientific advances or credible or actionable information.'[1]

Most people were unaware that the police had been searching
the moor since 2003, when Operation Maida was launched to find
Keith's grave. Detectives began by visiting Ian Brady, who refused to
cooperate, despite declaring his confidence in being able to pinpoint
the grave to 'within 20 yards'.[2] The search of Shiny Brook was
resumed using information 'already in the public domain', along with
Ian's photographs.[3] In the immediate aftermath of the announcement
confirming the end of Operation Maida, Ian wrote to Keith's mother:
'The Manchester Police, having bungled the search 20 years ago,
opposed my offer of assistance to the Yorkshire Police, fearing that it
might expose their former incompetence. Therefore, in the tenth year
of the force-fed by nasal-tube hunger strike, this is my last word on
the matter.'[4]

'Brady holds the key,' Joe Chapman declares. 'He is capable of standing on the grave and telling police he had no idea where Keith was. Chapman recalls Myra's words: 'His attention to detail was such that major landmarks on the horizon viewed from a particular vantage point on the roads across the moors provided a perfect grid reference for his trained mind . . . Ian had spent months planning the murders and plotting each location.'[5]

Standing on the rocks of Hollin Brown Knoll, Ian and Myra could survey their dominion: the graves of Pauline, Lesley and John were all within close sight, plotted in a wavering line. A photograph of Myra taken by a stream shows her clutching a map and compass; it isn't beyond the bounds of possibility that Ian, innately methodical, charted the graves with such precision. It was his 'landmarks' – the rocks of the Knoll, the peat bank and certain flat stones – that had enabled detectives to pinpoint the location of John Kilbride's grave. In her autobiography, Myra admitted that the graves of their victims were 'marked by photographs and not headstones'.[6] It was this macabre significance that lay behind Ian's fixation with retrieving the photographs after his arrest. 'The police on the original case returned the slides after about 18 months,' Myra wrote in her autobiography. 'Ian had them in prison, where he had permission to view them through a hand-sized projector.'[7] On one occasion when Peter Topping visited, Ian took out the photographs, murmuring that he wanted to see how the landscape had changed, then flicked slowly through them while the detective sat nearby.[8] In a 1988 letter to Ann West, Ian describes the tartan photograph album as 'my property for reference purposes'.[9]

Duncan Staff's 2004 documentary, *The Moors Murders Code*, discussed the use of photographs as grave markers. One previously unknown photograph was highlighted in the programme: it showed Myra Hindley hunkered down on a patch of grass with her dog on her knee. But the image has no landmark or detail within it and research into it 'proved to be fruitless', according to a police spokeswoman.[10] There is just one picture that resembles the infamous shot taken of Myra crouching on John Kilbride's grave. It was taken in a spot the couple visited often with their dogs, and where they photographed themselves at different times of the year, in snow and in sun, always showing the same clearly identifiable landmark in each shot: a tree, struck by lightning, on which the initials 'FW' have been carved. In one particular photograph, Myra Hindley kneels beside the tree, clutching her dog and staring straight at the ground. But as with the shot of her crouched on John's grave, the landmark is impossible to place – except to those already familiar with it.

'How many more trophy photographs were there?' former Detective Chief Superintendent Ian Fairley ponders. 'My view: somebody should speak to Brady now, before it's too late. When we locked him up in Hyde and he smoked all my Embassy fags, I told him, "One day you will have to tell the truth." Nothing to do with foresight. "One day you will have to tell the truth. And it will be easier for you when you do." I accept it could be a power thing for him. I'm in no doubt at all that he knows where Keith Bennett is buried. He's the type of fellow who *would* stand on the grave surrounded by police and get a kick out of saying, "Not here." Brady is the type of individual who leaves nothing to chance, although he misread David Smith. But everything else was thought through carefully. There *are* other trophy photographs and what you need is for Brady to say: that's of significance, that one.'[11] Mike Massheder agrees: 'I know for a fact that Joe Mounsey believed *all* the graves were marked this way. He felt very strongly that the relevant photographs were in our possession. Strangely enough, among the negatives was one which was cut in half. When we had it printed, it showed the scene at Hollin Brown Knoll, but the area where the grave was had been cut off. Just that one particular negative cut in half. After the grave was found, detectives went back up there and had a look around and said, yes, that's it, in that half of the negative. Why it had been chopped off I don't know.'[12]

At present, Ian Brady clearly isn't willing to divulge the whereabouts of Keith's grave; shorn of the 'power' of being able to stand on the moor and survey the cemetery of his making, retaining that knowledge is the last vestige of control he can exert. But is it possible that Myra deliberately withheld the whereabouts of Keith's grave? Her supporters are certain that she did all she could to assist Topping and his team, but we know now that she stuck to an impenetrable smokescreen: she told detectives that she hadn't known where any of the graves were located and made it clear that she didn't want the graves of Lesley or John pointed out to her during visits to the moor; she lied to Topping about the use of photographs as grave markers and used the promise of hypnosis as a bargaining tool, ultimately declining to submit to it.

Yvonne Roberts muses: 'I do wonder about Keith. I wonder if she actually did know where his body was buried but couldn't bear to let go of it. They were both committed to having pulled off the perfect murder. Perhaps she took the biggest secret with her to the grave quite deliberately.'[13] Fairley concurs: 'I don't trust Hindley. Much as I despise Brady, I would be more inclined to believe him than her. She has, on countless occasions, been proven to be a liar.'[14] Ian Brady told Topping that Myra knew the exact whereabouts of the undiscovered graves and – his own hypocrisy aside – in a letter to Ann West wrote that Myra 'had been deliberately misleading the police by "distancing" herself from the sites by not giving the *precise* locations, which she knows'.[15]

Myra wrote a curious letter to David Astor in February 1987; two lines imply that she was going to reveal more than she subsequently did: 'Everything will be resolved with satisfaction all round . . . things they have to know to clear this case up.'[16] But there are no letters to shed further light on the matter. Later that same year, when discussing Shiny Brook, Ian told Topping that Keith might well be buried in a completely different area of the moor. He referred obliquely to the original investigation, when 'the police had been close to the body of Pauline Reade and had not found it'.[17] During another conversation with Topping, Ian blurted out, 'Myra knows the location of [Keith's] grave on that slope.'[18] He went on to say that there was a railway sleeper on the side of the road where John Kilbride had been buried on the incline; he and Dave Smith had used the sleeper for target practice, but it was also 'a marker to other matters'.[19] Elsewhere, he mentioned murdering and burying a youth in 1964 (the year Keith was killed) not far from John Kilbride's grave. The victims at Hollin Brown Knoll were buried within a few hundred yards of each other; the two girls lay in the shadow of the black, molar-shaped rocks, while John Kilbride lay on the other side of the road, his grave partly hidden from the A635 by a peat bank.

Mike Massheder states, 'Hollin Brown Knoll is the burial ground. I believe that Keith Bennett is there. Kilbride, Downey and Reade were all buried together. Why would Brady bury that one child two miles away? He was methodical, remember. I'm not saying the police were *wrong* to search Shiny Brook – on the basis of the information Brady and Hindley gave them, they would have failed in their duty if they hadn't investigated it thoroughly. And I'm not necessarily saying they should stop looking there, but I know that if you spoke to anyone involved in the original search, they would say the same: look at Hollin Brown Knoll, where the other victims were. All right, they searched there before, but how diligently? Pauline wasn't found until 20 years later, yet I know they searched around there when Lesley was discovered. Everybody felt there were more victims in that area. For *years* afterwards, Joe Mounsey would disappear up to Hollin Brown Knoll. If he wanted a driver, he'd ring through and, if I was in, it was "Send Mash", because we'd worked together. We'd go up there and he'd stand and stare out across the moor, where John's grave had been, and potter about. It was always on his mind. He'd say, "There's *got* to be others around here, Mash." He wouldn't let it go. When I retired, a card went round and people wrote the usual daft comments. But he wrote on it: "A635, Joe Mounsey." That was the road past the graves.'[20]

Ian Fairley is in agreement: 'Brady knows where Keith's grave is, and if it was near John Kilbride's grave, somewhere on Hollin Brown Knoll, then I shouldn't be surprised. He knows where the others are too – because if you want my honest opinion, I'm certain there are other victims buried on the moor.'[21] Keith's mother, Winnie Johnson, concurs: 'I told Topping to stop looking in Shiny Brook. I've thought for a long time that Keith wasn't there. I still put flowers up there, but I think he's near the others. That makes sense, for him to be near John.'[22] Danny Kilbride holds the same view: 'They need to search in other places, not just Shiny Brook. Why don't they search where they found John? On that side of the road? I've written to Brady and he's written back, but he won't see me. I'd sleep in the same cell as him if he'd only admit he knows where Keith is buried. I want Brady to tell Winnie where Keith is. That's all I want. And if he doesn't, then he's a coward.'[23]

Chris Crowther, whose family own the land on which the other graves were found, recalls: 'I've seen Brady all over the moors here, but I told Topping: "You won't find Keith at Shiny Brook." I told him that more than once. We've always felt Keith is near John. Brady was a lazy beggar, wasn't he? He kept them close. Girls on one side of the road, boys on the other. John's grave was just under the lay-by there that we've created. Not far from the road at all. Those photos of Myra that were published recently, showing her with a map and a compass by a stream – that's not Shiny Brook. If you ask me, that's closer to here, not far from Rimmon Cottage. Birchen Clough, it might be – it looks like it. There used to be a road there down to Greenfield Brook.'[24]

In a letter to Lesley Ann Downey's stepfather, Ian described Keith's grave in a gully 'where a sheep pen is and a junction of two streams'.[25] On Hollin Brown Knoll, not far from John Kilbride's grave, the land slopes to the remains of dry-stone sheep pens, and two streams – Rimmon Pit Clough and Holme Clough – meet in a waterfall that drops down to Greenfield Brook. Nearby was the railway sleeper Ian and Dave had used for target practice but which Ian had said was also 'a marker for other matters'. Between John Kilbride's grave and Rimmon Pit Clough are the Standing Stones, a rock formation not unlike the one Myra described to her right as she sat on the plateau on the night of Keith's murder.

'There's a photograph of Myra standing on rocks at Hollin Brown Knoll, with the puppy in her coat, the same coat she was wearing on John Kilbride's grave,' Mike Massheder muses. 'In the distance is the hill – the Alderman. The day before they found John's grave, I was standing on that same side of the moor, but further down, towards the Alderman on a piece of spongy ground, and I got a whiff, you know, this distinctive whiff of putrefaction. It's a very distinctive smell – you can't mistake it for anything else. And I remember looking there – somebody was prodding around the Knoll – and I thought afterwards: that must have been a grave. It was in that area. They searched and found nothing, but they must have been just off the right spot. That odour didn't come from John's grave, it came from another.'[26]

Until he is found, there is no way of knowing if Keith Bennett lies in the Shiny Brook area, as Peter Topping thought, based on information given to him by the child's killers, or whether there are other victims, as those involved in the original investigation suspect. Topping's belief that 'W/H' referred to Wessenden Head may or may not be correct; it might just as easily refer to Woodhead, or to White Moss, which appears in large letters close to Hollin Brown Knoll on Ordnance

Survey maps from the mid 1960s.[27] However, among the photographs recovered by the police in 1965, there must be one indicating the grave of Keith Bennett, featuring some identifiable landmark – identifiable to his killers, at least. The detectives from the original investigation, as well as the farmer whose land was desecrated by the couple and the mother of their last-known victim, are all in agreement on one issue: while Shiny Brook undoubtedly had to be explored, the probability that Keith Bennett lies closer to the graves of those whose fate he shared is equally worthy of consideration.

Ian Brady and Myra Hindley were keen on codes, riddles and private jokes. There was a time when they planned their perfect murder, lying together on a picnic blanket behind the rocks on Hollin Brown Knoll. A time when they walked across the wind-harrowed hills where they buried their victims, scorning the 'maggots' down in the city. A time when they took photographs of each other in a slam of wind on the black boulders above the reservoir where the deserted mansion stood in the shadow of trees, as Motown music poured from the transistor radio. A time when they made a pact to share their secrets with no one else, when they were 'so close, we knew exactly what was in each other's minds. We were one mind.'[28]

In the weeks after their arrest, during the early days of her separation from Ian Brady, when she was hunting for literary allusions to the landscape they had left behind, Myra Hindley copied a poem by Charlotte Mew into an exercise book. Read with the knowledge that at least one of their victims remains in his secret grave, its meaning twists and darkens like the road through the stark hills of the green-lit moor:

Moorland Night

My face is against the grass – the moorland grass is wet –

My eyes are shut against the grass, against my lips there are the little blades,

Over my head the curlews call, And now there is the night wind in my hair;

My heart is against the grass and the sweet earth, – it has gone still, at last;

It does not want to beat any more,

And why should it beat?

This is the end of the journey.
The Thing is found.

This is the end of all the roads –
Over the grass there is the night-dew
And the wind that drives up from the sea along the moorland
    road,
I hear a curlew start out from the heath
And fly off calling through the dusk,
The wild, long, rippling call –:
The Thing is found and I am quiet with the earth;
Perhaps the earth will hold it or the wind, or that bird's cry,
But it is not for long in any life I know. This cannot stay,
Not now, not yet, not in a dying world, with me, for very
    long;
I leave it here:
And one day the wet grass may give it back –
One day the quiet earth may give it back –
The calling birds may give it back as they go by –
To someone walking on the moor who starves for love and
    will not know
Who gave it to all these to give away;
Or, if I come and ask for it again
Oh! then, to me.[29]

NOTES

Part I – Pariah: 20 November 2002

1

1. Myra Hindley, letter, 20 February 1997. From the David Astor archive, private collection.
2. National Archive, Myra Hindley Home Office files, HO 336/131.
3. Ibid.
4. Anon., 'Hindley Cremated in Private Funeral', BBC News online (21 November 2002).
5. Ryan Dilley, 'Few Witness Hindley's Final Journey', BBC News online (21 November 2002).
6. Anon., 'Jeers as Hindley Cremated', *London Evening Standard*, online edition (23 November 2002).
7. Bill Mouland, 'Myra Gets the Funeral Her Child Victims Were Denied', *Daily Mail*, online edition (21 November 2002).
8. Bridget Astor, author interview, London, 28 July 2009.
9. Neil Tweedie, 'Theme for Hindley's Funeral Was Repentance', *Daily Telegraph*, online edition (22 November 2002).
10. Father Michael Teader, author interview, Suffolk, 3 September 2009.
11. Anon., 'Date Set for Hindley Funeral', *Daily Mail*, online edition (19 November 2002).
12. Terri Judd, 'Controversy Over Final Resting Place for Hindley', *The Independent*, online edition (18 November 2002).
13. National Archive, Myra Hindley Home Office files, HO 336/114.
14. Some of the many epithets used to describe Myra Hindley over the years. 'A disgrace to womankind' is Hindley's own phrase, taken from a letter she wrote to Ann West in the 1990s.

15. Nicci Gerrard, 'The Face of Human Evil', *The Observer* (17 November 2002).
16. David Rowan and Duncan Campbell, 'Myra Hindley: My Life, My Guilt, My Weakness', *The Guardian* (18 December 1995).
17. Ian Brady was sentenced to three life sentences to run concurrently; Myra Hindley was sentenced to two life sentences and one sentence of seven years to run concurrently.
18. Brian Deer, 'First Degree Photocall Lifts Murderer's Image', *The Times*, online edition (29 October 1989).
19. Myra Hindley, autobiography. Reproduced with the kind permission of Andrew McCooey.
20. Duncan Staff, author interview, Bristol, 18 June 2009.

Part II – Gorton Girl: 23 July 1942 – 21 December 1960

2

1. Joe Chapman, *Out of the Frying Pan* (London: Chipmunka Publishing, 2009). Quotations from online edition (no page numbers): www.chipmunkapublishing.co.uk.
2. Myra Hindley and Nina Wilde, 'Older and Wiser', *Verdict* (January 1996).
3. Myra Hindley, autobiography. Reproduced with the kind permission of Andrew McCooey.
4. Chapman, *Out of the Frying Pan.*
5. Ibid.
6. Ibid.
7. Emlyn Williams, *Beyond Belief: The Moors Murderers – The Story of Ian Brady and Myra Hindley* (London: Pan, 1968), p. 113.
8. Chapman, *Out of the Frying Pan.*
9. David Rowan and Duncan Campbell, 'Myra Hindley: My Life, My Guilt, My Weakness', *The Guardian* (18 December 1995).
10. Chapman, *Out of the Frying Pan.*
11. Ibid.
12. Ibid.
13. Rowan and Campbell, 'Myra Hindley: My Life, My Guilt, My Weakness'.
14. Ibid.
15. Emlyn Williams Collection, Preliminary Notes, Ref: L3/4, National Library of Wales.

16. Myra Hindley, letter, 1988. From the David Astor archive, private collection.

17. Peter Topping, *Topping: The Autobiography of the Police Chief in the Moors Murders Case* (London: Angus and Robertson, 1989), pp. 134–5. Ian Brady strongly disputes Hindley's claim: 'It is fashionable nowadays to blame one's faults and crimes on abuse as a child. I had a happy childhood. But Myra Hindley's allegations obviously are framed to exploit a variation of the theme.' (Anon., 'Keep Hindley in Jail, Says Ex-Lover Brady', BBC News online, [27 August 1998].)

3

1. Myra Hindley, letter, 2 March 1999. From the David Astor archive, private collection.

2. Joe Chapman, *Out of the Frying Pan* (London: Chipmunka Publishing, 2009).

3. Duncan Staff, *The Lost Boy: The Definitive Story of the Moors Murders and the Search for the Final Victim* (London: Bantam Books, 2008), p. 67.

4. Chapman, *Out of the Frying Pan*.

5. Myra Hindley, autobiography. Reproduced with the kind permission of Andrew McCooey.

6. Staff, *The Lost Boy*, p. 71.

7. Chapman, *Out of the Frying Pan*.

8. Ibid.

9. David Rowan and Duncan Campbell, 'Myra Hindley: My Life, My Guilt, My Weakness', *The Guardian* (18 December 1995).

10. Chapman, *Out of the Frying Pan*.

11. Ibid.

12. Ibid.

13. Frances Hodgson Burnett, *The Secret Garden* (1911), online edition at the Free Library by Farlex (www.burnett.thefreelibrary.com).

14. Ibid.

15. Ibid.

16. Dominic Sandbrook, *Never Had It So Good: A History of Britain from Suez to the Beatles* (London: Abacus, 2006), p. 48.

17. Myra Hindley, autobiography. Reproduced with the kind permission of Andrew McCooey.

18. Chapman, *Out of the Frying Pan*.

19. Fred Harrison, *Brady and Hindley: The Genesis of the Moors Murders* (London: Grafton Books, 1987), pp. 47–8.

20. John Deane Potter, *The Monsters of the Moors: The Full Account of the Brady–Hindley Case* (New York: Ballantine Books, 1968), p. 243.

21. David Marchbanks, *The Moor Murders* (London: Leslie Frewin, 1966), p. 126.

22. Anne Murdoch, author interview, Manchester, 28 May 2009.

23. Jean Ritchie, *Myra Hindley: Inside the Mind of a Murderess* (London: Grafton Books, 1988), p. 5. With kind permission of Jean Ritchie, copyright 2010.

24. National Archive, Myra Hindley Home Office files, HO336/110.

25. Marchbanks, *The Moor Murders*, p. 122.

26. Allan Grafton, author interview, Manchester, 25 August 2009. Bob Hindley received financial compensation for his works accident, which enabled him to sponsor the football team.

27. Ibid.

28. In *The Lost Boy*, Staff mistakenly refers to Beasley Street and Bannock Street as if they were two separate places.

29. Chapman, *Out of the Frying Pan*.

30. Ibid.

31. Myra Hindley, autobiography. Reproduced with the kind permission of Andrew McCooey.

32. Mo Stratham, author interview, York, 26 March 2009.

33. *Gorton & Openshaw Reporter* (21 June 1957).

34. Ibid.

35. Ibid.

36. *Born to Kill?: Myra Hindley*, documentary (Stax Entertainment, 2006).

37. Harrison, *Brady and Hindley*, p. 47.

38. Chapman, *Out of the Frying Pan*.

39. Allan Grafton, author interview, Manchester, 25 August 2009.

40. Ibid.

41. Chapman, *Out of the Frying Pan*.

42. Ibid.

43. Ibid.

44. Ibid.

45. Rowan and Campbell, 'Myra Hindley: My Life, My Guilt, My Weakness'.

46. Chapman, *Out of the Frying Pan*.

4

1. *Gorton & Openshaw Reporter* (19 July 1957).
2. Dominic Sandbrook, *Never Had It So Good: A History of Britain from Suez to the Beatles* (London: Abacus, 2006) pp. 29–30.
3. Ibid. p. 460.
4. Ibid. p. 464.
5. Myra Hindley and Nina Wilde, 'Older and Wiser', *Verdict* (January 1996).
6. Joe Chapman, *Out of the Frying Pan* (London: Chipmunka Publishing, 2009).
7. Jean Ritchie, *Myra Hindley: Inside the Mind of a Murderess* (London: Grafton Books, 1988) p. 17.
8. Chapman, *Out of the Frying Pan*.
9. David Marchbanks, *The Moor Murders* (London: Leslie Frewin, 1966), p. 127.
10. Ritchie, *Myra Hindley*, p. 10.
11. Allan Grafton, author interview, Manchester, 25 August 2009.
12. Chapman, *Out of the Frying Pan*.
13. Marchbanks, *The Moor Murders*, p. 127.
14. Emlyn Williams Collection, Preliminary Notes, Ref: L3/4, National Library of Wales.
15. Ritchie, *Myra Hindley*, p. 12.
16. David Rowan and Duncan Campbell, 'Myra Hindley: My Life, My Guilt, My Weakness', *The Guardian* (18 December 1995).
17. Emlyn Williams Collection, Preliminary Notes, Ref: L3/4, National Library of Wales.
18. Allan Grafton, author interview, Manchester, 25 August 2009.
19. Chapman, *Out of the Frying Pan*.
20. Ibid.
21. Rowan and Campbell, 'Myra Hindley: My Life, My Guilt, My Weakness'.
22. Chapman, *Out of the Frying Pan*.
23. Ibid.
24. Rowan and Campbell, 'Myra Hindley: My Life, My Guilt, My Weakness'.
25. Chapman, *Out of the Frying Pan*.
26. Ibid.
27. Rowan and Campbell, 'Myra Hindley: My Life, My Guilt, My Weakness'.

Part III – This Cemetery of Your Making: 21 December 1960 – 6 October 1965

5

1.   David Rowan and Duncan Campbell, 'Myra Hindley: My Life, My Guilt, My Weakness', *The Guardian* (18 December 1995).
2.   Joe Chapman, *Out of the Frying Pan* (London: Chipmunka Publishing, 2009).
3.   Ibid.
4.   Jonathan Goodman, *The Moors Murders: The Trial of Myra Hindley and Ian Brady* (London: Magpie Books, 1994), p. 13.
5.   Chapman, *Out of the Frying Pan*.
6.   Earlier sources claim the engagement ended in 1960, but Hindley firmly dates the break-up as occurring during her first months at Millwards.
7.   Rowan and Campbell, 'Myra Hindley: My Life, My Guilt, My Weakness'.
8.   Chapman, *Out of the Frying Pan*.
9.   Ibid.
10. Duncan Staff, 'Portrait of a Serial Killer', *The Guardian* (18 November 2002).
11. Emlyn Williams Collection, Preliminary Notes, Ref: L3/4, National Library of Wales.
12. Rowan and Campbell, 'Myra Hindley: My Life, My Guilt, My Weakness'.
13. Emlyn Williams Collection, Preliminary Notes, Ref: L3/4, National Library of Wales.
14. Chapman, *Out of the Frying Pan*.
15. Ibid.
16. Ibid.
17. Emlyn Williams Collection, Preliminary Notes, Ref: L3/4, National Library of Wales.
18. Chapman, *Out of the Frying Pan*.
19. Rowan and Campbell, 'Myra Hindley: My Life, My Guilt, My Weakness'.
20. Ibid.
21. Dominic Sandbrook, *Never Had It So Good: A History of Britain from Suez to the Beatles* (London: Abacus, 2006), p. 572.

22. Rowan and Campbell, 'Myra Hindley: My Life, My Guilt, My Weakness'.

23. Ibid.

24. Janie Jones, *The Devil and Miss Jones: The Twisted Mind of Myra Hindley* (London: Smith Gryphon, 1988), pp.122–3.

25. Hindley told her prison therapist that it was months before she and Brady progressed sexually, but the account in her autobiography is one she frequently repeated elsewhere.

26. Chapman, *Out of the Frying Pan*. Although Myra does not give a precise date to which Christmas Eve, it must be 1961 since it was before the murders. By the end of 1962, she had renounced religion.

27. Myra Hindley, autobiography. Reproduced with the kind permission of Andrew McCooey.

28. Peter Topping, *Topping: The Autobiography of the Police Chief in the Moors Murders Case* (London: Angus and Robertson, 1989), p. 111.

29. Myra Hindley, autobiography. Reproduced with the kind permission of Andrew McCooey.

30. Emlyn Williams Collection, Preliminary Notes, Ref: L3/4, National Library of Wales.

31. Peter Gillman and Leni Gillman, 'I had a very happy childhood free of fear . . . I have no excuses – Ian Brady', *The Mail on Sunday* (15 May 2005).

32. Ibid.

33. Emlyn Williams Collection, Preliminary Notes, Ref: L3/4, National Library of Wales.

34. Chapman, *Out of the Frying Pan*.

35. Gillman and Gillman, 'I had a very happy childhood . . .'.

36. Rowan and Campbell, 'Myra Hindley: My Life, My Guilt, My Weakness'.

37. Chapman, *Out of the Frying Pan*.

38. Topping, *Topping*, p. 126.

6

1. Peter Gillman and Leni Gillman, 'I had a very happy childhood free of fear . . . I have no excuses – Ian Brady', *The Mail on Sunday* (15 May 2005).

2. Ibid.
3. Cal McCrystal, 'What Made the Gorbals Famous?', *The Independent* (31 January 1993).
4. Colin MacFarlane, *The Real Gorbals Story: True Tales from Glasgow's Meanest Streets* (Edinburgh: Mainstream Publishing, 2007), p. 15.
5. Emlyn Williams Collection, Preliminary Notes, Ref: L3/4, National Library of Wales.
6. In a probable publicity stunt, Italian solicitor Giovanni Di Stefano claims to have uncovered the truth about his client's father, whom he describes as 'a relatively well-known Scottish professional', but Brady has declared that he does not wish to know the man's identity.
7. Gillman and Gillman, 'I had a very happy childhood . . .'.
8. Jonathan Goodman, *The Moors Murders: The Trial of Myra Hindley and Ian Brady* (London: Magpie Books, 1994), p. 10.
9. Gillman and Gillman, 'I had a very happy childhood . . .'.
10. Fred Harrison, *Brady and Hindley: The Genesis of the Moors Murders* (London: Grafton Books, 1987), p. 22.
11. Gillman and Gillman, 'I had a very happy childhood . . .'.
12. Ian Brady, *The Gates of Janus: Serial Killing and its Analysis* (Los Angeles: Feral House, 2001), p. 198.
13. Peter Topping, *Topping: The Autobiography of the Police Chief in the Moors Murders Case* (London: Angus and Robertson, 1989), p. 245.
14. Brady, *The Gates of Janus*, p. 92.
15. Goodman, *The Moors Murders*, p. 11.
16. Robert Wilson, *Devil's Disciples: Moors Murders* (Dorset: Javelin Books, 1986), p. 22.
17. Brady, *The Gates of Janus*, p. 23.
18. Ibid.
19. Gillman and Gillman, 'I had a very happy childhood . . .'.
20. Ibid.
21. Goodman, *The Moors Murders*, p. 11.
22. Brady, *The Gates of Janus*, p. 8.
23. Ibid., p. 93.
24. Harrison, *Brady and Hindley*, p. 23. Brady's confessions to Fred Harrison should be treated with caution. Although he finally admitted to Harrison that he and Hindley had murdered Pauline Reade and Keith Bennett, he also provided Harrison with misleading information and falsely claimed accountability for several

other murders. Hindley, when questioned in the 1980s, told detectives Brady had never mentioned the 'Face of Death' to her.

25. Ibid. p. 24.

26. Ibid., p. 29.

27. Brady, *The Gates of Janus*, p. 8.

28. Emlyn Williams Collection, Preliminary Notes, Ref: L3/4, National Library of Wales.

29. Ibid.

30. David Marchbanks, *The Moor Murders* (London: Leslie Frewin, 1966), p. 117.

31. Ibid.

32. Harrison, *Brady and Hindley*, p. 26.

33. Christine Hart, *The Devil's Daughter* (Essex: New Author Publications, 1993), p. 225.

34. Bernard Mahoney, *Vice Magazine*, 'The A–Z of Law and Disorder' (July 2006). The Criminal Justice Act of 1982 abolished borstals and replaced them with youth custody centres.

35. Emlyn Williams, *Beyond Belief: The Moors Murderers – The Story of Ian Brady and Myra Hindley* (London: Pan, 1968), p. 93.

36. Journalists always refer to him as Philip Deare; Peter Topping, who investigated his death, insists his name was Gil Deares.

37. Brady, *The Gates of Janus*, p. 93.

38. Marchbanks, *The Moor Murders*, pp. 118–19.

39. Williams, *Beyond Belief*, p. 94.

40. Emlyn Williams Collection, Preliminary Notes, Ref: L3/4, National Library of Wales.

41. Ian Brady's landlady unwittingly rented out another of her properties in the street to a second murderer: Alfred Bailey, of 10 Westmoreland Street, was found guilty of strangling a six-year-old girl and was sentenced to life imprisonment in 1964.

42. Topping, *Topping*, p. 245.

43. Fyodor Dostoevsky, *Crime and Punishment* (1866), online edition at Google Books (www.books.google.co.uk).

44. Brady, *The Gates of Janus*, p. 39.

45. Harrison, *Brady and Hindley*, p. 26.

46. Marchbanks, *The Moor Murders*, pp. 133–4.

47. Dostoevsky, *Crime and Punishment*.

48. The term 'black light' is Brady's own, referring to the sexual impulse; see 'Colin Wilson at 70' by Geoff Ward, on Wilson's own website, www.colinwilsonworld.co.uk

7

1. Peter Topping, *Topping: The Autobiography of the Police Chief in the Moors Murders Case* (London: Angus and Robertson, 1989), p. 136.

2. Ian Brady disputes these nicknames, but family members and friends assert they were used. When she was imprisoned, Myra called a close friend by another *Goon*-inspired nickname: Eccles, played by Spike Milligan.

3. Ian Brady, *The Gates of Janus: Serial Killing and its Analysis* (Los Angeles: Feral House, 2001), p. 21.

4. Fred Harrison, *Brady and Hindley: The Genesis of the Moors Murders* (London: Grafton Books, 1987), p. 54.

5. Dominic Sandbrook, *Never Had It So Good: A History of Britain from Suez to the Beatles* (London: Abacus, 2006), p. 596.

6. Jean Ritchie, *Myra Hindley: Inside the Mind of a Murderess* (London: Grafton Books, 1988), pp. 34–5.

7. Harrison, *Brady and Hindley*, p. 57.

8. Myra Hindley, letter, 3 June 1998. From the David Astor archive, private collection.

9. Joe Chapman, *Out of the Frying Pan* (London: Chipmunka Publishing, 2009)

10. Ibid.

11. Ibid.

12. 'If you enjoy . . .', D.J. Enright, *Conspirators and Poets* (London: Chatto & Windus, 1966); 'If crime is . . .', Marquis de Sade, *Justine*, online edition at Globusz Publishing (www.globusz.com).

13. Chapman, *Out of the Frying Pan*.

14. Brady, *The Gates of Janus*, p. 214.

15. Chapman, *Out of the Frying Pan*.

16. Emlyn Williams Collection, Preliminary Notes, Ref: L3/4, National Library of Wales.

17. *The Guardian*, 'Myra Hindley in Her Own Words', 29 February 2000.

18. Helen Birch, *Moving Targets: Women, Murder and Representation* (London: Virago, 1993), p. 41.

19. Brady, *The Gates of Janus*, p. 43.

20. Duncan Staff, 'Myra Hindley in Her Own Words', *The Guardian* (29 February 2000).

21. Emlyn Williams Collection, Preliminary Notes, Ref: L3/4, National Library of Wales.

22. John Deane Potter, *The Monsters of the Moors: The Full Account of the Brady–Hindley Case* (New York: Ballantine Books, 1968), p. 250.

23. David Marchbanks, *The Moor Murders* (London: Leslie Frewin, 1966), p. 134.

24. *Born to Kill?: Myra Hindley*, documentary (Stax Entertainment, 2006).

25. Emlyn Williams Collection, Preliminary Notes, Ref: L3/4, National Library of Wales.

26. Staff, 'Myra Hindley in Her Own Words'.

27. Brady, *The Gates of Janus*, p. 43.

28. Chapman, *Out of the Frying Pan*.

29. Birch, *Moving Targets*, p. 42.

30. Chapman, *Out of the Frying Pan*.

31. Ibid.

32. David Rowan and Duncan Campbell, 'Myra Hindley: My Life, My Guilt, My Weakness', *The Guardian* (18 December 1995).

33. Ibid.

34. Chapman, *Out of the Frying Pan*.

35. Ibid.

36. Ibid.

37. Ibid.

38. Brady, *The Gates of Janus*, p. 23.

39. Chapman, *Out of the Frying Pan*.

40. Christine Hart, *The Devil's Daughter* (Essex: New Author Publications, 1993), p. 245.

41. Gil Deares was later the subject of a police investigation, when Brady claimed to have murdered him and Hindley was said to have told a fellow prisoner that she suspected Brady of his murder. In July 1962, Deares apparently drove to Manchester in a Jaguar coupe, which he passed on to another man for use as a getaway car, and visited Brady at the same time. In November, Deares left from home, telling his family he was going to meet a friend, and called on Brady, confiding that he was on the run: the man to whom he had passed on the Jaguar was arrested after failing to get rid of the vehicle and had given Deares's name to the police. He then disappeared. One Saturday Brady insisted on

driving to Deares's home, telling Hindley to knock on the door and pretend to be an ex-girlfriend keen to be in touch again; the family knew Brady and disapproved of his friendship with Gil. Hindley left them her name and address, and two weeks later received a letter from the Deares explaining that they still hadn't heard anything. Hindley steamed the letter open, despite knowing that Brady wanted to read it first. She handed it to him while they were out at a cinema in Oldham. When Brady realised she'd already opened it, he refused to speak to her for an entire week. As was their custom, he ended the silence between them with a gift as an apology. Hindley later claimed to a journalist that Brady and Deares had attempted a robbery, armed with knives, and that they fled the scene when the police arrived. Whatever the truth of that, Brady didn't murder Gil Deares, who drowned in a Sheffield reservoir in 1977.

42. National Archive, Assizes: Wales and Chester Circuit: Criminal Depositions and Case Papers, ASSI 84/427.

43. Ritchie, *Myra Hindley*, p. 38.

44. Loeb was murdered in prison by a fellow inmate. Leopold was released after serving 33 years. He found employment in a hospital and married a widowed florist; he died of a diabetes-related heart attack in 1971, after unsuccessfully trying to block the film version of *Compulsion*.

45. Brian Masters, *On Murder* (London: Coronet, 1994), p. 164.

46. Chapman, *Out of the Frying Pan*.

47. Ibid.

48. Ibid.

49. Steve Boggan, 'Brady Told Me that I Would be in a Grave', *The Independent* (15 August 1998).

50. Hart, *The Devil's Daughter*, p. 244.

51. Ibid.

52. Duncan Staff, *The Lost Boy: The Definitive Story of the Moors Murders and the Search for the Final Victim* (London: Bantam Books, 2008), p. 379.

53. Brady, *The Gates of Janus*, p. 102.

54. Chapman, *Out of the Frying Pan*.

55. W.H. Auden, *Collected Poems* (London: Faber and Faber, 2004).

8

1. Anon., 'Keep Hindley in Jail, Says Ex-Lover Brady', BBC News online (27 August 1998).
2. Steve Boggan, 'Brady Told Me that I Would be in a Grave', *The Independent* (15 August 1998).
3. Steve Boggan, 'Brady's Myra Time Bomb', *London Evening Standard* (7 November 2002).
4. Myra Hindley, letter, 3 June 1998. From the David Astor archive, private collection.
5. Ibid.
6. Boggan, 'Brady Told Me that I Would be in a Grave'.
7. Ibid.
8. Myra Hindley, letter, 3 June 1998. From the David Astor archive, private collection.
9. William Mars-Jones QC, 'The Moors Murders' address given to the Medico-Legal Society, 9 November 1967.
10. Myra Hindley, letter, 3 June 1998. From the David Astor archive, private collection.
11. Ibid.
12. Boggan, 'Brady Told Me that I Would be in a Grave'.
13. Myra Hindley, letter, 3 June 1998. From the David Astor archive, private collection.
14. Steve Boggan, 'Revealed: New Evidence that Might Free Myra Hindley', *The Independent* (15 August 1998).
15. Myra Hindley, letter, 3 June 1998. From the David Astor archive, private collection.
16. Ian Brady, *The Gates of Janus: Serial Killing and its Analysis* (Los Angeles: Feral House, 2001), pp. 21–2.
17. Fred Harrison, *Brady and Hindley: The Genesis of the Moors Murders* (London: Grafton Books, 1987), p. 60.
18. Duncan Staff, 'Myra Hindley in Her Own Words', *The Guardian* (29 February 2000).
19. Peter Topping, *Topping: The Autobiography of the Police Chief in the Moors Murders Case* (London: Angus and Robertson, 1989), p. 135.
20. Janie Jones, *The Devil and Miss Jones: The Twisted Mind of Myra Hindley* (London: Smith Gryphon, 1988), pp. 122–3.
21. Anon., 'Special Report – Myra Hindley: The Brady Letter', BBC News online (8 December 1997).

22. Harrison, *Brady and Hindley*, p. 153.

23. Joe Chapman, *Out of the Frying Pan* (London: Chipmunka Publishing, 2009).

24. Dominic Sandbrook, *Never Had It So Good: A History of Britain from Suez to the Beatles* (London: Abacus, 2006), p. 504.

25. Maureen Hindley, witness statement. The following (open) documents at the National Archives in Kew deal with Brady and Hindley's arrest, witness statements and trial transcripts: National Archive, Assizes: Wales and Chester Circuit: Criminal Depositions and Case Papers, ASSI ASSI 84/425 / ASSI 84/426 / ASSI 84/427 / ASSI 84/428 / ASSI 84/429 / ASSI 84/430 and also National Archive, Court of Criminal Appeal and Supreme Court of Judicature, Court of Appeal, Criminal Division: Case papers J82/668 and J82/669. Jonathan Goodman's *The Moors Murders: The Trial of Ian Brady and Myra Hindley* is a comprehensive account of the trial generally.

26. Harrison, *Brady and Hindley*, p. 45.

27. In his autobiography, Peter Topping states that Brady gave Hindley a copy of a record to commemorate Pauline's killing and that this was the theme music from a Sidney Lumet film, *The Hill*, starring Sean Connery as a soldier forced to participate in a brutal army exercise in the Libyan desert. Hindley told Topping that she and Brady had seen the film as part of a double bill with *The Day of the Triffids* in Oldham, but *The Hill* wasn't released until 1965; the film Hindley and Brady saw in Oldham two days after Pauline's murder was *The Legion's Last Patrol*, which was part of a nationwide double-bill release with *The Day of the Triffids*. See chapter 9 for further details.

28. Brady told Topping a different version of events. He said that the idea of flashing his lights was nonsense because there was no need to do so and it wasn't dark when they set off. The 'lost glove' theory is another peculiarity: although they claimed to have used the ploy effectively on other occasions, the fact remains that the only person who lost a glove that night was Pauline – before she was taken to the moor.

29. Staff, 'Myra Hindley in her own Words'.

30. Hindley's acquaintance Allan Grafton, who still lives in Gorton near Marie – now a married woman with children of her own – affirms: 'Marie was the one who got away. They would have

got her if she hadn't lived so close to Myra's mother. It happened a few streets from here. Whenever I see Marie, she always says to me, "I was the lucky one – I went home to my family that night."'

31. Duncan Staff, 'A Journey into Darkness', *The Guardian* (29 February 2000).
32. Chapman, *Out of the Frying Pan*.
33. Ibid.
34. Staff, 'Myra Hindley in her own Words'.
35. Brady told Topping that Hindley's version of events was all wrong; he claimed she parked in Cornwall Street and asked Pauline to help her carry some records to the van, but since he also asserts that it was more than an hour before he met them on the moor – a delay which Hindley would have found very difficult to explain to Pauline – Hindley's account seems the more likely.
36. Joan Reade forgot to mention the glove to the police in her agony over Pauline. She did look for the other glove eventually but never found it and only told the story to Fred Harrison in the mid 1980s. He explained in his book *Brady and Hindley: The Genesis of the Moors Murders* that the glove was lying about nine feet from the Reades' front door and to the left of the door – in the opposite direction of Pauline's walk away from the house. Harrison presents a reasonable theory that Pauline may have doubled back on her journey to the dance, visiting Maureen at her boyfriend Dave Smith's home in Wiles Street to see if she could persuade her to go with her to the club, but the theory falls apart in the light of Hindley's confession, which Brady largely echoes, and so the mystery of Pauline's glove remains.
37. Colin Wilson, Introduction in Brady, *The Gates of Janus*, p. 13.
38. Ian Brady, letter, 16 January 1990. From the David Astor archive, private collection.
39. Topping, *Topping*, p. 218. When Pauline's body was discovered 24 years later, the locket was missing. Hindley denied seeing the locket or having it in her possession, while Brady claims to have buried it the following day on a country road near Oldham.
40. Brady, *The Gates of Janus*, p. 254.
41. Hindley recalled moonlight when Brady led her onto the moor to look at Pauline's body, but the abduction occurred around

eight o'clock and it would have been light for at least a couple of hours after that.

42. Myra Hindley, autobiography. Reproduced with the kind permission of Andrew McCooey.

43. Staff, 'A Journey into Darkness'.

44. Apart from the issue of whether it was light or dark during Pauline's murder, there are other inconsistencies: Hindley and Brady's accounts differ, Pauline's lost glove remains a mystery and there are further discrepancies with the timescale. According to Fred Harrison's interviews with Joan and Paul Reade (both now deceased), when Paul arrived home from the cinema he turned off Taylor Street into Benster Street, where he saw Maureen Hindley having a row with her boyfriend Dave Smith. The two were standing in Charmers Street, at the top end of the entry behind Wiles Street. It was 9.30 p.m., yet Paul clearly recalled seeing Myra Hindley standing on the opposite corner, and as he turned into Wiles Street he glanced back to see Maureen crying and her sister walking over to break up the argument. Joan Reade also told Emlyn Williams, author of *Beyond Belief*, that she had seen Maureen Hindley in Wiles Street that night and that the girl was wearing a plaster cast after breaking her leg. Traumatic events can have a concertina effect on time, but the inconsistencies are perplexing.

45. David Rowan and Duncan Campbell, 'Myra Hindley: My Life, My Guilt, My Weakness', *The Guardian* (18 December 1995).

46. Topping, *Topping*, p. 86.

47. It isn't clear when they disposed of the spade. Hindley gave a verbal account of using the same spade for the first three murders, but, in writing, she stated that they bought another spade for the next murder.

48. Staff, 'Myra Hindley in her own Words'. In the account she gave to Duncan Staff, Hindley stated that she took a couple of Nembutals and put on clean underwear and a dressing gown before drifting off to sleep with Brady in front of the fire; they 'celebrated' with the Drambuie the following night.

49. Brady, *The Gates of Janus*, p. 44.

50. Chapman, *Out of the Frying Pan*.

9

1. David Rowan and Duncan Campbell, 'Myra Hindley: My Life, My Guilt, My Weakness', *The Guardian* (18 December 1995).
2. Joe Chapman, *Out of the Frying Pan* (London: Chipmunka Publishing, 2009).
3. Ian Brady, *The Gates of Janus: Serial Killing and its Analysis* (Los Angeles: Feral House, 2001), pp. 86–7.
4. Ibid., p. 53.
5. Chapman, *Out of the Frying Pan*.
6. Ibid.
7. Rowan and Campbell, 'Myra Hindley: My Life, My Guilt, My Weakness'.
8. Christine Hart, *The Devil's Daughter* (Essex: New Author Publications, 1993), p. 246.
9. *The Day of the Triffids/The Legion's Last Patrol* 1962 Press Sheet. Brady misremembers the film as *The Last Patrol*. It isn't clear whether he gave Hindley the record before or after Pauline's murder.
10. Allan Grafton, author interview, Manchester, 25 August 2009.
11. *Gorton & Openshaw Reporter* (19 July 1963).
12. Ibid.
13. Steve Boggan, 'Brady Told Me that I Would be in a Grave', *The Independent* (15 August 1998).
14. *Gorton & Openshaw Reporter* (2 August 1963).
15. Allan Grafton, author interview, Manchester, 25 August 2009.
16. *The Moors Murders*, documentary (Chameleon TV, 1999).
17. Duncan Staff, 'Hindley Tried to Join Police after First Killing', *The Guardian* (28 February 2000).
18. Ibid.
19. Ibid.
20. Emlyn Williams Collection, Preliminary Notes, Ref: L3/4, National Library of Wales.
21. Allan Grafton, author interview, Manchester, 25 August 2009.
22. David Marchbanks, *The Moor Murders* (London: Leslie Frewin, 1966), pp. 134–5.
23. Fred Harrison, *Brady and Hindley: The Genesis of the Moors Murders* (London: Grafton Books, 1987), p. 105.
24. Ibid., p. 106.

25. At their trial, Brady said the revolvers were bought in July 1964.
26. Boggan, 'Brady Told Me that I Would Be in a Grave'.
27. Myra Hindley, autobiography. Reproduced with the kind permission of Andrew McCooey.
28. Staff, 'Hindley Tried to Join Police after First Killing'. Norman Sutton left the police force when the news of his affair with Myra Hindley broke. He and his wife eventually divorced. Duncan Staff tracked him down to a nursing home in Blackpool where he had little to say about the relationship. In her prison cell, Hindley pinned *The Sun*'s front-page story about their affair to the wall above her bed. It was still there when she died.
29. Presumably Hindley either still had the use of the Ford Prefect van or had borrowed someone else's car; Brady's memory of the event is very clear.
30. Brady, *The Gates of Janus*, p. 53.
31. Harrison, *Brady and Hindley*, p. 104.
32. Emlyn Williams Collection, Preliminary Notes, Ref: L3/4, National Library of Wales. Mrs Kilbride was talking to Emlyn Williams. In *Beyond Belief*, he advanced the theory that Kennedy's assassination provided a psychological trigger for the murder of John Kilbride, but when Topping questioned Brady and Hindley separately about the matter, they both insisted that it was a coincidence. The abduction vehicle had already been hired for 23 November 1963.

10

1. Danny Kilbride, author interview, Manchester, 21 August 2009.
2. Ibid.
3. Robert Wilson, *Devil's Disciples: Moors Murders* (Dorset: Javelin Books, 1986), p. 28.
4. Danny Kilbride, author interview, Manchester, 21 August 2009.
5. Ibid.
6. Hindley told Peter Topping that she bought the wig after Pauline's murder, potentially contradicting her claim that she didn't realise other murders would follow.
7. Danny Kilbride, author interview, Manchester, 21 August 2009.
8. John Ryan, witness statement. See footnote 25, chapter 8.
9. Duncan Staff, *The Lost Boy: The Definitive Story of the Moors Murders and the Search for the Final Victim* (London: Bantam Books, 2008), p. 219.

10. Danny Kilbride, author interview, Manchester, 21 August 2009.
11. Ibid.
12. Hindley couldn't remember seeing Brady remove the spade from the boot when he and John walked onto the moor; if he had, then John would have realised that something was terribly wrong. But she insisted that Ian had buried John before returning to the car.
13. Wilson, *Devil's Disciples*, p. 29.
14. Peter Topping, *Topping: The Autobiography of the Police Chief in the Moors Murders Case* (London: Angus and Robertson, 1989), p. 180.
15. Ian Brady, *The Gates of Janus: Serial Killing and its Analysis* (Los Angeles: Feral House, 2001), p. 175.
16. Duncan Staff, 'Myra Hindley in Her Own Words', *The Guardian* (29 February 2000).
17. Ibid.
18. Mike Massheder, author interview, Preston, 1 July 2009.
19. Danny Kilbride, author interview, Manchester, 21 August 2009.
20. Peter Cantwell, witness statement. See footnote 25, chapter 8.
21. Brady, *The Gates of Janus*, p. 104.
22. Danny Kilbride, author interview, Manchester, 21 August 2009.
23. Ibid.
24. *Manchester Evening News* (29 November 1963).
25. *The Moors Murders*, documentary (Chameleon TV, 1999).
26. Staff, 'Myra Hindley In Her Own Words'.
27. Anon., 'Mass Hunt for a Boy', *The Reporter* (6 December 1963).
28. Emlyn Williams, *Beyond Belief: The Moors Murderers – The Story of Ian Brady and Myra Hindley* (London: Pan, 1968), p. 27.
29. Fred Harrison, *Brady and Hindley: The Genesis of the Moors Murders* (London: Grafton Books, 1987), p. 111.
30. Danny Kilbride, author interview, Manchester, 21 August 2009.
31. Ibid.
32. Staff, *The Lost Boy*, p. 224.

11

1. Dominic Sandbrook, *Never Had It So Good: A History of Britain from Suez to the Beatles* (London: Abacus, 2006), pxxv. Harold Macmillan resigned as Prime Minister in October 1963, citing ill health. His place was taken by the Conservative Alec Douglas-

Home until October 1964, when Labour's Harold Wilson came to power.

2. Ibid., pxxiii.

3. Ibid., p. 735.

4. Anon., 'We Had Finished Killing, Says Brady', *Manchester Evening News* (28 October 2005).

5. Emlyn Williams Collection, Preliminary Notes, Ref: L3/4, National Library of Wales.

6. Joe Chapman, *Out of the Frying Pan* (London: Chipmunka Publishing, 2009).

7. Peter Topping, *Topping: The Autobiography of the Police Chief in the Moors Murders Case* (London: Angus and Robertson, 1989), p. 94.

8. Jean Ritchie, *Myra Hindley: Inside the Mind of a Murderess* (London: Grafton Books, 1988), p. 54.

9. Peter Gould, 'Still Missing After Forty Years', BBC News online (16 June 2004).

10. Ritchie, *Myra Hindley*, p. 51.

11. Brady disputed Hindley's account to Topping: he insisted that she had picked Keith up on her own, then drove to Ardwick to meet him, coincidentally, at Bennett Street. Topping did not believe him.

12. Topping, *Topping*, p. 95.

13. Hindley told Topping that Brady definitely wasn't carrying a spade. She thought he must have hidden it earlier, alone, before they brought Keith Bennett to the moor.

14. Topping, *Topping*, p. 96.

15. Ibid.

16. Hindley insisted Brady buried the spade but doesn't explain how he managed to do so satisfactorily without the use of another implement; it would have needed to be buried deep to prevent its discovery. Shale, a sedimentary rock, isn't particularly easy to dig into by hand.

17. Ritchie, *Myra Hindley*, p. 52.

18. Anon., 'Tracker Dogs Join Hunt for Lost Boy', *Manchester Evening News* (19 June 1964).

19. Ibid.

20. Anon., 'Missing Boys and the Two Mothers Who Wait', *Manchester Evening News* (June 1964).

21. Ritchie, *Myra Hindley*, p. 53.

22. Ibid., pp. 53–4.
23. Ibid.
24. Anon., 'Longsight Boy Still Missing', *Gorton & Openshaw Reporter* (3 July 1964).
25. Ritchie, *Myra Hindley*, p. 54.
26. Fred Harrison, *Brady and Hindley: The Genesis of the Moors Murders* (London: Grafton Books, 1987), p. 116.
27. Anon., 'Galway Man Who Turned in the Moors Murderers', *Ireland on Sunday* (undated).
28. Harrison, *Brady and Hindley*, p. 115.
29. Anon., 'Smith Alleges He Saw Brady Kill Youth in House with Axe', *The Reporter* (10 December 1965).
30. Harrison, *Brady and Hindley*, p. 113.

12

1.   David Marchbanks, *The Moor Murders* (London: Leslie Frewin, 1966), p. 57.
2.   *Myra: The Making of a Monster*, documentary (Map-TV, 2003).
3.   Fred Harrison, *Brady and Hindley: The Genesis of the Moors Murders* (London: Grafton Books, 1987), p. 116.
4.   William Mars-Jones QC, 'The Moors Murders' address given to the Medico-Legal Society, 9 November 1967.
5.   Jean Ritchie, *Myra Hindley: Inside the Mind of a Murderess* (London: Grafton Books, 1988), p. 58.
6.   Harrison, *Brady and Hindley*, p. 117.
7.   Ibid.
8.   David Rowan and Duncan Campbell, 'Myra Hindley: My Life, My Guilt, My Weakness', *The Guardian* (18 December 1995).
9.   Emlyn Williams Collection, Preliminary Notes, Ref: L3/4, National Library of Wales.
10. Ritchie, *Myra Hindley*, p. 62.
11. John Deane Potter, *The Monsters of the Moors: The Full Account of the Brady–Hindley Case* (New York: Ballantine Books 1968), p. 266.
12. Emlyn Williams Collection, Preliminary Notes, Ref: L3/4, National Library of Wales.
13. Anon., 'Special Report – Moors Murderers Jailed for Life', BBC News online (6 May 1966).

14. Emlyn Williams Collection, Preliminary Notes, Ref: L3/4, National Library of Wales.

15. Ibid.

16. Patricia Ann Hodges, witness statement. See footnote 25, chapter 8.

17. Emlyn Williams Collection, Preliminary Notes, Ref: L3/4, National Library of Wales.

18. Anon., 'Special Report: Moors Murderers Jailed for Life'.

19. Patricia Ann Hodges, witness statement. See footnote 25, chapter 8.

20. Emlyn Williams Collection, Preliminary Notes, Ref: L3/4, National Library of Wales.

21. Ian Brady, *The Gates of Janus: Serial Killing and its Analysis* (Los Angeles: Feral House, 2001), p. 151.

22. Emlyn Williams Collection, Preliminary Notes, Ref: L3/4, National Library of Wales.

23. Ibid.

24. James Stansfield, 'Diary of a Supercop: The Mounsey Memoirs', *Evening Gazette* (2 August 1988).

25. Ibid.

26. Margaret Mounsey, author interview, Preston, 14 July 2009.

27. Mike Massheder, author interview, Preston, 1 July 2009.

28. Margaret Mounsey, author interview, Preston, 14 July 2009.

29. Danny Kilbride, author interview, Manchester, 21 August 2009.

30. Emlyn Williams Collection, Preliminary Notes, Ref: L3/4, National Library of Wales.

31. Potter, *The Monsters of the Moors*, p. 280.

32. Emlyn Williams Collection, Preliminary Notes, Ref: L3/4, National Library of Wales.

33. Ibid.

34. Ibid.

35. Ibid.

36. Ibid.

37. Patricia Ann Hodges, witness statement. See footnote 25, chapter 8.

38. Topping, *Topping*, p. 101.

13

1. Hindley clearly recalled 'Little Red Rooster' was playing as they watched Lesley by the dodgems.

2. Peter Topping, *Topping: The Autobiography of the Police Chief in the Moors Murders Case* (London: Angus and Robertson, 1989), p. 103.

3. The transcript is included in full here, both because it was the most damning piece of evidence against Hindley and because there has been so much speculation about its content.

4. Jonathan Goodman, *The Moors Murders: The Trial of Myra Hindley and Ian Brady* (London: Magpie Books, 1994), pp. 113–7.

5. The music was taken from the 1962 album by Ray Conniff and the Ray Conniff Singers, *We Wish You a Merry Christmas*. Brady made two recordings of the original tape. Three issues remain unclear: why Lesley Ann had given her surname incorrectly (although that can be explained by the little girl's terror); why she called her abusers 'mum' and 'dad' – whether that had been at their instigation; and the truth behind Brady's slip in the witness box, when he said that after the photographs were taken 'we all got dressed and went downstairs'. Under cross-examination, Brady refused to admit he had said it. But if it was a genuine slip of the tongue, it calls into question Hindley's version of events following the photographs being made.

6. Lesley is alone in the photographs. Topping asked Hindley if there were other photographs – featuring her or Brady or both of them with the little girl – but Hindley insisted there were none.

7. Joe Chapman, *Out of the Frying Pan* (London: Chipmunka Publishing, 2009).

8. Ibid.

9. Robert Verkaik, 'The Death of Myra Hindley: The Letters', *The Independent* (16 November 2002).

10. Ian Brady, *The Gates of Janus: Serial Killing and its Analysis* (Los Angeles: Feral House, 2001), p. 15.

11. Chapman, *Out of the Frying Pan*.

12. Goodman, *The Moors Murders*, p. 111.

13. Ibid., p. 111.

14. Chapman, *Out of the Frying Pan*.

15. Ibid.

16. Myra Hindley, letter, 3 June 1998. From the David Astor archive, private collection.
17. Hindley could not recall what happened to the bloodstained sheet, but Hattersley was a smokeless zone so it could not have been burnt at home. Nonetheless, it wasn't found with Lesley's body when she was discovered a year later.
18. Anon., 'Tracker Dogs Join Giant Search for Girl', *Manchester Evening News* (28 December 1964).
19. Anon., 'Lesley: 100 Police with Dogs in Big Hunt', *Manchester Evening News* (31 December 1964).
20. Anon., 'Have You Seen 10 Year Old Lesley? Big Search for Lost Girl', *Gorton & Openshaw Reporter* (1 January 1965).
21. Patty Hodges testified at the trial that Myra had taped their conversation, not Ian.
22. National Archive, Assizes: Wales and Chester Circuit: Criminal Depositions and Case Papers, ASSI 84/427.
23. Jean Ritchie, *Myra Hindley: Inside the Mind of a Murderess* (London: Grafton Books, 1988), p. 67.
24. Robert Wilson, *Devil's Disciples: Moors Murders* (Dorset: Javelin Books, 1986), p. 42.
25. David Marchbanks, *The Moor Murders* (London: Leslie Frewin, 1966), p. 24.
26. Ibid., p. 24.
27. Maureen Hindley, witness statement. See footnote 25, chapter 8.
28. Ibid. Hindley later refuted Maureen's accusation. She told Peter Topping that she and Maureen had discussed the matter years after the trial and that Maureen had told her she must have confused the facts. Topping was unable to verify her claim; Maureen had died five years before.

14

1. Peter Topping, *Topping: The Autobiography of the Police Chief in the Moors Murders Case* (London: Angus and Robertson, 1989), p. 137.
2. Anon., 'We Had Finished Killing, Says Brady', *Manchester Evening News* (28 October 2005).
3. Ibid.
4. Anon., 'Galway Man Who Turned in the Moors Murderers', *Ireland on Sunday* (undated).

5. Trial transcripts. See footnote 25, chapter 8.

6. William Mars-Jones QC, 'The Moors Murders' address given to the Medico-Legal Society, 9 November 1967.

7. Emlyn Williams Collection, Preliminary Notes, Ref: L3/4, National Library of Wales.

8. Fred Harrison, *Brady and Hindley: The Genesis of the Moors Murders* (London: Grafton Books, 1987), p. 121.

9. Emlyn Williams Collection, Preliminary Notes, Ref: L3/4, National Library of Wales. When Topping asked if she ever suspected Brady was homosexual, Hindley replied that she used to wonder what he did all night with Dave. Otherwise, she felt that when Brady wasn't with her he was probably with other women. But when Topping questioned Brady himself, Brady admitted with his head bowed that he was bisexual. It was probably men, not women, that he was interested in when he went out alone without her.

10. Emlyn Williams Collection, Preliminary Notes, Ref: L3/4, National Library of Wales.

11. Patricia Ann Hodges, witness statement. See footnote 25, chapter 8.

12. Ann West, *For the Love of Lesley: Moors Murders Remembered by a Victim's Mother* (London: W.H. Allen & Co., 1989), p. 59.

13. Jean Ritchie, *Myra Hindley: Inside the Mind of a Murderess* (London: Grafton Books, 1988), p. 71.

14. *Myra: The Making of a Monster*, documentary (Map-TV, 2003).

15. Emlyn Williams Collection, Preliminary Notes, Ref: L3/4, National Library of Wales.

16. Anon., 'Galway Man Who Turned in the Moors Murderers'.

17. Harrison, *Brady and Hindley*, p. 120.

18. The house was demolished in 1981.

19. Robert Bottomley, 'The Babysitter with Blue Hair', *Manchester Evening News* (18 November 2002).

20. John Deane Potter, *The Monsters of the Moors: The Full Account of the Brady–Hindley Case* (New York: Ballantine Books, 1968), p. 280.

21. Ibid.

22. Ritchie, *Myra Hindley*, p. 74.

23. Despite her insistence that she didn't speak to Hindley or Brady after February 1965, Patty very loosely resumed her friendship with them, as indicated by photographs taken later that year.

24. Emlyn Williams Collection, Preliminary Notes, Ref: L3/4, National Library of Wales.

25. Ibid.

26. Potter, *The Monsters of the Moors*, p. 277.

27. *The Reporter* (17 December 1965).

28. Ibid.

29. Topping, *Topping*, p. 212.

30. Harrison, *Brady and Hindley*, p. 125.

31. Ian Brady, *The Gates of Janus: Serial Killing and its Analysis* (Los Angeles: Feral House, 2001), p. 154.

32. Christine Hart, *The Devil's Daughter* (Essex: New Author Publications, 1993), p. 258.

33. David Smith, witness statement. See footnote 25, chapter 8. Maureen was never party to the discussions.

34. Ibid.

35. Ibid.

36. David Marchbanks, *The Moor Murders* (London: Leslie Frewin, 1966), p. 60.

37. David Smith, witness statement. See footnote 25, chapter 8.

38. Brady, *The Gates of Janus*, p. 16.

39. Harrison, *Brady and Hindley*, p. 126.

40. Ibid. Fred Harrison dates the conversation about Tony Latham as summer, yet places it after Brady first mentioned to David Smith that he had already killed – a conversation that, according to the court transcripts, didn't occur until September.

41. Brady, *The Gates of Janus*, p. 93.

42. Brady told Topping that he had killed an English hitch-hiker when he and Hindley were driving through the village of Arrochar, near Loch Long; he claims to have shot the man, but there is no trace of the murder.

15

1. David Smith, witness statement. See footnote 25, chapter 8.

2. Ibid.

3. Ibid.

4. Ibid.

5. Author interview with Anne Murdoch, Manchester, 28 May 2009.

6.   David Smith, witness statement. See footnote 25, chapter 8. In
        light of the known pattern of the murders, Brady's comment
        is puzzling; if there was no murder that summer, then he was
        'overdue', unless he meant that he had not killed that summer
        and only intended to murder again in November or December, as
        before.

7.   Ibid.

8.   Ibid.

9.   Robert Wilson, *Devil's Disciples: Moors Murders* (Dorset: Javelin
        Books, 1986), p. 52.

10.   David Smith, witness statement. See footnote 25, chapter 8.

11.   Dominic Sandbrook, *Never Had It So Good: A History of Britain
        from Suez to the Beatles* (London: Abacus, 2006), p. 600. The
        Sexual Offences Act of 1967 only partially decriminalised male
        homosexuality.

12.   Ibid., p. 601.

13.   Together with the disposal plan, the gift is further proof, if it were
        needed, that Edward's murder was premeditated. Hindley never
        admitted fully to this and the version of the murder recounted in
        Duncan Staff's *The Lost Boy* is drawn from her writings. Edward's
        killing had a dual purpose for Brady: it was a means of proving
        himself to Dave and a test of Dave himself, to discover just how
        deeply he had taken on board his 'tutoring'.

14.   *The Reporter* (17 December 1965).

15.   Ibid.

16.   Wilson, *Devil's Disciples*, p. 52.

17.   Letter from rent man, read to court. See footnote 25, chapter 8.

18.   David Smith, witness statement. See footnote 25, chapter 8.

19.   Jean Ritchie, *Myra Hindley: Inside the Mind of a Murderess*
        (London: Grafton Books, 1988), p. 76.

20.   Maureen Smith, witness statement. See footnote 25, chapter 8.

21.   Duncan Staff, *The Lost Boy: The Definitive Story of the Moors
        Murders and the Search for the Final Victim* (London: Bantam
        Books, 2008), p. 247.

22.   David Smith, police statement. See footnote 25, chapter 8. Smith's
        police statement is also quoted in Mars-Jones's address to the
        Medico-Legal Society.

23.   Anon., 'Galway Man Who Turned in the Moors Murderers',
        Ireland on Sunday (undated).

24. No one else admitted to hearing Edward's screams that night. Brady and Hindley's next-door neighbours, the Braithwaites, told the police they never heard anything other than 'domestic noises'.
25. David Smith, police statement. See footnote 25, chapter 8.
26. *Myra: The Making of a Monster*, documentary (Map-TV, 2003).
27. David Smith, police statement. See footnote 25, chapter 8.
28. Ibid. This can only refer to Lesley Ann Downey since, as far as is known, all the other victims, apart from Edward Evans, were killed on the moor.
29. Anon., 'Galway Man Who Turned in the Moors Murderers'.
30. David Smith, police statement. See footnote 25, chapter 8.
31. Anon., 'Galway Man Who Turned in the Moors Murderers'.
32. *Myra: The Making of a Monster*, documentary (Map-TV, 2003).
33. Ritchie, *Myra Hindley*, p. 81.
34. Anon., 'Galway Man Who Turned in the Moors Murderers'.
35. David Smith, police statement. See footnote 25, chapter 8.
36. Ibid., p. 32.
37. Emlyn Williams Collection, Preliminary Notes, Ref: L3/4, National Library of Wales.
38. Anon., 'Galway Man Who Turned in the Moors Murderers'.
39. William Mars-Jones QC, 'The Moors Murders' address given to the Medico-Legal Society, 9 November 1967.

Part IV – The Shadow of the Rope: 6 October 1965 – 6 May 1966

16

1. Ian Fairley, author interview, Norfolk, 20 July 2009.
2. Ibid.
3. Ibid.
4. Ibid.
5. Ibid.
6. Emlyn Williams Collection, Preliminary Notes, Ref: L3/4, National Library of Wales.
7. Ian Fairley, author interview, Norfolk, 20 July 2009.
8. Robert Talbot, witness statement. See footnote 25, chapter 8.
9. David Rowan and Duncan Campbell, 'Myra Hindley: My Life, My Guilt, My Weakness', *The Guardian* (18 December 1995).

10. Nicola Dowling, 'Myra and I Planned Suicide', *Manchester Evening News* (28 March 2006).

11. Ian Fairley, author interview, Norfolk, 20 July 2009.

12. Robert Talbot, witness statement. See footnote 25, chapter 8.

13. Ibid.

14. Ibid.

15. Ibid.

16. Jean Ritchie, *Myra Hindley: Inside The Mind of a Murderess* (London: Grafton Books, 1988), p. 84.

17. Ian Fairley, author interview, Norfolk, 20 July 2009.

18. Ibid.

19. Ritchie, *Myra Hindley*, p. 86.

20. Ian Fairley, author interview, Norfolk, 20 July 2009.

21. National Archive, Assizes: Wales and Chester Circuit: Criminal Depositions and Case Papers, ASSI 84/427.

22. Ritchie, *Myra Hindley*, p. 83.

23. Myra Hindley, police interview. See footnote 25, chapter 8.

24. Ibid.

25. Ibid.

26. Peter Topping, *Topping: The Autobiography of the Police Chief in the Moors Murders Case* (London: Angus and Robertson, 1989), p. 122.

27. Sandra Ratcliffe, 'Why Myra Must Never Be Freed', *Daily Record* (29 October 1997).

28. Emlyn Williams Collection, Preliminary Notes, Ref: L3/4, National Library of Wales.

29. Journalist Clive Entwistle recalls: 'Very soon after the arrest, I spoke to Tom Roden, who lived with his wife Kitty behind Brady and Hindley on Wardle Brook Walk. He told me that on the night that Evans was murdered, Myra's car was parked outside, on the road. Tom was taking his dog for a walk and he was nearby, just at the back of the pub, and he saw figures coming out of the house, carrying something. But then they saw him and went back in. Tom felt certain afterwards that he had seen them in the process of taking Evans to the car in order to bury him on the moors.' (Clive Entwistle, author interview, Leeds, 3 August 2009).

30. Ian Fairley, author interview, Norfolk, 20 July 2009.

31. Ibid.

32.   Ian Brady, police interview. See footnote 25, chapter 8.
33.   Janie Jones, *The Devil and Miss Jones: The Twisted Mind of Myra Hindley* (London: Smith Gryphon, 1988), p. 142.
34.   David Marchbanks, *The Moor Murders* (London: Leslie Frewin, 1966), p. 78.
35.   *Manchester Evening News* (7 October 1965).

17

1.   *Manchester Evening News* (8 October 1965). That same issue featured an article on eleven murders that had taken place in Manchester city centre within the last ten years. All were adults.
2.   Clive Entwistle, author interview, Leeds, 3 August 2009.
3.   Robert Wilson, *Devil's Disciples: Moors Murders* (Dorset: Javelin Books, 1986), p. 52.
4.   Ian Fairley, author interview, Norfolk, 20 July 2009.
5.   Ibid.
6.   Emlyn Williams Collection, Preliminary Notes, Ref: L3/4, National Library of Wales.
7.   By then, working hours at Millwards had altered. The staff worked longer hours through the week and had Saturdays off. Brady and Hindley had signed a petition for the change, which was put into place immediately after their arrest. It isn't clear how she got in, unless someone was already there to admit her.
8.   The contents are unknown. Topping suggested incriminating photographs, which Hindley denied, insisting that it was nothing to do with the murders but instead plans for robberies. The theory in *The Lost Boy* by Duncan Staff is that it was body disposal plans, but that's extremely unlikely since the police had the last disposal plan and Brady would have already destroyed the others ('destroy all lists'). Fairley disputes that Hindley had any opportunity to dispose of evidence.
9.   Emlyn Williams, *Beyond Belief: The Moors Murderers – The Story of Ian Brady and Myra Hindley* (London: Pan, 1968), p. 323.
10.   Ian Fairley recalls: 'I found the name of John Kilbride in the notebook. Dixie Dean had nothing else to do with the murder inquiry. He didn't find the name of John Kilbride in the notebook. This is what I've said; the names have been changed. Dean didn't look at that notebook in the house. It was among the exhibits as

they came into the inquiry room.' (Ian Fairley, author interview, Norfolk, 20 July 2009).

11. James Stansfield, 'Diary of a Supercop: The Mounsey Memoirs', *Evening Gazette* (2 August 1988).

12. Danny Kilbride, author interview, Manchester, 21 August 2009.

13. *The Moors Murders*, documentary (Chameleon TV, 1999).

14. Margaret Mounsey, author interview, Preston, 14 July 2009.

15. Ian Brady, police interview. See footnote 25, chapter 8.

16. Emlyn Williams Collection, Preliminary Notes, Ref: L3/4, National Library of Wales.

17. Myra Hindley, police interview. See footnote 25, chapter 8.

18. Myra Hindley, autobiography. Reproduced with the kind permission of Andrew McCooey.

19. Hindley was told to stand, not shoved into a chair as she claimed in a letter to journalist Duncan Staff.

20. Ian Brady, evidence given at trial. See footnote 25, chapter 8.

21. Ibid.

22. Ibid.

23. David Rowan and Duncan Campbell, 'Myra Hindley: My Life, My Guilt, My Weakness', *The Guardian* (18 December 1995).

24. A member of staff at Longsight Library noticed that Brady was late in returning his books; his fines amounted to 4s 3d. She sent him a reminder, but the postcard was sent back marked, 'Gone away.'

25. Hindley told Peter Topping that she thought Brady had kept the receipt in his wallet; it was only later that she admitted to knowing where it was hidden.

26. Williams, *Beyond Belief*, p. 323.

27. Clive Entwistle, author interview, Leeds, 3 August 2009.

28. Williams, *Beyond Belief*, p. 323.

29. Jean Ritchie, *Myra Hindley: Inside the Mind of a Murderess* (London: Grafton Books, 1988), p. 38.

30. In his notes for *Beyond Belief*, Emlyn Williams wrote: 'Terrific funerals for children but Evans hardly noticed.'

31. Myra Hindley, police interview. See footnote 25, chapter 8.

32. Williams, *Beyond Belief*, p. 352.

33. Emlyn Williams Collection, Myra Hindley, letter, 14 October 1965, ref: L3/6A, National Library of Wales.

34. After her daughter's disappearance, Ann asked to be re-housed by the council. Her new home was at Bowden Close, Hattersley

– a few streets from the house where her daughter had been murdered.

35. Danny Kilbride, author interview, Manchester, 21 August 2009.

36. The road is named after a pub on the moor that was destroyed by fire.

37. Ritchie, *Myra Hindley*, p. 92.

38. Carol and David Waterhouse were also questioned by the police but were unable to contribute anything to the investigation.

39. Ian Fairley, author interview, Norfolk, 20 July 2009.

40. Ibid.

41. Ibid.

18

1. Clive Entwistle, author interview, Leeds, 3 August 2009.

2. Ian Fairley, author interview, Norfolk, 20 July 2009. Fairley disputes how the discovery of the cases has been reported: 'Talbot wasn't there, and the photos weren't in a halibut-oil tin – not the ones we saw. They were in a bundle. What was written about how they were found is bollocks. I'm sure there *was* a roll of prints in a halibut-oil tin, but I know for a fact that's not how we found them, and apart from Clive Entwistle's father-in-law we were the first people to go through those suitcases.'

3. Ibid.

4. Ian Fairley, author interview, Norfolk, 20 July 2009.

5. Ibid.

6. *The Moors Murders*, documentary (Chameleon TV, 1999).

7. Sandra Ratcliffe, 'Why Myra Must Never Be Freed', *Daily Record* (29 October 1997).

8. Bob Spiers, author interview, Preston, 15 July 2009.

9. Dr David Gee, witness statement. See footnote 25, chapter 8.

10. Ibid.

11. Tom McVittie, telephone interview, 25 July 2009.

12. Clive Entwistle, author interview, Leeds, 3 August 2009.

13. Bob Spiers, author interview, Preston, 15 July 2009.

14. Dr David Gee, witness statement. See footnote 25, chapter 8.

15. Ann West, *For the Love of Lesley: Moors Murders Remembered by a Victim's Mother* (London: W.H. Allen & Co., 1989), pp. 74–6.

16.   Ian Brady, *The Gates of Janus: Serial Killing and its Analysis* (Los Angeles: Feral House, 2001), p. 278.

17.   Ian Brady, police interview. See footnote 25, chapter 8.

18.   Hindley later told Peter Topping that she didn't know Lesley had been found when the detectives played her the tape, but Lesley's clothes were shown to her on this same date.

19.   Clifford Haigh, witness statement. See footnote 25, chapter 8.

20.   Peter Topping, *Topping: The Autobiography of the Police Chief in the Moors Murders Case* (London: Angus and Robertson, 1989), p. 102.

21.   Ibid., p. 142.

22.   Janie Jones, *The Devil and Miss Jones: The Twisted Mind of Myra Hindley* (London: Smith Gryphon, 1988), p. 146.

19

1.   Anon., *Manchester Evening News* (19 October 1965). The press felt Brady and Hindley might be responsible for Susan's disappearance and the *Manchester Evening News* ran an article about her alongside their 'moor report': 'Heartbroken mother of a missing Manchester teenage girl, Mrs Margaret Ormrod, today told of attempts by her daughter to sell two girls' suits and of a visit to a house in Denton. For four months since her daughter Susan vanished from her home . . . Mrs Ormrod prayed for a clue to her whereabouts. Mrs Ormrod said the week before Susan vanished she was highly nervous and frightened of somebody. She brought the clothes home and asked me, did I know anyone who would buy them? When I asked whose they were, she would not say. But I was later told by a friend that she had told her, "If I don't sell these, he will murder me." Mrs Ormrod was also told of a visit to a house in Denton. "When I went to visit it, the woman next door told me the screams of girls who went in were shocking." Susan, who looks much older than her actual age, disappeared shortly after giving her notice at the hotel where she had worked since leaving Newall Green Secondary School.' Susan was 5 ft 6 in. tall, with gold-tinted hair. In his 1966–7 notes, Emlyn Williams refers to: 'Pauline Reade, 16, Keith Bennett, 12, Susan Ormrod, 16.'

Prosecutor William Mars-Jones also discussed Pauline, Keith and Susan as potential victims of Brady and Hindley, while in other notes Williams writes: 'Also police search for John Betteridge (8), Fallowfield. WHAT HAPPENED TO HIM?' (Emlyn Williams Collection, Preliminary Notes, Ref: L3/4, National Library of Wales).

2. James Stansfield, 'Diary of a Supercop: The Mounsey Memoirs', *Evening Gazette* (2 August 1988).

3. Mike Massheder, author interview, Preston, 1 July 2009.

4. Emlyn Williams Collection, Preliminary Notes, Ref: L3/4, National Library of Wales.

5. Anon., *Manchester Evening News* (20 October 1965).

6. Ibid.

7. Ibid.

8. Ibid.

9. Several books, including *The Lost Boy*, wrongly date the discovery of the left luggage receipt as occurring on Friday, 15 October.

10. Mike Massheder, author interview, Preston, 1 July 2009.

11. Ibid.

12. John Chaddock, witness statement. See footnote 25, chapter 8.

13. Mike Massheder, author interview, Preston, 1 July 2009.

14. Ibid.

15. Ibid.

16. Margaret Mounsey, author interview, Preston, 14 July 2009.

17. Danny Kilbride, author interview, Manchester, 21 August 2009.

18. *The Moors Murders*, documentary (Chameleon TV, 1999).

19. Ibid.

20. Anon., *Gorton & Openshaw Reporter* (29 October 1965).

21. A question mark hangs over whether or not Myra's old home on Bannock Street was searched. In *Beyond Belief*, Emlyn Williams claimed it had already been razed, but, according to Manchester City Corporation records, the odd-numbered houses in Bannock Street were not demolished until August 1972. Benfield told Fred Harrison that he believed the house had been searched, while Talbot, then retired in Cheshire, refused to be drawn on the subject. Among the Emlyn Williams archives is a letter dated 23 September 1968, from Canon Lewis of St James's Rectory in Gorton to Williams's publisher, stating that the house had not yet been pulled down as part of the slum clearances: '... we are

still waiting for that happy event to reach Gorton. The house
in question, and others around it, were cleared to make a site
for a new Church secondary school to replace St James', among
others.' (Emlyn Williams Collection, Preliminary Notes, Ref:
L3/4, National Library of Wales.)

22. Robert Wilson, *Devil's Disciples: Moors Murders* (Dorset: Javelin
 Books, 1986), p. 83.

23. Ibid.

24. Anon., *Gorton & Openshaw Reporter* (29 October 1965).

25. Wilson, *Devil's Disciples*, p. 87.

26. No charges were brought against either of the men. Patrick
 Downey bought himself a gun but was persuaded to give it up by
 his wife. He and his brother were told not to attend the main trial.

27. Wilson, *Devil's Disciples*, p. 87.

28. Unless otherwise stated, Brady and Hindley's interviews with the
 police are based on the accounts given in Goodman, *The Moors
 Murders*.

29. Margaret Mounsey recalls: 'When we lived in Ashton-under-
 Lyne, at the time of the search, I remember going with a couple
 of the other police wives into this shop where we all bought our
 make-up and the girl behind the counter said, "Hey, you know
 that woman who's up for murder? She comes in here to buy
 her make-up too." Myra definitely shopped in Ashton-under-
 Lyne, although she tried to convince the prosecution otherwise.'
 (Margaret Mounsey, author interview, Preston, 14 July 2009.)

30. Mike Massheder, author interview, Preston, 1 July 2009.

31. David Marchbanks, *The Moor Murders* (London: Leslie Frewin,
 1966), p. 84.

32. Mike Massheder, author interview, Preston, 1 July 2009.

33. Contrary to common belief, Brady could drive a car and admitted
 that to detectives Haigh and Talbot on 18 October. He said he
 only drove on private land.

34. *The Moors Murders*, documentary (Chameleon TV, 1999).

35. Tom McVittie, telephone interview, 25 July 2009.

36. Myra Hindley, police interview. See footnote 25, chapter 8.

37. Ian Brady, police interview. See footnote 25, chapter 8.

38. Myra Hindley, letter, 27 July 1998. From the David Astor archive,
 private collection.

39. Emlyn Williams Collection, Preliminary Notes, Ref: L3/4, National Library of Wales.

40. Danny Kilbride, author interview, Manchester, 21 August 2009.

41. Marchbanks, *The Moor Murders*, p. 110.

42. Ibid.

20

1. Author interview with Anne Murdoch, Manchester, 28 May 2009.

2. Allan Grafton, author interview, Manchester, 25 August 2009.

3. Myra Hindley, letter, 5 November 1965. Reproduced with the kind permission of Andrew McCooey.

4. Ibid.

5. Ian Fairley, author interview, Norfolk, 20 July 2009.

6. Margaret Mounsey, author interview, Preston, 14 July 2009. Apart from Keith Bennett and Pauline Reade, Brady asserts that he was questioned about Veronica Bondi (1963), Ben Marsden (1959) and William Cullen, who was killed in 1965. Cullen's murder was solved in 1984, although Brady falsely claimed responsibility for it. In a post-arrest letter, Brady referred to his 'dear friend in Bradford' – probably alluding to Gil Deares, whose disappearance he and Hindley were also questioned about. There is a curious note among Emlyn Williams's papers from his interviews: 'Benfield: "These families obviously well-known to Ian Brady?????"' (Emlyn Williams Collection, Preliminary Notes, Ref: L3/4, National Library of Wales.) The child victims are thought to have been chosen at random, but a peculiarity of the case is that the first known victim, teenager Pauline Reade, was indeed familiar to Hindley, while Brady claimed to have known the last victim, teenager Edward Evans.

7. At that time, the full prosecution case had to be presented before magistrates in order to decide whether to send a case to trial. The press were permitted to report proceedings unless instructed otherwise. Philip Curtis, representing Hindley, and David Lloyd-Jones, representing Brady, asked for the evidence to be heard in camera but only the prosecution's opening submission was kept from the press and public.

8. Robert Wilson, *Devil's Disciples: Moors Murders* (Dorset: Javelin Books, 1986), p. 114.

9. David Rowan and Duncan Campbell, 'Myra Hindley: My Life, My Guilt, My Weakness', *The Guardian* (18 December 1995).

10. Myra Hindley, letter, December 1965. Reproduced with the kind permission of Andrew McCooey.

11. Ibid.

12. Anon., *The Reporter* (17 December 1965).

13. Myra Hindley, letter, December 1965. Reproduced with the kind permission of Andrew McCooey.

14. National Archive, Myra Hindley Home Office files, HO336/148.

15. Jean Ritchie, *Myra Hindley: Inside the Mind of a Murderess* (London: Grafton Books, 1988), p. 103.

16. Wilson, *Devil's Disciples*, p. 117.

17. Duncan Staff, *The Lost Boy: The Definitive Story of the Moors Murders and the Search for the Final Victim* (London: Bantam Books, 2008), p. 285.

18. Bob Spiers, author interview, Preston, 15 July 2009.

19. Myra Hindley, December 1965, letter. Reproduced with the kind permission of Andrew McCooey.

20. Steve Boggan, 'Brady's Myra Time Bomb', *London Evening Standard* (7 November 2002).

21. Ibid.

22. Ibid.

23. Myra Hindley, letter, 27 July 1998. From the David Astor archive, private collection.

24. *The Moors Murders Code*, documentary (Duncan Staff for BBCTV, 2004).

25. William Wordsworth, 'Tintern Abbey' in *The Collected Poems* (London: Wordsworth Editions, 1994).

26. William Shakespeare, *King Lear* in *The Complete Works* (Oxford: OUP, 2005).

27. William Shakespeare, *Richard III* in *The Complete Works* (Oxford: OUP, 2005).

28. Myra Hindley, letter, December 1965. Reproduced with the kind permission of Andrew McCooey.

29. William Mars-Jones QC, 'The Moors Murders' address given to the Medico-Legal Society, 9 November 1967.

30. Myra Hindley, letter, 1966. Reproduced with the kind permission of Andrew McCooey.

31. Staff, *The Lost Boy*, p. 290.

32. Ritchie, *Myra Hindley*, p. 159.
33. Jonathan Goodman, *The Moors Murders: The Trial of Myra Hindley and Ian Brady* (London: Magpie Books, 1994), p. 94.
34. Myra Hindley, letter, April 1966. Reproduced with the kind permission of Andrew McCooey.

21

1. Pamela Hansford Johnson, *On Iniquity: Some Personal Reflections Arising Out of the Moors Murder Trial* (London: Macmillan, 1967) p. 18.
2. Ibid.
3. Dominic Sandbrook, *Never Had It So Good: A History of Britain from Suez to the Beatles* (London: Abacus, 2006), p. 183.
4. Ibid., p. 453.
5. Ibid.
6. Trial transcripts. See footnote 25, chapter 8.
7. Hansford Johnson, *On Iniquity*, p. 21.
8. In *The Lost Boy*, Duncan Staff erroneously credits Fenton Atkinson ('Fenton-Atkinson') as having overseen the Nuremberg Trials.
9. Fred Harrison, *Brady and Hindley: The Genesis of the Moors Murders* (London: Grafton Books, 1987), p. 150.
10. Ibid.
11. Hansford Johnson, *On Iniquity*, p. 23.
12. Ibid., p. 22.
13. Clive Entwistle, author interview, Leeds, 3 August 2009.
14. Jean Ritchie, *Myra Hindley: Inside the Mind of a Murderess* (London: Grafton Books, 1988), p. 55.
15. Danny Kilbride, author interview, Manchester, 21 August 2009.
16. Brady later tried to seek revenge on both David Smith and Myra Hindley by claiming he had fathered the baby Maureen was carrying at the trial; the story was reported in the *Sunday Mirror*, but in reality there was never any doubt about the child's parentage.
17. Trial transcripts. See footnote 25, chapter 8.
18. Ritchie, *Myra Hindley*, p. 111.
19. Margaret Campion suffered a breakdown after the conclusion of the Moors investigation and eventually left the police force.

20. Emlyn Hoosen QC, MP, opening speech. See footnote 25, chapter 8.
21. Ian Brady, evidence given at trial. See footnote 25, chapter 8.
22. Ibid.
23. Trial transcripts. See footnote 25, chapter 8.
24. Mr Justice Fenton Atkinson, summing up. See footnote 25, chapter 8.
25. The Right Hon. Sir Frederick Elwyn Jones QC, MP, trial transcripts. See footnote 25, chapter 8.
26. Ibid.
27. Ian Brady, evidence given at trial. See footnote 25, chapter 8.
28. The Right Hon. Sir Frederick Elwyn Jones QC, MP, trial transcripts. See footnote 25, chapter 8.
29. Ian Brady, evidence given at trial. See footnote 25, chapter 8.
30. Ibid.
31. Ibid.
32. Myra Hindley, letter, April 1966. Reproduced with the kind permission of Andrew McCooey.
33. Peter Topping, *Topping: The Autobiography of the Police Chief in the Moors Murders Case* (London: Angus and Robertson, 1989), p. 143.
34. Ritchie, *Myra Hindley*, p. 113.
35. Myra Hindley, evidence given at trial. See footnote 25, chapter 8.
36. Ibid.
37. Ibid.
38. Ibid.
39. Ibid.
40. The Right Hon. Sir Frederick Elwyn Jones QC, MP, trial transcripts. See footnote 25, chapter 8.
41. Ibid.
42. Myra Hindley, evidence given at trial. See footnote 25, chapter 8.
43. The Right Hon. Sir Frederick Elwyn Jones QC, MP, trial transcripts. See footnote 25, chapter 8.
44. Myra Hindley, evidence given at trial. See footnote 25, chapter 8.
45. The Right Hon. Sir Frederick Elwyn Jones QC, MP, trial transcripts. See footnote 25, chapter 8.
46. *Panorama: Myra Hindley*, documentary (BBC, 24 November 1997).
47. Topping, *Topping*, p. 142.

48. Myra Hindley, evidence given at trial. See footnote 25, chapter 8.
49. The Right Hon. Sir Frederick Elwyn Jones QC, MP, trial transcripts. See footnote 25, chapter 8.
50. Myra Hindley, evidence given at trial. See footnote 25, chapter 8.
51. G. Heilpern QC, trial transcripts. See footnote 25, chapter 8.
52. The Right Hon. Sir Frederick Elwyn Jones QC, MP, trial transcripts. See footnote 25, chapter 8.
53. Ibid.
54. Ibid.
55. Mr Justice Fenton Atkinson, summing up. See footnote 25, chapter 8.
56. Myra Hindley, letter, May 1966. Reproduced with the kind permission of Andrew McCooey.
57. Mr Justice Fenton Atkinson, summing up. See footnote 25, chapter 8.
58. Ibid.
59. Trial transcripts. See footnote 25, chapter 8.
60. Ibid.
61. Ibid.
62. Ian Brady, statement to court. See footnote 25, chapter 8.
63. Trial transcripts. See footnote 25, chapter 8.
64. Mr Justice Fenton Atkinson, summing up. See footnote 25, chapter 8.
65. Janie Jones, *The Devil and Miss Jones: The Twisted Mind of Myra Hindley* (London: Smith Gryphon, 1988), p.148.
66. Mr Justice Fenton Atkinson, sentencing. See footnote 25, chapter 8. When Brady and Hindley left the dock, the judge praised the detective work done on the case in general; he singled out Tyrrell alone for special mention. Although Tyrrell had found the left luggage receipt, without doubt the most crucial work was carried out by Jock Carr, Joe Mounsey, Mike Massheder and Dennis Barrow. None of the men were ever given public recognition for their achievements in the case.
67. Judge Gerald Sparrow, *Satan's Children* (London: Odhams Books, 1966), p. 102.
68. Anon., *The Gorton & Openshaw Reporter* (13 May 1966).
69. Hansford Johnson, *On Iniquity*, p. 89.
70. Ritchie, *Myra Hindley*, p. 107.
71. Francis Wyndham, *The Sunday Times* (8 May 1966).

72. David Rowan and Duncan Campbell, 'Myra Hindley: My Life, My Guilt, My Weakness', *The Guardian* (18 December 1995).

PART V – God Has Forgiven Me: 7 May 1966 – 15 November 2002

22

1. Jean Ritchie, *Myra Hindley: Inside the Mind of a Murderess* (London: Grafton Books, 1988), p. 131.
2. Ibid., p. 132.
3. Marshall Palmer, report, 21 September 1966. National Archive, Myra Hindley, J82/669.
4. Ritchie, *Myra Hindley*, p. 134.
5. Ibid., p. 133.
6. Joe Chapman, *Out of the Frying Pan* (London: Chipmunka Publishing, 2009).
7. David Rowan and Duncan Campbell, 'Myra Hindley: My Life, My Guilt, My Weakness', *The Guardian* (18 December 1995).
8. Ann West, *For the Love of Lesley: Moors Murders Remembered by a Victim's Mother* (London: W.H. Allen & Co., 1989), p. 115.
9. William Mars-Jones QC, 'The Moors Murders' address given to the Medico-Legal Society, 9 November 1967.
10. Lady Tree is the founder of Fine Cell Work, a charity that employs prisoners to make skilled needlework and tapestry, which is sold through 'premium' outlets such as the shop at Highgrove or via commissions. There are currently 350 prisoners involved in the scheme.
11. Lady Anne Tree, Peter Stanford interview for the *Independent on Sunday Review*.
12. Ibid.
13. Ibid.
14. Ibid.
15. Joe Chapman, author interview, Oxford, 18 July 2009.
16. Myra Hindley, letter, 1967. Reproduced with the kind permission of Andrew McCooey.
17. Nellie had been using the name Hettie Moulton for some time, but to avoid confusion she is referred to throughout this book as Nellie.
18. The 1968 Theatres Act abolished censorship.

19. Ann West was left cold by Williams' method of interviewing, as was Danny Kilbride, who refused to allow his name to be included in the book. Williams wanted to include two chapters about Keith Bennett and Pauline Reade but was dissuaded by his publisher's lawyers.

20. Myra Hindley, letter, 15 June 1968. Hull University; Brynmore Library.

21. Ibid. On 24 June 1967, Benfield wrote to Emlyn Williams, heading his letter 'Extremely Confidential', to ask him about his sources. His main concerns were the pornographic photos of Brady and Hindley, and her diary. Williams replied that Maureen had given him a copy of the diary, but on his own typewritten copy of the diary he'd scribbled, 'Found in wardrobe, 16.' He claimed to have been given the pornographic photos by 'Bill', whose real name he'd forgotten and whose address he'd lost. However, in a very jolly letter written to Williams' wife in 1969, William Mars-Jones's wife stated that her husband and Emlyn were great pals and the four of them should have lunch. She signed her letter, 'Yours sincerely, Sheila Mars-Jones ("Mrs Bill")'. (Emlyn Williams Collection, Preliminary Notes, Ref: L3/4, National Library of Wales.)

22. Myra Hindley, letter, 15 June 1968. Hull University; Brynmore Library.

23. Lady Anne Tree, Peter Stanford interview for the *Independent on Sunday Review*.

24. Tania Branigan, 'High Profile Allies Led Call for Release', *The Guardian* (16 November 2002).

25. Robert Wilson, *Devil's Disciples: Moors Murders* (Dorset: Javelin Books, 1986), p. 161.

26. Myra Hindley, letter, 1967. Reproduced with the kind permission of Andrew McCooey.

27. *Myra Hindley: The Prison Years*, documentary (Granada Anglia, 2006).

28. Internal memo, 13 January 1969. National Archive, Myra Hindley Home Office files, HO336/86.

29. Internal memo, 14 January 1969. National Archive, Myra Hindley Home Office files, HO336/86.

30. Fred Harrison, *Brady and Hindley: The Genesis of the Moors Murders* (London: Grafton Books, 1987), p. 156.

31. Ritchie, *Myra Hindley*, p. 233.
32. Myra Hindley, letter, 1966. Reproduced with the kind permission of Andrew McCooey.
33. Harrison, *Brady and Hindley*, p. 156.
34. Wilson, *Devil's Disciples*, p. 161.
35. Ritchie, *Myra Hindley*, p. 168.
36. Ibid., p. 155.
37. Myra Hindley, letter, 1969. Reproduced with the kind permission of Andrew McCooey.

23

1. Myra Hindley, letter, 1970. Reproduced with the kind permission of Andrew McCooey.
2. Robert Wilson, *Devil's Disciples: Moors Murders* (Dorset: Javelin Books, 1986), p. 162.
3. Fred Harrison, *Brady and Hindley: The Genesis of the Moors Murders* (London: Grafton Books, 1987), p. 154.
4. Wilson, *Devil's Disciples*, p. 163.
5. Jean Ritchie, *Myra Hindley: Inside the Mind of a Murderess* (London: Grafton Books, 1988), p. 152.
6. Wilson, *Devil's Disciples*, p. 163. Note: Ritchie has Myra writing this after an outing to Hampstead Heath with Dorothy Wing.
7. Ritchie, *Myra Hindley*, p. 158.
8. Ibid., p. 234.
9. According to Robert Wilson's book *Devil's Disciples*, Tricia exchanged letters with Myra at Nellie's address using the name Glynis Moors.
10. Ian's foster mother died of heart failure in 1970, and his foster brother, Robert Sloan, died from the same complaint in middle age. His foster sister, May, contracted tuberculosis and her sister, Jean, took an overdose in 1988. Journalists tracked down his foster brother, John, in 2005, but he refused to speak to them.
11. Peter Topping, *Topping: The Autobiography of the Police Chief in the Moors Murders Case* (London: Angus and Robertson, 1989), p. 131.
12. Wilson, *Devil's Disciples*, p. 164.
13. Ibid.
14. Duncan Staff, 'Dangerous Liaison', *The Guardian* (14 October 2006).

15. Ann West, *For the Love of Lesley: Moors Murders Remembered by a Victim's Mother* (London: W.H. Allen & Co., 1989), p. 104.

16. Ritchie, *Myra Hindley*, p. 165.

17. It was usual, but not regulatory, for the governor to obtain Home Office permission first.

18. Myra Hindley, letter, 1972. Reproduced with the kind permission of Andrew McCooey.

19. Ritchie, *Myra Hindley*, p. 166. A life sentence was then reckoned as twenty-one years, with any long-term prisoner entitled to apply for parole after serving a third of their sentence; that left Myra within six months of being legally eligible to apply.

20. Ibid., pp.166–7.

21. Norman Luck, 'Hearts and Flowers' (22 February 2008). Gentlemen Ranters website: www.gentlemenranters.com.

22. Ritchie, *Myra Hindley*, p. 175.

23. Following the trial, the Home Office reviewed the information given by Pat Ali and awarded her £1,500 as compensation for her lost remission.

24. Danny Kilbride, author interview, Manchester, 21 August 2009.

25. Wilson, *Devil's Disciples*, p. 168.

26. Myra Hindley, letter, 1974. Reproduced with the kind permission of Andrew McCooey.

27. Ritchie, *Myra Hindley*, p. 187.

28. Wilson, *Devil's Disciples*, p. 168.

29. Janie Jones, *The Devil and Miss Jones: The Twisted Mind of Myra Hindley* (London: Smith Gryphon, 1988), pp. 158–9.

30. Wilson, *Devil's Disciples*, p. 169.

31. Internal memos, November 1975. National Archive, Myra Hindley Home Office files, NA, 336/26.

32. Sara Trevelyan, author interview, Edinburgh, 24 June 2009.

33. On 8 November 1972, *The Times* reported David Smith's acquittal at Manchester Crown Court for the murder of his father, who was in the last stages of cancer when Dave gave him a drink mixed with 20 sodium amytal tablets. He received a nominal two-day sentence.

34. Ritchie, *Myra Hindley*, p. 235.

35. Ibid., p. 238.

36. Ibid.

37. Ibid., p. 243.

38. Internal memo, 26 March 1976. National Archive, Myra Hindley Home Office files, HO336/141.

39. Jones, *The Devil and Miss Jones*, p. 164.

40. Ibid., pp. 114–5.

41. Internal memo, 26 September 1976. National Archive, Myra Hindley Home Office files, HO336/141.

42. Pat Carlen, *Criminal Women* (Cambridge: Polity Press, 1985), pp. 157–8.

43. Internal memo, 28 September 1976. National Archive, Myra Hindley Home Office files, HO336/141.

44. Ritchie, *Myra Hindley*, p. 190.

45. Carlen, *Criminal Women*, pp. 157–8.

46. Myra Hindley, letter, 6 October 1976. National Archive, Myra Hindley Home Office files, HO336/141.

47. 'Find that . . .' Ritchie, *Myra Hindley*, p. 191; 'both laughed . . .' internal memo, 28 February 1977. National Archive, Myra Hindley Home Office files, HO336/141. After her release from jail, Josie worked for the charity Women in Prison, but ended up inside again. She died in Bulwood prison in October 1997, found slumped in a pool of blood in the prison's healthcare unit. She had a severed artery in her wrist and a lethal level of sedatives in her blood. Two inquests failed to reach a conclusive verdict about her death.

48. Peter Stanford, *The Outcasts' Outcast: A Biography of Lord Longford* (Gloucester: Sutton Publishing Ltd, 2006), p. 348.

49. Ibid., pp. 348–9.

50. Anne Maguire, author interview, London, 29 July 2009.

51. Ibid.

52. Internal memo, 28 February 1977. National Archive, Myra Hindley Home Office files, HO336/141.

53. Sara Trevelyan, author interview, Edinburgh, 24 June 2009.

54. Anne Maguire, author interview, London, 29 July 2009.

55. There had already been one play about the Moors case; in 1970, a theatre in Germany staged *Pre-Paradise Sorry Now*, which has recently been revived.

56. Myra Hindley, letter, 16 May 1977. National Archive, Myra Hindley Home Office files, HO336/148. The correspondent's name has been blacked out by the censor.

57. Wilson, *Devil's Disciples*, p. 172.

58. Ibid.
59. Jones, *The Devil and Miss Jones*, p. 218.
60. Myra Hindley, letter, 1 August 1977. National Archive, Myra Hindley Home Office files, HO336/110.
61. Wilson, *Devil's Disciples*, p. 173.
62. Ibid.
63. Myra Hindley, letter, 26 April 1978. National Archive, Myra Hindley Home Office files, HO336/110.
64. Internal memo, 24 October 1978. National Archive, Myra Hindley Home Office files, HO336/22.
65. Internal memo, 24 October 1978. National Archive, Myra Hindley Home Office files, HO336/22.
66. Internal memo, 18 December 1978. National Archive, Myra Hindley Home Office files, HO336/22.
67. Ritchie, *Myra Hindley*, p. 202.
68. Jones, *The Devil and Miss Jones*, p. 134.
69. Ritchie, *Myra Hindley*, pp. 202–3.
70. Myra Hindley, letter, 16 January 1979. National Archive, Myra Hindley Home Office files, HO336/22.
71. Myra Hindley letter, 18 January 1979. National Archive, Myra Hindley Home Office files, HO336/22.
72. Internal memo, 13 March 1979. National Archive, Myra Hindley Home Office files, HO336/22.

24

1. Robert Wilson, *Devil's Disciples: Moors Murders* (Dorset: Javelin Books, 1986), p. 175.
2. David Smith paid a moving visit to his ex-wife, at Bill's request – he hoped Dave's presence might rouse Maureen from her coma. Eventually, Dave and his wife Mary, together with their daughter Jodie and three sons, moved from Hyde to Lincoln after becoming the focus of a hate campaign by residents in Hyde. Although they were resistant to giving in to such tactics, they decided to leave for the sake of their children.
3. Jean Ritchie, *Myra Hindley: Inside the Mind of a Murderess* (London: Grafton Books, 1988), p. 240.
4. Elizabeth Longford also wrote to Myra's mother: '. . . I do understand the agony of a mother like yourself. It seems so terribly unnatural that a young and happy girl should leave this world

before her own mother.' (Duncan Staff, 'Dangerous Liaison', *The Guardian* [14 October 2006]).

5. Anne Maguire, author interview, London, 29 July 2009.

6. Myra Hindley letter, 11 July 1980. National Archive, Myra Hindley Home Office files, HO336/86.

7. Ritchie, *Myra Hindley*, p. 241.

8. Joe Chapman, *Out of the Frying Pan* (London: Chipmunka Publishing, 2009).

9. Myra Hindley letter, 27 January 1981. National Archive, Myra Hindley Home Office files, HO336/86.

10. Ritchie, *Myra Hindley*, p. 186.

11. Internal report, 3 November 1981. National Archive, Myra Hindley Home Office files, HO336/145.

12. Ritchie, *Myra Hindley*, p. 206.

13. Revd Peter Timms, author interview, Sussex, 28 July 2009.

14. Bridget Astor, author interview, London, 28 July 2009.

15. Revd Peter Timms, author interview, Sussex, 28 July 2009.

16. Ibid.

17. David Astor, 14 December 1982. From the David Astor archive, private collection.

18. Sara Trevelyan, author interview, Edinburgh, 24 June 2009.

19. Ritchie, *Myra Hindley*, p. 209. According to David Staff's *The Lost Boy*, in July 1982 Linda Melvern visited Hindley's mother and offered to pay her gas bill in return for the tartan album.

20. Wilson, *Devil's Disciples*, p. 180.

21. Sara Trevelyan, author interview, Edinburgh, 24 June 2009. Jimmy Boyle has since become a celebrated sculptor and novelist. He and Sara had two children before their divorce in 2000; they remain on amicable terms.

22. Myra Hindley, letter, 9 August 1983. From the David Astor archive, private collection.

23. Ibid.

24. Bridget Astor, author interview, London, 28 July 2009.

25. Patrick Downey, letter, 29 February 1984. National Archive, Myra Hindley Home Office files, HO336/26.

26. Internal memo, March 1984. National Archive, Myra Hindley Home Office files, HO36/26.

27. Myra Hindley, letter, 20 May 1984. National Archive, Myra Hindley Home Office files, HO336/26.

28. Janie Jones, *The Devil and Miss Jones: The Twisted Mind of Myra Hindley* (London: Smith Gryphon, 1988), p. 228.

29. Wilson, *Devil's Disciples*, p. 184.

30. Hindley was granted the privilege of naming her toiletries and cosmetics on account of her 'lifer' status.

31. Ritchie, *Myra Hindley*, p. 229.

32. Wilson, *Devil's Disciples*, p. 180.

33. Fred Harrison, *Brady and Hindley: The Genesis of the Moors Murders* (London: Grafton Books, 1987), p. 72.

34. Anne Maguire, author interview, London, 29 July 2009.

35. Ritchie, *Myra Hindley*, pp. 229–30.

36. Danny Kilbride, author interview, Manchester, 21 August 2009.

37. Anon., 'My Myra Should Die in Prison', *The Sun* (20 June 1985).

38. Myra Hindley, letter, 1985. Reproduced with the kind permission of Andrew McCooey.

39. Wilson, *Devil's Disciples*, p. 190.

40. Brady, *The Gates of Janus: Serial Killing and its Analysis* (Los Angeles: Feral House, 2001), p. 18.

41. Ritchie, *Myra Hindley*, p. 258.

42. Ibid., pp. 260–1.

43. Internal memo, November 1986. National Archive, Myra Hindley Home Office files, HO336/26.

44. Ibid.

45. Myra Hindley, letter, 3 November 1986. From the David Astor archive, private collection.

46. Revd Peter Timms, author interview, Sussex, 28 July 2009.

47. Topping also had the dog handler visit woods at Whaley Bridge and Taxal, knowing that those were also favourite spots for Brady and Hindley.

48. Peter Topping, *Topping: The Autobiography of the Police Chief in the Moors Murders Case* (London: Angus and Robertson, 1989), p. 41.

49. Ritchie, *Myra Hindley*, p. 263.

50. David Astor, 20 November 1986. From the David Astor archive, private collection.

51. Revd Peter Timms, author interview, Sussex, 28 July 2009.

52. Topping also consulted the original detectives who worked on the case. Ian Fairley recalls, 'It wasn't done properly. A chap called [Detective Inspector] Geoff Knupfer came to see me and asked what I could tell them. I said, "What do you want to know?" But

he didn't know. That's what it came down to – he didn't really know what to ask. Topping was so secretive ... I could have told Knupfer more, but he didn't know what he wanted.' Topping himself spoke to Joe Mounsey, who had been promoted to Chief Superintendent, Head of Lancashire CID, two years after the Moors trial. His widow, Margaret, remembers, 'Joe was interested in the new search, definitely. Topping contacted him, and I think he and Joe corresponded, but Joe basically said to him, "You've got the maps," and that was about it. When they took Brady up to the moors, Joe said, "He won't tell them a bloody thing. He won't help."' (Ian Fairley, author interview, Norfolk, 20 July 2009).

53. Ritchie, *Myra Hindley*, pp. 265–6.

54. David Smith was also taken to the moor without being told where he was going. He was unable to help, except to tell Topping that he remembered parking at Hoe Grain with Brady and Hindley on occasion.

55. Journalist Robert Wilson covers the story of the case and the renewed search in his books *Devil's Disciples* and *Return to Hell*. He spoke to Edward Evans's mother, Edith, then 64 and living alone in a council house in a quiet Manchester suburb. She had little to say, except that she wished her son's killers had been hung.

56. Ritchie, *Myra Hindley*, p. 268.

57. Myra Hindley, letter, 5 February 1987. From the David Astor archive, private collection. Author's italics.

58. Ibid., author's italics.

59. Topping, *Topping*, p. 73.

60. Gerard Seenan, 'Catholic Girl Turned Killer Whose Pleas for Redemption Fell on Deaf Ears', *The Guardian* (16 November 2002).

61. Duncan Staff, 'A Journey into Darkness', *The Guardian* (29 February 2000).

62. Topping, *Topping*, p. 89.

63. Myra Hindley, autobiography. Reproduced with the kind permission of Andrew McCooey.

64. Topping, *Topping*, p. 144.

65. Ibid., p. 147.

66. Ibid.

67. Ibid.

68. Revd Peter Timms, author interview, Sussex, 28 July 2009.

69. Myra Hindley, letter, 31 March 1987. National Archive, Myra Hindley Home Office files, HO336/28.

70. Myra Hindley, petition, 15 April 1987. National Archive, Myra Hindley Home Office files, HO336/28.

71. Sara Trevelyan, author interview, Edinburgh, 24 June 2009.

72. Psychiatric report, the Bethlehem Royal Hospital and the Maudsley Hospital. From the David Astor archive, private collection.

73. Ibid.

74. In the aftermath of the visit, Ian sent a letter to the BBC claiming responsibility for five other killings, which the police investigated without result.

75. Ritchie, *Myra Hindley*, p. 277.

76. Topping, *Topping*, p. 203.

77. Ibid., p. 209.

78. Ibid., p. 237.

79. Deed of Trust, The Open Hand. From the David Astor archive, private collection. The trust was in name only; the book was never published.

80. Ritchie, *Myra Hindley*, p. 279.

81. Myra Hindley, letter to Peter Stanford, 4 February 1987.

82. Ibid.

83. Peter Stanford, author interview, London, 24 June 2009.

84. Ibid.

85. Ibid.

86. Myra Hindley, letter, 3 December 1987. From the David Astor archive, private collection.

87. Bernard Black, author interview, Portsmouth, 19 August 2009.

88. Margaret Black, author interview, Portsmouth, 19 August 2009. Bernard lost contact with Hindley around 1999 when he suffered a stroke.

89. Myra Hindley, 28 April 1988. From the David Astor archive, private collection.

90. Baroness Helena Kennedy QC is the author of *Eve Was Framed* and *Just Law*. Myra contributed to neither book.

91. Myra Hindley, letter, 2 June 1988. From the David Astor archive, private collection.

92. Myra Hindley, letter, 28 July 1988. From the David Astor archive, private collection.

93. Diana Athill, *Stet: An Editor's Life* (London: Grove Press, 2002), p. 96.

94. Ibid., p. 97.

95. Ibid., p. 97.

96. Andrew McCooey, telephone interview, 11 August 2009.

97. Myra Hindley, letter, 29 September 1988. From the David Astor archive, private collection.

98. Myra Hindley, letter, 4 November 1988. From the David Astor archive, private collection.

99. Myra Hindley, letter, 18 November 1988. From the David Astor archive, private collection.

100. Ritchie, *Myra Hindley*, p. 16.

101. Myra Hindley, letter, 18 November 1988. From the David Astor archive, private collection.

102. Myra Hindley, letter, 19 September 1989. Reproduced with the kind permission of Peter Stanford.

103. Peter Stanford, author interview, London, 24 June 2009.

104. Ibid.

105. Myra Hindley, letter, 20 April 1989. Reproduced with the kind permission of Peter Stanford.

106. Myra Hindley, letter, 2 December 1988. Reproduced with the kind permission of Peter Stanford.

107. Myra Hindley, letter, 7 December 1988. From the David Astor archive, private collection.

108. Ibid.

109. Myra Hindley, letter, 3 April 1989. From the David Astor archive, private collection.

110. Ibid.

111. Myra Hindley, letter, 1 May 1989. From the David Astor archive, private collection.

112. David Astor, letter, 18 July 1989. From the David Astor archive, private collection.

113. Unsigned report on the Hindley manuscript. From the David Astor archive, private collection.

114. Yvonne Roberts, author interview, London, 27 July 2009.

115. Ibid.

116. Myra Hindley, letter, 8 October 1989. From the David Astor archive, private collection. Alan Bennett also corresponded with Ian Brady in the hope that he would reveal information leading to the discovery of Keith's grave.

117. Revd Peter Timms, author interview, Sussex, 28 July 2009.
118. Myra Hindley, letter, 11 December 1989. From the David Astor archive, private collection.
119. Myra Hindley, letter, 26 November 1989. From the David Astor archive, private collection.

25

1. Ian Brady, letter, 16 January 1990. From the David Astor archive, private collection.
2. Andrew McCooey, letter, 12 June 1991. From the David Astor archive, private collection.
3. On New Year's Day 1992, Longford wrote to her: 'Thank you very much for the Christmas card, with its message of friendship for Elizabeth and me. I cannot resist telling you how much I miss coming to see you but understand your feeling that it is better not to.' (From the David Astor archive, private collection.)
4. Joe Chapman, author interview, Oxford, 18 July 2009.
5. Bridget Astor, author interview, London, 28 July 2009.
6. Myra Hindley, undated correspondence. From the David Astor archive, private collection.
7. Geraldine Bedell, 'Profile: Beyond Forgiveness? Myra Hindley', *The Independent* (18 April 1993).
8. Ibid.
9. Joe Chapman, author interview, Oxford, 18 July 2009.
10. Ibid.
11. Ibid.
12. Ibid.
13. Ibid.
14. Steve Boggan, 'How I Fell in Love with Myra: Nina Wilde', *The Independent* (9 February 1997).
15. Joe Chapman, *Out of the Frying Pan*, (London: Chipmunka Publishing, 2009).
16. Ibid.
17. Joe Chapman, author interview, Oxford, 18 July 2009.
18. Chapman, *Out of the Frying Pan*.
19. Myra Hindley, solicitor correspondence, 24 June 1994. From the David Astor archive, private collection.

20. Myra Hindley, campaign correspondence, 1994. From the David Astor archive, private collection.
21. Ibid.
22. Myra Hindley, letter, 7 December 1994. From the David Astor archive, private collection.
23. Ibid.
24. Joe Chapman, author interview, Oxford, 18 July 2009.
25. Chapman, *Out of the Frying Pan*.
26. Ibid.
27. Ibid.
28. Ibid.
29. Internal memo, 1994. National Archive, Myra Hindley Home Office files, HO336/34.
30. Ibid.
31. Topping intended to brief the hypnotist first as to where he believed the grave might be, thereby leaving little room for a location other than Shiny Brook to be considered.
32. Hindley had written previously to David Astor about press reports that Paul McKenna would hypnotise her to find Keith's grave: 'I've never even heard of Paul McKenna and wrote to the PCC [Press Complaints Commission] myself to say I hadn't.'
33. Chapman, *Out of the Frying Pan*.
34. Ibid.
35. Ibid.
36. Myra Hindley, letter, 30 May 1995. From the David Astor archive, private collection.
37. Chapman, *Out of the Frying Pan*.
38. Internal memo, 26 July 1995. National Archive, Myra Hindley Home Office files, HO336/34.
39. Ibid.
40. David Astor, letter, 12 October 1995. From the David Astor archive, private collection.
41. Myra Hindley, letter, 14 November. From the David Astor archive, private collection.
42. David Rowan and Duncan Campbell, 'Myra Hindley: My Life, My Guilt, My Weakness', *The Guardian* (18 December 1995).
43. Ibid.
44. Myra Hindley, solicitor correspondence, 29 August 1996. From the David Astor archive, private collection.

45. David Astor, letter, 9 September 1996. From the David Astor archive, private collection.

46. Myra Hindley, letter, 10 November 1996. From the David Astor archive, private collection.

47. Myra Hindley, letter, 20 February 1997. From the David Astor archive, private collection.

48. David Astor, letter, 20 October 1997. From the David Astor archive, private collection.

49. Chapman, *Out of the Frying Pan*.

50. Ibid.

51. Margaret Mounsey, author interview, Preston, 14 July 2009.

26

1. Myra Hindley, letter, 2 March 1998. From the David Astor archive, private collection.

2. Myra Hindley, letter, 30 June 1998. Reproduced with the kind permission of Bernard Black.

3. Father Michael Teader, author interview, Suffolk, 3 September 2009.

4. Ibid.

5. Ibid.

6. Alan Watkins, 'Hindley – An Icon of Evil: The Myra I Knew', *Sunday Mirror* (17 November 2002).

7. Myra Hindley, letter, 2 March 1998. From the David Astor archive, private collection.

8. Myra Hindley, letter, July 1998. From the David Astor archive, private collection.

9. Ibid.

10. Robert Verkaik, 'The Death of Myra Hindley: The Letters', *The Independent* (16 November 2002).

11. Steve Boggan, 'Revealed: New evidence that might free Myra Hindley', *The Independent* (15 August 1998).

12. Steve Boggan, 'Hindley Happy to Kill, Says Brady', *The Independent* (28 August 1998).

13. Anon., 'Myra Went to the Ends of the Earth for Brady . . . They Were Bonded by Blood', *Daily Mirror* (9 February 1999).

14. Myra Hindley, letter, August 1998. From the David Astor archive, private collection.

15. Ibid.
16. Myra Hindley, letter, 2 September 1998. From the David Astor archive, private collection.
17. Myra Hindley, letter, 7 December 1998. From the David Astor archive, private collection.
18. David Astor and Terry Waite, letter, 23 December 1998. From the David Astor archive, private collection.
19. Myra Hindley, letter, 6 January 1999. From the David Astor archive, private collection.
20. Myra Hindley, letter, 22 January 1999. Reproduced with the kind permission of Bernard Black.
21. Joe Chapman, *Out of the Frying Pan* (London: Chipmunka Publishing, 2009).
22. Joe Chapman, author interview, Oxford, 18 July 2009.
23. Anon., 'Victim's Mother Determined Hindley Should Not Be Released', BBC News online (17 December 1997).
24. David Astor, 30 May 1998. From the David Astor archive, private collection.
25. Bridget Astor, author interview, London, 28 July 2009.
26. Ibid.
27. Father Michael Teader, author interview, Suffolk, 3 September 2009.
28. Duncan Staff, author interview, Bristol, 18 June 2009.
29. Andrew McCooey, telephone interview, 11 August 2009.
30. Internal memo, 20 December 2000. National Archive, Myra Hindley Home Office files, HO336/145.
31. Internal memo, March 2001. National Archive, Myra Hindley Home Office files, HO336/114.
32. Myra Hindley, letter, 20 August 2001. From the David Astor archive, private collection.
33. Ibid.
34. Father Michael Teader, author interview, Suffolk, 3 September 2009.
35. Myra Hindley, letter, 6 December 1999. From the David Astor archive, private collection.
36. Peter Stanford, author interview, London, 24 June 2009.
37. Bridget Astor, author interview, London, 28 July 2009.
38. Andrew McCooey, telephone interview, 11 August 2009.
39. Anon., 'Hindley's Ashes to Be "Thrown Away"', *The Mail on Sunday* (17 November 2002).

40. Father Michael Teader, author interview, Suffolk, 3 September 2009.

41. Ibid.

42. Sue Doolan, letter, 20 December 2002. National Archive, Myra Hindley Home Office files, HO336/114.

27

1. Stuart Millar, Sarah Hall and Jamie Wilson, 'Death of Moors Murderer Lets Blunkett off the Hook', *The Guardian* (16 November 2002).

2. Tania Branigan, 'High Profile Allies Led Call for Release', *The Guardian* (16 November 2002).

3. Peter Stanford, 'Myra Hindley, Notorious Child Murderer Whose Protestations of Repentance Failed to Assuage Public Revulsion', *The Guardian* (16 November 2002).

4. Sara Trevelyan, author interview, Edinburgh, 24 June 2009.

5. David Sapsted, 'Authorities Rush to Get Rid of Hindley's Remains', *The Telegraph* (18 November 2002).

6. *The Moors Murders*, documentary (Chameleon TV, 1999). Pauline Reade's brother, Paul, died of a brain tumour in 2004.

7. Danny Kilbride, author interview, Manchester, 21 August 2009.

8. Ian Herbert, 'Memories Cut through the Murderous Mists of Saddleworth', *The Independent on Sunday* (17 November 2002).

9. Father Michael Teader, author interview, Suffolk, 3 September 2009.

10. In October 2002, Brady was taken under guard to Manchester Royal Infirmary to visit his dying mother. The Home Office issued a statement: 'Leave was agreed for completely compassionate reasons in accordance with the wishes of Mrs Brady. Ian Brady's mother is dying and a last meeting was at her request. She is not a criminal and does have human rights, which is why the Home Secretary agreed. It's a one-off deathbed wish and it's difficult, but we should not deny the innocent mother's dying wish.' Brady spent an hour with his mother before she died.

11. Duncan Staff, author interview, Bristol, 18 June 2009.

12. Helena Kennedy, *Eve Was Framed: Women and British Justice*, (London: Vintage, 2005), p. 257.

13. Myra Hindley, letter, 4 February 1987. Reproduced with the kind permission of Peter Stanford.

14. Joe Chapman, author interview, Oxford, 18 July 2009.

15. Diana Athill, *Stet: An Editor's Life* (London: Grove Press, 2002), p. 97.

16. Yvonne Roberts, author interview, London, 27 July 2009.

17. Peter Stanford, author interview, London, 24 June 2009.

18. Anon., 'Myra Hindley's Portrait Plea', *The Guardian*, letters page (31 July 1997).

19. Marina Warner, 'Peroxide Mug Shot', *London Review of Books* (1 January 1998). A portrait of Myra Hindley created by artist Gary Cartwright using bloodstained carpet and ropes hangs in the Greater Manchester Police Museum.

20. Rachel Bletchley, 'Myra Hindley's Twelve Faces of Evil', *The People* (15 September 2002).

21. Kennedy, *Eve Was Framed*, p. 18.

22. Kay Carmichael, *Sin and Forgiveness: New Choices in a Changing World* (Farnham: Ashgate, 2003), pp. 9–10.

23. Andrew McCooey, telephone interview, 11 August 2009.

24. Kennedy, *Eve Was Framed*, p. 254.

25. Joe Chapman, *Out of the Frying Pan* (London: Chipmunka Publishing, 2009).

26. Myra Hindley, autobiography. Reproduced with the kind permission of Andrew McCooey.

27. Michael Fisher, letter, 28 July 1987. From the David Astor archive, private collection.

28. Janie Jones, *The Devil and Miss Jones: The Twisted Mind of Myra Hindley* (London: Smith Gryphon, 1988), p. 141.

29. Unsigned report on the Hindley manuscript. From the David Astor archive, private collection.

30. David Astor, letter, 27 January 1999. From the David Astor archive, private collection.

31. Revd Peter Timms, letter, 1 November 1989. From the David Astor archive, private collection.

32. Danny Kilbride, author interview, Manchester, 21 August 2009.

33. Christine Joanna Hart, *Searching for Daddy* (London: Hodder & Stoughton, 2008), p. 257.

34. Ian Brady, *The Gates of Janus: Serial Killing and its Analysis* (Los Angeles: Feral House, 2001), p. 151.

35. Myra Hindley, 21 January 1997. From the David Astor archive, private collection.

36. David Rowan and Duncan Campbell, 'Myra Hindley: My Life, My Guilt, My Weakness', *The Guardian* (18 December 1995).

37. Jean Ritchie, *Myra Hindley: Inside the Mind of a Murderess* (London: Grafton Books, 1988), pp. 201–2.

38. Helen Birch, *Moving Targets: Women, Murder and Representation* (London: Virago, 1993), p. 41.

39. Robert Wilson, *Devil's Disciples: Moors Murders* (Dorset: Javelin Books, 1986), p. 184.

40. Birch, *Moving Targets*, p. 60.

41. Jonathan Goodman, *The Moors Murders: The Trial of Myra Hindley and Ian Brady* (London: Magpie Books, 1994), pp. 20–4.

42. Ian Fairley, author interview, Norfolk, 20 July 2009.

43. Nicci Gerrard, 'The Face of Human Evil', *The Observer* (17 November 2002).

44. Myra Hindley, letter, 1985. Reproduced with the kind permission of Andrew McCooey.

45. Carmichael, *Sin and Forgiveness*, p. 129.

46. Sara Trevelyan, author interview, Edinburgh, 24 June 2009.

47. Lady Anne Tree, Peter Stanford interview for the *Independent on Sunday Review*.

48. Danny Kilbride, author interview, Manchester, 21 August 2009.

49. Brian Masters, 'The Other Side of Evil', *The Independent* (17 November 2002).

Appendix: He Kept Them Close

1. Anon., 'Moors Murder Victim Keith Bennett Search Ended by Police', *Daily Telegraph* (1 July 2009).

2. Carol Midgley, 'A Letter from Hell', *The Times* (26 April 2006).

3. Anon., 'Moors Murder Victim . . .'.

4. Mike McCarthy, 'Moors Murderer Brady: No More Help from Me', Sky News online (10 July 2009).

5. 'Brady holds . . .' Joe Chapman, author interview, Oxford, 18 July 2009; 'His attention . . .' Joe Chapman, *Out of the Frying Pan* (London: Chipmunka Publishing, 2009).

6. Myra Hindley, autobiography. Reproduced with the kind permission of Andrew McCooey.

7. Myra Hindley, autobiography. Reproduced with the kind permission of Andrew McCooey.

8. More recently, detectives asked for a warrant to search Brady's cell in order to examine the photographs, but, because he has never been charged with Keith's murder, their request was refused.

9. Ann West, *For the Love of Lesley: Moors Murders Remembered by a Victim's Mother* (London: W.H. Allen & Co., 1989), p. 176.

10. Russell Jenkins, 'Desolate Moors Confounded Experts' Search for Body of Keith Bennett', *The Times* (2 July 2009).

11. Ian Fairley, author interview, Norfolk, 20 July 2009.

12. Mike Massheder, author interview, Preston, 1 July 2009.

13. Yvonne Roberts, author interview, London, 27 July 2009.

14. Ian Fairley, author interview, Norfolk, 20 July 2009.

15. West, *For the Love of Lesley*, p. 175.

16. Myra Hindley, letter, 5 February 1987. From the David Astor archive, private collection.

17. Peter Topping, *Topping: The Autobiography of the Police Chief in the Moors Murders Case* (London: Angus and Robertson, 1989), p. 230.

18. Ibid., p. 215.

19. Ibid., p. 229.

20. Mike Massheder, author interview, Preston, 1 July 2009.

21. Ian Fairley, author interview, Norfolk, 20 July 2009.

22. Winnie Johnson, author interview, Manchester, 7 September 2009.

23. Danny Kilbride, author interview, Manchester, 21 August 2009.

24. Chris Crowther, author interview, Saddleworth, 7 September 2009.

25. West, *For the Love of Lesley*, p. 162.

26. Mike Massheder, author interview, Preston, 1 July 2009.

27. Brady was a keen cinemagoer; in April 1960, *Hell Is a City* premiered at the Apollo in Ardwick Green. The film, starring Stanley Baker as a detective on the trail of a gang of Manchester thieves, features the dumping of a girl's body on the moors and was shot on location at Wessenden Head – two years before Brady and Hindley began visiting the area.

28. Fred Harrison, *Brady and Hindley: The Genesis of the Moors Murders* (London: Grafton Books, 1987), p. 153.

29. Charlotte Mew, 'Moorland Night', in *Charlotte Mew: Collected Poems and Prose* (Manchester: Carcanet Press, 2003).

BIBLIOGRAPHY

BOOKS

Athill, Diana, *Stet: An Editor's Life* (London: Grove Press, 2002).

Auden, W.H., *Collected Poems* (London: Faber and Faber, 2004).

Birch, Helen, *Moving Targets: Women, Murder and Representation* (London: Virago, 1993).

Brady, Ian, *The Gates of Janus: Serial Killing and its Analysis* (Los Angeles: Feral House, 2001).

Carlen, Pat, *Criminal Women* (Cambridge: Polity Press, 1985).

Carmichael, Kay, *Sin and Forgiveness: New Choices in a Changing World* (Farnham: Ashgate, 2003).

Chapman, Joe, *Out of the Frying Pan* (London: Chipmunka Publishing, 2009).

Dostoevsky, Fyodor, *Crime and Punishment* (London: Penguin, 2003).

Enright, D.J., *Conspirators and Poets* (London: Chatto & Windus, 1966).

Goodman, Jonathan, *The Moors Murders: The Trial of Myra Hindley and Ian Brady* (London: Magpie Books, 1994).

Hansford Johnson, Pamela, *On Iniquity: Some Personal Reflections Arising Out of the Moors Murder Trial* (London: Macmillan, 1967).

Harrison, Fred, *Brady and Hindley: The Genesis of the Moors Murders* (London: Grafton Books, 1987).

Hart, Christine, *The Devil's Daughter* (Essex: New Author Publications, 1993); rev. edn, as Hart, Christine Joanna, *Searching for Daddy* (London: Hodder & Stoughton, 2008).

Hodgson Burnett, Frances, *The Secret Garden* (London: Puffin Books, 2008).

Jones, Janie, *The Devil and Miss Jones: The Twisted Mind of Myra Hindley* (London: Smith Gryphon, 1988).

Kennedy, Helena, *Eve Was Framed: Women and British Justice* (London: Vintage, 2005).

MacFarlane, Colin, *The Real Gorbals Story: True Tales from Glasgow's Meanest Streets* (Edinburgh: Mainstream Publishing, 2007).

Maguire, Anne, *Why Me? One Woman's Fight for Justice and Dignity* (London: HarperCollins, 1994).

Marchbanks, David, *The Moor Murders* (London: Leslie Frewin, 1966).

Marquis de Sade, *Justine* (London: HarperPerennial, 2009).

Masters, Brian, *On Murder* (London: Coronet, 1994).

Mew, Charlotte, *Charlotte Mew: Collected Poems and Prose* (Manchester: Carcanet Press, 2003).

Potter, John Deane, *The Monsters of the Moors: The Full Account of the Brady–Hindley Case* (New York: Ballantine Books, 1968).

Ritchie, Jean, *Myra Hindley: Inside the Mind of a Murderess* (London: Grafton Books, 1988).

Sandbrook, Dominic, *Never Had It So Good: A History of Britain from Suez to the Beatles* (London: Abacus, 2006).

Shakespeare, William, *The Complete Works* (Oxford: OUP, 2005).

Sparrow, Judge Gerald, *Satan's Children* (London: Odhams Books, 1966).

Staff, Duncan, *The Lost Boy: The Definitive Story of the Moors Murders and the Search for the Final Victim* (London: Bantam Books, 2008).

Stanford, Peter, *The Outcasts' Outcast: A Biography of Lord Longford* (Gloucester: Sutton Publishing Ltd, 2006).

Topping, Peter, *Topping: The Autobiography of the Police Chief in the Moors Murders Case* (London: Angus and Robertson, 1989).

West, Ann, *For the Love of Lesley: Moors Murders Remembered by a Victim's Mother* (London: W.H. Allen & Co., 1989).

Williams, Emlyn, *Beyond Belief: The Moors Murderers – The Story of Ian Brady and Myra Hindley* (London: Pan, 1968).

Wilson, Robert, *Devil's Disciples: Moors Murders* (Dorset: Javelin Books, 1986).

Wordsworth, William, *The Collected Poems* (London: Wordsworth Editions, 1994).

NEWS SOURCES AND JOURNALS

Anon., 'Special Report – Moors Murderers Jailed for Life', BBC News online (6 May 1966).

Anon., 'My Myra Should Die in Prison', *The Sun* (20 June 1985).

Anon., 'Myra Hindley's Portrait Plea', *The Guardian*, letters page (31 July 1997).

Anon., 'Special Report – Myra Hindley: The Brady Letter', BBC News online (8 December 1997).

Anon., 'Victim's Mother Determined Hindley Should Not Be Released', BBC News online (17 December 1997).

Anon., 'Keep Hindley in Jail, Says Ex-Lover Brady', BBC News online (27 August 1998).

Anon., 'Myra Went to the Ends of the Earth for Brady . . . They Were Bonded by Blood', *Daily Mirror* (9 February 1999).

Anon., 'Hindley's Ashes to Be "Thrown Away"', *The Mail on Sunday* (17 November 2002).

Anon., 'Date Set for Hindley Funeral', *Daily Mail*, online edition (19 November 2002).

Anon., 'Hindley Cremated in Private Funeral', BBC News online (21 November 2002).

Anon., 'Jeers as Hindley Cremated', *London Evening Standard*, online edition (23 November 2002).

Anon., 'We Had Finished Killing, Says Brady', *Manchester Evening News* (28 October 2005).

Anon., 'Moors Murder Victim Keith Bennett Search Ended by Police', *Daily Telegraph* (1 July 2009).

Anon., 'Galway Man Who Turned in the Moors Murderers', *Ireland on Sunday* (undated).

Bedell, Geraldine, 'Profile: Beyond Forgiveness? Myra Hindley', *The Independent* (18 April 1993).

Bletchley, Rachel, 'Myra Hindley's Twelve Faces of Evil', *The People* (15 September 2002).

Boggan, Steve, 'How I Fell in Love with Myra: Nina Wilde', *The Independent* (9 February 1997).

Boggan, Steve, 'Brady Told Me that I Would be in a Grave', *The Independent* (15 August 1998).

Boggan, Steve, 'Revealed: New Evidence that Might Free Myra Hindley', *The Independent* (15 August 1998).

Boggan, Steve, 'Hindley Happy to Kill, Says Brady', *The Independent* (28 August 1998).

Boggan, Steve, 'Brady's Myra Time Bomb', *London Evening Standard* (7 November 2002).

Bottomley, Robert, 'The Babysitter with Blue Hair', *Manchester Evening News* (18 November 2002).

Branigan, Tania, 'High Profile Allies Led Call for Release', *The Guardian* (16 November 2002).

Deer, Brian, 'First Degree Photocall Lifts Murderer's Image', *The Times*, online edition (29 October 1989).

Dilley, Ryan, 'Few Witness Hindley's Final Journey', BBC News online (21 November 2002).

Dowling, Nicola, 'Myra and I Planned Suicide', *Manchester Evening News* (28 March 2006).

Gerrard, Nicci, 'The Face of Human Evil', *The Observer* (17 November 2002).

Gillman, Peter and Gillman, Leni, 'I Had a Very Happy Childhood Free of Fear ... I Have No Excuses – Ian Brady', *The Mail on Sunday* (15 May 2005).

Gould, Peter, 'Still Missing After Forty Years', BBC News online (16 June 2004).

Herbert, Ian, 'Memories Cut through the Murderous Mists of Saddleworth', *The Independent on Sunday* (17 November 2002).

Hindley, Myra and Wilde, Nina, 'Older and Wiser', *Verdict* (January 1996).

Jenkins, Russell, 'Desolate Moors Confounded Experts' Search for Body of Keith Bennett', *The Times* (2 July 2009).

Judd, Terri, 'Controversy Over Final Resting Place for Hindley', *The Independent*, online edition (18 November 2002).

Mahoney, Bernard, 'The A–Z of Law and Disorder', *Vice Magazine* (July 2006).

Masters, Brian, 'The Other Side of Evil', *The Independent* (17 November 2002).

McCarthy, Mike, 'Moors Murderer Brady: No More Help from Me', Sky News online (10 July 2009).

McCrystal, Cal, 'What Made the Gorbals Famous?', *The Independent* (31 January 1993).

Midgley, Carol, 'A Letter from Hell', *The Times* (26 April 2006).

Millar, Stuart, Hall, Sarah and Wilson, Jamie, 'Death of Moors Murderer Lets Blunkett off the Hook', *The Guardian* (16 November 2002).

Mouland, Bill, 'Myra Gets the Funeral Her Child Victims Were Denied', *Daily Mail*, online edition (21 November 2002).

Ratcliffe, Sandra, 'Why Myra Must Never Be Freed', *Daily Record* (29 October 1997).

Rowan, David and Campbell, Duncan, 'Myra Hindley: My Life, My Guilt, My Weakness', *The Guardian* (18 December 1995).

Sapsted, David, 'Authorities Rush to Get Rid of Hindley's Remains', *The Telegraph* (18 November 2002).

Seenan, Gerard, 'Catholic Girl Turned Killer Whose Pleas for Redemption Fell on Deaf Ears', *The Guardian* (16 November 2002).

Staff, Duncan, 'Hindley Tried to Join Police after First Killing', *The Guardian* (28 February 2000).

Staff, Duncan, 'A Journey into Darkness', *The Guardian* (29 February 2000).

Staff, Duncan, 'Myra Hindley in Her Own Words', *The Guardian* (29 February 2000).

Staff, Duncan, 'Portrait of a Serial Killer', *The Guardian* (18 November 2002).

Staff, Duncan, 'Dangerous Liaison', *The Guardian* (14 October 2006).

Stanford, Peter, 'Myra Hindley, Notorious Child Murderer Whose Protestations of Repentance Failed to Assuage Public Revulsion', *The Guardian* (16 November 2002).

Stansfield, James, 'Diary of a Supercop: The Mounsey Memoirs', *Evening Gazette* (2 August 1988).

Tweedie, Neil, 'Theme for Hindley's Funeral Was Repentance', *Daily Telegraph*, online edition (22 November 2002).

Verkaik, Robert, 'The Death of Myra Hindley: The Letters', *The Independent* (16 November 2002).

Warner, Marina, 'Peroxide Mug Shot', *London Review of Books* (1 January 1998).

Watkins, Alan, 'Hindley – An Icon of Evil: The Myra I Knew', *Sunday Mirror* (17 November 2002).

Wyndham, Francis, *The Sunday Times* (8 May 1966).

DOCUMENTARIES

Body Hunt: The Search for Keith Bennett (BBC2, 15 November 2001).

Born to Kill?: Myra Hindley (Stax Entertainment, 2006).

Martina Cole's Ladykillers: Myra Hindley (Free@Last TV, 2008).

Modern Times: Myra Hindley (BBC1, 1 March 2000).

The Moors Murders (Chameleon Production for Channel Five.

First aired on Channel Five, beginning 30 September 1999, in three parts: 'Web of Evil', 'The Investigation' and 'Lambs to the Slaughter').

The Moors Murders Code (BBC2, 8 September 2004).

Myra: The Making of a Monster (Map-TV for Channel Five, 2003).

Myra Hindley: The Prison Years (Granada Anglia, 2006).

Panorama: Myra Hindley (BBC, 24 November 1997).

OTHER MEDIA

Mars-Jones QC, William, 'The Moors Murders' address given to the Medico-Legal Society (9 November 1967).

INDEX